D0084878

Controlling Chemicals

Controlling Chemicals

The Politics of Regulation in Europe and the United States

RONALD BRICKMAN

SHEILA JASANOFF

THOMAS ILGEN

CORNELL UNIVERSITY PRESS *Ithaca and London*

First published 1985 by Cornell University Press.

International Standard Book Number 0-8014-1677-9
Library of Congress Catalog Number 84-29340
Printed in the United States of America
*Librarians: Library of Congress cataloging information
appears on the last page of the book.*

*The paper in this book is acid-free and meets the guidelines for
permanence and durability of the Committee on Production Guidelines
for Book Longevity of the Council on Library Resources.*

Contents

Preface		7
Principal Abbreviations and Foreign Terms		11
1	Introduction	19
2	The Comparison of National Policies	28
3	Legislative Politics	54
4	Administrative Implementation	74
5	Policy Making in the Courts	100
6	The Development of the Scientific Base	129
7	Expertise and Decision Making	157
8	The Politics of Scientific Uncertainty	187
9	The Chemical Industry: Regulatory Challenges and Adaptive Strategies	218
10	The Advocates of Regulation	250
11	Domestic Policy and International Cooperation	274
12	Cross-National Analysis and Regulatory Reform	301
	Appendix Tables of Regulated Substances	319
	Index	337

Preface

We present in this book a systematic comparison of the policies and politics of toxic chemical regulation in the United States, Great Britain, France, and the Federal Republic of Germany. We examine the methods by which public officials in these countries have dealt with the scientific and political controversies that accompanied the emergence of chemical control into the political limelight. Our objective is to identify significant areas of convergence and divergence in national policy making and to interpret these in the light of variations among the political, legal, and scientific institutions of the four countries. We also assess the influence of private interest groups and international organizations on policy formulation in each country. Our analysis is based on research into four areas of chemical regulation: food additives, pesticides, chemicals in the workplace, and industrial chemicals subject to premarket testing and notification requirements. Throughout the book, we devote special attention to the regulatory dilemmas presented by chemicals suspected of causing cancer.

A research project of this size and scope demanded the cooperation of many individuals and organizations. We gratefully acknowledge the assistance of all those who agreed to be interviewed in the course of the project. Several dozen experts, including public officials, scientists, industrialists, public interest activists, trade union leaders, and representatives of international organizations, gave us information that was not always publicly available, as well as their candid opinions about current issues in the field of chemical regulation. Without their generous help, this book could never have been written. We thank them here collectively and regret that it is not possible to name them all individually.

A number of professional colleagues with experience in comparative policy studies gave us invaluable advice and encouragement. We are particularly grateful to Edward Burger, Brendan Gillespie, Rüdiger Lummert, Axel Murswieck, Dorothy Nelkin, Jürgen Schmandt, and David Vogel. We also thank the following individuals who agreed to serve as members of an advisory committee and offered helpful comments on early drafts of the book: Martin Alexander, Donald Buffington, T. Colin Campbell, Hans Falk, John Ficke, and Ingo Walter. While we have endeavored to incorporate their suggestions into our analysis, we retain full responsibility for any misinterpretations or errors of fact that remain.

Several students ably served as research assistants in the course of the project. We thank Christopher Allen, Wayne Edisis, Erich Latniak, Wendy Lovett, Lori Todd, and John Wooding for their contributions. We are also indebted to Coraleen Rooney who, with unfailing patience and skill, typed the manuscript in its earlier versions.

The research on which this book is based was funded by grants from the National Science Foundation and the Stiftung Volkswagenwerk. The preliminary results of the research were submitted to these two organizations as a report entitled *Chemical Regulation and Cancer: A Cross-National Analysis of Policy and Politics.* The report contains a somewhat more detailed description of the chemical control strategies of the four governments and was distributed by the National Technical Information Service.

We would like to thank the German Marshall Fund of the United States for individual fellowships awarded to two of the authors for research on related topics. The Program on Science, Technology and Society at Cornell University, the Mazer Fund for faculty research at Brandeis University, the Hoover Institution, and the American Enterprise Institute provided complementary administrative or financial support.

In August 1983 we convened an international conference to pursue some of the themes concerning science and public decision making that originated in this book. The conference, hosted by the Rockefeller Foundation at the Villa Serbelloni in Bellagio, Italy, received additional funding from the Russell Sage Foundation, the National Science Foundation, and the German Marshall Fund of the United States. We are indebted to these organizations for their support, and to the participants for making the conference a stimulating intellectual experience. The results of the Bellagio conference will be published separately.

This book represents the culmination of an interdisciplinary collaboration spread over a period of several years. Our goal was to produce, from different disciplinary perspectives, a cohesive account of the determinants and implications of alternative national approaches to chemical control. Toward this end, each author participated fully in all aspects of the study, from the initial design through the cross-national fieldwork to the final integrative analysis. This collaboration is reflected in the joint authorship of chapters 1, 2, and 12. Responsibility for drafting the more specialized chapters was allocated as follows, reflecting the disciplinary background and intellectual interests of each author: chapters 3, 4, 5, 8, Jasanoff; chapters 6, 7, and 10, Brickman; chapter 9, Ilgen; and chapter 11, Ilgen and Brickman.

RONALD BRICKMAN
Vanderbilt University

SHEILA JASANOFF
Cornell University

THOMAS ILGEN
Brandeis University

Principal Abbreviations and Foreign Terms

United States

ACGIH	American Conference of Governmental Industrial Hygienists
AIHC	American Industrial Health Council
APA	Administrative Procedure Act
ATSAC	Administrator's Toxic Substances Advisory Committee
CEQ	Council on Environmental Quality
CMA	Chemical Manufacturers Association
CPSC	Consumer Product Safety Commission
DHEW	Department of Health, Education, and Welfare
DHHS	Department of Health and Human Services [formerly DHEW]
EDF	Environmental Defense Fund
EPA	Environmental Protection Agency
FDA	Food and Drug Administration
FDCA	Food, Drug, and Cosmetic Act
FIFRA	Federal Insecticide, Fungicide, and Rodenticide Act
FR	*Federal Register*
GAO	General Accounting Office
IRLG	Interagency Regulatory Liaison Group
ITC	Interagency Testing Committee
NACA	National Agricultural Chemicals Association

NACOSH	National Advisory Committee on Occupational Safety and Health
NAS	National Academy of Sciences
NCI	National Cancer Institute
NIEHS	National Institute of Environmental Health Sciences
NIH	National Institutes of Health
NIOSH	National Institute for Occupational Safety and Health
NRC	National Research Council [National Academy of Sciences]
NRDC	Natural Resources Defense Council
NTP	National Toxicology Program
OCAW	Oil, Chemical, and Atomic Workers
OMB	Office of Management and Budget
OPTS	Office of Pesticides and Toxic Substances [EPA]
OSHA	Occupational Safety and Health Administration
OSH Act	Occupational Safety and Health Act
OTA	Office of Technology Assessment
TSCA	Toxic Substances Control Act
TSSC	Toxic Substances Strategy Committee

Great Britain

ACP	Advisory Committee on Pesticides
ACTS	Advisory Committee on Toxic Substances
ASTMS	Association of Scientific, Technical, and Managerial Staffs
BAA	British Agrochemical Association
BIBRA	British Industrial Biological Research Association
CIA	Chemical Industries Association
DHSS	Department of Health and Social Security
DOE	Department of the Environment
EMAS	Employment Medical Advisory Service
FACC	Food Additives and Contaminants Committee
GMWU	General and Municipal Workers' Union
HSC	Health and Safety Commission
HSE	Health and Safety Executive
HSW Act	Health and Safety at Work Etc. Act
ICI	Imperial Chemical Industries
MAFF	Ministry of Agriculture, Fisheries, and Food
MRC	Medical Research Council
NUAAW	National Union of Agricultural and Allied Workers
PSPS	Pesticide Safety Precaution Scheme
TUC	Trades Union Congress

France

	Comité d'Homologation des Produits Antiparasitaires à Usage Agricole et des Produits Assimilés	Authorization Committee for Agricultural Pesticides and Related Products
	Commission d'Etude de la Toxicité des Produits Antiparasitaires à Usage Agricole et des Produits Assimilés	Study Committee on the Toxicity of Agricultural Pesticides and Related Products
	Commission d'Evaluation de l'Ecotoxicité des Substances Chimiques	Evaluation Committee for the Ecotoxicity of Chemical Substances
	Commission des Produits Antiparasitaires à Usage Agricole	Agricultural Pesticides Committee
CHSP	Conseil Supérieur de l'Hygiène Publique	Higher Council of Public Hygiene
CSPRP	Conseil Supérieur de la Prévention des Risques Professionnels	Higher Council for the Prevention of Occupational Risks
FFSPN	Fédération Française des Sociétés de Protection de la Nature	French Federation of Nature Protection Societies
INRS	Institut National de Recherche et de Sécurité	National Institute of Research and Safety
	Service du Contrôle des Produits	Service of Products Control
	Service de la Protection des Végétaux	Service of Plant Protection
	Service de la Répression des Fraudes et du Contrôle de la Qualité	Service of Fraud Repression and Quality Control
UFC	Union Française des Consommateurs	French Consumers Union
UIC	Union des Industries Chimiques	Chemical Industry Association

Federal Republic of Germany

AGA	Ausschuss für Gefährliche Arbeitsstoffe	Committee on Hazardous Substances in the Workplace
AGV	Arbeitsgemeinschaft der Verbraucherverbände	Society of Consumer Associations
BAU	Bundesanstalt für Arbeitsschutz und Unfallforschung	Federal Institute for Occupational Safety and Accident Research
BBA	Biologische Bundesanstalt für Land- und Forstwirtschaft	Federal Biological Research Center for Agriculture and Forestry

BGA	Bundesgesundheitsamt	Federal Health Office
BMAS	Bundesministerium für Arbeit und Sozialordnung	Ministry for Labor and Social Affairs
BMJFG	Bundesministerium für Jugend, Familie, und Gesundheit	Ministry for Youth, Health, and Family Affairs
ChemG	Chemikaliengesetz	Chemicals Act
DFG	Deutsche Forschungsgemeinschaft	German Research Society
DKFZ	Deutsches Krebsforschungszentrum-	German Cancer Research Center
DVS	Deutscher Verbraucherschutzverband	German Consumer Protection Association
RSU	Rat von Sachverständigen für Umweltfragen	Council of Experts on Environmental Questions
UBA	Umweltbundesamt	Federal Environmental Agency
VCI	Verband der Chemischen Industrie	Chemical Industry Association

International

CEFIC	Conseil Européen des Fédérations de l'Industrie Chimique	European Council of Chemical Industry Federations
EC		European Community
ECETOC		European Chemical Industry Ecology and Toxicology Centre
FAO		Food and Agricultural Organization
IARC		International Agency for Research on Cancer
ILO		International Labor Organization
IPCS		International Program on Chemical Safety
IRPTC		International Register of Potentially Toxic Chemicals
OECD		Organization for Economic Cooperation and Development
UN		United Nations
WHO		World Health Organization

Technical Terms

ADI		acceptable daily intake
GLP		good laboratory practices
GRAS		generally regarded as safe

MAK	Maximale Arbeitsplatzkonzent-ration	maximum concentration in the workplace
MPD		minimum premarketing data
MTD		maximum tolerated dose
NOEL		no-effect level
PMN		premanufacture notification
RPAR		rebuttable presumption against registration
TLV		threshold limit value
TRK	Technische Richtkonzentration	technical guiding concentration

Controlling Chemicals

1

Introduction

Social Regulation and Technological Change

By the end of the 1960s, worldwide concern about the harmful effects of industrialization and technological change coalesced into insistent public demands for remedial state action. The governments of the advanced industrial nations responded with ambitious programs of "social regulation" to protect public health and the environment. Wide-ranging statutes were enacted granting broad new regulatory powers to executive agencies. Environmental and labor groups mobilized to extend the regulatory agenda and press for faithful implementation of the law. Confronted with costly and onerous legal obligations, industries sought to contain the scope of state intervention by intensifying their efforts to influence public authorities. In little more than a decade, these activities changed the face of regulatory policy and politics in every industrialized country.

The environmental movement won particularly dramatic successes in the United States. Congress passed sweeping legislation designed to reduce air pollution, clean up rivers and lakes, protect wilderness and coastal areas, and limit public exposure to toxic substances. New agencies such as the Environmental Protection Agency (EPA) and the Occupational Safety and Health Administration (OSHA) were entrusted with ambitious regulatory programs, while older agencies, such as the Food and Drug Administration (FDA), saw their duties expanded and redefined. In no country was the banner of social regulation taken up with greater fanfare and promise.[1]

By the late 1970s, however, serious questions arose about the direction and impact of the new programs. In the context of a flagging economy, American industry complained of exorbitant regulatory costs and sharpened its attack on big government. Advocates of tighter environmental and health protection standards were dismayed at government's repeated failure to meet deadlines and to respond forcefully to recognized hazards. All parties were caught up in a maze of procedures that stretched out regulatory controversies and impeded harmonious resolution of conflict. A crossfire of claims that regulators were doing either too little or too much deepened public skepticism about the federal government's capacity to formulate or execute a workable regulatory strategy.

This growing disillusionment helped move regulatory policy to the forefront of American political debate in the late 1970s, stimulating demands for reform. One strong current of opinion held that the federal government had exceeded the bounds of permissible intervention and that the cure should be sought in deregulation, decentralization, and a more careful accounting of the costs of regulation. Some analysts favored recourse to a more market-oriented policy, using effluent charges and other economic incentives to encourage pollution abatement. Others called for an overhaul of the major regulatory statutes to make them clearer, simpler, and more consistent. Environmentalists and labor leaders, in turn, campaigned for stricter enforcement of statutory standards and timetables and a more emphatic public commitment to the reduction of risk.[2]

This book was conceived at a time when the need for changes in U.S. policy was painfully obvious but directions for reform were far from clear. Our guiding premise was that the debate about regulatory reform in the United States could be enriched by comparing American policy initiatives with the

---

[1] For analyses of American social regulation, see, inter alia, *Ecology Law Quarterly,* 7, no. 2 (1978) (entire issue); William Lilley III and James C. Miller III, "The New 'Social Regulation'," *Public Interest,* no. 47 (Spring 1977), pp. 49–61; James Q. Wilson, ed., *The Politics of Regulation* (New York: Basic Books, 1980); and Eugene Bardach and Robert A. Kagan, eds., *Social Regulation: Strategies for Reform* (San Francisco: Institute for Contemporary Studies, 1982).

[2] For background on this debate, see GAO, "Government Regulatory Activity: Justifications, Processes, Impacts and Alternatives," Washington, D.C., June 3, 1977; Timothy B. Clark, Marvin H. Kosters, and James C. Miller III, eds., *Reforming Regulation* (Washington, D.C.: American Enterprise Institute, 1980); Senate Committee on Governmental Affairs, *Study on Federal Regulation,* vols. 1–6, 95th Cong., 2d sess., 1977–78; Donald P. Jacobs, ed., *Regulating Business: The Search for an Optimum* (San Francisco: Institute for Contemporary Studies, 1978); Steven Kelman, *What Price Incentives?* (Boston: Auburn House, 1981); Eugene Bardach and Robert A. Kagan, *Going by the Book: The Problem of Regulatory Unreasonableness* (Philadelphia: Temple University Press, 1982).

way other liberal democracies have approached similar problems. Cross-national comparison, in our view, offers a fresh vantage point from which to analyze the development of American social regulation and to evaluate its performance. It permits us to address a series of questions bearing on regulatory reform. Are the deepening political conflicts, the polarizing technical disputes, the widening gaps between promise and accomplishment, unique to U.S. policy? Or are these the inevitable consequences of governmental efforts to restrain the development of socially valued technologies? Have other nations succeeded any better in attaining the objectives of social regulation? If so, what features of their approach—their institutional arrangements, their management of scientific and political conflict, or their tools of intervention—are responsible for their greater success? And to what extent can these techniques be borrowed or adapted for use by American regulators?

Answering these questions requires more than a comparison of regulatory style and performance. It demands a probing of the wellsprings of governmental action in response to the hazards of technological development. Our assumption in this book is that policy choices are conditioned by identifiable features in each country's domestic and international political environment. We therefore explore and compare those features that exert greatest influence on the shape and direction of national policy: governmental structure and legal tradition, science and scientific institutions, interest group politics, and international developments. The book thus goes beyond the highly descriptive or narrowly focused studies that dominate the existing literature on comparative regulatory policy. It offers a comprehensive assessment of the forces that define different national approaches to the regulation of technological risk.

The Design of the Study

With these general objectives in view, we examine the policies developed by the United States, Great Britain, France, and West Germany to limit public exposure to toxic chemicals. Special attention is given to the efforts made by these countries to identify and control cancer-causing substances. Hazardous chemicals, and carcinogens in particular, present national authorities with some of the most intractable dilemmas of social regulation. Chemical production and trade are indispensable to the vitality of modern industrial economies, yet the chemical disasters of the past few decades attest to real dangers presented by toxic substances to human health and the environment. Efforts to assess these risks and design appropriate control policies are beset with uncertainties, and the high stakes riding on such decisions engender bitter political controversy. Decision making, under these circumstances, can become more a matter of crisis management than of developing rational, long-term strategies.

In all four countries, toxic chemicals are subject to multifaceted programs of intervention under both general pollution control laws and legislation directed at specific product categories. This book focuses on four distinct frameworks of regulation aimed at hazards to which the public is involuntarily exposed: food additivies, pesticides, chemicals in the workplace, and industrial chemicals subject to notification and testing requirements. In the first three regulatory sectors, the principle of governmental intervention has been established for some time, but recent scientific advances have uncovered new hazards and added greater urgency to the search for adequate control policies. In contrast, programs for the testing and notification of industrial chemicals represent a significant extension of prior policies and a novel attempt to bring all aspects of chemical production under a uniform regulatory blanket. Examination of these four areas can thus be expected to yield a comprehensive picture of each country's chemical control initiatives and to reveal the most distinctive features of each national approach.[3]

The four countries selected for this study share an economic and political tradition that leads us to anticipate similar responses to the problems of chemical control. With some variation, all have embraced market-oriented economies, though each accords government a limited role in the management of economic activity. All four countries have achieved comparable levels of economic and technological development, with the postwar chemical industry figuring prominently in that achievement. Politically, all four share such fundamental Western values as the protection of private rights against undue governmental intrusion, participation by citizens in administrative decision making, and a commitment to government under law. Protection of public health and the environment is accepted in each country as a legitimate sphere of state action.

At the same time, the four countries offer significant contrasts in their political organization and behavior. The classic parliamentary systems of Britain and West Germany contrast with the presidential regimes of the United States and France. West Germany and the United States are founded on a federal structure, with power constitutionally divided between state and national governments, while state authority in Britain and France is more

---

[3] In effect, the analysis of four regulatory sectors in each of four countries has the potential for generating sixteen "cases" from which to search for patterns of policy making. In reality, however, there are fewer than sixteen cases. In the United Kingdom, for example, premarket notification requirements for industrial chemicals have grown from general legislation addressing occupational health and safety rather than from separate legislation devising new regulatory arrangements, as in the United States.

centralized. The three European countries belong to a supranational federation, the European Community (EC), which is charged with harmonizing the laws and regulations of its members. Political parties are differently organized in the four countries and support different roles for bureaucrats and elected officials. Legal traditions also differ among the four, with the administrative courts and jurisprudence of France and Germany finding no precise counterpart in Britain or the United States. This wide array of institutional and political differences can be expected to foster divergences in the four national approaches to chemical control.

The first task of comparison, then, is simply to describe the chemical control policies of the four countries in a way that permits identification of significant similarities and differences. This analysis, presented in chapter 2, reveals that although U.S. and European governments have addressed the problem of chemical control at roughly the same times and have assumed similar responsibilities, they have developed markedly different procedures for reaching regulatory decisions. Two distinct patterns emerge. American regulatory processes stand apart in the complexity of their procedures, the heavy reliance on formal analysis of risks and benefits, the openness of administrative decision making, and the active supervision of executive agencies by Congress and the courts. European processes, despite some notable differences among them, share simpler administrative procedures, greater informality in the analysis of evidence, less complete public access to decision makers, and relatively little oversight by parliament or the courts. Yet one of our most intriguing conclusions is that these contrasting methods of decision making have led to remarkably similar policy choices, particularly in the selection of specific chemicals as targets of regulation.

These findings point to the central analytical puzzles addressed in this book. Why have toxic substances provoked a nearly contemporaneous burst of regulatory activity in so many countries? How do we account for the very different strategies employed by governments to control these hazards? And why are there such notable similarities in their regulatory records? These questions are explored in chapters 3–11 through an examination of four key factors: the organization and processes of national political institutions; the production and use of scientific information; the political strategies of private interest groups; and the chemical control policies of international organizations.

The choice of these explanatory factors is guided by several bodies of scholarly literature that offer insights into the workings of modern governments as they adjust to economic and social change. Some of the earliest and most influential work in political science emphasized the role of institutions and constitutional traditions, showing that these fundamental arrangements produce important differences in the alignment of political forces and the resolution of conflict.[4] After a period of relative neglect, this line of scholarship again seems highly relevant to what some political scientists have termed a "rediscovery of the state," signaling their renewed interest in the institutions that link state and society in the management of complex policy issues.[5] From different disciplinary perspectives, economic and social historians have also devoted attention to the state's role in the process of modernization and economic development.[6] Recent work in these areas suggests that governments that efficiently organize and coordinate their relations with affected social interests achieve more satisfactory policy results than states in which these relations are less capably managed.[7]

Neocorporatism, a pattern of orderly, tightly knit state-society relationships, characterizes a broad range of policy processes in Western Europe.[8] Major social interests are organized into large representative hierarchies by the state and are drawn into close association with public decision makers. By contrast, the pluralist tradition of American politics continues to favor a more laissez-faire approach to the involvement of private interests in policy mak-

[4]C. J. Friedrich, *Constitutional Government and Democracy* (Boston: Ginn, 1946); Herman Finer, *Theory and Practice of Modern Government* (New York: British Book Center, 1949); and S. N. Eisenstadt, *Essays on Comparative Institutions* (New York: Wiley, 1965).

[5]"Restoring the State to Political Science" was the theme of the 1981 American Political Science Convention, a sometimes reliable indicator of trends in political science research. Some recent notable contributions to this trend are Charles Tilley, ed., *The Formation of National States in Western Europe* (Princeton: Princeton University Press, 1975); Theda Skocpol, *States and Social Revolutions* (Cambridge: Cambridge University Press, 1979); Peter Katzenstein, ed., *Between Power and Plenty: Foreign Economic Policies of Advanced Industrialized States* (Madison: University of Wisconsin Press, 1978); Eric Nordlinger, *On the Autonomy of the Democratic State* (Cambridge: Harvard University Press, 1981); Stephen Skowronek, *Building a New American State: The Expansion of National Administrative Capacities, 1877–1920* (Cambridge: Cambridge University Press, 1982).

[6]Among the most influential works are Barrington Moore, *Social Origins of Dictatorship and Democracy: Lord and Peasant in the Making of the Modern World* (Boston: Beacon Press, 1966); Alexander Gerschenkron, *Economic Backwardness in Historical Perspective: A Book of Essays* (Cambridge, Mass.: Belknap Press, 1962); Samuel P. Huntington, *Political Order in Changing Societies* (New Haven: Yale University Press, 1968); Andrew Shonfield, *Modern Capitalism: The Changing Balance of Public and Private Power* (London: Oxford University Press, 1970).

[7]See Katzenstein, op. cit. Much of the appeal of industrial policy prescription in the United States follows from this reasoning. See, for example, Robert Reich, *The Next American Frontier* (New York: Times Books, 1983); and John Zysman and Laura Tyson, eds., *American Industry in International Competition* (Ithaca: Cornell University Press, 1983).

[8]See P. C. Schmitter and G. Lehmbruch, eds., *Trends Toward Corporatist Intermediation* (Beverly Hills, Calif.: Sage, 1979); R. Harrison, *Pluralism and Corporatism: The Political Evolution of Modern Democracy* (London: George Allen and Unwin, 1980); and Suzanne D. Berger, ed., *Organizing Interests in Western Europe: Pluralism, Corporatism, and the Transformation of Politics* (Cambridge: Cambridge University Press, 1981).

ing. In chapters 3, 4, and 5, we trace the impact of these institutional differences on policy development in the legislative, administrative, and judicial arenas.

Scientifically validated assessments of risk play a crucial part in any government's efforts to protect the public from hazardous chemicals. To the extent that scientific research expands the base of common knowledge about chemicals, it can be expected to operate in favor of cross-national convergence. Explorations of the growing number of science-based policy problems faced by modern governments frequently call attention to the imperatives and limitations that science and technology create for policy makers.[9] However, the massive uncertainties surrounding chemical risk assessment mitigate the power of science as a harmonizing force and open the door to political manipulation of the objectives and results of scientific research. The ways in which expertise is introduced into decision making assume special significance in the context of uncertainty. Whether scientists are cast in the role of impartial experts or of advocates for particular policy results substantially influences their credibility. These issues are examined at length in chapters 6, 7, and 8. Chapter 6 analyzes the impact of political decision making on the development and utilization of research relevant to carcinogen regulation in the four countries; chapter 7 examines the role of experts in the policy process, and chapter 8 focuses on the way political considerations impinge on the resolution of scientific uncertainty in different decision-making environments.

Since the New Deal and the rise of the modern administrative state, the relationship between regulators and affected industries has been a subject of enduring interest to American students of regulation and regulatory reform. Almost all the early research in this area concluded that regulators were eventually co-opted or "captured" by the interests they were supposed to regulate.[10] More recently, these findings have been extended by studies show-

[9] The role of science and technology as a factor of convergence has been explored in Clark Kerr et al., *Industrialism and Industrial Man* (Cambridge: Harvard University Press, 1960); Z. Brzezinski and Samuel P. Huntington, *Political Power: USA/USSR* (New York: Viking Press, 1963); Robert Lane, "The Decline of Politics and Ideology in a Knowledgeable Society," *American Sociological Review,* 31 (October 1966), 649–62; Daniel Bell, *The Coming of Post-Industrial Society* (New York: Basic Books, 1973); Alvin M. Weinberg, "Can Technology Replace Social Engineering?" *University of Chicago Magazine,* 59 (October 1966), 6–10.

[10] Marver Bernstein, *Regulating Business by Independent Commission* (Princeton: Princeton University Press, 1955); Gabriel Kolko, *Railroads and Regulation, 1877–1916* (Princeton: Princeton University Press, 1965); Roger Noll, *Reforming Regulation* (Washington, D.C.: Brookings, 1971); and George J. Stigler, "The Theory of Economic Regulation," *Bell Journal of Economics and Management Science,* no. 2 (Spring 1971), pp. 3–21.

ing the decisive influence of public interest groups on mission-oriented agencies implementing social regulation.[11] But although examples of capture are commonplace in the United States, few attempts have been made to compare the influence of American pressure groups with similar organizations in Europe, which are known to behave very differently in their choice of goals and strategies. How, for example, do varying patterns of interest group interaction affect such critical policy choices as the setting of the regulatory agenda or the selection of control instruments? Does the theme of capture arise with the same frequency in countries with entirely different traditions of business-government relations? In addressing these issues, chapter 9 compares industry strategies for adjusting to the demands of chemical regulation, while chapter 10 examines the efforts of labor and public interest groups to gain fuller protection against hazardous substances.

Each country's policies for chemical control are influenced, as well, by developments outside its own borders. Strong pressures for harmonization arise from the growing interdependence of modern societies.[12] The global integration of chemical markets cautions governments against imposing regulatory burdens that would damage the competitiveness of their industries or throw up harmful barriers to trade. International ties among scientists and public interest groups also encourage parallelism in national regulatory initiatives. These incentives for harmonization receive added strength from the formal efforts of such international organizations as the European Community, the Organization for Economic Cooperation and Development (OECD), and the United Nations (UN), all of which have taken up the issue of chemical control. Chapter 11 discusses these international efforts and examines the

---

[11] Paul Sabatier, "Social Movements and Regulatory Agencies: Toward a More Adequate—and Less Pessimistic—Theory of 'Clientele Capture'," *Policy Sciences,* 6, no. 3 (1975), 301–42. For efforts to explore the politics and economics of different regulatory arrangements see James Q. Wilson, op. cit., and Barry M. Mitnick, *The Political Economy of Regulation* (New York: Columbia University Press, 1980).

[12] The process of promoting cross-national cooperation and harmonizing national policies received early attention from students of European economic integration: David Mitrany, *A Working Peace System* (Chicago: Quadrangle, 1966), and Ernst B. Haas, "International Integration: The European and the Universal Process," *International Organization,* 15, no. 3 (1961), 366–92. As the bonds of interdependence draw tighter, the case for the cooperative resolution of common problems becomes stronger. See, for example, Robert Keohane and Joseph S. Nye, "International Interdependence and Integration," in Fred I. Greenstein and Nelson W. Polsby, eds., *Handbook of Political Science,* vol. 8, *International Politics* (Reading, Mass.: Addison-Wesley, 1975), pp. 363–414, and Richard Cooper, *The Economics of Interdependence* (New York: McGraw-Hill, 1968). More recent work on the prospects and possibilities of cross-national cooperation has centered on the dynamics of international "regimes," sets of agreed-on rules and procedures that facilitate the management of a wide variety of common problems. See, especially, Stephen D. Krasner, ed., "International Regimes," *International Organization* (special issue), 36, no. 2 (Spring 1982).

degree to which individual states are prepared to subordinate their national approaches to multilateral policy initiatives.

The final chapter of the book weaves the strands of the foregoing analysis into a composite explanation of similarities and differences in the U.S. and European approaches to chemical regulation. We reaffirm the importance of institutions, arguing that each country's institutional arrangements define the allocation of power not only among governmental actors, but between governmental and societal interests. These distributions of power, in turn, account for the striking differences we observe in the process by which regulatory conflict is resolved in the four countries. Institutional links between government and citizens also influence aspects of chemical control policy that have not previously been analyzed in these terms. The role of scientists and other experts in the policy process, the resolution of scientific uncertainty, and the strategies of competing interest groups can be plausibly traced to different institutional patterns for dispersing or concentrating the powers of the state.

In the final pages, we return to our point of departure by asking what Americans concerned about the failures of social regulation might learn from the experiences of other countries. Our conclusions emphasize the difficulty of transplanting regulatory approaches from one national setting to another, since each country's policies are rooted in unique political traditions and practices. Yet comparison of regulatory policies brings the advantages and disadvantages of the American approach into sharper relief and raises some new issues that should inform discussions of reform. American policies have tended to magnify the uncertainties and deepen the value conflicts inherent to the regulation of health and environmental risks. If Europeans have achieved comparable levels of protection against chemical hazards at substantially lower economic and political cost, their methods merit study by anyone who is concerned about good government. As U.S. policy makers struggle to chart a new course over the next decade, they cannot afford to ignore the experiences of those who have discovered a smoother road across equally troubled terrain.

2

The Comparison of National Policies

The term *policy* is usually defined as a plan or course of action designed to influence specific decisions. Governmental policies, however, are both more haphazard and more dynamic than the dictionary definition suggests. They are aggregates of critical choices made over time by changing constellations of governmental actors operating only in loose concert with one another. It is a daunting task to identify distinctive policy approaches among kaleidoscopic patterns of decision making across four countries and four sectors of regulation; yet such an analysis must be undertaken if meaningful comparisons of regulatory politics in Europe and the United States are to be made.

Despite the surge of interest in public policy analysis in the past decade, there is little scholarly agreement about the components and boundaries of policy.[1] Analytical guidelines are particularly deficient in the case of regulatory policy. For example, since legislatures rarely foresee the full range of regulatory issues at the stage of policy formulation, administrative authorities enjoy considerable discretionary power to make decisions that are essentially legislative in character. In this context, the classic distinction between *policy* and *implementation* appears relatively unimportant. Both the procedures

[1] General works on policy analysis include Ira Sharkansky, ed., *Policy Analysis in Political Science* (Chicago: Markham, 1970); Kenneth Dolbeare, ed., *Public Policy Evaluation* (Beverly Hills, Calif.: Sage, 1975); Thomas R. Dye and Virginia Gray, eds., *Determinants of Public Policy* (Lexington, Mass.: Lexington Books, 1980).

used to resolve regulatory conflict and the individual decisions reached by administrative agencies become defining characteristics of the state's overall approach to regulation. The impacts of regulatory policy are equally difficult to characterize. Unlike other spheres of governmental action, such as social services, public works, or taxation, regulatory policy seeks welfare objectives and imposes changes in private behavior that have no readily calculated price tag. Accordingly, it is a major challenge for regulatory policy analysts to establish valid criteria for measuring the effectiveness of state intervention.[2]

Cross-national comparison of regulatory policies raises additional special difficulties. The field of comparative public policy, still in its infancy, has not yet developed firm theoretical or methodological guidelines.[3] Available studies seldom focus on regulation, and few attempt a general characterization of national regulatory styles.[4] There are thus few scholarly precedents for

---

[2] See Paul A. Sabatier, "Regulatory Policy-Making: Towards a Framework of Analysis," *Natural Resources Journal,* 17 (July 1977), 415–60.

[3] Useful contributions to the growing field of comparative policy analysis include Harold L. Wilensky, *The Welfare State and Equality* (Berkeley and Los Angeles: University of California Press, 1975); Richard Rose, ed., *The Dynamics of Public Policy: A Comparative Analysis* (Beverly Hills, Calif.: Sage, 1975); A. Heidenheimer, Hugh Heclo, and Carolyn Adams, *Comparative Public Policy: The Politics of Social Change in Europe and America* (New York: St. Martin's Press, 1975); Douglas E. Ashford, ed., *Comparing Public Policies: New Concepts and Methods,* vol. 4 of Sage Yearbooks in Politics and Public Policy (Beverly Hills, Calif.: Sage, 1978); Howard M. Leichter, *A Comparative Approach to Policy Analysis: Health Care Policy in Four Nations* (Cambridge: Cambridge University Press, 1979); Peter Flora and Arnold J. Heidenheimer, eds., *The Development of Welfare States in Europe and America* (New Brunswick, N.J.: Transaction Books, 1981).

[4] Cross-national analyses that are most relevant to the subject matter of this study include Ronald Brickman, Sheila Jasanoff, and Thomas Ilgen, *Chemical Regulation and Cancer: A Cross-National Study of Policy and Politics,* NTIS No. PB-83-206771 (Springfield, Va.: National Technical Information Service, 1983) (in part the basis for the present work). See also Steven Kelman, *Regulating America, Regulating Sweden: A Comparative Study of Occupational Safety and Health Policy* (Cambridge, Mass.: MIT Press, 1981); Lennart J. Lundqvist, *The Hare and the Tortoise: Clean Air Policies in the United States and Sweden* (Ann Arbor: University of Michigan Press, 1980); Donald R. Kelley, Kenneth R. Stuckel, and Richard R. Wescott, *The Economic Superpowers and the Environment* (San Francisco: W. H. Freeman, 1976); Elliot J. Feldman and Jerome Milch, *Technocracy vs. Democracy* (Boston: Auburn House, 1981); Lawrence E. Rose, "Consumer Protection Policy Making in Norway and the United States: A Research Note," *West European Politics,* 3, no. 3 (October 1980), 421–30; Sam Gusman et al., *Public Policy for Chemicals: National and International Issues* (Washington, D.C.: Conservation Foundation, 1980); Roger Williams, "Government Regulation of the Occupational and General Environments in the United Kingdom, the United States, and Sweden," Science Council of Canada Background Study no. 40, Ottawa, 1977; Joseph L. Badaracco, "A Study of Adversarial and Cooperative Relationships between Business and Government in Four Countries," Report prepared for the Office of Technology, Strategy, and Evaluation, U.S. Department of Commerce, Washington, D.C., 1981. See also David Vogel and Veronica Kun, "The Comparative Study of Environmental Policy: A Review of the Literature" (Paper presented at Science Center, Berlin, December 1983), and David Vogel, "Cooperative Regulation: Environmental Protec-

dealing with the problems of equivalence and comprehensiveness that inevitably arise when complex patterns of national decision making are compared. Growing out of different institutional, political, and legal settings, the chemical control policies adopted by the four governments frequently do not fit into the same conceptual categories. What is legislated in one country corresponds to administrative action in another. One country accords to the courts a continuous role in policy making that is unknown elsewhere. Regulatory outcomes take the form of legally binding rules in some countries and informal agreements between industry and government in others.

These analytical difficulties are partly offset by the intellectual rewards of cross-national comparison. For the policy analyst, a comparative approach reveals functional equivalents of regulatory policies that might be overlooked in studies focusing on a single country. Features that are taken for granted in one nation take on a new significance through their absence in other national settings. Cross-national comparison is thus a uniquely effective method for distinguishing what is generic in governmental regulation from what is conditioned by particular institutions or political cultures.

With these issues in mind, we undertake in this chapter a comparison of national chemical control policies structured by three ground rules. First, we define chemical control policy broadly as the sum of three more or less discrete stages of decision making: the decision of the state to define or expand its regulatory authority through the establishment of legislative goals and priorities; the process of implementation in which broad policy mandates are narrowed and given individual application; and the outcome and enforcement of administrative decision making. Second, our analysis is comparative throughout, in keeping with the goal of uncovering the most important areas of convergence and divergence among the four countries. Third, our description of policy is not exhaustive, but is intended only as a preliminary overview in which broadly differentiated patterns of policy choice can be distinguished. The main descriptive findings, summarized in a concluding section, set the stage for extended investigation and explanation in the chapters that follow.

The Definition of Regulatory Goals

During the last two decades, the regulatory agendas of the industrialized nations have expanded to include the control of toxic chemicals in virtually

tion in Great Britain," *Public Interest,* no. 72 (Summer 1983), pp. 88–106. Two studies that address more the politics than the policies of environmental control are Cynthia Enloe, *The Politics of Pollution in Comparative Perspective* (New York: McKay, 1975), and Dorothy Nelkin and Michael Pollak, *The Atom Besieged: Extraparliamentary Dissent in France and Germany* (Cambridge, Mass.: MIT Press, 1981).

every environmental pathway and product category. Though extraordinary in their scope, these initiatives are embedded in a centuries-old tradition of state intervention to protect the health and safety of the general public against harmful private conduct. This "police power" has found expression in some of the oldest recorded legal texts, particularly those concerning the wholesomeness of food and water. The laws of the ancient Hittites dating from around 1500 B.C., for example, stipulated that a person be fined three half-shekels of silver for putting filth into a cistern, and the Bible mentions laws prohibiting the adulteration of food. The British first enacted an anti-adulteration statute in 1266.[5]

In the postwar period, an exponential rise in chemical production and use, accompanied by rapid advances in scientific knowledge about the hazards of pollution, spurred public efforts to control these newly discovered threats to health and the environment. To start with, governments relied on legal and policy instruments already in place for safeguarding public health. In the United States, the Federal Food and Drugs Act of 1906 provided an early conceptual framework for controlling hazards transmitted through food. Similarly, in Germany and France, legislation directed against the adulteration of food has been in place since 1879 and 1903, respectively. With significant amendment and modification, these laws have been transformed into more general instruments for regulating food safety, including the hazards presented by chemical additives.

Worker safety also has been a recurrent concern of legislatures in the industrialized countries since the mid-nineteenth century. Though the locus and instruments of regulatory control have varied over the years, frameworks of the past supplied the basis for modern programs to regulate chemicals in the workplace. Regulatory concern with the environmental and health effects of pesticides boasts a shorter history, corresponding to their relatively recent widespread use in agriculture. Nevertheless, pesticides and other agricultural poisons have been subject to public control for several decades in all four countries.

The 1970s witnessed a worldwide sharpening of interest in toxic substances, and chemical risk assessment and regulation were elevated to new prominence on national legislative agendas. Pressured by highly publicized chemical disasters at Minamata (Japan), Seveso (Italy), and Hopewell, Virginia (United States), and by dozens of lesser incidents, the leading chemical-producing nations of the world debated and adopted legislation to fill gaps in the existing network of controls. A new generation of laws created far-reaching obligations for the chemical industry to test new products before

---

[5]Peter B. Hutt, "The Basis and Purpose of Government Regulation of Adulteration and Misbranding of Food," *Food Drug Cosmetic Law Journal,* 33, no. 10 (1978), 506.

releasing them for commercial use.[6] In 1976 the U.S. Congress enacted the Toxic Substances Control Act (TSCA). The European Community followed suit in September 1979 by incorporating into its existing directive on the classification, packaging, and labeling of dangerous substances a new framework for chemical testing and notification. Member states established conforming national programs within a few years. This flurry of legislation rounded off the long history of parallel policy development which brought specific classes of chemicals—food additives, pesticides, chemicals in the workplace—under regulatory control in Europe and the United States at roughly the same times.

Assumptions Underlying Chemical Control

Modern chemical control policies rest on a shared assumption that chemical risks to health and the environment can be mitigated through preventive regulation. Yet the costs of producing relevant information and adopting control measures can be extremely high. The allocation of these costs is an important dimension in the state's definition of regulatory policy. In general, all four governments have endorsed the "polluter pays principle,"[7] which holds polluting enterprises responsible for undesirable externalities associated with their operations. To date, however, there are relatively few statutory schemes requiring the chemical industry to set aside funds for compensating those who are injured by its products. One limited exception is the U.S. "Superfund" law,[8] which provides money from an industry-financed fund for cleaning up after chemical disasters.

Conceptually related to the "polluter pays principle" is the rule that manufacturers be required to demonstrate that their products are "safe" before they market them. In legal terms, this means that the burden of proving the safety of new products rests with the manufacturer. In all four countries there has been a notable shift away from earlier policies that permitted relatively uncontrolled introduction of new chemicals into commercial use. New products are no longer presumed safe until public authorities prove that they are harmful. In removing the presumption of safety, modern chemical control

---

[6]These include Sweden (1973, 1979), Japan (1973), United Kingdom (1974), Canada (1975), Norway (1976), United States (1976), France (1977), Denmark (1979), Germany (1980), Austria, Australia, and the remaining members of the European Economic Community. See, generally, Sam Gusman et al., op. cit., pp. 10–16.

[7]See OECD, "The Polluter Must Pay Principle," Paris, 1974, and Recommendation of OECD Council on Guiding Principles Concerning International Economic Aspects of Environmental Policies, July 6, 1972.

[8]Comprehensive Environmental Response, Compensation, and Liability Act, Public Law (hereafter P.L.) no. 98–510 (1980).

laws impose higher costs on manufacturers, since the burden of establishing product safety can only be met through expensive programs of testing and research which delay commercialization.

In the case of food additives and pesticides, most countries have elected a legally enforceable permitting or registration process as the mechanism for imposing premarket testing obligations on manufacturers. Firms cannot sell such products without obtaining the government's approval in advance. In the 1980s only Britain controls pesticide safety by means of a voluntary screening program, the Pesticide Safety Precaution Scheme (PSPS), which rests on an informal agreement between the pesticide industry and government. But the PSPS is merely the exception that proves the rule, for the scheme is scarcely less binding than a statutory program. Few manufacturers could think of marketing a new pesticide without "voluntary" clearance under PSPS, and the European Community has accepted it as an enforceable registration program.

Some observers see the permitting programs for pesticides and food additives as part of a more general shift from a "caveat emptor" to a "caveat vendor" philosophy of marketing consumer goods. But if such a change is in progress, thus far it extends only to those classes of chemicals (pesticides, food additives, drugs) for which innovation is relatively slow and the range of uses is well known at the time of manufacture. For new industrial chemicals, the laws of all four countries establish notification schemes rather than registration programs. Under these frameworks the manufacturer's responsibility ends with the production of data pertinent to the assessment of health and environmental risks. It is then up to the regulatory authority to evaluate this information and to determine whether the substance presents a risk sufficient to trigger governmental intervention. With respect to toxic substances in the workplace, the distribution of regulatory burdens is even more lopsided. Except in Britain, where employers have the primary duty to develop protective measures, a governmental agency is responsible for both identifying hazards and formulating control measures.

Safety Concepts: The Criteria for Intervention

Chemical control policies define not only the responsibilities of manufacturers and users, but also the limits on the government's power to intervene. The central decision to undertake or forego regulation is usually controlled by a legislated standard that establishes the circumstances justifying state intervention. This standard can function as an effective check on the implementing agency, particularly if it is enforced through legislative oversight or judicial review. Standards used in toxic substance control laws are ordinarily expressed in terms of risk to public health or the environment: governmental action is authorized only if the risk presented by a chemical is legally sufficient to warrant intervention. Terms like *risk, safety,* and *danger* are thus frequently used in the chemical control laws of all four countries, but national legislatures differ considerably in the specificity with which they define these terms.

During the last twenty years, U.S. chemical control laws have spelled out in increasing detail the criteria that decision makers must apply in deciding whether a risk is serious enough to regulate. The idea of "safety" was discussed at length in 1958 when Congress comprehensively revised the existing law on food additives. It was clearly recognized that "safety" is not an absolute concept, for even apparently harmless substances like water and salt can be deadly if they are consumed in sufficient quantity.[9] The new law accordingly permitted the use of food additives as long as manufacturers could show that they were "reasonably certain" not to harm human health. But Congress adopted a more stringent "zero risk" policy for potentially carcinogenic food additives. An anticancer amendment proposed by Congressman James Delaney required the Food and Drug Administration to ban any additive found to induce cancer in humans or test animals.

More recent chemical control legislation has mandated a broader approach to risk assessment, requiring implementing agencies to weigh economic and social considerations along with public health in reaching regulatory decisions. Federal pesticide legislation adopted in 1972, for example, requires the Environmental Protection Agency to take into account "economic, social, and environmental costs and benefits" in deciding whether to ban or restrict such substances. The Occupational Safety and Health Act (OSH Act) of 1970, as interpreted by the Supreme Court, does not require formal cost-benefit analysis in setting standards for toxic substances, but it does demand that "health and safety goals be capable of economic and technological accomplishment."[10] The 1976 Toxic Substances Control Act provides even more explicit guidance. TSCA specifies not only that EPA consider costs and benefits during the regulatory process, but also that the agency take into account particular factors such as the impact of regulation on the national economy, small business, and technological innovation.

Terms like *risk* and *safety* in European legislation are seldom accompanied by explicit instructions to weigh the costs of regulation. The French law on pesticide registration, for example, specifies only that candidate substances be examined for their "harmlessness with respect to public health, users,

[9]H.R. Rep. no. 2284, 85th Cong., 2d sess. (1958), pp. 4–5 (reprinted in Charles W. Dunn, ed., *Legislative Record of 1958 Food Additives Amendment to Federal Food, Drug, and Cosmetic Act* [New York: Commerce Clearing House, 1958], p. 39).

[10]*American Textile Manufacturers Institute, Inc. v. Donovan,* 452 *U.S.* 490 (1981).

crops and animals." Similarly, the 1977 law concerning premarket notification and control of industrial chemicals expresses an intent to "protect man and his environment from the risks that can result from chemical substances." These laws on their face are silent about the role of economic considerations in decision making. In this respect, they are strongly reminiscent of the 1958 U.S. legislation on food additives.

Risk standards in German chemical control legislation also apparently limit the regulator's attention to issues of health or environmental damage. The German Chemicals Act (ChemG), for example, authorizes regulatory action whenever there is a "substantial hazard to human life or health or the environment." The provisions of the law vary as to whether such a hazard must be "demonstrated" or only substantially or reasonably probable and whether factual findings are required to support the determination of "substantial hazard." Similarly, to be accepted for registration, pesticides not only must be "adequately effective," but also must "cause no harmful effects on human and animal health" when properly used. Such formulations leave little apparent scope for administrators to consider economic impacts.

British regulatory standards for toxic substances are less consistent than those of the other three countries. The Food and Drugs Act of 1955, for example, follows conventional norms in requiring merely that food be "safe to consume." By contrast, British legislation on occupational safety and health explicitly incorporates the notion of economic costs. The Health and Safety at Work Etc. Act (HSW Act) of 1974, a broad enabling statute, assigns to employers the responsibility for maintaining health and safety in the workplace only "so far as is reasonably practicable" using the "best practicable means." As construed by the courts, this language permits employers to balance only the costs and inconvenience associated with specific control measures against risks to employee health and safety.[11]

Priorities: The Emphasis on Existing Chemicals and Carcinogens

Priority setting is a particularly important component of chemical control policy. The number of chemical substances in current use is estimated to lie anywhere between thirty-five thousand and one hundred thousand, and several hundred new compounds enter commerce each year.[12] The task of

[11] George Applebey, "British Legislation on Health and Safety at Work: A Reappraisal after Five Years," *Les Cahiers de Droit,* 20 (1979), 702–3.

[12] The number varies owing to differences in the definition and classification of chemical substances and the size of the market under consideration. The Commission of the European Community has published a list of some thirty-five thousand chemicals believed to be on the European market. The EPA inventory of chemicals subject to TSCA, published in

evaluating and controlling these substances puts severe strains on public resources and makes the establishment of priorities almost indispensable. Priorities often emerge spontaneously as regulators are forced to act on newly revealed hazards. In a smoothly functioning process, however, priorities represent disciplined and reasoned choices about the investment of limited resources. Viewed cross-nationally, two basic regulatory orientations emerge as significant: the degree of attention devoted to substances already on the market and the emphasis on carcinogens relative to other toxic chemicals.

The policies of the four governments express similar commitments to regulating new food additives, pesticides, and industrial chemicals. But there are striking differences in their concern with substances cleared for use in the past. The United States has by far the most fully developed legal framework for discovering and controlling existing chemical hazards. TSCA, for example, establishes a framework for dealing with both new and existing industrial chemicals. Pursuant to TSCA's broad mandate, EPA can demand information from industry on the production, distribution, and use of existing chemicals, as well as data on exposure and health and environmental effects. The agency can use this information to regulate any substance found to pose an unreasonable risk. Although EPA was slow to implement these provisions,[13] by the end of 1980 it had made appreciable progress toward targeting existing chemicals for regulatory action.[14]

July 1980, came to over fifty-five thousand substances. The International Register of Potentially Toxic Chemicals, a UN program (see chapter 11), reports that a more inclusive list of chemicals on the U.S. market, based on the TSCA inventory and the NIOSH Registry of Toxic Effects of Chemical Substances, comes to sixty-six thousand. Another estimated twenty thousand chemicals were not included in the TSCA inventory because of the limited quantity prepared. Over ten thousand additional chemicals are estimated to be in use outside the United States. See IRPTC, "Instructions for the Selection and Presentation of Data for the International Register of Potentially Toxic Chemicals," UN Environment Program, Geneva, 1979, p. 1.

[13] See, for example, House Committee on Commerce, Science, and Transportation, Subcommittee on Science, Technology and Space, *Hearings on Toxic Substances Control Act of 1976,* 96th Cong., 1st sess., 1979; *New York Times,* May 6, 1980; GAO, "EPA Is Slow to Carry Out Its Responsibility to Control Harmful Chemicals," Washington, D.C., October 28, 1980.

[14] These included final regulations on PCBs, the only class of chemicals to be named in the act, and a ban on nonessential uses of chlorofluorocarbons in joint action with FDA and CPSC. EPA also completed its inventory of existing substances, required and obtained health effects data on ten chemicals, proposed rules calling for exposure data on some twenty-three hundred substances and for health effects on sixty-one substances, and completed an initial screen of approximately one thousand existing chemicals for their possible harmful effects. Testing requirements had been proposed for chloromethane and the chlorinated benzenes, and a timetable was issued for proposing test rules on another thirty-seven substances or classes of chemicals. See GAO, ibid.; EPA, *TSCA Chemicals-in-Progress Bulletin,* 1, nos. 1–4 (1980).

Notification statutes in Europe give much less attention to existing chemicals. The European Community's Sixth Amendment makes no reference to old substances, and earlier directives concerning the classification, packaging, and labeling of hazardous chemicals did not require extensive testing of substances already in commerce. The 1977 French chemicals law requires industry to notify public authorities only when a new danger arises in connection with existing substances. The corresponding German law authorizes the federal government to demand testing for particular existing substances that indicate a real hazard, but, unlike TSCA, it does not require systematic testing or hazard assessment, and these provisions were not accorded high priority in the initial stages of the law's implementation. Conforming to the EC directive, British regulations on chemical notification do not consider existing substances, although the HSW Act provides sufficient legal authority for doing so.

In the case of pesticide regulation, all governments except the British require manufacturers to renew their product licenses after a specified number of years (ten in France and Germany, five in the United States). Moreover, all have procedures for reexamining cleared products if new risks are suspected or if an application for extended use is received. But reappraisals are often perfunctory in European countries, and regulatory attention is most often oriented toward the assessment of new ingredients and preparations.[15] In the United States, in contrast, the 1972 Federal Environmental Pesticide Control Act required EPA to examine for reregistration some thirty-five thousand pesticides then on the market. When the agency proved unable to meet this requirement, two procedures were introduced to accelerate the review process. The Federal Pesticide Act of 1978 allowed EPA to develop generic registration standards for active ingredients. Another procedure, the Rebuttable Presumption against Registration (RPAR) program, authorized EPA to determine if a suspected pesticide meets one or more criteria of excess risk; if it does, the agency initiates a proceeding that may eventually lead to cancellation.[16]

Cross-national disparities in the treatment of existing chemicals are somewhat less pronounced in the area of food additives. In Britain, for example,

[15] Interviews with pesticide registration officials in France, Germany, and Britain. Also Ministère de l'Agriculture, Direction de la Qualité, "Rapport général d'activité," Paris, 1979, p. 25.

[16] Despite lags in implementation, both the RPAR and the generic standard programs focus far greater attention on pesticides already in use than is customary in the three European countries. By the end of 1979, more than two hundred pesticides had gone through some stage of the RPAR process, although only thirty of these had actually reached the stage of an RPAR notice. See GAO, "Delays and Unresolved Issues Plague New Pesticide Protection Programs," Washington, D.C., February 15, 1980.

periodic review of approved additives has resulted in the issuance of over twenty reports since 1965, including assessments of antioxidants, flavorings, and food colors.[17] However, FDA's program for reviewing previously permitted food additives in the United States appears considerably more extensive. In 1970 FDA embarked on a reevaluation of some three hundred and fifty substances "generally regarded as safe" (GRAS). It has also commenced a review of some twenty-one hundred flavorings and, under the 1960 color additive amendment, has reexamined two hundred food colors.[18]

In recent years the preoccupation with existing chemicals in the United States has translated into an almost exclusive focus on carcinogens. Unlike European legislatures, the U.S. Congress has repeatedly directed governmental agencies to treat carcinogens as substances of special concern. The most dramatic action along these lines was the adoption in 1958 of the Delaney amendment to the federal Food, Drug, and Cosmetic Act (FDCA). This statutory provision has been construed by both public interest groups and officials in the government as an invitation to pursue especially stringent policies in regulating carcinogens. In 1976 Congress again singled out carcinogens, as well as mutagens and teratogens, for special attention under TSCA. Legislative interest in carcinogens has been amplified by the efforts of federal agencies such as the Occupational Safety and Health Administration and the Interagency Regulatory Liaison Group (IRLG)[19] to establish special generic procedures for identifying and regulating these substances.

The heavy U.S. emphasis on carcinogens is reflected as well in the extensive chemical testing programs of the regulatory agencies and the federal health research institutes. By far the largest volume of this research is directed toward identifying carcinogens. For example, by 1981 the animal testing program of the National Cancer Institute (NCI), now administered by the National Toxicology Program (NTP), had examined the carcinogenic effects of more than two hundred substances. Additional chemicals are being reviewed at the rate of thirty to forty-five each year. This program has no parallel in any of the European countries.

French and British policies concerning carcinogens have developed in piecemeal fashion; in neither country has a consistent desire been displayed to place these substances in a prominent slot on the regulatory agenda. In

[17] MAFF, Food Additives and Contaminants Committee, *Interim Report on the Review of the Colouring Matter in Food Regulations, 1973* (London: HMSO, 1979).

[18] GAO, "Need for More Effective Regulation of Direct Additives to Food," Washington, D.C., August 14, 1980.

[19] This group was formed during the Carter administration, under an interagency cooperative agreement, to coordinate federal activities in the area of chemical regulation. As finally constituted, IRLG represented five agencies: EPA, FDA, OSHA, CPSC, and the Food Safety and Quality Service (FSQS), Department of Agriculture.

keeping with a low legislative concern, the idea of a specific "carcinogens policy" finds little active support in either French or British administrative circles. Authorities in both countries regard carcinogenicity as only one of many possible toxic effects though they concede it is one of the most serious.[20]

In Germany, however, carcinogens have been recognized for years as a separate category for purposes of regulating workplace health and safety. A commission of the German Research Society (Deutsche Forschungsgemeinschaft, DFG), which designates tolerance levels for most occupational chemicals, decided some years ago that no valid numerical exposure thresholds can be established for carcinogens. The commission issues an annually updated list of carcinogens, for which an expert advisory committee of the labor ministry determines "technically achievable" (rather than "safe") ambient standards.[21] This process in effect constitutes an occupational "cancer policy." Significantly, the initiative for treating carcinogens in this fashion was supplied by an autonomous scientific committee rather than parliament or the administrative agencies.

The Regulatory Process

In sum, there are substantial similarities among the four countries at the initial stages of policy formulation. Responsibility for protecting the public from chemical hazards was assumed and expanded at comparable times, and similar strategies were adopted for allocating regulatory duties and costs between the public and private sectors. One observes greater differentiation in the limits imposed on the state's powers of intervention, particularly with respect to requirements that economic costs be balanced against public health considerations. Some divergences are also detectable in priority setting, with the United States displaying the greatest preoccupation with existing substances and carcinogens. Among the statutory provisions examined here, only the Delaney amendment states the obligation to regulate carcinogens in unequivocal terms.

Turning to the implementation process, however, we find that the policies of the four governments diverge quite markedly, with the American approach in sharpest contrast. A series of procedural features, from reliance on formal

---

[20] This attitude explains the British HSE's decision not to update the Carcinogenic Substances Regulations of 1967, which placed strict controls on four chemicals in the benzidine dye family.

[21] Additional protective requirements are specified by the Industrial Injuries Insurance Institute for the chemical industry, a public law corporation with legal authority to make occupational safety and health regulations.

analysis to rules of public participation, distinguish American regulatory decision making from standard European practices.

Economic and Scientific Analysis of Regulatory Options

Regulators in the United States rely much more than their European counterparts on formal quantitative methodologies such as economic analysis and risk assessment. U.S. agencies have been forced to evaluate the economic and social costs of regulation not only by their statutory mandates, but also by recurring presidential directives. Guidelines issued under Presidents Nixon and Ford required the federal agencies to calculate the economic consequences of major regulatory proposals. The Carter administration also directed the agencies to prepare economic impact analyses and to balance the "burdens" of proposed regulations against their "gains."[22] President Reagan's Executive Order 12291, issued in February 1981, reaffirmed presidential support for "regulatory impact analysis." The order went further than its predecessors by providing for centralized enforcement through the Office of Management and Budget (OMB) and by recommending wider use of quantified cost-benefit analysis.

Economic analysis is a routine component in the development of U.S. toxic substances regulations. EPA, for example, has undertaken economic impact analysis on such measures as the standard for benzene emissions, rules for premanufacture notification and testing under TSCA, and pesticide registration guidelines. OSHA, too, has commissioned economic analyses of such initiatives as exposure standards for individual substances (for example, DBCP, acrylonitrile, beryllium), the hazard notification program, and the generic "cancer policy."

The virtual neglect of formal cost-benefit analysis in European decision making presents a striking contrast. Of the European agencies considered in this study, only Britain's Health and Safety Commission (HSC) has explicitly acknowledged the need to prepare economic assessments of proposed rules.[23] But although such appraisals are now standard practice in HSC's rule making, they tend to be more qualitative than quantitative and are much briefer than comparable evaluations by U.S. agencies. As of 1982, no directive to account for the costs and benefits of chemical control had been issued in Germany or France.

---

[22] For a more detailed account of these Ford and Carter initiatives, see Michael S. Baram, "Regulation of Health, Safety, and Environmental Quality and the Use of Cost-Benefit Analysis," Report to the Administrative Conference of the United States, September 7, 1978.

[23] HSC, *Cost/Benefit Assessment of Health, Safety, and Pollution Controls* (London: HMSO, 1982).

With respect to scientific analysis, as well, American regulators go well beyond their European counterparts in quantifying their risk assessments and in making public the data, hypotheses, and reasoning underlying their actions. These tendencies have become more pronounced in recent years. The Food and Drug Administration's decision to ban cyclamates in 1969 was accompanied by relatively little discussion of scientific issues. In contrast, an extensive scientific record was compiled to support the proposed ban on saccharin a mere ten years later. EPA, OSHA, and the Consumer Product Safety Commission (CPSC) have also tended to provide more detailed scientific explanations over time. For example, OSHA's record in support of its generic policy on occupational carcinogens covered almost three hundred pages in the *Federal Register,* of which more than half were devoted to analyzing disputed scientific issues and explaining the agency's choices among competing arguments. The publication capped more than three years of regulatory development, summarized the views of at least fifty-four experts in the field of cancer research, and distilled a total record of over two hundred and fifty thousand pages. In recent years, all the major health and environmental agencies have accepted the utility of quantitative risk assessments.

The scientific rationales published by European chemical control agencies appear thinner, less systematic, and less formal. In Germany, scientific analysis of hazards and of regulatory options is generally performed by "subordinate authorities" structured within each ministry. As a rule, the findings and recommendations of these agencies are not made public. Documented reports are occasionally issued with respect to issues of particular regulatory concern, such as the Federal Biological Research Center's (BBA) 1978 review of the safety of the herbicide 2,4,5-T.[24] Similarly, the Federal Environmental Agency (UBA) prepared a lengthy report on asbestos in 1980, but unlike the 2,4,5-T report, this study did not attempt to justify a specific regulatory decision.

The scientific commissions of the DFG which play a prominent role in German chemical regulation follow a more open policy with regard to publication. As members of the nation's leading research organization, these groups are strongly opposed to secrecy in the pursuit of knowledge. Symptomatic of their commitment to "transparency" is the decision of the commission on hazardous substances in the workplace to publish its evaluations of toxicological data along with the standards it recommends. In the commission's view, numerical exposure standards make sense only if they are read in light of the accompanying scientific record.

British scientific advisory bodies vary widely in their attitudes toward the

---

[24]BBA, "Stellungnahme zur Anwendung von 2,4,5-T bei der Unkrautbekämpfung im Forst," Berlin, 1978.

publication of scientific assessments. The Food Additives and Contaminants Committee (FACC), for example, regularly publishes the scientific basis for the recommendations it makes to the Ministry of Agriculture, Fisheries, and Food (MAFF). Compared with similar documentation in the United States, these explanations appear extremely terse, merely summarizing the arguments supporting the decision. The FACC, however, is more open than the Advisory Committee on Pesticides (ACP), which ordinarily does not justify its scientific conclusions in public.[25] The Health and Safety Commission and its advisory bodies have also followed an ad hoc approach to scientific justification. Only for substances of intense regulatory concern, such as asbestos, has the HSC published detailed evaluations.

Expert advisory bodies do most of the technical work for French regulatory authorities, but the basis for their advice consistently remains secret. One minor exception was the brief discussion of Tris in the 1978 annual report of the Higher Council of Public Hygiene (Conseil Supérieur de l'Hygiène Publique, CSHP), an advisory committee on public health issues.

Generic Procedures

Generic procedures represent a framework for decision making that falls conceptually between broad legislative statements of objectives and particularized agency decisions on specific chemicals. These procedures seek to standardize decision making by establishing general principles for evaluating the adequacy of evidence and assessing risk. During the 1970s, American regulators invested considerable energy in developing such procedures. The most comprehensive attempt was OSHA's 1980 "cancer policy," a regulation designed to identify and categorize all carcinogens found in the workplace. OSHA expected its policy to streamline risk assessments and to establish sensible priorities among potential regulatory targets. Less ambitious attempts to formulate "cancer principles" have been episodically undertaken by EPA and the President's Office of Science and Technology Policy.

European reaction to these U.S. initiatives has ranged from incredulity to principled rejection. European regulatory officials challenge the scientific basis for the generic approach, stressing that it ignores important variations among chemical compounds and prevents accurate assessments of risk. In keeping with these views, efforts to develop standardized principles of car-

---

[25] One exception was ACP's report on 2,4,5-T, which it issued in December 1980. The document, written in response to public controversy about the herbicide in Britain and other Western countries, surveyed the scientific information about the substance in considerably greater detail than did an earlier report dating from March 1979. See ACP, *Further Review of the Safety for Use in the U.K. of the Herbicide 2,4,5-T* (London: HMSO, 1980), and idem, *Review of the Safety for Use in the U.K. of the Herbicide 2,4,5-T* (London: HMSO, 1979).

cinogen risk assessment are virtually nonexistent in European regulatory and scientific circles.

Public Participation

In highly contentious areas of public policy making, such as chemical regulation, rules of participation take on overriding significance. Access to regulatory authorities permits private interest groups to shape the policy agenda and influence individual decisions. The regulatory process in all four countries admits the views of nongovernmental participants, but the extent, format, and timing of participation vary considerably.

The U.S. administrative process provides by far the most generous opportunities for even marginally interested groups to take part in regulatory proceedings. Many recent environmental and health and safety statutes authorize concerned persons to petition for specific regulatory action. In addition, these statutes provide for public hearings at which citizen groups, as well as industrial interests, can express their viewpoints. TSCA even authorizes EPA to fund public interest intervenors who are likely to make a positive contribution to decision making.

German channels for public intervention are significantly narrower. A requirement to consult named interests may be imposed by law, as for example in the case of the food safety statute, which requires regulators to consult with "a circle of experts to be selected from science, consumer interests and the affected industry." But even when consultation is not mandatory, German agencies seek advice from multipartite expert committees, such as the labor ministry's committee on hazardous substances in the workplace. Participation in the French regulatory system follows a similar pattern. In the regulatory sectors reviewed here, governmental agencies rely on pluralistic advisory groups to provide a range of views on regulatory issues.[26] Representatives of groups favoring regulation usually form only a small minority on such bodies. The major exception is the area of worker safety, where five of fourteen members of the dangerous substances committee represent workers' unions.

Public participation in Germany and France differs in three notable respects from the U.S. model. First, categories of interests to be consulted during regulatory proceedings are often identified by law or regulation. Second, the administrative authority has almost complete discretion to decide which interest group representatives it will hear, since the law specifies at

---

[26]The 1978 consumer protection law explicitly provides for consultation with consumer groups and industry (Law no. 78–23 on the Protection and Information of the Consumer, 1978).

most that certain classes of interests must be heard. Third, participation is usually channeled through established "peak" organizations (trade associations, consumer groups, labor unions), and opportunities for individuals or minor interest groups to take part in regulatory proceedings are usually minimal. Overall, the consultative process offers greatest access to expert or informed opinion; amateurs or generalists have no assured place in such proceedings.

Consultation in Britain follows a less structured pattern than it does in Germany or France, though it is an equally central element of the decision-making process. Major regulatory proposals are circulated to other governmental departments, to affected industries, and to consumer or public interest groups regarded as competent by regulatory authorities. Comments made by these parties are carefully considered in reaching final decisions, so that groups drawn into the consultative process exert considerable influence on policy making. Conversely, groups not recognized as important by public authorities remain outside the administrative process and exercise little or no influence. In the context of worker health and safety, Britain has adopted a "tripartite" institutional structure as required by the HSW Act of 1974. This means that workers enjoy equal representation with industry and local government on all decision-making and advisory bodies.

Public Access to Information

The effectiveness of private intervention in regulatory proceedings depends in large part on access not only to the decision maker but also to relevant sources of information. The U.S. regulatory process is notable for exposing such information to public scrutiny. The Freedom of Information Act (FOIA) establishes an overarching presumption of openness: information in the federal government's control is regarded as accessible unless it is protected by a specific exemption. One of these exemptions preserves the traditional confidentiality of commercial information. In the case of toxic chemicals, however, even this protection has been somewhat narrowed by TSCA, which provides for the release of health and safety studies regardless of claims of confidentiality. The records compiled in the course of rule-making proceedings are generally available for public review, and agencies are required to publish their evaluation of this information when making a regulatory decision.

In contrast, European governments continue to carry out their regulatory business under a presumption of confidentiality. The edifice of secrecy is most firmly grounded in Britain, where any unauthorized disclosure of official information is punishable as a criminal offense under the Official Secrets Act. In France, a law enacted in 1978 established a citizen's right to information and granted access to nonpersonal administrative documents. The exceptions to the French law, however, seem on their face more extensive than those of the American FOIA, particularly the exemption for documents whose disclosure would bring prejudice to the "secrecy of the deliberation of government and of the authorities in the executive branch."

Legislative and Judicial Supervision

The schoolbook notion of policy making presumes that the role of the legislature ends with the enactment of laws, while the responsibility of the courts is confined to post hoc corrections of unlawful decision making. This neat compartmentalization often holds true in Europe, but in the U.S. context it loses almost all validity. Both Congress and the courts closely supervise the process of implementation to a degree that is unimaginable in Europe.

Relations between the U.S. Congress and the federal administrative agencies, not complacent in the best of circumstances, are exceptionally demanding and competitive in matters relating to chemical control. These tensions are reflected in a proliferation of adversarial proceedings: legislative hearings, the appropriations process, reauthorization and amendment, investigations by special oversight committees and the General Accounting Office (GAO), and formal or informal inquiries. Federal agencies implementing toxic substance policies spend considerable time each year preparing for and participating in these interchanges. For example, in 1978 the Food and Drug Administration took part in fifty-one hearings before twenty-four different congressional committees and subcommittees. In the same year, GAO issued eight investigative reports on issues affecting FDA, and the agency responded to 4,463 written inquiries from Congress.

Turning to Europe, one finds a vastly diminished number and variety of interactions between the legislature and the executive during the implementation of chemical control programs. Special investigations, a recognized form of parliamentary intervention, generally address only the broadest policy issues. The parliamentary question is virtually the only device for calling ministers to account for more specific administrative decisions, such as actions on hazardous chemicals. Questions usually focus on the government's response to individual substances, particularly suspected carcinogens, but they also occasionally address broader policy choices, such as the government's strategy for controlling occupational cancer.

Apart from the watchful eye of Congress, U.S. regulators must contend with an extremely active judiciary. The power of the federal courts is invoked not only by manufacturers seeking invalidation of onerous regulations, but also by consumer groups, labor unions, and environmentalists wishing to compel speedier or more stringent regulatory action. Indeed, resort to the courts by one or another interest group has become so commonplace that major regulatory issues are seldom settled without litigation. As a result, the courts enjoy an unparalleled opportunity to second-guess the agencies in the implementation of chemical control laws.

Even a casual observer is struck by the vastly lower level of judicial involvement in European regulatory processes. The courts in Europe provide numerous back-up services to regulatory authorities: violators of chemical control laws can be prosecuted in court, and judges are sometimes called on to order remedial action. Suits against governmental agencies by private parties, however, are extremely rare, even when regulatory action seriously impinges on private economic interests. German administrative and constitutional courts have occasionally confronted regulatory issues relating to toxic substances in the environment, but they have been only minimally involved in the process of chemical product regulation.

Policy Outcomes

Our analysis of the regulatory process for chemical control underscores the uniqueness of the American approach. With remarkable consistency across several regulatory sectors, the United States has opted for open and indiscriminate access of private citizens to decision making. The U.S. process also demonstrates a striking preference for formal analysis of regulatory options, including quantitative risk assessment. Congress and the courts join the regulatory agencies as major players in policy implementation. Notwithstanding some significant differences across countries and programs, European chemical control processes diverge from these U.S. practices in virtually every respect.

One might expect that such differences in regulatory decision making, in combination with the different priorities cited earlier, would lead to significant differences in policy outcomes. To test this hypothesis, the following section reviews some of the more significant dimensions of the state's regulatory output: the instruments selected to control chemicals, the substances singled out for regulatory action, and the effectiveness of the state's enforcement strategies.

The Choice of Control Instrument

National authorities have at their disposal a wide variety of instruments for controlling chemicals, ranging from outright bans on production or use to compulsory warnings for prospective users. The most restrictive measures are often directed at carcinogens, such as the ban on cancer-causing food additives mandated by the Delaney clause of the U.S. Food, Drug, and Cosmetic Act. For some additives prohibited under the Delaney clause, such as Red Dye No. 2, European officials have chosen the less extreme solution of restricting usage to certain categories of foods at specified maximum doses. In all four countries, labeling figures prominently among strategies for controlling food additives, but the requirement that saccharin-containing products carry a label specifically alerting consumers to the risk of cancer is unique to the United States.

For pesticides and related products, the four governments have generally adopted similar control measures: complete or partial prohibitions on use, labeling and other restrictions on permitted uses, and provisional clearance for experimental trials. But within this common pattern, there are notable differences in approach and emphasis. Since the British pesticide clearance scheme rests on a voluntary agreement between government and industry, controls on pesticide use have no legal force, but are developed only as recommended guidelines. With respect to pesticide residues, Great Britain is the only country that has not yet mandated legal standards establishing maximum allowable levels in food. British policy is based on the assumption that if guidelines on application and use are properly followed, residue levels will remain within acceptable limits.

The four countries differ most strikingly in the instruments they use to regulate chemicals in the workplace. The United States and West Germany rely more heavily than the other two countries on numerical standards defining the permissible limits of exposure. Since 1970, OSHA has regulated a small but significant group of substances by means of exposure standards, including a number of known human carcinogens. In Germany, legally binding exposure limits are in effect for a larger list of hazardous substances, including more than forty recognized carcinogens. The British, however, prescribe exposure limits primarily in the form of recommendations, and by 1980 the French had adopted legally enforceable exposure limits for only four substances, three of which are carcinogens (asbestos, benzene, vinyl chloride).

The use of medical surveillance to protect worker health also varies across the four countries. In Germany and France, industry is legally obliged to provide medical care and periodic check-ups for workers, including those exposed to toxic substances. The British worker safety agency maintains its own corps of physicians and nurses to conduct obligatory medical examinations of exposed workers. All three European governments must be notified whenever a worker is afflicted with an identifiable occupational disease. Federal law in the United States requires monitoring of workers exposed to regulated substances, but it does not impose more extensive medical care obligations on employers.

To date the three European governments have also gone further than the

United States in promoting worker safety through such indirect means as creating channels for workers to deal with management on health and safety issues. These measures include the appointment of worker-designated safety representatives in Britain, the establishment of health and safety councils in France, and the extension of the codetermination (worker participation) principle to workplace safety in Germany. All four countries have public training and information programs for workers and require the labeling of dangerous chemicals. OSHA's rule on labeling appeared in 1983, long after such provisions were in force in the three European countries. Finally, it is worth mentioning that none of the four countries uses market incentives such as taxes, charges, or marketable permits to control toxic substances in the workplace or under any of the other three regulatory frameworks.

Controls on Specific Substances

Because national authorities use different means to achieve their ends, it is difficult to make straightforward comparisons among the controls imposed on specific substances. Work practice requirements in one country, for example, may correspond to standards based on engineering controls in another. The fragmented, overlapping, and dynamic character of administrative rules pertaining to individual chemicals makes cross-national comparisons all the more difficult. Some regulations, such as labeling orders, cover thousands of compounds and use different naming conventions, making precise comparison almost impossible.

Nevertheless, by suitably narrowing the field of comparison, it is possible to draw some preliminary conclusions about the regulatory output of the four governments. The regulation of carcinogens offers especially fruitful comparisons because it is relatively easy to delimit the class of target compounds and to trace official response to these substances in the four countries. Our analysis here rests on three groups of chemicals independently recognized as carcinogens by at least one regulatory or scientific authority. The first group consists of substances officially regulated as carcinogens in each country under each of the four regulatory frameworks. The second includes fourteen suspected or confirmed human carcinogens which have generated scientific and policy interest in at least one of the four countries, and for which detailed regulatory histories can be compiled. The third and largest group consists of substances designated as known or suspected carcinogens by the International Agency for Research on Cancer (IARC), the cancer research arm of the World Health Organization (WHO) (see the Appendix).

With few exceptions, all four governments had by the end of 1980 taken some regulatory action on all fourteen substances in the second group and on a subset of the substances on the IARC list. Complete bans or nearly complete bans on these substances have been rare, except in the case of a few food additives in the United States and France and certain pesticides in every country except Britain. Only the United Kingdom has effectively banned any occupational carcinogen included in this set, although standards and use restrictions elsewhere may be equally severe in effect.

The United States has officially recognized more substances as carcinogens than the European countries. In most cases, however, the same substances have also been controlled abroad, although not always on the same grounds. All four countries show the greatest inclination to designate substances as carcinogens and to regulate them stringently when they are found in the workplace. Of the fourteen substances studied in detail, only four are controlled by means of exposure standards in all four countries: asbestos, benzene, vinyl chloride, and nitrates. Germany has set the lowest standards for asbestos, nitrates, and benzene, and the United States the lowest for vinyl chloride.

The United States has been the first to take significant restrictive action on many of the fourteen substances, with one or more European governments following suit. Examples include acrylonitrile, amaranth (Red Dye No. 2), asbestos, and vinyl chloride. But in several instances, particularly for pesticides, the Europeans have adopted final controls before the United States. After promulgation by an administrative agency, American regulations are more often amended, altered, or suspended than comparable policy measures in Europe. At least for carcinogens, then, the overall impression is of roughly comparable regulatory outputs among the four governments. Notwithstanding discrepancies in the handling of particular substances, no country appears notably more or less aggressive than another when regulatory records are compared over a period of years.

Enforcement of Regulatory Decisions

The chemical control policies of all four countries contain measures to ensure that regulated parties will carry out their state-imposed duties. Each country has constructed an institutional framework for inspecting regulated products and industries and a system of penalties to punish and deter violations of the law. The organization of inspection programs, the powers of inspectors, and the stringency of sanctions, however, differ considerably across countries and across regulatory sectors.

Under West Germany's federal system of government, enforcement obligations are constitutionally delegated to the states (Länder), even in areas where legislative power belongs to the federal government. In the context of chemical regulation, this means that the eleven Länder are responsible for enforcement functions ranging from inspecting factories to monitoring agricultural products for pesticide residues. Since the Länder vary greatly in the resources they commit to these tasks, unequal enforcement of federal policy has emerged as a serious regulatory problem. The problem is less critical in Britain and France, where regional inspection units work under more powerful central coordination. In France, the Service of Fraud Repression oversees the enforcement of food additive and pesticide residue regulations, while the Service of Plant Protection coordinates the regional monitoring of pesticide application. In Britain, the major inspectorates responsible for worker protection belong to a single central organization, the Health and Safety Executive (HSE), which provides unified guidance to inspectors in the field.

In the American federal system, enforcement authority is often divided between state and federal governments, but according to no fixed institutional paradigm. Federal toxic substance laws frequently provide for optional state enforcement of chemical control policies, typically requiring federal approval for state administrative programs. The OSH Act, for example, permits any state with an approved plan to develop and enforce occupational safety and health standards, even with respect to hazards already regulated by OSHA. The Federal Insecticide, Fungicide, and Rodenticide Act (FIFRA) sets forth conditions under which states must assume primary enforcement responsibility for pesticide use violations. TSCA authorizes the EPA administrator to make grants to the states for the development of programs designed to reduce risks associated with toxic substances.

The powers of inspectors vary from country to country and even from one regulatory scheme to another. The inspector's right to enter premises and to issue enforcement orders is usually defined by statute, but these powers may also be subject to constitutional limitations, as in the United States. Moreover, inspection practices are constrained by tradition as well as by law, and a wide grant of power does not necessarily mean that inspectors exercise their fullest authority against regulated industries.[27]

Penalties for violations also vary notably from one regulatory framework to another. Not surprisingly, the more recently enacted laws, such as those governing chemical notification, include the stiffest penalties. Thus, the German Chemicals Act of 1980 authorizes fines of up to one hundred thousand marks for violations of premarket notice requirements, and more serious offenses are punishable with prison sentences of up to five years. In contrast, the Plant Protection Law of 1968 provides for fines of up to five thousand marks for ordinary violations and ten thousand marks for intentional viola-

---

[27] It has been said of the British Alkali Inspectorate, for example, that "though the Inspectors are empowered to visit works 'at all reasonable times by day and night, without giving previous notice', they are not known to be nocturnal, and excessive night time pollution is a frequent complaint." Social Audit, "The Alkali Inspectorate," London, 1974, p. 15.

tions. A similar discrepancy exists in the United States between penalties authorized by FIFRA and TSCA.

The stringency of statutory penalties, however, does not necessarily correlate well with their effectiveness. There are many indications that penalty provisions are underused by administrative authorities, particularly those involving criminal sanctions. For example, in the first six years after the passage of the OSH Act, only four criminal prosecutions were instituted against individual and corporate employers.[28] In each case, the penalty ultimately imposed was far lighter than those obtained in civil proceedings growing out of similar offenses. Reluctance to resort to prosecution appears even more deeply ingrained in Britain. Since the mid-nineteenth century, British inspectors have relied much more on negotiation and conciliation than on litigation in enforcing health and safety laws.[29] The efficacy of these informal methods is difficult to evaluate, since they do not ordinarily appear on an agency's formal enforcement record.[30]

Britain's preference for informal persuasion elevates to the status of a fundamental policy principle a practice that all governments are compelled to follow. Since resources for enforcement are always limited, the four governments must rely to a greater or lesser extent on voluntary compliance and civic-mindedness, directing their enforcement efforts, often on an ad hoc, intuitive basis, to areas of suspected low compliance or high risk. Yet this strategy may produce quite different results in different countries, since respect for law and state authority, as well as industry's sense of social responsibility, vary across national boundaries. German public officials and industrialists, for example, assert that extensive policing is not required to secure compliance with regulatory prescriptions. In the United States, in contrast, the assumption is that regulated parties will comply only under close supervision and under threat of punitive sanctions.[31]

In the final analysis, the effectiveness of chemical control policies has to be

[28] See Michael H. Levin, "Crimes against Employees: Substantive Criminal Sanctions under the Occupational Safety and Health Act," *American Criminal Law Review,* 14 (1977), 717–45.

[29] Social Audit, op. cit., pp. 18–19. See also W. G. Carson, "White Collar Crime and the Enforcement of Factory Legislation," *British Journal of Criminology,* 10 (1970), 383–98; Peter Bartrip, "Safety at Work: The Factory Inspectorate in the Fencing Controversy, 1833–1857," Working Paper no. 4 (Oxford: Centre for Socio-Legal Studies, 1979), pp. 22–25.

[30] Another peculiarity of the British approach to enforcement is the reliance on market-based surveys to establish the extent of food contamination by pesticide residues. Those who defend the absence of pesticide residue tolerance levels in Britain cite these surveys as an adequate control mechanism. See Consumers' Association, *Pesticide Residues and Food* (London: Consumers' Association, 1980).

[31] See Steven Kelman, "Occupational Safety and Health Administration," in James Q. Wilson, ed., *The Politics of Regulation* (New York: Basic Books, 1980), pp. 255–56.

assessed in terms of their success in meeting the stated objective of protecting the public and the environment from harm. But evaluating the impact of regulation on public health is a difficult task under the best of circumstances. In the case of cancer, such an evaluation is greatly complicated by the special nature of the disease: its long latency period, the multistage theory of causation involving initiators and promoters, the unknown extent of synergistic effects, and the inadequacy of exposure data. Moreover, the preventive impact of carcinogen regulation, however large in absolute terms, is not likely to show up in aggregated mortality or morbidity statistics, which appear broadly similar across the four countries.[32] Without great advances both in the understanding of cancer causation and in techniques of record keeping, any assessment of policies in terms of their success in reducing the incidence of cancer must remain largely speculative.

Conclusion: Patterns of Policy Convergence and Divergence

The foregoing comparison of chemical control policies reveals certain broad patterns. First, the greatest similarities among the four countries are in the form and timing of the state's assumption of regulatory responsibility and in the selection of substances for control. In creating chemical control programs, all four governments were guided by similar concerns about public health and the environment and similar philosophies about allocating the costs of preventive regulation. The four countries differ somewhat in their regulatory priorities, especially with respect to existing substances and carcinogens. Over time, however, all four have compiled similar records in controlling substances suspected of causing cancer in humans.

There are striking differences, however, in the way American and European authorities carry out their regulatory responsibilities. The American approach is notable for its legal and procedural complexity. Elaborately detailed statutes, formal rule-making procedures, extensive scientific and economic analysis, and widespread use of generic decision-making rules, legislative oversight, and judicial review all place heavy burdens on the regulatory process. Interested parties enjoy liberal access to information and opportunities to participate at all stages of decision making, so that important decisions, whether scientific or political, cannot be reached without sophisticated public debate.

The European approach to chemical regulation appears far less complicated. Enabling legislation is written in schematic language, without complex standards and procedural requirements. Administrators review sub-

---

[32] IARC, *Cancer Incidence in Five Continents,* vol. 4 (Lyon: IARC, 1981).

stances case by case, rejecting generic approaches, and seldom employ formal risk assessment or cost-benefit analysis. Information is closely guarded. The administrative process offers few opportunities for broad public involvement, usually limiting participation to designated experts and interest group representatives.

While differences among the European countries are generally less pronounced, one contrast is worth noting explicitly. Britain and Germany differ strikingly in their preference for law and formality in defining regulatory duties and relationships. The British carry flexibility to the extreme, developing policy wherever possible through close, informal contacts among government officials and private groups. Flexibility characterizes policy outcomes as well, with guidelines, recommendations, and informal persuasion substituting as far as possible for statutory orders and prosecutions. The Germans, by contrast, insist on a precise formulation of public and private regulatory responsibilities, usually by means of statutory instruments. The national bias toward precision is reflected both in the consultation process, which tends to be more structured and formal than that in Britain, and in the use of numerically exact standards for chemicals in the workplace and pesticide residues.

The following chapters seek explanations for these patterns of convergence and divergence, focusing particularly on the reasons for the marked deviation of the U.S. approach from that followed in Europe. We first examine the role of national political and legal institutions in policy making, and then compare the impact of science, experts, private interest groups, and international organizations on regulatory action in each country.

3

Legislative Politics

Among the differences between European and American policy described in chapter 2, the variations in the character of legislation stand out as especially significant. While the laws of all four countries express a similar intent to control chemical hazards, the American formulations are consistently the most ambitious and detailed. They require regulation of both existing and new substances and include extensive provisions relating to administrative rule making and judicial review. By contrast, European legislation carves out more modest regulatory objectives and leaves administrators free to design their own procedural approach to rule making. This chapter examines the political and institutional constraints on lawmaking in the four countries in an effort to explain these divergences in legislative policy.

The first part of the chapter examines the legislative histories of recent chemical control statutes in Europe and the United States. The object is to shed light on those points in the legislative process at which crucial policy choices are made and to explain, with reference to the institutional framework in which legislative disputes are resolved, why different countries formulate their statutory agendas in systematically different ways. The respective roles of the legislature and the executive branch are of primary interest in this analysis. The distribution of power between these two branches is advanced as an explanation for many of the policy discrepancies observed in chapter 2.

Another potentially significant factor is the subdivision of authority between different levels of government within a single country. The second part of this chapter studies the impact of federal-state relations on chemical control policy in Germany and the United States. On the whole, the influence of these relationships on each country's legislation has been far less pronounced than the impact of the European Community, a supranational federation, on the legislative politics of its member states.

The final section of the chapter traces certain features of modern chemical control laws, such as the variations in the manner of specifying the state's obligations, to the larger traditions of public law in each of the four countries.

Executive and Legislative Relations in Lawmaking

While the impetus for new legislation frequently comes from the executive branch in all four countries, the legislature's power to develop independent positions and to modify the substance of executive policy differs greatly between Europe and the United States. In parliamentary governments, the legislature is controlled by a political majority acting through the prime minister and the cabinet. Though parliament is constitutionally designated as the lawmaking authority, in practice it seldom breaks out of its subservient role to enact policies different from those favored by the administration. In contrast, the American political system fosters genuine competition between the executive and legislative branches, allowing Congress to assert substantial control over the content of legislation.

Elected independently of the chief executive, Congress enjoys a degree of autonomy that is quite exceptional from the standpoint of the three European legislatures. Through liberal construction of its implied powers, Congress enjoys an unparalleled right to oversee and investigate all executive activities related to the administration of federal law. Equally important in the context of chemical control are the resources that permit members of Congress to acquire independent expertise on technical issues. Congress can draw on the Congressional Research Service for sophisticated analysis of emerging legislation and the General Accounting Office for informed evaluation of policy implementation. On matters involving the management of technology, Congress can commission specialized studies from the Office of Technology Assessment (OTA).[1] Legislators and their committees employ expert staffs that are skilled in manipulating the technical and political complexities of the legislative process. With such resources at their command, powerful mem-

---

[1] Recent studies carried out by OTA on aspects of carcinogen regulation include *Cancer Testing Technology and Saccharin* (Washington, D.C.: GPO, 1977) and *Technologies for Determining Cancer Risks from the Environment* (Washington, D.C.: GPO, 1981).

bers of Congress can easily challenge measures introduced by the administration or by legislators representing different parties and interests.

In the three European countries, the bonds of party affiliation greatly reduce both the autonomy of parliament and the likelihood of serious discord between the executive and the parliamentary majority. In West Germany, direct election of the chancellor by the Bundestag formally expresses the identity of political interests between parliament and the administration. Effectively the same pattern obtains in Britain, where the prime minister is also the leader of the majority party in Parliament. In both political settings, the possibility of the legislative majority adopting positions distinct from those of the executive is remote.

The separate elections of parliament and the president in France suggest a competitiveness in executive-legislative relations that approaches the situation in the United States. In reality, however, the French parliament in the Fifth Republic has always been led by a majority that includes the president's own party, and there has been no serious challenge to the president's leadership in policy formulation. By constitutional arrangement, moreover, the French legislature has less power in relation to the executive, particularly the president, than do the parliaments of the other two European countries. The 1958 Constitution not only confers on the president a sweeping right to dissolve the National Assembly, but also narrowly delimits the legislature's power to originate policy. Parliament can act only on those issues listed in Article 34 as falling into the domain of "laws."[2] All matters not specifically enumerated in Article 34, including virtually all institutional and procedural aspects of policy implementation, must be decided by the executive through regulatory decrees and ordinances. The government's right to determine the agenda for legislative action further weakens parliamentary control over lawmaking, allowing governmental proposals to take precedence over private members' bills. Finally, the constitutionally authorized "blocked vote" procedure permits the government to request a vote on proposed measures without offering parliament any opportunity for amendment.

In the United States, the relatively equal stature of the two houses of Congress enhances the potential for conflict in the legislative process. In the three European countries, the upper houses of parliament, none of which are elected by popular vote, represent a narrower range of interests and possess more limited powers than the lower houses. The German Bundesrat, for example, revives a nineteenth-century institution consisting of delegates from the state governments. Its principal function is to protect Länder interests and guard against radical shifts of legislative power to the federal government.

---

[2] See L. Neville Brown and J. F. Garner, *French Administrative Law* (London: Butterworths, 1973), pp. 6–7.

In Britain, the powers of the House of Lords have been whittled away under successive Parliament Acts,[3] and the French Senate's involvement in lawmaking is likewise subject to control through a variety of procedural devices. Unlike the U.S. Senate, none of these European bodies serves as a powerful, independent forum for the development of legislative policy.

The legal and institutional factors that predispose the U.S. Congress to compete internally and with the president are thus largely absent in Europe. Cooperation between the two policy-making branches is the rule in European politics, with the legislature possessing neither the expertise nor the separate political base needed to support policy innovation. The legislative histories of major chemical control statutes show that the procedures used to negotiate compromises among lawmakers reinforce the basic patterns of competition in the United States and cooperation in Europe. The legislative process in Europe concentrates power in the already dominant executive branch, whereas in the United States power is dispersed both between Congress and the president and within Congress. These dynamics account for some major differences in the form and content of legislation.

The passage of the 1970 Occupational Safety and Health Act typified the highly competitive nature of U.S. legislative politics. Bills mandating federal regulation of workplace hazards were first introduced into Congress in the final year of the Johnson administration. Although no legislation emerged from these initiatives,[4] the movement gathered force during the Nixon years, when the political cleavages between a Congress controlled by Democrats and the Republican president gave rise to two substantially different occupational safety and health bills. One of these, sponsored by Harrison Williams, then a Democratic senator from New Jersey, was a conceptual descendant of earlier Democratic initiatives and was enthusiastically supported by organized labor. Business groups, however, predictably threw their support behind the administration's proposal.

With rival positions worked out in minute detail, hopes for piecing together an acceptable draft depended on major compromises by all parties. No one argued with the act's broad purpose: "to assure . . . every working man and woman in the Nation safe and healthful working conditions." But bitter political battles developed over the design of institutions and rule-making procedures. Prolabor forces won a sizeable victory by delegating implementing authority to the Department of Labor rather than to the weaker, independent

---

[3] In particular, the Parliament Act of 1911, as amended in 1949, permits the House of Commons, after it complies with specified procedures, to pass a bill into law without the consent of the House of Lords.

[4] For a history of the OSH Act, see Joseph A. Page and Mary Win O'Brien, *Bitter Wages* (New York: Grossman, 1973), and the Bureau of National Affairs, *The Job Safety and Health Act of 1970* (Washington, D.C.: BNA, 1971).

occupational safety and health board favored by the Republicans. The law's strict sanctions for noncompliance also catered primarily to Democratic interests. Republicans, for their part, prevented the Department of Labor from gaining control over enforcement. The Republicans also introduced the concept of "feasibility" into the standard-setting provision for toxic substances, thereby ensuring that economic and technical considerations would influence regulatory decisions on chemicals in the workplace. Legislative horse trading produced some peculiar procedural complexities. For example, the OSH Act included its own rule-making procedures, independent of the Administrative Procedure Act (APA), and a novel standard for judicial review[5] which has occasioned considerable difficulty for the courts.

Party alignments played a less visible role in the development of TSCA, but the history of this statute manifests the same competitive interplay between rival centers of power, leading to similarly unwieldy legislation. In response to an influential report by the Council on Environmental Quality (CEQ), chemical control legislation was introduced in both the 92d and 93d Congresses, but a sharp split between the House and the Senate over the premanufacture requirements of section 5 impeded progress until 1976. Originally, the Senate preferred a restrictive, registration-like process, leaving the EPA administrator great freedom to select appropriate regulatory responses for identified hazards. The House, on the other hand, favored automatic clearance, without notification, for all new chemicals except those specially listed by the administrator.[6] The effort to satisfy these conflicting demands led to the complex procedures outlined in sections 5(e) and 5(f). Section 5(e) followed the wishes of the Senate in authorizing the administrator to determine, without recourse to court action, whether additional information should be required to evaluate the health and environmental risks presented by a new chemical. At the same time, the provision bowed to the promanufacturer concerns of the House by providing a thirty-day period for filing objections to any EPA order restricting manufacture or distribution. In order to proceed in the face of such objections, the administrator must seek a court injunction against the manufacturer. Thus an elaborate system of procedural checks and cross-checks was enacted to compensate for disagreements in Congress over fundamental policy goals.

Another symptom of congressional inability to produce effective substantive compromises is the frequent use of cost-benefit standards to guide the

---

[5] The OSH Act provides for substantial evidence review, although it calls for use of informal rule-making procedures with certain modifications. The standard of "substantial evidence" is usually applied in reviewing adjudicatory or trial-type rule making.

[6] See Kevin Gaynor, "The Toxic Substances Control Act: A Regulatory Morass," *Vanderbilt Law Review*, 30, no. 6 (1977), 1149–90.

regulation of toxic substances.[7] U.S. laws require administrators to weigh economic and technical considerations against health risks, but they provide only vague instructions on how to strike the final balance. The effect of these provisions is to delegate large policy decisions to the executive, arguably overstepping constitutional limits on the administration's lawmaking powers. The vagueness of these standards also undermines the capacity of executive agencies to develop authoritative interpretations and, as we shall see in chapters 4 and 5, leaves them vulnerable to recurrent legal and political challenge.

The histories of the OSH Act and TSCA underscore the dearth of mechanisms for promoting consensus in the U.S. legislative process. The long period of gestation for major bills, which undergo many mark-ups, creates multiple opportunities for intervention. In the absence of effective coalition-building procedures and strict party discipline, it is possible for strong-willed minorities, or even individuals, to advance their own positions at the expense of more broadly representative policies. The addition of the Delaney amendment to the FDCA in 1958 is a striking illustration of this.

The landmark anticancer provision was drafted by Congressman Delaney, who, as chairman of the House Select Committee to Investigate the Use of Chemicals in Food, was well placed to promote his longstanding personal interest in banning carcinogenic food additives. Delaney formally proposed his amendment after the Committee on Interstate and Foreign Commerce completed its consideration of the food additives bill and reported it to the full House.[8] Given the intense public fear of cancer, the proposal carried enormous political appeal and, despite procedural irregularities, little could be done to block its enactment. Although the legislative record indicates less than wholehearted support,[9] the Department of Health, Education, and Welfare (DHEW) ultimately approved the amendment, recognizing that opposing Delaney on this issue could jeopardize passage of the entire bill. Congress thus adopted a far-reaching policy that never underwent thorough legislative scrutiny or commanded genuine executive support.

Though open and vigorous parliamentary debate is a treasured feature of European politics, the lawmaking process as a whole ensures that proposals

---

[7] For a further exploration of why such standards are found in American but not European statutes, see Ronald Brickman and Sheila Jasanoff, "Concepts of Risk and Safety in Toxic Substances Regulation: A Comparison of France and the United States," *Policy Studies Journal,* 9, no. 3 (1980), 394–403.

[8] Richard Merrill, "Regulating Carcinogens in Food: A Legislator's Guide to the Food Safety Provisions of the Federal Food, Drug, and Cosmetic Act," *Michigan Law Review,* 77, no. 2 (1978), 180.

[9] HEW, on behalf of FDA, originally objected to the inclusion of the anticancer clause in the food-additives legislation but later withdrew its objection, stating that, in the department's view, "the bill reads and means the same with or without the inclusion of the clause referred to" (S. Rep. no. 2422, 85th Cong., 2d sess., 1958, pp. 10–11).

in which the executive branch has a major stake will not be substantially modified by parliament. The history of the German Chemicals Act illustrates the point. Preliminary work by the Ministry of the Interior led to a draft proposal on premarket testing of new chemicals in early 1977. Subsequently, an interministerial committee led by the Ministry for Youth, Health, and Family Affairs (Bundesministerium für Jugend, Familie, und Gesundheit, BMJFG) prepared a revised draft for parliamentary consideration. This proposal was widely circulated and debated within the administration. For example, the prestigious Council of Experts on Environmental Questions (Rat von Sachverständigen für Umweltfragen, RSU) reviewed it in an advisory capacity and recommended substantial revisions. Only in 1979, following legislative action by the EC (see chapter 11), was a considerably modified version of the original cabinet draft laid before the Bundestag.

The ensuing parliamentary process, terminating with the passage of the Chemicals Act in July 1980, followed a fundamentally different pattern from comparable deliberations in the United States. Acting under pressure of time,[10] and with very limited resources at its command, the subcommittee responsible for reviewing the draft law confined its "fact finding" to two sets of hearings at which it heard experts from selected government, industry, and public interest organizations. Parliamentary consideration was dominated by the administration's well-rehearsed proposal, with the Bundestag cast more as a critical reviewer than as an equal partner in policy formulation. While the administration bill did not sail through parliament without controversy, most of the changes made by the Bundestag were minor and took the form of deletions rather than additions or substitutions. For example, a draft provision authorizing the establishment of a national cancer register was eliminated on the ground that such a scheme would run counter to constitutional principles of federalism.[11]

Only once did the Bundestag fashion an independent response to a political pressure group. To satisfy Germany's vocal animal protection lobby, all express endorsements of animal testing were deleted from the statute.[12] Otherwise, the legislature simply followed the administration's lead, leaving undisturbed such central provisions as the authorization to control existing

---

[10] Under the terms of the EC Sixth Amendment adopted in September 1979, member states were required to have their own implementing legislation and administrative provisions in place no later than September 18, 1981. Although it was enacted in 1980, the Chemicals Act did not take effect until January 1, 1982.

[11] Interview, BMJFG, Bonn, August 18, 1980.

[12] In a statement of legislative intent, the Bundestag instructed the government to seek alternatives for animal testing in hazard assessment. Deutscher Bundestag, Beschlussempfehlung und Bericht zu dem Chemikaliengesetz, Drucksache 8/4243 (June 18, 1980), p. 3.

substances, the safety standards and permissible forms of governmental intervention, and the schedule of penalties and sanctions. On many of these issues, the Bundestag's freedom to act was sharply constrained by the 1979 EC directive on testing and notification. But even on issues left open by the EC directive, the Bundestag remained passive. For example, it went along with the administration in rejecting the concept of an independent scientific commission to recommend testing requirements for new chemicals.[13]

As in the German case, the French law requiring notification of new chemicals developed from an initial phase of interministerial negotiation and compromise. The Act on the Control of Chemical Products was the result of a policy initiative that began with the publication of a report on chemical pollution of the environment in 1973. The report drew attention to inadequacies in existing French law with respect to premarket testing and control of industrial chemicals. In December 1973, the Interministerial Action Committee for Nature and the Environment, a body formed to oversee national environmental policy and to administer a national fund for environmental improvement,[14] called on the minister of the environment to address this problem through appropriate legal instruments. A technically qualified interministerial task force was formed to study the issue. This group published its final report, accompanied by draft legislation on chemical control, toward the end of 1975. It was not until November 1976, however, that the government completed its internal deliberations and laid a draft bill before the National Assembly. Since this proposal differed in important details from the recommendations of the working group, it must be assumed that there was a critical period of political infighting before the bill ever reached the legislature.

During parliamentary debate, opposition political parties proposed a number of changes designed to strengthen the act's regulatory reach. After an unsuccessful motion to defeat the bill, socialists demanded a more specific statement of the notification requirements, a provision explicitly demanding the evaluation of mutagenic, teratogenic, and carcinogenic risks, and authorization for the government to verify test results in its own laboratories. These moves were all rejected, partly on the ground that such detailed prescriptions would contravene the constitutional limits on parliament's lawmaking powers under Article 34. Two other opposition proposals—establishing a presumption of public availability for toxicological data and creating an advisory

[13]Interview, Federal Economics Ministry, Bonn, August 18, 1980. The Bundestag apparently bought the government's argument that decision making under the Chemicals Act should remain in the hands of politically accountable agencies.

[14]The Comité Interministeriel d'Action pour la Nature et l'Environnement is an interministerial committee presided over by the prime minister.

committee with consumer representatives—met a similar fate. In the end the enacted law differed little in substance from the bill developed by the administration.

The sovereignty of Parliament is a central dogma of British government and deeply influences judicial interpretations of the law. There is little in the history of chemical control, however, to suggest that this theoretical preeminence translates into independent legislative action. As in Germany and France, legislative politics in Britain leaves little room for policy innovation outside the executive branch. The history of the HSW Act of 1974, under which Britain now administers both the general program for occupational safety and health and the notification scheme for new industrial chemicals, illustrates the almost complete domination of the legislative process by the executive branch.

By the late 1960s, British politicians of both major parties agreed that the existing framework of worker protection laws, much of it inherited from the nineteenth century, badly needed overhauling. In line with established British tradition, the government appointed a blue-ribbon committee, chaired by Lord Robens, to prepare a dispassionate analysis of the problem. Over a two-year period, the committee heard testimony from employer, employee, and governmental organizations with the express purpose of constructing a balanced, nonpartisan set of policy proposals. Its findings were received with a respect rarely accorded to American presidential commissions and laid much of the conceptual groundwork for the 1974 statute.[15] The committee emphasized the need to streamline the existing tangle of laws, to replace legal obligations by means of self-regulation and voluntary codes of practice, and to create institutionalized opportunities for labor-management consultation on health and safety issues. In sum, these recommendations repudiated Britain's earlier ad hoc, fragmented approach to health and safety regulation.

The Robens Committee proposed a number of specific policies to control toxic substances in the workplace. It recommended a statutory obligation for manufacturers to test their products prior to marketing and to notify the government of risks disclosed through testing.[16] It also called for a standing Advisory Committee on Toxic Substances (ACTS), modeled on the existing committees for food additive and pesticide regulation, to help administer the chemical notification scheme. In developing these proposals, the committee was influenced by the testimony of industrial health and safety inspectors, whose enforcement efforts had long been frustrated through lack of adequate information about hazardous chemicals. Their experiences, detailed in the annual reports of the chief inspector of factories, convinced the Robens Com-

---

[15]Robens Committee, *Safety and Health at Work* (London: HMSO, 1972).
[16]Ibid., pp. 106–7.

mittee of the need for more extensive premarket testing. Parliament, in turn, endorsed the committee's conclusions by providing legal authorization for premarket testing and notification in the HSW Act.[17]

It is a tribute to the Robens Committee's success in accommodating disparate points of view that the potentially volatile issue of occupational safety and health did not produce serious controversy in Parliament. The committee's apparent impartiality and its reliance on acknowledged experts, such as the industrial health and safety inspectors, ensured bipartisan support. Although trade unions and their supporters criticized the emphasis on voluntary controls,[18] Parliament approved the report's major premises in 1974, its deliberations unhindered by an intermediate change in government. Thus parliamentary consideration of the HSW Act was marked by little of the political pressure and counterpressure, accompanied by patchwork revision and compromise, that characterize the passage of similar legislation in the United States.

These legislative histories demonstrate one point with surprising clarity. The task of balancing interests and striking compromises, classically a function of the legislature, is performed in Europe more often under the umbrella of the executive than in parliament. Because of this shift in function, the legislature enters the lawmaking process much later in Europe than in the United States. Thus, in three of the four countries—Britain, France, and the United States—chemical notification laws received their initial impetus from a report produced under governmental sponsorship. Although each recommended new regulatory policy, the documents issued by the Robens Committee, the French environmental committee, and the CEQ were handled quite differently in the legislative process. In the United States, the draft legislation accompanying CEQ's report was almost immediately placed before Congress. Thereafter, congressional politics governed the course of legislation, and four years passed before a compromise acceptable to major interest groups was forged. Even then, the result was more an elaborate system of procedural checks on administrative discretion than a genuine bipartisan agreement on a coherent set of policy prescriptions.

In contrast, both the Robens report and the French report on toxic substances led to legislative drafts that were first heavily circulated within the government. In Germany, as well, interministerial consultation preceded parliamentary consideration of the Chemicals Act. In each of these cases, the executive agencies ultimately responsible for implementing policy played a

---

[17] The British premarket notification regulations were developed under authority of section 6 of the HSW Act, which requires that substances for use at work be tested to ensure that they will be safe when properly used.

[18] *The Times,* London, September 6, 1972, p. 4.

dominant role in drafting legislation. As a result, policy goals reflected a consistent administration viewpoint and were written with an eye to workability. Moreover, through the intervention of three or four powerful ministries, major social interests were indirectly drawn into a conciliation process that preceded parliamentary debate. Consequently, parliament received a legislative proposal already incorporating substantial compromises among the parties most interested in the policy outcome.

The negotiations carried out within the executive branch in Europe are fundamentally different in character from the bargaining that takes place in the U.S. legislative forum. Access to ministerial circles tends to be limited to established interest groups with traditionally strong ties to government and a well-defined role in policy making. Acting in a relatively private arena and in close contact with the bureaucracy, these groups can freely make deals with little need for public justification. In their turn, the ministries for industry, commerce, or labor are free to negotiate on behalf of their established clienteles without serious interference from marginal or new coalitions, including most environmental or consumer groups. Parliament remains the only forum in which these groups can present their policy demands. The German animal protection lobby, for example, could intervene in the legislative process only when the draft Chemicals Act reached the Bundestag. The mainstream of European interest group participation, however, is channeled into the more restricted and disciplined framework of interministerial deliberations. By limiting participation to "major" interests, particularly in the crucial early rounds of negotiation, European governments produce legislative accords that are not easily disturbed by the vagaries of parliamentary politics. Legislation is thus proof against much of the fragility and incoherence that characterize the policies emanating from America's more competitive and more widely participatory legislative process.

Federalism

In the United States and Germany, the power to make law is not only shared de facto between the executive and the legislature, but is also constitutionally divided between the federal government and the states. In Germany, principles of federalism relieve the national government of the need to legislate detailed enforcement programs and curtail the scope of toxic substance control policies in certain substantive respects. In the United States, too, federalism serves as a check against total preemption of chemical regulation by Congress, but it is rarely invoked to limit federal authority once the federal government decides to legislate. Federalism in the United States also provides an excuse for continually varying the state and federal roles with respect to enforcement.

Although the commerce clause provides authority for Congress to regulate toxic substances, federal chemical control legislation in fact remains "interstitial," conforming to a more general pattern:

> Federal legislation, on the whole, has been conceived and drafted on an *ad hoc* basis to accomplish limited objectives. It builds upon legal relationships established by the states, altering or supplanting them only so far as necessary for the special purpose. Congress acts, in short, against the background of the total *corpus juris* of the states in much the same way that a state legislature acts against the background of the common law, assumed to govern unless changed by legislation.[19]

The supplementary character of federal policies is particularly evident in the field of worker protection, where preventive policy making was taken over by the federal government only in 1970, and compensation programs continue to be administered under state law. Similarly, federal laws enacted to ensure premarket control of pesticides, food additives, and industrial chemicals have left largely undisturbed the rules of state law governing the duties and potential liability of manufacturers toward consumers and users. Several years of unresolved debate concerning a national compensation program for toxic substance victims attest to the difficulty of federalizing these traditional preserves of state regulation and common law.

Legislative politics in the United States offers few opportunities for the states to limit the scope of federal preemption. The effectiveness of existing state programs is often cited by interests seeking to forestall centralized administration of regulatory policies. Once the federal legislative process gathers momentum, however, proponents of states' rights are routinely appeased by the delegation of residual enforcement or standard-setting functions to the states; indeed, numerous federal chemical control laws authorize the states to carry out these functions under plans approved by the federal government. While federal standards and policies provide minimum levels of control,[20] states are free to pursue stricter regulatory alternatives. Though states often seem reluctant to exercise their independent regulatory rights, Congress continues to experiment with such delegations. Encouraging state involvement without a fixed blueprint for state-federal cooperation contributes to the diversity and complexity of toxic substance legislation.

[19] Henry M. Hart and Herbert Wechsler, *The Federal Courts and the Federal System,* 2d ed. (Mineola, N.Y.: Foundation Press, 1973), pp. 470–71.

[20] See, for example, OSH Act §18 (state jurisdiction and state plans).

Since adoption of the Basic Law (Grundgesetz) in 1949, West Germany has been committed to a federal system that not only grants extensive powers to the Länder, but also protects and effectuates these powers through specialized institutions. Like the U.S. Constitution, the Basic Law divides legislative power between two levels of government,[21] but diverging from the U.S. model, it also grants the Länder exclusive authority to enforce both federal and state laws.[22] By virtue of their monopoly on enforcement, the German Länder enjoy a potentially more powerful position in relation to the federal government than do the American states. They derive additional strength through representation in the Bundesrat, which safeguards Länder interests both in the course of legislation and in administrative rule making; for example, the Bundesrat's consent is required prior to the issuance of most federal toxic substance regulations.

German chemical regulation builds on a highly structured framework of federal-state relationships. Apart from the Bundesrat, a host of lesser intergovernmental institutions offer opportunities for formal state-federal negotiations in the implementation and enforcement of regulatory policy. In defining the enforcement duties of the Länder, federal laws can therefore use "framework" provisions that provide just enough legal guidance to secure uniform interpretation across the Länder. Details of organization and management, for example, monitoring programs for hazardous substances in the workplace or in food, are left open for negotiation.

The membership of Britain, France, and West Germany in the European Community raises questions about the impact of federalism on legislation at a supranational level. Under Articles 2 and 100 of the EC Treaty, the EC Council enjoys broad powers to harmonize the economic policies of member states. Though opinion varies as to the precise limits of these powers, the Council has interpreted them freely in recent years to include matters such as food safety, environment, and worker protection, which impinge less directly on the economic concerns of member states. EC members have generally gone along with the effort to harmonize environmental policies, agreeing in March 1973 to inform the European Commission, the technical arm of the European Community, in advance of significant new policies designed to protect the environment.[23] The Commission may then block further national action by developing a proposal of its own within a five-month period. Although the 1973 agreement is not legally binding—it is sometimes charac-

[21] Basic Law, Articles 70–75.
[22] Ibid., Article 83.
[23] Agreement of March 5, 1973, on information for the Commission and for the Member States with a view to possible harmonization throughout the communities of urgent measures concerning the protection of the environment, *Official Journal of the European Communities* (hereafter *OJEC*), 16, C9 (March 15, 1973), 1.

terized as a gentlemen's agreement—formal compliance with its terms has been reasonably high.[24]

Through its power to preempt and harmonize national legislation, the EC opens up opportunities for legislative maneuvering that affect the balance of power between parliament and the executive in member states. Community legislation is developed through closed-door negotiations that tend to concentrate power in the hands of a small group of bureaucrats representing key ministries. Their influence, particularly in the field of chemical control, is enhanced by expertise in the technical aspects of regulating environmental pollution. Pressed to the limit, bureaucratic control of policy making in Brussels can be used by national governments to widen their already substantial advantages over the legislature. With EC negotiations in process, the overriding need for harmonization can be cited to quell minority and dissenting opinion in parliament. Policies drafted by a handful of technically competent bureaucrats can even be handed to parliament as a fait accompli: as a European directive that must be implemented by national legislation within specified time limits and with little room for modification. Though this may be an extreme scenario, the EC's legislative activity undoubtedly reinforces the European executive's traditionally tight control over policy development.

While negotiations at the European Community level tend to diminish the role of national parliaments, they by no means rule out unilateral policy actions by the governments of member states. In a number of instances involving toxic chemicals, domestic forces favoring legislation have prevailed over pressures for communal policy development. France, for example, adopted the notification scheme for new industrial chemicals without waiting for parallel initiatives at the EC to bear fruit. Germany adopted a statutory ban on DDT in 1972 and a strict limitation on the lead content of automobile fuels in 1976. Neither country fully explored the potential for joint EC decisions on these matters, although France delayed implementation of the chemical control law pending the outcome of EC negotiations on the premarket testing directive (see chapter 11).

Legal System and Legal Tradition

Some of the cross-national differences in chemical control legislation noted in chapter 2 are difficult to explain purely in terms of contemporary political organization and process. Why, for example, has Britain alone decided to

---

[24] Sixteen notifications were submitted to the Commission in 1980, including five from Germany, one from France, and two from the United Kingdom. Commission of the EC, *General Report* no. 14 (1980), p. 158.

shift regulatory responsibility to the private sector in the HSW Act? Why do German laws seem more detailed and legalistic than French statutes of comparable scope? And why does the United States display such a marked preference for legal instruments in controlling administrative discretion? In addressing these questions, it becomes necessary to look to much older theories and instruments of government intervention. This section sets modern chemical control policies against the historical backdrop of each country's public law tradition.

In view of their shared common-law heritage, it is surprising that Britain and the United States are furthest removed from each other in their preference for legislation as a policy instrument. Britain, at one extreme, either avoids statutory controls altogether (pesticides, pesticide residues) or enacts enabling laws that confer open-ended regulatory authority on governmental departments. In the notable case of the 1974 HSW Act, Britain paradoxically used new legislation to reduce the government's regulatory role and to give greater prominence to private regulation of workplace conditions. The United States, on the other hand, has adopted detailed legislation covering every important sector of chemical control. These laws define the obligations of governmental officials much more precisely than do comparable British statutes, and they are heavily freighted with procedural requirements.

Britain's relative reluctance to spell out the government's regulatory obligations through law has been attributed by Nevil Johnson to the relationship between concepts of law and concepts of state in that country.[25] Britain has maintained a strict dualism between the positive law declared by Parliament and the common law handed down by judges as interpretations of social custom. Historically, the positivist view encouraged a pragmatic, incremental approach to legislation, with legislators focusing on specific social problems as they arose rather than attempting to define the nature and limits of governmental authority in broader terms. The pattern of incremental lawmaking dominated nineteenth-century factory legislation and provided the basis for British worker protection policies prior to 1974: "This century of experience in factory legislation affords a typical example of English practical empiricism. We began with no abstract theory of social justice or the rights of man. We seem always to have been incapable even of taking a general view of the subject we were legislating upon. Each successive statute aimed at remedying a single ascertained evil."[26] The common law provides no independent basis

---

[25] Nevil Johnson, "Law as the Articulation of the State in Western Germany: A German Tradition Seen from a British Perspective," *West European Politics*, 1, no. 2 (May 1978), 177–92.

[26] Sidney Webb, preface to B. L. Hutchins and E. Harrison, *A History of Factory Legislation*, 3d ed. (New York: Kelly, Reprints of Economic Classics, 1966).

for legal characterizations of the state and its relations to society. To the extent that common-law principles are invoked to regulate state action, the state is cast essentially in the role of a private litigant asserting private rights or responsibilities. The use of the common law thus bypasses a central problem of public law: to define how the state's activities differ from those of private individuals.

It appears, then, that British concepts of law do not allow the close identification of "government" with "law" that characterizes the German Rechtsstaat and, to a lesser extent, the U.S. constitutional system. Indeed, British public law often shies away from an overly precise definition of the state's role, so that one observes "an increasing tendency for statute law conferring powers on public authorities of one kind and another to do so in a manner which is ambiguous, suggestive of persuasion, conciliation, the exercise of influence rather than a clear allocation of powers and a concomitant definition of responsibilities."[27] One example of this trend is the HSW Act, which, as mentioned earlier, conceives of private self-regulation as the appropriate means for securing worker health and safety. In this framework, the primary duty of public authorities is to encourage nongovernmental regulatory initiatives through behind-the-scenes influence and, where necessary, coercion.

The description "government of laws" applies with particular force to the American federal government. The rights and duties of each of its branches, as well as the limits on their powers, are derived from a system of explicit legal rules distinct from the common law and the laws of the fifty states. That these rules are rooted in a written constitution is itself symptomatic of America's early preference for defining the powers of government through legal instruments.

Given this history of legalism, it comes as no surprise that American regulatory statutes are much more detailed and specific in delineating public responsibilities than are their British counterparts. This factor alone, however, fails to account for the extreme complexity that distinguishes U.S. chemical control laws from comparable enactments in Europe. Indeed, elaborate standards and formal rule-making procedures are relatively recent components of U.S. regulatory legislation. Statutes delegating authority to turn-of-the-century federal agencies, and again to those created during the New Deal, were considerably simpler in form.[28] In comparison with recent environmental and health and safety laws, these earlier statutes appear to be virtually stan-

---

[27] Johnson, op. cit., p. 190.

[28] See, for example, Paul MacAvoy, *The Regulated Industries and the Economy* (New York: Norton, 1979), and Paul J. Quirk, *Industry Influence in Federal Regulatory Agencies* (Princeton: Princeton University Press, 1981).

dardless delegations of power, much closer in form to European legislative delegations.

Two mutually reinforcing lines of explanation can be offered for the discrepancies between the "old" and the "new" U.S. regulatory statutes. One view holds that Congress enacted more detailed mandates and judicially enforceable standards in the later laws to forestall the "capture" of implementing agencies by regulated interests that allegedly took place under less carefully constructed statutory frameworks. By defining the responsibilities of the new agencies with greater precision, Congress not only gave them firmer guidance, but created standards against which they could be held accountable, either by Congress itself or by the courts.

A second explanation focuses on the unprecedented breadth of the newer regulatory statutes and the controversy and divisiveness that surrounded their enactment. As has been documented above, the complexity of chemical control legislation in the United States stems in part from the inability of Congress to agree on how actively the federal government should regulate the affairs of the chemical industry. Failing to agree on the substance of regulatory policy, opposing interests in Congress fell back time and again on procedural safeguards and complex standards in order to ensure that they and their political clients would have the means of intervening at every stage of administrative decision making.

In Germany and France, there has been no detectable shift from one pattern of regulatory lawmaking to another. This relative stability is partly explained by the existence in the civil law jurisdictions of a separate and well-developed body of law governing the conduct of public authorities. These public law norms, which sometimes take the form of unwritten rules enforced by the administrative courts, reduce both the need and the incentive to legislate controls on administrative behavior in every new statute. For example, though German chemical control statutes do not explicitly demand cost-benefit analysis, administrators are required to weigh costs and benefits pursuant to a general provision of administrative law that regulatory means be "proportional" to ends.[29] German law also incorporates a general requirement that the administrative agencies choose the least burdensome means of effectuating their regulatory purposes. American administrative law contains no such general stricture, so that Congress is free to debate statute by statute whether or not administrators should be compelled to use the "least burdensome requirements."[30]

---

[29] See, for example, David P. Currie, "Air Pollution Control in West Germany," *University of Chicago Law Review,* 49, no. 2 (1982), 359–60.

[30] TSCA §6 contains such a provision, and regulatory analysts have urged that similar requirements apply to the implementation of other federal statutes, as well. See, for example, James C. Miller III, "Occupational Safety and Health Administration," *Regulation* (November/December 1980), 22–23.

French regulatory statutes are just as unspecific as German laws in their procedural provisions and perhaps even less detailed on substantive issues. Their skeletal structure reflects the rigorous enforcement of the constitutional separation of powers in French legislative politics. By all indications, the administration intervenes actively in the legislative process to prevent parliament from usurping the authority to specify the details of policy implementation.[31] German legislation, on the other hand, is pushed toward greater specificity by one of the cardinal principles of the Rechtsstaat: government may not infringe on the rights of private individuals without explicit authorization in law. To effectuate this principle, the Basic Law demands that a statute clearly indicate its intent to abridge any substantive right guaranteed by the constitution. The German legal tradition also requires all permissible forms of regulatory action to be explicitly set forth in the enabling legislation.

Whatever their differences of detail, chemical control laws in all three European countries are remarkably similar in their reluctance to state the government's positive regulatory duties with precision. They confer more or less specific powers on the regulatory agencies, but they do not stipulate either the conditions under which the government must act or the procedures it must follow. As we see in the next chapter, established patterns of bureaucratic decision making in Europe fill in the gaps left open by the legislature. The United States, in contrast, uses detailed legal prescriptions not only to ensure that the government will undertake regulatory action, but also to specify how and when it should act. These procedures compensate, in part, for the inexperience and political instability of the highest administrative ranks in the regulatory agencies.

Conclusion

Legal traditions in the four countries explain some underlying differences in their conceptualization of the state's role. But divergences in the goals of chemical control and the procedural rigor imposed by law are more convincingly related to differences in the configuration of power between the legislature and the executive branch. Structurally and functionally, the U.S. Congress is more independent and competitive in relation to the executive, even when both are led by the same party, than are any of the three European

---

[31] The legislative history of the 1977 Chemicals Control Law, discussed above, tends to support this conclusion. See also Michel Prieur, "The Rights of Associations for the Protection of Nature and the Environment in France," in Stephen McCaffrey and Robert Lutz, eds., *Environmental Pollution and Individual Rights: An International Symposium* (Deventer, The Netherlands: Kluwer, 1978), pp. 71–72. Prieur mentions a decision of the Constitutional Council determining that the choice of the competent authority to grant approval to environmental associations is a matter of regulatory, not legislative, power.

legislatures. In Europe, party discipline virtually guarantees that the administration will command a parliamentary majority in support of important policy proposals. Executive control over policy making is reinforced by the tactics of legislative negotiation. Delaying the legislature's entry into the lawmaking process and channeling draft legislation through a tight interministerial structure enables European governments to develop bills that closely mirror their actual agenda of action. Marginal and unorganized interests are excluded from the all-important early rounds of discussion, so that their demands do not exert the fragmenting pressure associated with interest group politics in the United States. Membership in the European Community promotes a further centralization of national policy making, since governments can point to accords produced in Brussels to deter excessive parliamentary revision of legislative proposals.

In contrast, American government maintains a real, though by no means perfect, separation of powers between the executive and the legislative branches. One consequence is that chemical control policies can be formulated by the legislature with a disregard for problems of implementation that would be unthinkable in Europe. It is in this light that the emphasis of American law on "old" substances can best be explained. Congress has found it politically expedient to endorse the remedying of past insults to health and the environment. Laws enacted in the last dozen years have therefore laid out impossibly optimistic goals: elimination of pollutant discharges into water by 1985, stepwise upgrading of existing sources of air and water pollution, reregistration of thousands of pesticides in use since the last world war, regulation of existing as well as new toxic substances. For reaching these objectives, Congress has provided stringent timetables that fall somewhere between the merely unrealistic and the wholly fantastic. Yet if goals are not met in timely fashion, Congress bears no direct responsibility. Indeed, as we see in the next chapter, legislative oversight provides Congress an unparalleled means of making political capital out of agency failure.

The compromises struck in Congress are markedly more fragile than the policies developed in the highly disciplined European legislative process. The enactment of a law signifies, at least in a formal sense, that disparate political interests have submerged their differences and agreed to move forward on a specified set of social objectives. In the recent mass of environmental and health and safety legislation, much of it directed at problems of chemical control, there are numerous indications that the consensus achieved in Congress falls short of such genuine accommodation. In particular, by requiring agencies to balance economic, social, and public health considerations according to ill-defined standards, Congress merely transfers difficult policy decisions to the executive forum. The complaint that Congress makes legislators, not law, is not wholly unfounded in the context of toxic substance control.

Congressional reluctance to plant firmer guideposts for policy makers is compounded by the ready availability of procedural mechanisms in the storehouse of American law. As the example of TSCA's premanufacture notice provision indicates, the inability to agree on substantive policy may lead Congress to exert a kind of negative control. This takes the form of complicated procedural checks and balances whose function is to limit the freedom of both the regulator and the regulated interests. By stipulating that agencies hold hearings and make explicit their findings, and by expanding the scope of judicial involvement, Congress creates a framework for regulatory policy that puts enormous pressure on agency resources and helps push all participants toward a day in court. The next two chapters contrast U.S. administrative and judicial responses to this intrusive style of legislation with those triggered by Europe's less demanding legislative mandates.

4

Administrative Implementation

Toxic substance laws, no matter how specific or detailed, rarely stipulate what controls should be imposed on particular chemicals. Applying a general legal mandate to specific cases is a quintessentially administrative task, and in each country this function is performed by specialized agencies that determine what chemicals to regulate, in what order, by what means, and how stringently. Given the complex scientific issues involved in decision making, administrators in all four regulatory systems must also solicit a broad range of expert opinion and decide how much weight to give to divergent assessments of risk. Within this common framework of duties and responsibilities, the administrative practices of U.S. and European agencies sharply part company, deepening and reinforcing the differences between American and European policy that originate in the legislative process. In dealing with existing chemicals, for example, U.S. agencies have developed the most ambitious agendas, as in the case of generic cancer policies developed by OSHA and EPA. The American preoccupation with speeding up the regulation of existing substances also contrasts markedly with the business-as-usual attitude of most European administrators.

U.S. administrators have often gone beyond strict statutory requirements in implementing the procedural provisions of toxic substance laws. In many cases, procedures not mandated by law, such as cross-examination and scientific peer review, have been adopted in an effort to strengthen the credibility of the decision-making record. Over time, U.S. agencies have tended to explain their regulatory decisions in increasing detail, especially through advance announcement of the principles they use in risk assessment. Examples of such activity include OSHA's generic principles for identifying and classifying carcinogens and the guidelines for assessing carcinogenic risk issued by the Interagency Regulatory Liaison Group during the Carter administration. These initiatives have set the U.S. regulatory process far apart from the informal, consultative approach to rule making favored in Europe.

A final area in which European and American practices differ noticeably is the selection of risk management techniques. On the whole, U.S. administrators have made greatest use of relatively burdensome control options, such as technology-based ambient standards and complete or partial bans on individual substances. This tendency cannot be explained in terms of unique characteristics of the legal authority conferred on U.S. agencies. Both American and European regulators are legally empowered to restrict production or to impose engineering controls in order to achieve desired levels of protection against chemical hazards. And statutes of comparable scope in Europe and the United States, such as TSCA and the German Chemicals Act, generally authorize similar forms of intervention: bans on production; regulation of production methods, storage, and distribution; and packaging and labeling requirements.

In this chapter, the divergent regulatory practices of American and European agencies are traced to different institutional structures and different traditions of political accommodation in the four countries. The first part of the chapter examines the agencies and explains how differences in their organization, experience, and resources lead to different patterns of decision making. The second part studies the impact of the political controls to which agencies are subjected by other governmental institutions and by private interest groups.

The Regulatory Institutions

In each of the four countries, chemical control agencies have been established on an ad hoc basis to meet changing political and administrative demands. Nevertheless, there are systematic differences among the four countries with respect to the ways in which the agencies are structured within the executive branch, their institutional histories, and their budgetary and staff resources.

Administrative Agencies: Structural Considerations

The independent regulatory agency is one of the more remarkable features of American government.[1] Its history in the federal government begins with

[1] Although independent regulatory agencies are not unknown in Europe—Sweden, for example, has made use of such entities since the seventeenth century—the United States is

the creation of the Interstate Commerce Commission (ICC) in 1887 and continues into the 1970s. The agencies created at the turn of the century and during the New Deal were similar to one another in structure and function. They were established on an industry-by-industry basis, their concerns were economic and allocative (rates, routes, frequencies), and their mandates included protection as well as control of the regulated industry. They stood, for the most part, outside the direct purview of the cabinet departments, and their independence was protected through limits on the president's power to dismiss their heads without cause.

The rise of social regulation in the last few decades spawned a new generation of federal agencies that are functionally independent, even when they are not organized along the lines of the ICC. Some, like the Nuclear Regulatory Commission or the Consumer Product Safety Commission, are independent regulatory agencies of the classic type. Others, like the Environmental Protection Agency, deviate somewhat from the traditional pattern. Although EPA is not subject to control by a cabinet department, its administrator may be removed by the president. OSHA, by contrast, is located within the Department of Labor and is thus not structurally independent. But both OSHA and FDA, now a part of the Department of Health and Human Services (DHHS),[2] are situated in a larger administrative hierarchy that is basically sympathetic to their regulatory missions.

Along with independence, the new agencies enjoy regulatory powers considerably more generous than those granted to the New Deal institutions. The jurisdiction of the new agencies typically extends across a wide range of industries. Their mission is to improve the nation's quality of life, if necessary at considerable cost to industry. In pursuit of such goals as clean air, clean water, and safe products and places of work, the new agencies are authorized to intrude into aspects of business management over which the older agencies exercised little or no control. In regulating occupational carcinogens, for example, OSHA may prescribe not only exposure limits achievable by engineering and work practice controls, but a host of secondary restrictions, such as monitoring, record-keeping, and notification requirements, medical surveillance, and employee information and training programs. Similarly, to prevent injury from industrial chemicals, EPA may use a variety of techniques ranging from warning labels to prohibitions on manufacture or marketing.[3]

---

the only one of the four countries included in this study which relies extensively on this institutional format.

[2] FDA resides in DHHS, following a restructuring of its earlier organizational home, DHEW. Created by administrative order in 1906, FDA was originally located in the Department of Agriculture, and subsequently in the Federal Security Administration, until the creation of DHEW.

[3] TSCA §6.

The legislation conferring these extensive powers leaves the administrative agencies free to choose from a wide range of technically and economically feasible control strategies. As a result, highly controversial technology-forcing policies, such as EPA's decision to press for scrubbers in coal-fired power plants or catalytic converters in automobiles, are implemented without specific authorization by Congress.[4] In the area of chemical control, neither the decision of the Consumer Product Safety Commission to regulate chronic hazards under the Federal Hazardous Substances Act[5] nor OSHA's promulgation of a generic cancer policy was mandated by law. Each has been called into question as exceeding the agency's legal authority.[6] Multiple statutory objectives also provide numerous opportunities for the agencies to alter their regulatory priorities. The potential for extreme swings in policy is illustrated by OSHA's decision in 1977 to shift from safety regulation to a concerted attack on occupational carcinogens[7] and its subsequent decision to repudiate the painstakingly developed generic cancer policy. Finally, resource limitations provide an excuse for agencies to implement statutes selectively and without regard to congressional intent. EPA, for example, gives unquestioned priority to new over existing chemicals in implementing TSCA, even though the statute did not authorize an unequal distribution of administrative effort.[8]

---

[4] While some administrative decisions of this magnitude have won subsequent political acceptance, sometimes in the form of express congressional ratification, others have notably failed. In the former category is the offset policy developed by EPA to permit sources of air pollution to locate in nonattainment areas. This was approved with modifications by Congress in the 1977 Clean Air Act amendments. On the other hand, the transportation control program launched by EPA under the 1970 Clean Air Act met with both congressional and judicial disapproval and had to be abandoned. For an analysis of this failure which attributes a significant share of the blame to the U.S. legislative process, see John Quarles, "The Transportation Control Plans: Federal Regulation's Collision with Reality," *Harvard Environmental Law Review*, 2 (1977), 241–63.

[5] 15 U.S.C. §1261.

[6] Supporting the Reagan proposal to dismantle CPSC, OMB Director David Stockman criticized the agency in February 1981 for venturing too far in its chronic hazards program. The American Industrial Health Council has argued that OSHA's cancer policy goes beyond the authority conferred on it by the OSH Act. See AIHC, "Post-Hearing Brief re OSHA Generic Cancer Policy," October 1978, pp. 41–46.

[7] OSHA's performance in its first six years attracted critical reviews from a variety of commentators who called attention, inter alia, to the agency's excessive bias toward safety questions in relation to health hazards. See, for example, Nicholas A. Ashford, *Crisis in the Workplace* (Cambridge, Mass.: MIT Press, 1976), pp. 294–99, and R. S. Smith, *The Occupational Safety and Health Act* (Washington, D.C.: American Enterprise Institute, 1976), pp. 74–77.

[8] In a preappointment interview, John Todhunter, later EPA's assistant administrator for toxic substances, indicated that regulation should be based on the degree of hazard presented rather than whether a substance is new or already on the market. See *BNA International Environment Reporter*, 4, no. 8 (August 12, 1981), 974. But the promised integrated approach to implementing TSCA never fully materialized.

In contrast to EPA or CPSC, most European regulatory agencies still operate under the political umbrella of an established ministry or department. This arrangement has not changed with the assumption of wider regulatory powers by the health, safety, and environmental agencies. In all three European countries, for example, the agriculture ministry remains responsible for pesticide registration, although in the United States this function was transferred to EPA from the Department of Agriculture under a 1972 law.[9] Agriculture ministries have historically served as advocates of grower and producer interests. According to the prevailing American view, placing regulatory responsibilities within these institutions invites capture by the very interests they were designed to control. U.S. environmentalists in the 1970s were convinced that an independent, mission-oriented agency like EPA was needed to resist capture by industrial interests, although EPA's pro-industry orientation in the early 1980s shows that these hopes were misplaced. Perhaps organized labor was more realistic when it fought to bring OSHA within the Department of Labor, believing that a structurally independent board would be more easily co-opted by employer interests.

Interministerial negotiation provides a line of defense against capture in European countries. In Germany, for example, pesticide regulations developed by the federal agriculture ministry are valid only if they are approved by the health ministry as well.[10] The latter's sensitivity to public health issues acts as a counterweight to the former's possible bias against strict regulation of agrochemicals. Interdepartmental consultation serves a similar function in Britain. Such discussions routinely take place during the rule-making process even without express statutory requirement.[11] The system of interministerial cooperation is perhaps most fully developed in France through such techniques as required cosigning of regulations and joint representation on regulatory committees. Formal arrangements of this sort are notably scarce on the U.S. scene. Ad hoc interdepartmental bodies are occasionally formed by statute or on the initiative of the president and the executive agencies themselves, but the interests represented in such groups are more often complementary than conflicting, and the groups' role is limited to giving advice. IRLG, for example, represented five agencies that had a definite commitment to regulating toxic substances. The Interagency Testing Committee (ITC) established by TSCA includes one representative from the Department of Commerce as well as seven from various scientific and public health agencies.

---

[9] Federal Environmental Pesticide Control Act, P.L. no. 92–516 (1972).

[10] Plant Protection Act (Pflanzenschutzgesetz) §8 provides that decisions concerning the health effects of pesticides must be taken jointly by BBA and BGA.

[11] Although the power to take executive action in Britain is vested in the individual ministers, it is an established political convention that ministers bear collective responsibility for decisions. This rule tends to favor wide consultation among governmental departments.

The Toxic Substances Strategy Committee (TSSC) convened by President Carter included a wider range of interests, but it was much more clearly restricted to an advisory role.

Interministerial consultation reinforces the authoritative character of chemical regulation by putting the government as a whole behind decisions to intervene. It also constrains the health and safety agencies to follow more middle-of-the-road policies than would be advocated by their political allies in the environmental, labor, and consumer movements. In the United States, however, the social regulatory agencies of the 1970s can interpret law and develop policy with very little interference from executive departments with countervailing policy interests. While formal rule making requires U.S. agencies to hear a broad range of views, statutory mandates are usually flexible enough to permit systematic downgrading of considerations that the agencies see as extraneous to their central goal of protecting public health and safety. As a result, it has fallen to the White House to correct what some perceive as a tendency toward overzealous regulation by the newer federal agencies. The presidential cost-benefit directives discussed later in this chapter can best be understood as an attempt by the White House to regain control over the regulatory process and to force the agencies, through explicit analysis of economic impacts, to arrive at more balanced policy outcomes.

Administrative Agencies: Experience and Expertise

The U.S. preference for independent regulatory agencies is coupled with a marked propensity for creating new agencies to administer new federal programs. As a result, the landscape of American administration has undergone sweeping changes in the last dozen years. According to one count, seven major federal agencies were established between 1970 and 1975 to implement distinct programs of social regulation.[12] This factor helps explain some of the more radical features of American chemical control policy in the 1970s. On the one hand, these agencies approached their tasks with considerable creativity and zeal, unconstrained by established tradition or bureaucratic inertia. On the other, their effectiveness was diluted by inexperience, inadequate resources, and vacillation among competing regulatory objectives.

Among the federal agencies responsible for chemical control, EPA is by far the most important. Established in 1970 shortly after the passage of the National Environmental Policy Act (NEPA),[13] EPA became the lead agency for

---

[12] See William Lilley III and James C. Miller III, "The New 'Social Regulation'," *Public Interest*, no. 47 (Spring 1977), 49–61.

[13] EPA was created on December 2, 1970, pursuant to President Nixon's Reorganization Plan no. 3.

implementing a broad range of federal environmental programs. Within a half-dozen years, the fledgling institution was authorized to regulate air pollution, radiation in the environment, water pollution, ocean dumping, noise, pesticides, drinking water, toxic substances, and disposal of solid and hazardous wastes. The control of chemical substances or products is one of EPA's prime responsibilities under all of these regulatory programs.

On a less dramatic scale, the establishment of a federal administrative structure for occupational safety and health regulation also illustrates the U.S. penchant for entrusting new legislation to new agencies. The 1970 OSH Act provided for three new agencies to administer federal policy. It authorized the creation of a separate administrative machinery within the Department of Labor to implement the standard-setting provisions.[14] A second institution, the Occupational Safety and Health Review Commission (OSHRC), was formed to adjudicate claims against employers. Congress also established a supporting research institution, the National Institute for Occupational Safety and Health (NIOSH) located within DHEW, now the Department of Health and Human Services.

The distinctive U.S. approach to regulating carcinogens is largely the result of initiatives undertaken by the new administrative agencies. In proceedings relating to the chlorinated hydrocarbon pesticides at EPA, battle lines were quickly drawn between traditional and nontraditional approaches to evaluating animal evidence of carcinogenicity. Gillespie et al. have noted that EPA's innovative search for "cancer principles" in this period was orchestrated by the new, environmentally conscious staff in the Office of General Counsel (OGC) over the objections of former U.S. Department of Agriculture scientists in the Office of Pesticide Programs (OPP).[15] OGC lawyers sought out fresh scientific opinion on the interpretation of cancer bioassays to counteract the more traditional analyses offered by OPP scientists.

OSHA's elaboration of the EPA principles in its own cancer policy proceedings again illustrates the relative flexibility of new regulatory institutions. In 1976 OSHA was under attack for promulgating rigid and trivial standards that curtailed business freedom without measurably benefiting workers. Following a presidential election and a change in leadership, the agency was ready for a drastic reorientation of its priorities. Under Eula Bingham, OSHA not only shifted its focus from safety to health, but also redirected the bulk of its resources toward developing a generic cancer policy. According to one for-

[14] OSH Act §§29 and 30 provided for the appointment of an assistant secretary for occupational safety and health and the creation of twenty-five additional positions within the Department of Labor to implement the act.
[15] See Brendan Gillespie et al., "Carcinogenic Risk Assessment in the United States and Great Britain: The Case of Aldrin/Dieldrin," *Social Studies of Science,* 9, no. 3 (1979), 265–301.

mer OSHA official, the agency's freedom from commitment to a prior regulatory strategy explains why it took up the cancer policy challenge, though it was not necessarily best qualified to do so from the standpoint of experience and expertise.[16]

The pattern of activity displayed by EPA and OSHA in carcinogen regulation contrasts markedly with that of FDA, the oldest health and safety agency in the U.S. government. In implementing the Delaney clause, the first statutory provision demanding special sensitivity toward carcinogens, FDA is required to decide whether experimental results are based on "appropriate" methodology. However, throughout the 1960s, the agency followed a low-key approach to reviewing scientific information, and never explicitly stated what principles it was using to evaluate test protocols or interpret laboratory data. More recently, in a string of controversies involving carcinogens—saccharin, nitrites, and caffeine, among others—FDA was compelled to explain its decisions in greater detail.[17] On the formation of IRLG, FDA was also drawn into collaboration with several of the newer agencies to develop explicit risk assessment guidelines. Without these external pressures, FDA very probably would not have recognized the need for a systematically articulated policy on carcinogens.

Regulatory programs are established with much less visible delegation of authority in Europe than in the United States. New administrative responsibilities tend to be distributed within existing administrative structures, although the three European countries differ somewhat in their preference for particular institutional forms. There are, however, one or two new regulatory agencies in Europe that call for explicit comparison with their closest American counterparts.

In Britain, two institutions dominate the field of chemical control. Though one is "old" and the other "new," both represent a continuity of experience rarely found in the American social regulatory agencies. The Ministry of Agriculture, Fisheries, and Food regulates food additives and pesticides, while the Health and Safety Commission within the Department of Employment controls toxic hazards in the workplace and premarket testing of new chemicals. With some organizational changes, MAFF assumed the duties of a board of agriculture that was established toward the end of the nineteenth

---

[16] Interview, Clement Associates, Washington, D.C., April 24, 1981.

[17] In the cases of both saccharin and nitrite, controversy was triggered by the claims of scientists outside the agency that these substances cause cancer in laboratory animals. The agency's responses in both cases suggest that it was not fully prepared for the consequences of such disclosures. For more complete accounts of these incidents, see Reginald W. Rhein, Jr., and Larry Marion, *The Saccharin Controversy* (New York: Monarch Press, 1977), and R. Jeffrey Smith, "Nitrites: FDA Beats a Surprising Retreat," *Science,* 209, no. 4461 (1980), 1100–1101.

century. Both HSC and its enforcement arm, the Health and Safety Executive, are new agencies that were established under authority of the 1974 Health and Safety at Work Act.

HSC is different from older British regulatory agencies in that it is formally tripartite, containing equal representation from local government, labor, and management. But this new institutional format left undisturbed another extremely influential component of Britain's regulatory structure for worker protection. The major health and safety inspectorates, incorporating well over a century of practical regulatory experience, were merely consolidated under a single roof, HSE.[18] Cohesively organized, the inspectorates retain a dominant role in policy making and ensure a continuity of approach to both standard setting and enforcement. In the long run the new tripartite institutions may enlarge the leverage of worker groups in the policy process. This, at any rate, was the assessment of British agricultural workers, who began demanding in the early 1980s that policies affecting their safety and health also be developed by a tripartite agency.[19] With HSE there to counterbalance HSC, however, any reorientation of policy priorities in Britain is bound to be slower than it is in the leading U.S. chemical control agencies.

Between 1971 and 1980 the German parliament enacted a series of laws giving effect to the comprehensive "Environment Program" announced by the federal government. These activities culminated with the 1980 Chemicals Act, which authorizes both premarket testing and notification of industrial chemicals and the control of toxic substances in the workplace. In ratifying these programs, parliament showed little inclination to experiment with new institutional structures. Instead, new regulatory powers were delegated to existing federal ministries and their network of subordinate technical agencies. In the German paradigm for policy making, the technical agencies are responsible for virtually all policy decisions short of issuing binding legal instruments. Among their many responsibilities are making decisions about the nature and amount of information to be demanded from chemical producers and determining the principles to be used in risk assessment. The minister is responsible only for the promulgation of a final chemical control decision.

This pattern of decision making is encountered in purest form in the regulation of food additives and pesticides, where it has persisted essentially unchanged since the nineteenth century. The Federal Biological Research Center (BBA), the technical arm of the agriculture ministry, supervises the

---

[18] For a general history of these influential institutions, see Gerald Rhodes, *Inspectorates in British Government* (London: George Allen and Unwin, 1981).

[19] Interview, NUAAW, London, July 17, 1980. See also John Mathews, "Unions Press for Herbicide Ban," *New Scientist*, 85, no. 1195 (1980), 558–60.

testing of pesticide efficacy and administers the registration program. The Federal Health Office (BGA) performs toxicological evaluations and advises the federal health and agriculture ministries on the regulation of pesticide residues and new food additives.

Institutional arrangements for worker protection are more complex, though here again current German practice is rooted in past experience. Authority to regulate workplace conditions is divided between the Federal Ministry for Labor and Social Affairs (BMAS) and, for each major industrial sector, the appropriate industrial injuries insurance institute (Berufsgenossenschaft, BG). The labor ministry is responsible for developing policies of general application, including exposure standards for hazardous substances, while the BGs establish health and safety requirements at the plant level, inspect workplaces, maintain records, train safety personnel, and administer employee insurance funds. Created under a law of 1884, the BGs bring to the field of occupational safety and health a length of experience similar to that of the British inspectorates,[20] but their regulatory powers are considerably greater. They have played an active role in controlling chemicals. In 1976, for example, the BG-Chemie, which insures the chemical industry, adopted a program on hazardous substances in the workplace[21] which devoted particular attention to occupational carcinogens.

Conforming to the usual German pattern, administrative officials in the labor ministry draw expert advice from the ministry's technical arm, the Federal Institute for Occupational Safety and Accident Research (Bundesanstalt für Arbeitsschutz und Unfallforschung, BAU). In comparison with the two technical agencies involved in food additive and pesticide control, BAU is a relative newcomer on the regulatory scene.[22] Its expertise on occupational disease, particularly the health effects of chemical exposure, is still quite limited. This explains why the labor ministry continues to rely on an independent scientific committee for advice on toxic substances in the workplace. Exposure standards for noncarcinogenic chemicals are developed by a DFG commission and are incorporated by reference into the ministry's regulations.

The initial plan for implementing the Chemicals Act illustrates the extraordinary influence of the German subordinate technical agencies on regulatory policy making. According to this plan,[23] new chemical notifications are first forwarded to BAU in Dortmund. Thereafter, hazard assessments on various properties of notified substances are carried out by technical agencies in their

---

[20] For a descriptive overview of their organization and activities, see Brenda McCall, "How West Germany Protects Its Workers," *Job Safety and Health,* 5, no. 7 (1977), 21–25.

[21] Interviews at BG-Chemie, Heidelberg, August 15, 1980, and July 15, 1981.

[22] BAU was created in 1972.

[23] Interview at BAU, July 22, 1981. See also *BNA International Environment Reporter,* 4, no. 7 (July 8, 1981), 922–23.

own areas of expertise: BGA (human toxicology), BBA (ecotoxicology in soil), UBA (ecotoxicology in air, water), and the Federal Office for Materials Testing (flammability, explosivity). Complex new regulatory tasks are thus totally accommodated within the existing institutional structure.

Of the five institutions involved in chemical hazard assessment, the newest is the Federal Environmental Agency. Like EPA, UBA was created in response to the environmental activism of the 1970s, but its powers are much slighter than those of the American agency.[24] Though it functions as the technical branch of the Federal Ministry of the Interior on environmental matters, UBA possesses neither delegated regulatory responsibilities nor a developed in-house research capacity. Critics of the agency charge that this is no accident, since UBA is simply a child of "Berlin politics," created to enlarge the federal government's presence in West Berlin.[25] Whatever the truth of this allegation, UBA's lack of specific regulatory power has kept it from winning the backing of any powerful client group.[26] The agency has been an active presence in international negotiations, participating in both EC and OECD discussions on chemical control, but its impact on domestic regulatory policy has remained, to date, relatively weak.

In France, only the policies concerning chemicals in the workplace are developed in collaboration by ministry officials and a supporting technical institution, the National Institute of Research and Safety (INRS). In other sectors of chemical control, French regulatory officials derive scientific and technical support primarily from advisory committees. Recent legislative authorization to control toxic substances has produced little change in French institutional structure. The regulatory schemes for food additives and pesticides, for example, continue to be administered by the Service of Fraud Repression and the Service of Plant Protection, both established divisions of the Ministry of Agriculture. The 1976 Act on the Prevention of Accidents in the Workplace authorized an important new regulatory program—a notification scheme for occupational chemicals—but it created no new implementing agencies. The more comprehensive French chemical notification law of 1977 likewise produced no significant institutional change. Implementation responsibilities were delegated to the Division of Nuisance and Pollution Prevention of the Ministry of the Environment.

---

[24] UBA's history, structure, and activities are described in greater detail in the agency's own publication *Federal Environmental Agency* (Berlin: UBA).

[25] Interview, RSU, Bonn, June 12, 1980.

[26] Indeed, UBA's role in the international harmonization process is called into question by chemical industry representatives who deny the importance of the agency's contributions to OECD negotiations. In industry's view, genuinely important harmonization decisions must be worked out in a political forum, such as the EC, where UBA is not a particularly influential participant. Interview at Hoechst, Frankfurt, July 17, 1981.

Institutional conservatism goes a long way toward explaining why the European approach to regulating carcinogens has remained static over the years. But the relatively low receptivity of European regulators to policy change is also a function of national policies for recruiting personnel. Positions at the highest levels of the administrative hierarchy are ordinarily filled by civil servants on the basis of seniority and merit. Although ministers are nominally accountable for the decisions of all departments under their supervision, important policies are in fact developed by the cadre of higher civil servants, who are themselves largely insulated against the pressure of electoral politics and changes in government. While political considerations, especially party affiliation, may play a part in the selection of senior officials, bureaucrats are seldom chosen for their particular regulatory ideology or their views on specific policy issues. Finally, in spite of national differences in the patterns of recruitment, training, and promotion, civil servants in all three European countries tend to make their careers within a single governmental department.[27] Staffing practices in Europe thus contribute to a decision-making environment that is resistant to shifting political currents and radical change.

In the United States, by contrast, presidential appointments at the highest levels respond openly to political demand and are often designed to achieve specific goals and policies. In the 1970s, for example, the power of the environmental movement influenced the appointments of administrators William Ruckelshaus and Russell Train, whose strong, mission-conscious leadership established EPA from the start as an active regulatory presence. Similarly, the appointments of Eula Bingham and Donald Kennedy to head OSHA and FDA, respectively, catered to an increasing national preoccupation with health issues and were aimed at spurring these two agencies to greater activism.

Because many top positions at governmental agencies are appointive, it is relatively easy for succeeding administrations to undo the initiatives of their predecessors. Senior Reagan appointees, including the EPA administrator, the interior secretary, and the assistant secretary in charge of OSHA, were able to channel federal policy in a direction quite different from that established by past administrations. Moreover, the president's control over appointments extends significantly below the level of agency head. The position of EPA's assistant administrator for toxic substances, for example, was awarded under Reagan to John Todhunter, a chemistry professor and former director of the American Council on Science and Health (ACSH) who attracted public attention through his criticisms of Carter administration deci-

[27] See F. F. Ridley, ed., *Government and Administration in Western Europe* (New York: St. Martin's Press, 1979).

sions on hazardous chemicals. The appointment helped ensure that the new administration's overall regulatory philosophy would be realized at the level of actions taken against specific toxic substances.

Resources

In cross-national analysis, it is difficult to pinpoint the relationship between the resources committed to the regulatory process and the nature of policy outcomes. Financial and manpower statistics for governmental departments are not generally broken down by program area, making exact comparison difficult. Judging the adequacy of regulatory budgets is equally problematic, since both the size and the scope of regulatory programs vary greatly from one country to another. Nevertheless, the available staffing data for one regulatory program, the testing and notification of industrial chemicals, reveal a clear difference of scale between the United States and the three European countries.

The 1981 German federal budget authorized seventy-five new positions for the first year of the chemical notification scheme.[28] As the designated notification office, BAU was to receive about forty-six of these, and the remainder were to be divided between BGA and UBA. The French notification program is administered by the environment ministry's Service of Products Control. In the fall of 1979, two years after passage of the chemical notification law and nine months after adoption of the first implementing decree, this group commanded a professional staff of only three individuals.[29] By mid-1981, Britain's technical secretariat for reviewing chemical notifications was not yet in place. HSC's annual reports, however, give a rough indication of the average yearly personnel changes at HSE. In 1978–79, HSE received about eighty additional staff members "for the fuller implementation of the requirements of the Health and Safety at Work Act 1974."[30] Only a fraction of these were assigned to tasks specifically connected with chemical notification.

Compared with these figures, the personnel increases at EPA during the first four years after the enactment of TSCA appear phenomenal. From 1977 to 1980, the number of authorized positions in the Office of Pesticides and Toxic Substances (OPTS) rose from 88 to 510, while the number of places actually filled rose to 423.[31] But a critical report by the General Accounting

[28] *BNA International Environment Reporter,* 4, no. 7 (July 8, 1981), 922–23.
[29] Interview, Service of Chemical Products, Ministry of the Environment, Paris, November 12, 1979.
[30] HSC, *Report, 1978–79* (London: HMSO, 1980), p. 42.
[31] GAO, "EPA Is Slow to Carry Out Its Responsibility to Control Harmful Chemicals," Washington, D.C., GPO, 1980, pp. 11–12. The following discussion of EPA's performance in implementing TSCA is based on this report.

Office pointed out that, even with 423 new positions, EPA was not effectively meeting its wide-ranging responsibilities under TSCA. GAO found the agency's record on existing chemicals particularly deficient in view of its failure to issue testing requirements for any substances on the Interagency Testing Committee's priority list. Overall, GAO concluded that EPA's progress in identifying and controlling hazardous chemicals had been "disappointing."

This comparison of resource commitments reconfirms our general observations about U.S. and European policies. In staffing the agencies, as in writing law, the U.S. tendency is to think big. Large resources are set aside for the implementation of even larger regulatory policies, so that public expectations are aroused without ever being fully satisfied. The shortfall between promise and actuality, so open and obvious in the United States and so much less noticeable in Europe, helps account for the unique vulnerability of American agencies to challenge from all quarters.

Delegated Legislation: Discretion and Legitimacy

Regulatory agencies should not, of course, be treated as discrete political institutions, independent of the setting in which they operate. Their legitimacy depends on their relationships within a broader political context defined by other governmental actors and the public. In Europe as in the United States, the threat to the legitimacy of regulatory agencies arises from their exercise of quasi-legislative power without direct electoral control. Each country has developed processes designed to legitimate agency behavior by imposing a form of democratic control on administrative lawmaking. The following is a comparison of two such processes across the four countries: public participation in regulatory proceedings and political supervision of administrative rule making by the legislature and the executive.

The Processes and Impact of Participation

Public participation is in some ways the closest substitute for direct electoral control of administrative policy making. Participation by a broad range of interests guards against bias in any one direction and reduces the possibility of capture by powerful pressure groups. Participation by a cross section of the public also broadens the agency's information base and helps ensure that decisions are reached in a rational, nonarbitrary manner. As we saw in chapter 2, all four countries implicitly acknowledge these benefits in controlling chemicals, though they use widely divergent procedures to secure public involvement in administrative proceedings. Here we relate these different participation rules to larger procedural traditions in each country and assess the impact of divergent participation models on the formulation of administrative policy.

The rules of participation in U.S. chemical control laws reflect a longstanding national preference for constraining administrative discretion through mandatory decision-making procedures. Basic procedural requirements applicable to all federal agencies were adopted in the Administrative Procedure Act of 1946. Briefly, the APA provides that administrative agencies must give notice of proposed rule making through publication in the *Federal Register* and offer interested persons an opportunity to comment.[32] In adjudicatory proceedings, where individual interests are at stake, the APA provides for stronger procedural safeguards, such as a formal trial-type hearing and a written transcript.[33] These provisions give American citizens much more extensive rights to participate in administrative proceedings than are conferred by the due process clause of the Constitution.

Once the idea of legalized procedures took hold, Congress proved all too willing to experiment with these requirements, using procedural checks and balances as a substitute for clear substantive standards.[34] The result is that APA provisions, once designed to bring uniformity into administrative practice, have come to be regarded more as procedural minima, to be supplanted as needed by additional requirements. As we shall see in chapter 5, the federal courts have encouraged this development by demanding a variety of "hybrid" procedures that require more than notice and comment but less than the full panoply of an adjudicatory hearing.[35] Federal regulatory proceedings have accordingly moved in the direction of the adjudicatory model, in which evidence is developed through adversarial techniques such as cross-examination.

Apart from specific action by Congress or the courts, the threat of litigation

---

[32] 5 U.S.C. §553.

[33] 5 U.S.C. §554.

[34] For a critical and pessimistic analysis of this history, see Antonin Scalia, "Vermont Yankee: The APA, the D.C. Circuit, and the Supreme Court," *Supreme Court Review* (1978), pp. 386–88, 400–407.

[35] The development of hybrid rule making through judicial intervention has generated a considerable body of scholarly comment, both positive and negative. See, for example, Kenneth C. Davis, *Administrative Law of the Seventies* (Rochester: Lawyers Co-Operative Publishing Co., 1976), §6; Stephen F. Williams, "'Hybrid Rulemaking' under the Administrative Procedure Act: A Legal and Empirical Analysis," *University of Chicago Law Review*, 42, no. 3 (1975), 401–56; Paul Verkuil, "Judicial Review of Informal Rule-Making," *Virginia Law Review*, 60, no. 2 (1974), 185–249; J. Skelly Wright, "New Judicial Requisites for Informal Rulemaking," *Administrative Law Review*, 29, no. 1 (1977), 59–64; Carl A. Auerbach, "Informal Rule Making: A Proposed Relationship between Administrative Procedures and Judicial Review," *Northwestern University Law Review*, 72, no. 1 (1977), 15–68; Note, "The Judicial Role in Defining Procedural Requirements for Agency Rulemaking," *Harvard Law Review*, 87, no. 1 (1974), 782–806.

has given American administrators a strong incentive to adopt formal procedures in rule making. In areas of high technical uncertainty, such as chemical control, administrative agencies recognize that their decision-making records will frequently be subjected to judicial scrutiny. Rather than risk remand for inadequacies in the record, administrators prefer to develop evidence as fully as possible from the outset, often employing supplementary procedures for the purpose. In implementing the OSH Act, for example, the secretary of labor "voluntarily move[d] his procedures significantly toward the formal model. He directed that (1) a qualified hearing examiner should preside over the oral hearing, (2) cross-examination should be permitted, and (3) a verbatim transcript made."[36] While these supplementary procedures do not necessarily increase the number of participants in rule making, they do affect the quality of participation. Formal hearings cast opposing interests as adversaries and put a premium on their knowledge and expertise.

The use of formal procedures carries far-reaching consequences for U.S. regulatory policy. The most obvious effect is to protract the period required to develop a final rule. It takes several years to issue a major federal regulation in final form. OSHA's generic cancer policy, for example, first appeared as a proposed rule in October 1977, but it was not promulgated as a final regulation until January 1980. Time lags of this magnitude make nonsense of statutory timetables. By 1980, EPA had not issued any testing rules for substances designated for priority testing by the Interagency Testing Committee, though TSCA requires EPA to begin rule making within one year after an ITC recommendation. EPA's own estimates showed that it would take eighteen months to issue an Advance Notice of Proposed Rulemaking and up to five years to promulgate a final rule.[37]

Formal rule making is also expensive. Federal agencies expend enormous resources in collecting data, commissioning expert analyses, maintaining detailed records, and making public the reasons for their regulatory decisions. A less tangible cost of adversarial administrative hearings is the polarization of expert witnesses and a weakening of public confidence in scientific objectivity (discussed more fully in chapter 8).

On the plus side of the ledger, careful use of hearings, cross-examination, and a written record help U.S. administrators identify scientific uncertainties and define clear policy options, furthering rational decision making. OSHA's cancer policy hearings provided an unmatched exploration of the issues involved in regulating carcinogens. The airing of such issues, the publication of a record, and access to supporting documents place public interest groups on a more equal footing with experts in industry. Admirers of the American

[36]*Industrial Union Department, AFL-CIO v. Hodgson*, 499 F. 2d 474 (D.C. Cir., 1974).
[37]GAO, op. cit., p. 30.

administrative process thus see formal participation as an essential safeguard against government by experts or special interests, and as the primary avenue to the Jeffersonian ideal of decision making by an enlightened and informed public.[38]

In the matter of administrative procedure, as in most other aspects of regulation, Britain has adopted a course diametrically opposed to that of the United States. Specifically, the British regulatory system has repudiated the attempt to legislate procedural rules except where administrative rule making directly impinges on individual rights.[39] In the very year the APA was enacted in the United States, Britain abolished an existing requirement of prior publication for administrative regulations. Terminating tentative movement toward a British APA, the Statutory Instruments Act of 1946 firmly established informal consultation as the preferred means for drawing the public into administrative proceedings.[40] In Germany, the Administrative Procedures Act of 1976[41] and the Administrative Court Ordinance[42] make the administrative process more uniform and formal than it is in Britain, but both statutes are primarily concerned with adjudicatory proceedings affecting individual rights.

Apart from procedural rights created by specific statutes, a variety of unwritten rules have been developed by the courts in all three European countries to protect individuals against arbitrary administrative action. These include the general legal principles articulated by the French Conseil d'Etat, parallel provisions in German administrative law, and common-law principles of natural justice. With respect to determinations of a legislative nature, however, none of these procedural safeguards compares in sweep to the APA rule-making provisions. As a result, German and French rule-making practices are scarcely more formal than those of Britain. Although environmental and health and safety laws (including chemical control laws) sometimes stipulate that certain private interests be consulted, such provisions do not confer a right to participate on any interest group. Moreover, procedures for securing public input are left entirely to the administrator's discretion. For all

---

[38] Judge Bazelon of the D.C. Circuit Court of Appeals has long been an articulate spokesman for these views. See, for example, David L. Bazelon, "Risk and Responsibility," *Science*, 205, no. 4403 (1979), 277–80.

[39] The Tribunals and Inquiries Act 1971, for example, prescribes procedures for certain classes of disputes between individuals and state agencies. In addition, planning law in Britain, as in France and Germany, provides for administrative proceedings ("public inquiries") to develop scientific or technical data and information about local or regional conditions.

[40] See H. W. R. Wade, *Administrative Law* (Oxford: Clarendon Press, 1977), pp. 728–30.

[41] Administrative Procedures Act (Verwaltungsverfahrensgesetz) of 25 May 1976 (*BGBl.* I p. 1253), as amended.

[42] Administrative Court Ordinance (Verwaltungsgerichtsordnung) of 21 January 1960 (*BGBl.* I p. 17; III pp. 340-1).

practical purposes, therefore, administrators in Germany and France enjoy as much freedom as their British counterparts to decide who should be heard and under what circumstances.

The preponderance of informal procedures in European rule making offers administrators a number of advantages that are foregone in the more rule-bound U.S. administrative process. The European approach is better suited to building consensus; the absence of confrontational procedures permits public authorities to work toward negotiated settlements without inducing the hardening of positions that is characteristic of more adversarial proceedings. Confidentiality is easier to maintain. Governmental officials not only act as gate-keepers, regulating entry into the consultation process, but also control the flow of information to and among the concerned parties. On the whole, the European consultative processes appear more compatible with the political aspects of administrative decision making than the open and formal procedures of the United States. Since compromises can be struck and deals made out of public view, European administrators do not feel pressured to justify essentially political decisions in the artificially rational language of science or economics.

We alluded above to the enormous costs of gathering and disseminating information in the American regulatory system. A glance at the documentary basis for European regulatory decisions helps drive this point home. In Britain, a written draft of a proposed major regulation or code of practice is often circulated for public comment. This "consultative document" superficially resembles an American proposed rule in that it discusses the basis and purpose of a projected action. Thus, the HSC's first consultative document on the notification of new substances[43] briefly reviewed the history and objectives of the HSW Act, rehearsed the background of chemical control initiatives in the EC and its member states, and discussed the economic impact of the British proposals. But all these matters were treated with a brevity that would be viewed as unacceptable in U.S. agency practice. The discussion of economic impacts, for example, was limited to little more than a page, a remarkable feat if one recalls the multivolume regulatory impact studies prepared by American agencies. In Germany and France, where the work of political accommodation is more frequently carried out within pluralistic expert committees, the decision-making record is even sparser than it is in Britain. The analogue of the consultative document either is not produced at all or is even less readily available for public review.

As in the legislative process, limiting public access to the administrative agencies enhances the government's control over policy outcomes. Since the issuing agency determines who should review regulatory proposals, it can

---

[43] HSC, *Notification of New Substances* (London: HMSO, 1981).

limit the public's right to comment on rules during their formative stages. While neocorporatist traditions guarantee established interest groups a place in regulatory consultations, the position of the newer public interest associations is more precarious. These must establish their right to be consulted on a case-by-case basis. The risk inherent in this approach is that the administrative agency may consciously or inadvertently exclude from consultation a group whose participation is essential to an unbiased exploration of the issues or to the formation of a viable consensus.

In all three European countries, regulators take certain precautions to guard against this risk. British administrators, for example, show great respect for the opinions of organized lobbies that have a demonstrated stake in specific regulatory issues. Both governmental officials and citizen groups acknowledge that expertise is the most effective key to unlocking the door of consultation proceedings. This provides an incentive for public interest representatives to increase their expertise on major policy questions. A favorite British success story is the case of Friends of the Earth (FOE), a group with branches in the United States and Britain. Once dismissed by public authorities as "eco-nuts," FOE has now established its credibility (and earned the right to be consulted) on a number of environmental issues, including sperm whales, marine pollution, and nuclear power.[44]

As described by German and French administrators, the criteria they use in selecting participants for administrative proceedings sound a shade more democratic than those applied in Britain. Breadth of representation is the key to participation in these two countries, rather than the more subjective and elitist criterion of expertise. In Germany, for example, two nationally organized environmental groups, the Bund für Umwelt and Naturschutz Deutschland (BUND) and the Bundesverband Bürgerinitiativen Umweltschutz (BBU), are now regularly consulted on matters relating to environmental protection.[45] In France, the notions of representation and participation have been formally linked in recent years through legislation conferring participation and litigation rights on "approved" associations. One criterion for approval under these laws is the association's status as a genuinely representative group. In accordance with a decree of 1977, an environmental association must demonstrate "a certain number of contributing members,

[44] Interview, Department of the Environment, London, July 18, 1980.

[45] The right to participate in the administrative process in Germany is limited by the fact (as discussed in chapter 5) that the denial of such rights does not automatically provide grounds for judicial review. See, for example, Eckard Rehbinder, "Private Recourse for Environmental Harm: Federal Republic of Germany," in Stephen McCaffrey and Robert Lutz, eds., *Environmental Pollution and Individual Rights: An International Symposium* (Deventer, The Netherlands: Kluwer, 1978), p. 40.

continuity in the administration of the association, regularity in accounting, and frequent activities or publications of certain importance."[46]

In addition to excluding potentially significant political opinion, European consultative processes tend to restrict the criticism of expert testimony by public interest representatives. Since consultation precludes open debate or cross-examination, the assumptions and theories of technical experts are rarely exposed to critical public scrutiny. Thus, consultation preserves the apparent neutrality of expert opinion, concealing the fact that such opinion may be colored by unexpressed political biases and value preferences. The consequences for European policy making on carcinogens are discussed at greater length in chapter 8.

The Imposition of Political Control

Legislative Supervision of Administrative Action   While legislatures in all four countries delegate substantial regulatory power to the executive branch, they are not equally zealous in supervising the exercise of this power. The U.S. Congress not only constrains administrative discretion most severely through procedural controls, but keeps closest watch over the implementation process through its far-reaching oversight activities. European parliaments, by contrast, rely primarily on well-placed questions to call executive officials to account. Predictably enough, the effect of these divergent styles of legislative supervision is to make American administrators more vulnerable and more dependent on technical support for their actions than are officials of comparable rank in Europe.

PARLIAMENTARY QUESTIONS   In all three European countries, the parliamentary question is a popular technique for criticizing governmental policies, even in technically complex areas such as chemical regulation. The substantive impact of parliamentary questions, however, seems insignificant. Two factors chiefly account for this. Formal rules for submitting parliamentary questions often insulate the government against genuinely embarrassing inquiries. On technical issues, moreover, disparities in the information available to legislators and that available to ministers make it difficult for the former to pose pertinent and effective questions.

Parliamentary questions in Britain are governed by an especially bewildering array of conventions concerning both form and substance.[47] Certain sub-

---

[46] Michel Prieur, "The Rights of Associations for the Protection of Nature and the Environment in France," in McCaffrey and Lutz, op. cit., p. 70.

[47] See Charles Medawar, *Parliamentary Questions—and Answers* (London: Social Audit, 1980).

jects, such as matters before the courts, are simply taboo. More generally, questions are accepted by the government only if they are framed directly and without ambiguity and address issues within the jurisdiction of the minister to whom they are addressed. Even if questions are posed in proper form, MPs have no established right to receive an answer. Because of its rule-bound character, the questioning process demands more gamesmanship than strict command of substance, especially in the handling of oral questions. Correspondingly, successful parliamentary questions are more likely to score general political points than to change specific policy decisions.

Parliamentary questions concerning chemical regulation most frequently focus on substances whose health effects have aroused particular public or scientific concern. Carcinogens thus figure prominently in the parliamentary questions of all three European countries. As the following examples suggest, however, most questions only seek information and hence receive little more than conventional assurances from the concerned ministry.

France:

> 28 August 1978. A study having recently been published, showing that sodium nitrite used in preserving foods, particularly meat and fish, has been revealed to be carcinogenic, M. Palmero asks the Minister of Health and the Family what measures for protection of consumers exist in this regard.
> Reply. The Minister of Health and the Family informs the honorable member of parliament that sodium nitrite is authorized as an additive in certain foods to prevent the development of clostridium botulinum and its toxins, which are responsible for a most serious infection, botulism. Public authorities limit to the strictly necessary level the quantities of nitrite permitted in food. Since the adoption of the arrêté of 8 December 1964, the tolerance level of sodium nitrite is limited to 150 mg/kg in cured foods, sausages and preserved meats. This tolerance is, moreover, internationally accepted.[48]

Britain:

> 16 November 1976. Mrs. Chalker asked the Minister of Agriculture, Fisheries and Food what advice he has for people wishing to dispose of the herbicide known as 245; and if he will wish to make a statement about its future use.
> Mr. Strang: The hon. Member is presumably referring to 2,4,5-T and I welcome this opportunity of dispelling any unnecessary anxiety about it. This herbicide has been cleared by the expert and independent Advisory

---

[48] France, Parlement, Assemblée Nationale, Débats Parlementaires no. 6 Législature, 1978, p. 3923.

Committee on Pesticides and Other Toxic Chemicals and contrary to any impression which may have been conveyed by recent presentation in the media it can safely be used in the recommended way for the recommended purposes. . . . [Remainder of answer omitted.][49]

Germany:

> Representative Schäfer (Offenburg, SPD) (Drucksache 8/2273 Question A13): Is it known to the Federal Government whether it is true that more than 15 chemical workers in the Badische Anilin- und Sodafabrik (BASF) in Ludwigshafen have contracted bronchial cancer since 1969 when they worked with Dichloromethylether and that 11 of them have died in the interim; and, according to the present state of knowledge in the Federal Government, are further cases of cancer deaths to be feared in the chemical industry?
>
> 15 November 1978. Answer of Parliamentary Secretary of State Buschfort: As the Insurance Association for the chemical industry has informed us, Dichloromethylether was produced in the years from 1952 until 1971 in the Badische Anilin- und Sodafabrik (BASF) for use in experimental products. In 1971 it became known from the U.S.A. that this substance is carcinogenic. BASF then immediately stopped its production.
>
> According to information given by the Insurance Association for the chemical industry, 11 deaths (bronchial cancer) have thus far resulted from handling this substance. Ten cases have been compensated and the eleventh case has been notified to the Insurance Association.
>
> Since a long period of time can elapse between the influence of an occupational carcinogen [on health] and the appearance of the disease, the exposed BASF employees from that period will continue to be monitored by the industrial medical division of BASF.[50]

CONGRESSIONAL OVERSIGHT While parliamentary questions are by nature oriented to single issues, congressional oversight subjects an agency's entire implementation record to critical review. Major modifications in U.S. chemical control policy are often preceded by detailed congressional probing of existing programs. In 1975 and 1976, for example, Congress held extensive hearings on EPA's implementation of the 1972 pesticide legislation.[51] A con-

---

[49] *Parliamentary Debates* (Commons), *Hansard,* vol. 919, November 16, 1976, column 514.

[50] Deutscher Bundestag, 8th Electoral Period, 116th sess., November 15, 1978, pp. 9073–74.

[51] House Committee on Agriculture, *Hearings on Federal Insecticide, Fungicide, and Rodenticide Act Extension,* 94th Cong., 1st sess., 1975; Senate Committee on Commerce, Subcommittee on the Environment, *Hearing on Federal Environmental Pesticides Control Act,* 94th Cong., 1st sess., 1975 House Committee on Government Operations, *Hearings on EPA's Implementation of the Pesticides Control Act,* 94th Cong., 2d sess., 1976.

cern that surfaced prominently in these hearings was that EPA was paying insufficient attention to the agricultural benefits of pesticide use. Congressional inquiry led to a strengthening of ties between USDA and EPA under the 1975 amendments to FIFRA. The 1977 saccharin hearings brought FDA's regulation of carcinogens under sharp attack.[52] Although the immediate result was to exempt the artificial sweetener from prohibition under the Delaney clause, the deluge of amendments to the FDCA proposed since that date suggests that the hearings sparked widespread legislative discontent with the existing state of the law.

In theory, congressional oversight could legitimate the actions of administrative agencies by demonstrating that administrators are subject to guidance by elected officials. Regular exchanges with the legislature could also help administrators to remain in touch with changing congressional perspectives, particularly following major political swings of the kind signaled by the 1980 election. In practice, however, the confrontational character of congressional activity erodes rather than shores up public confidence in the performance of the regulatory agencies. Legislators intent on increasing their own visibility use hearings as occasions for political grandstanding. The most dramatic agency shortcomings are seized on for protracted and intense investigation. The entire process publicly reaffirms the view that the agencies are incompetent and incapable of acting in the public interest unless driven by Congress. Thus, the 1977 saccharin hearings and overruling of FDA's proposed saccharin ban deepened public mistrust of the agency's chemical control policies. For the newer agencies, congressional supervision, often backed up by critical GAO investigations, has proved even more devastating. Both EPA and OSHA have had their scientific expertise and political wisdom challenged, sustaining significant losses in public esteem.

For many years, Congress experimented with the legislative veto as its ultimate mechanism for reasserting control over regulatory policy making. Disenchantment with perceived regulatory excesses in the late 1970s intensified congressional efforts to widen the veto authority of Congress and a number of bills were introduced to give one or both houses the final word in declaring the validity of federal regulations.[53] Uncertainty about the wisdom

---

[52] House Committee on Interstate and Foreign Commerce, Subcommittee on Health and the Environment, *Hearing on Proposed Saccharin Ban: Oversight,* 95th Cong., 1st sess., 1977; House Committee on Interstate and Foreign Commerce, Subcommittee on Health and the Environment, *Hearing on Moratorium on Saccharin Ban: Oversight,* 95th Cong., 1st sess., 1977.

[53] Examples of such proposals in the 95th Congress include H.R. 460, H.R. 495, H.R. 532, H.R. 1858 and S. 1463. A study on federal regulation carried out during the 95th Congress recommended against the use of the legislative veto. Senate Committee on Governmental Affairs, *Study on Federal Regulations,* vols. 1–4, 95th Cong., 2d. sess., 1977–78.

and constitutionality of these initiatives[54] was partly resolved by several Supreme Court decisions in 1983 declaring some two hundred federal legislative veto provisions unconstitutional.[55] But although these decisions obstructed an important avenue of congressional intervention, they did little to alter the fundamentally competitive dynamics of legislative-executive relations.

It could be argued that the rejection of the legislative veto has brought the balance of legislative and executive power in the United States closer to that in Europe, since some European parliaments still enjoy veto authority over regulations. In Britain, for example, regulations that have undergone ministerial approval must generally be accepted formally by Parliament. Under German law, most major chemical control regulations must be ratified by the Bundesrat. But these formal procedures scarcely compare in impact with the rigorous and systematic supervision of the U.S. regulatory agencies by Congress. The British Parliament rarely makes serious modifications in regulations that have passed cabinet review, particularly when they are technically complex. Submission to the Bundesrat guarantees administrative respect for Länder interests but does not otherwise detract from the federal administrative agencies' right to develop autonomous policy. The French system, with its stronger centralization of power in the executive branch, does not offer parliament even the semblance of political control over bureaucratic rule making. Instead, administrative policy is supervised and coordinated by the Conseil d'Etat, whose prestige and experience contribute powerfully to the legitimation of executive decisions.

Control by the Chief Executive   The chief executive's power to set general policy guidelines and to appoint and remove administrative officials imposes additional political controls over administrative behavior. Since the early seventies, these indirect controls have been supplemented in the United States by a series of presidential orders more directly influencing the decision-making processes of the federal regulatory agencies. Four successive administrations have directed the agencies to prepare economic analyses of proposed regulations under close supervision by the Office of Management and Budget or other White House agencies.[56] The primary aim of these direc-

---

[54] See, for example, Harold Bruff and Ernest Gellhorn, "Congressional Control of Administrative Regulation: A Study of Legislative Vetoes," *Harvard Law Review,* 90, no. 7 (1977), 1369–1440; Carl McGowan, "Congress, Court, and Control of Delegated Power," *Columbia Law Review,* 77, no. 8 (1977), 1119–74; OTA, *Assessment of Technologies for Determining Cancer Risks from the Environment* (Washington, D.C.: GPO, 1981), pp. 186–87.

[55] *Immigration and Naturalization Service v. Chadha,* 103 S. Ct. 2764 (1983); *United States Senate v. FTC,* 103 S. Ct. 3935 (1983).

[56] See, for example, Ford Executive Order (E.O.) 11821 (1974), extended by E.O. 11949 (1976); Carter E.O. 12044 (1978); Reagan E.O. 12291 (1981).

tives was to reduce the economic impact of health, safety, and environmental regulations by forcing agencies to elect the least costly means of achieving their policy objectives.

Criticism of the economic analysis directives has focused primarily on their legality; some analysts view them as an impermissible overlay on procedures mandated by the APA and specific agency statutes.[57] The wisdom of basing regulatory decisions on cost-benefit analysis has also been widely questioned. Setting these legal and methodological problems aside, we note that the American president's preferred technique for asserting political control reinforces the already pronounced formal and adversarial tendencies of American regulation. Mandatory economic analysis, performed under OMB's watchful eye, adds a layer of procedure to the rule-making process and fosters competitive relations within the executive branch. Even if these procedures lead to better, more balanced decisions, they cannot help exacerbating the delays and conflicts endemic to American regulation.

The low demand for similar analytical procedures in European policy circles can be attributed to traditions of corporatist and interministerial negotiation, coupled with generally cooperative relations between government and industry. An emphasis on negotiated dispute resolution tends to slow the pace of regulatory activity and often leads to a more flexible regulatory response.[58] For European industry, these gains are more significant than the somewhat questionable advantages that would be gained through analytical procedures.

Conclusion

Our comparison of the administrative systems of the four countries highlights several features that contribute to the differences between American and European policy described in earlier chapters: the structure and experience of regulatory agencies, the traditions of public participation, and the relationship of the agencies with the legislature and higher executive authorities. Generally, the problems created by ambitious statutory mandates in the United States are heightened by the bureaucratic and scientific inexperience of the new regulatory agencies and the complex procedures they are required to follow. Although broad participation and congressional supervision could make administrative decision making appear more legitimate, in practice both

[57] See Morton Rosenberg, "Presidential Control of Agency Rulemaking: An Analysis of Constitutional Issues That May Be Raised by Executive Order 12291," Congressional Research Service, June 15, 1981.

[58] Sheila Jasanoff, "Negotiation or Cost-Benefit Analysis: A Middle Road for U.S. Policy?" *Environmental Forum*, 2, no. 3 (1983), 37–43.

processes produce more nearly the opposite effect. Both focus attention on the scope of discretionary authority granted to the agencies but challenge the right of administrators to wield autonomous political authority. Congressional oversight, in particular, emphasizes the legislature's sovereign control over policy and implies that agencies must be continually supervised to keep their decisions in line with the popular will.

Many of the features that prompt urgent questions about the legitimacy of administrative action in the United States are absent in the European countries. We have seen that European administrators are entrusted with less divisive mandates in the field of health and safety regulation than are their American counterparts. In addition, both the structure of European institutions and their procedural practices tend to diffuse the sense of accumulated power that clings to American agencies such as EPA and OSHA. European administrative systems separate the minister, who is politically responsible for decisions, from the bureaucracy that performs the technical work of drafting regulations. This separation is most effective in Germany, where important policy-making functions are carried out by technical agencies that are organizationally and, by implication, functionally separated from the political wing of the ministry. Further, the negotiating mode of European regulation, whether through informal consultation or institutionalized representation, prevents an isolation and clear identification of the regulatory agency's own role in the process. European administrators exercise power, but they do not call attention to it in the American manner, and they are consequently spared the intense scrutiny drawn by U.S. agencies.

Despite problems of legitimacy, however, the U.S. administrative process has made notable contributions to the public appraisal of chemical hazards, particularly those associated with carcinogens. Innovation by EPA and OSHA led to the first generic policies for regulating carcinogens. Although their proposals were not immediately or widely accepted, they focused more systematic regulatory interest on these substances in the United States and other industrial countries (see chapter 8). The sophistication of current public debate about assessing and controlling carcinogenic risk is due in large part to the clarity and detail of the scientific and policy arguments developed in American chemical control proceedings.

5

Policy Making in the Courts

Litigation against governmental agencies responsible for chemical regulation is a distinctively American phenomenon. Although individuals who are injured by administrative decisions are entitled to judicial redress in all four countries, lawsuits against administrators based on chemical control decisions are virtually unknown in Britain and France and at best infrequent in Germany. In the United States, by contrast, regulatory action is often undertaken only when someone takes the agency to court. At the other end of the process, major chemical control decisions are rarely allowed to stand unchallenged by industry, labor, or concerned public interest groups.

The differences between the American and European patterns of litigation suggest two lines of inquiry which are pursued in this chapter. First, we seek to explain why, despite the existence of a general presumption of reviewability, administrative decisions concerning chemicals are so rarely brought before the courts in Europe. This chapter argues that part of the explanation is to be found within the legal doctrines concerning standing and scope of review that the courts have developed, with varying degrees of support from legislatures. Viewed in the larger context of state-society relationships, these doctrines seem to reflect fundamental national attitudes about the importance of building and maintaining consensus among major political actors. Thus, the liberal rules of standing and review in America seem natural extensions of the competitive and divisive tendencies observed throughout the U.S. regulatory process.

The second part of the chapter looks more generally at judicial review as a technique for legitimating regulatory decision making. Our analysis in this section is based primarily on American cases involving the regulation of carcinogens. This record shows that judicial power can be used to elicit more complete explanations for agency actions, including decisions not to act. Ultimately, however, the elaborate reasoning and documentation required by the U.S. courts seem to undermine rather than enhance administrative capability. They expose the often fragile scientific basis for regulatory decisions, making agency actions appear unmotivated and arbitrary.

The Judiciary and the Administration

In France and Germany, a separate hierarchy of administrative courts handles disputes between citizens and the government, whereas in Britain and the United States a single court system deals with both public and private legal controversies. One might expect the existence of specialized administrative courts to lead to greater cooperation between the judiciary and the administration in the civil law countries than is possible in the two common law jurisdictions. In reality, however, the courts of each country are organized in distinctive national configurations that rule out easy generalizations concerning judicial-administrative relations. A comparison of the four judicial structures only suggests that the greatest unity of purpose between courts and administration is likely to be found in France and the least in the United States. French administrative courts enjoy a peculiarly close relationship with the executive agencies because of the unique hybrid institution, the Conseil d'Etat, which heads the hierarchy. A historical distrust of judges meddling in administrative affairs[1] led to the creation, within the executive branch, of an institution capable of ensuring the legality of administrative action. The Conseil d'Etat, however, is much more than a conventional court. Only one of its five sections engages in the appellate review of administrative cases. The remaining four serve as general advisers to government, assisting both in drafting and implementing legislation and in supervising public administration.

Unlike courts in the other three countries, the Conseil participates directly in the administrative process through its nonlitigation sections. It is a primary duty of the Conseil to ensure that administrative authority is exercised within the limits prescribed by the 1958 Constitution. Consultation with the Conseil is therefore a mandatory step in the preparation of many regulatory instru-

---

[1] Henry J. Abraham, *The Judicial Process,* 3d ed. (New York: Oxford University Press, 1977), pp. 255–56.

ments. On other matters of sufficient importance, administrative officials often turn to the Conseil for advice even if they are not required to do so by law.[2] Since the Conseil's recommendations remain secret in most cases, it is difficult to judge their precise impact, but observers of the institution believe that a regulation submitted to one of the Conseil's administrative sections for review is unlikely to be annulled by the judicial section on legal grounds.[3] Prior review by the Conseil thus acts as a powerful legitimating influence on French administration.

Because of its complexity of form and function, the Conseil mediates between law and politics, administrative theory and practice, as no ordinary court can. It is hardly surprising that the institution has no parallel in another country. In Margherita Rendel's words:

> It is inconceivable that anyone should have "invented" the Conseil d'Etat. It has grown and developed. To this extent, therefore, it cannot be copied or transplanted. The institution has attracted attention and many countries have tried to create a Conseil d'Etat of their own. But the Conseil is not simply an institution. It has also a tradition, an original method of working and an unusual relationship with other departments of State.[4]

The German administrative courts originally grew out of an administrative structure in which higher supervisory authorities controlled the decisions of lower units.[5] Since the adoption of the Basic Law, however, the administrative courts have enjoyed complete independence from the political hierarchy of the executive branch.[6] The appointment of administrative civil servants to the court system keeps judges informed about routine problems of administration[7] and helps create a coherent administrative-judicial outlook on regulatory problems. Because they lack the equivalent of a Conseil d'Etat, however, the German administrative courts play no active part in the development of regulations. Their role is limited to after-the-fact checks on the legality of governmental decisions, so that their relations with the executive departments are on the whole more typical of Britain or the United States than France.

---

[2] Charles E. Freedman, *The Conseil d'Etat in Modern France* (New York: Columbia University Press, 1961), p. 97.

[3] Ibid., pp. 97–100.

[4] Margherita Rendel, *The Administrative Functions of the French Conseil d'Etat* (London: Weidenfeld and Nicolson, 1970), p. 253.

[5] David Southern, "Germany," in F. F. Ridley, ed., *Government and Administration in Western Europe* (New York: St. Martin's Press, 1979), p. 150.

[6] Dieter Lorenz, "The Constitutional Supervision of the Administrative Agencies in the Federal Republic of Germany," *Southern California Law Review,* 53, no. 2 (1980), 572.

[7] Southern, op. cit., p. 151.

Though the idea of separate administrative courts is repugnant to Anglo-American law, one U.S. court has recently emerged as an authoritative interpreter of administrative law. Under a number of environmental and health and safety statutes, significant administrative decisions are reviewed from the start by the courts of appeals rather than the district courts.[8] In almost all of these cases, a petition for review may be filed in the D.C. Circuit Court of Appeals, and in a few instances review is possible only in that court.[9] Partly as a consequence of these provisions and partly because of its strategic location, the D.C. Court of Appeals has become the most important forum for the resolution of controversies involving the federal administrative agencies. Since Supreme Court review is available only for a small percentage of circuit court decisions, the D.C. Court of Appeals frequently speaks as the highest judicial authority on major questions of administrative law. Its influence has been most strongly felt in the area of health, safety, and environmental decision making, including the field of chemical control.

In spite of its growing involvement in administrative affairs, the relationship of the D.C. Court of Appeals to the regulatory agencies remains fundamentally adversarial. Its role, as before, is to ensure that administrators are held to appropriate legal standards, particularly in their exercise of discretionary authority. Unlike the Conseil d'Etat, or even the German administrative courts, the judges of the D.C. Court of Appeals bear no responsibility for the managerial aspects of administration, including the cost or efficiency of rule making. Freedom from those constraints makes it easier for a body like the D.C. Court of Appeals to interpret administrative law doctrines in ways that increase the length and complexity of the regulatory process.

Keeping Administrative Conflicts out of the Courts

All four countries recognize that both the administrative process and the judicial process would irretrievably break down if all administrative decisions were subjected to judicial review. Moreover, automatic review would simply substitute judicial decisions for administrative ones, thereby eroding the functional separation that each country seeks to preserve between "policy" and "law," the former articulated by administrators and the latter by judges. Two sets of legal techniques are used to prevent excessive encroachment by judges on the sphere of administrative policy making. The first consists of rules

[8] For example, the U.S. courts of appeals have exclusive jurisdiction to review most rules promulgated under §§ 4, 5, 6, and 8 of TSCA. See TSCA §19.

[9] For example, §307(b)(1) of the Clean Air Act of 1970 provides that petitions for judicial review of most standards promulgated by EPA may be filed only in the United States Court of Appeals for the District of Columbia.

designed to keep conflicts out of the courts, whereas the second limits the extent to which judges may question or overrule administrative decisions that they have agreed to review. In comparing the use of these techniques in the four countries, we focus particularly on the activism of the courts themselves in expanding or constricting the doctrines governing review.

Jurisdictional Limits on Review

Whether an administrative action is reviewable in court is a matter that each legal system approaches somewhat differently. In France and Germany, the existence of separate administrative and ordinary courts requires a threshold inquiry into the nature of the challenged decision, since only those actions that are properly "administrative" may be controlled by the administrative courts. Under French law, reviewable administrative acts (actes administratifs) include regulatory decisions of general application, such as decrees and regulations, as well as actions affecting individuals.[10] Roughly the same range of administrative actions is considered reviewable in the two common law countries.

Judicial review in Britain is regarded as "merely the practical application of the rule of law."[11] To effectuate the premise of parliamentary supremacy, the courts must make sure that administrative officials exercise their delegated legislative powers within limits designated by Parliament. In principle, therefore, any action of an administrative body may be reviewed by the courts and invalidated if it falls beyond lawful limits (ultra vires). In the United States, the common law basis for judicial review has been overtaken to a much greater extent by statutory provisions than in Britain. A baseline for judicial review of administrative decisions is provided by the Administrative Procedure Act,[12] which merely codifies the common law presumption of reviewability established in American law prior to 1946.[13] In addition, the major health and safety laws of the seventies include their own review provisions, specifying the parties that may petition for review, the courts in which they may lodge their claims, and the possible grounds for review. These provisions authorize the courts to review virtually all regulatory decisions of both general and individualized application.

In Germany, as in France, "administrative acts" are subject to review by

[10] L. Neville Brown and J. F. Garner, *French Administrative Law* (London: Butterworths, 1973), p. 82.

[11] Bernard Schwartz and H. W. R. Wade, *Legal Control of Government* (Oxford: Clarendon Press, 1972), p. 210.

[12] 5 U.S.C. §551 et seq.

[13] Louis L. Jaffe, *Judicial Control of Administrative Action* (Boston: Little, Brown, 1965), p. 372.

the administrative courts, but the class of reviewable decisions is more narrowly defined than it is in the other three countries. Judicial review in Germany is primarily an instrument for safeguarding the rights of private persons against state action. To put it in somewhat different terms: "No act of the executive which affects the rights of the citizens can be immune from judicial review."[14] What this formulation captures is that review is always available for administrative decisions that have an individualized impact, but not for regulations of general application. The promulgation of an ambient standard for an airborne chemical, for example, is not subject to judicial review. However, a subsequent administrative act, such as the issuance of a permit to a facility emitting the chemical, can be challenged on the grounds that the emissions are hazardous to the health of nearby residents. In a lawsuit initiated on these grounds, the court can review the standards and invalidate the permit if the emissions are deemed unlawful.

The sovereignty of the legislature in both France and Britain implies that parliament may, if it chooses, shield administrative actions from judicial supervision. Statutory limitations on review are virtually unknown in France.[15] It has been suggested that British judges are more willing to decline review in deference to the perceived will of Parliament than are their French counterparts,[16] but there is little in the case law to support this assertion. The British Parliament has over the years enacted a variety of "ouster clauses" to remove delegated legislation from the jurisdiction of the courts. On the whole, however, the courts have proved adept at circumventing such exclusionary clauses.[17] In a 1969 decision[18] termed "a high water mark of judicial control,"[19] the House of Lords, Britain's highest court of appeals, agreed to review an administrative determination despite a provision stating that such determinations "shall not be called in question in any court of law."

In the United States, there are two exceptions to the APA's general rule in favor of reviewability. Review is available "except to the extent that (1) statutes preclude judicial review; or (2) agency action is committed to agency discretion by law."[20] Both exemptions have been narrowly construed.[21] It is clear, for example, that review may not be cut off simply because a statute fails to provide explicitly for judicial review or because a statute uses discre-

---

[14] Administrative Court Ordinance (Verwaltungsgerichtsordnung) §42 and 10 BVerfGE 267 (1960). The principle of reviewability is based on Art. 19, para. 4, of the Basic Law.
[15] Brown and Garner, op. cit., p. 90.
[16] Ibid., p. 91.
[17] See H. W. R. Wade, *Administrative Law* (Oxford: Clarendon Press, 1977), pp. 566–76.
[18] *Anisminic Ltd. v. Foreign Compensation Commission* [1969] 2 A.C. 147.
[19] Wade, op. cit., p. 571.
[20] 5 U.S.C. §701.
[21] See, for example, Schwartz and Wade, op. cit., pp. 272–73.

tionary language to describe an administrative duty. Thus, although the Federal Insecticide, Fungicide, and Rodenticide Act says nothing about the reviewability of negative actions, the D.C. Court of Appeals agreed to review a decision by the EPA administrator not to begin cancellation proceedings against DDT. The court saw no clear legislative intent to preclude review "in the mere fact that a statute is drafted in permissive rather than mandatory terms."[22]

It appears, then, that in Britain, France, and the United States, neither legal theory nor statutory law imposes serious restrictions on the power of the courts to review administrative decisions. In both Britain and the United States, the courts have actively repudiated legislative attempts to restrict their jurisdiction by narrowly construing ouster clauses and other statutory provisions designed to foreclose review. Only in Germany, where judicial review is most closely identified with the protection of individual rights, is a significant category of administrative decisions—rules and policies of general application—excluded from direct review.

Standing

The frequency of litigation in each country depends not only on the theoretical extent of the reviewing power, but also on a variety of technical rules developed by the courts and the legislature to control the volume and flow of litigation. In most jurisdictions, for example, the courts will only hear challenges to a final administrative decision. They may also require that the plaintiff exhaust all available administrative remedies before approaching the courts. Though the use of such screening devices is generally similar across the four countries, there are some striking differences in the rules by which courts decide who has standing to seek judicial review of governmental decisions. These rules reveal fundamentally different national attitudes about the circumstances under which private groups or individuals should be permitted to challenge the outcome of administrative decision making.

In all four countries, persons adversely affected by administrative regulations are entitled to seek relief from the courts. The law of standing therefore presents no barrier to litigation by corporations subject to chemical control decisions. Parties who are less directly affected, however, may be barred from seeking judicial review unless national law recognizes their "interest" in the regulatory proceeding as sufficient to give them standing. The requisite interest has been defined most narrowly in Germany, in line with that country's restrictive use of judicial review to protect individual rights. Under

---

[22] *Environmental Defense Fund, Inc. (EDF) v. Hardin,* 428 F. 2d 1093, 1098 (D.C. Cir., 1970).

German law, only plaintiffs who can assert an infringement of their legal rights are granted standing to challenge decisions of the administrative agencies.[23] No lesser violation is considered sufficient for purposes of allowing an appeal to the courts. The rights in question can flow from either the Basic Law or a particular statute.[24] In the latter case, the language of the law must clearly indicate that it was enacted to protect the rights of the complaining party.[25] The standing test is thus substantially more rigorous than the requirements for participating in regulatory proceedings affecting the environment.[26] All this accords well with the theory, widely accepted by German legal scholars, that judicial review should not be used merely as a vehicle for ensuring the legality, fairness, or rationality of public administrative decisions.

In the United States, the issue of standing is decided either by specific statutory provisions, such as TSCA's authorization of citizen suits, or by judicial doctrines based, in part, on the cases or controversies requirement of the Constitution.[27] Whatever their precise legal basis, American standing rules allow considerably greater access to the courts than do the corresponding German doctrines. Both Congress and the judiciary have proved willing to open the courthouse doors to petitioners who have only an indirect or impersonal stake in the outcome of administrative decision making.

In the earliest of its modern standing decisions, *Association of Data Processing Services v. Camp,*[28] the Supreme Court rejected the view that a complainant must have a "legal interest" in order to seek judicial review. Instead, the court announced a new test requiring petitioners to show an "injury in fact, economic or otherwise" falling "arguably within the zone of interests to be protected or regulated by the statute or constitutional guarantee in question."[29] The lower federal courts have paid greater attention to the existence

[23] Lorenz, op. cit., pp. 576–77.

[24] Eckard Rehbinder, "Private Recourse for Environmental Harm: Federal Republic of Germany," in Stephen McCaffrey and Robert Lutz, eds., *Environmental Pollution and Individual Rights: An International Symposium* (Deventer, The Netherlands: Kluwer, 1978), p. 42.

[25] Ibid. Mere injury in fact under a statute enacted in the public interest is not sufficient to confer standing. This follows from the so-called "protective law theory," which holds that the rule of law allegedly violated must have been enacted specifically in the interests of the individual claiming an injury, as well as in the interests of the public.

[26] Ibid., pp. 39–40. Recent U.S. Supreme Court decisions on standing have also raised the theoretical possibility that a participant in an administrative proceeding may not meet the constitutional test for standing and hence be denied judicial review.

[27] See, for example, *Simon v. Eastern Kentucky Welfare Rights Organization,* 426 U.S. 26 (1976); *Village of Arlington Heights v. Metropolitan Housing Development Corp.,* 429 U.S. 252 (1977).

[28] 397 U.S. 150 (1970).

[29] Ibid., p. 152. The "injury in fact" test represents a relaxation of the earlier "legal interest" rule, which granted standing, as in Germany, only when a legal interest of the plaintiff was invaded by governmental action.

of an injury in fact than to the second prong of the *Data Processing* rule,[30] and they have generally interpreted the notion of injury expansively. Injuries that justify standing have been held to include not only economic harm, but also injury to "aesthetic, conservational and recreational" interests.[31] The Supreme Court has indicated, moreover, that an inquiry into the plaintiff's interests serves only as a preliminary screening mechanism.[32] It need not set the substantive boundaries for the ensuing judicial proceeding. Once granted standing, the plaintiff may seek to protect not only his own personal interests, but also public interests in which he has no personal stake. This development makes it much easier for citizens to act as private attorneys general representing the public interest. Congress, too, has endorsed the private attorney general concept through the citizen suit provisions of such statutes as the Clean Air Act and TSCA. In this respect, American law is diametrically opposed to the German view that private plaintiffs should have standing only to represent their personal rights, a position that effectively rules out a significant role for environmental or consumer groups in litigation.[33]

In Britain, standing has never received as much sustained judicial attention as it has in the United States, and explicit principles are correspondingly difficult to identify. Nevertheless, it is clear that standing rules made by British judges are more liberal than those made in Germany, though they are less expansive than standing rules in the United States. In theory, petitioners challenging an administrative act or omission that does not affect their personal rights may make use of a device that effectively bypasses the standing problem. This is the so-called "relator action," in which the attorney general, the Crown official entrusted with enforcement of the law, nominally pursues an action at the behest of a private plaintiff. As a technique for securing judicial review, however, the relator action has many drawbacks. The attorney general's consent to such an action cannot be obtained in cases involving a minister or central government department, although permission is more freely granted in cases against local authorities.[34] Moreover, since the decision to permit a relator action is entirely discretionary, the attorney general's refusal to act on behalf of a private party cannot be appealed to any court.[35]

---

[30] Kenneth C. Davis, *Administrative Law Text*, 3d ed. (St. Paul, Minn.: West Publishing, 1972), pp. 432–35. But see *Tax Analysts and Advocates v. Blumenthal*, 566 F.2d 130 (D.C. Cir., 1977).

[31] See Frederick R. Anderson, *NEPA in the Courts* (Baltimore: Johns Hopkins University Press, 1973), pp. 29–34. Standing based on both noneconomic and nonenvironmental interests was recognized in *Arlington Heights* (cited above in n. 27).

[32] *Sierra Club v. Morton*, 405 U.S. 727, 739 (1972); *Duke Power Co. v. Carolina Environmental Study Group*, 438 U.S. 59 (1978).

[33] Rehbinder, op. cit., p. 44.

[34] Wade, op. cit., p. 511.

[35] *London County Council v. Attorney-General* [1902] A.C. 165, 169.

Where the relator action is unavailable and the plaintiff must proceed in his own name, standing may be granted on something less than a showing of a direct legal interest. In the area of planning law, for example, any person "aggrieved" by a local authority's decision may challenge it in court. According to one recent case, this means that anyone with a "legitimate bona fide reason" to object to a planning decision has standing to do so in court.[36] A relatively relaxed test of interest may also apply when the plaintiff desires one of the "prerogative remedies" traditionally invoked to control governmental activity.[37] In one or two mandamus actions, for example, the plaintiff has established a sufficient interest to support standing by participating in legal or administrative proceedings leading to the challenged act.[38] On the other hand, when the remedy sought is a declaration or injunction, standing is still likely to be denied unless the plaintiff is advancing some legal right.[39] It is thus premature to speculate that an across-the-board relaxation of standing requirements is underway in British law.

The separation of ordinary and administrative courts in France has given rise to somewhat different principles of standing for civil litigation in the ordinary courts and for challenging governmental actions in the administrative courts. Primarily concerned to prevent abuses of power, the administrative courts have on the whole taken a more liberal attitude to standing requirements than have the ordinary courts. For example, suits by associations representing collective rather than individual private interests have been tolerated by the French administrative courts for some time.[40] Specific legislation was needed, however, to give environmental associations and consumer groups standing to enforce pollution control laws against private defendants.[41]

The degree of "interest" required to support standing has obvious implications for public interest groups seeking judicial review. To the extent that the law demands a showing of personal injury, it tends to exclude private associations whose members are not directly affected by governmental action. Only in Germany, however, is the "personal interest" test applied so stringently as to exclude all citizen group litigation on environmental issues. Since judicial review is available only to vindicate individual legal rights, associations representing group interests are not permitted to engage in litigation against governmental agencies. This logic has been carried to the extreme in cases

---

[36] *R. v. Hammersmith and Fulham Borough Council ex parte People Before Profit Ltd.*, 80 Local Government Reports 322 (1982).
[37] Wade, op. cit., pp. 543–46, 608–10.
[38] *R. v. Manchester Corporation* [1911] 1 K.B. 560; *R. v. Cotham* [1898] 1 Q.B. 802, 804.
[39] *Gouriet v. Union of Post Office Workers* [1978] A.C. 435.
[40] Brown and Garner, op. cit., pp. 86–87.
[41] Michel Prieur, "The Rights of Associations for the Protection of Nature and the Environment in France," in McCaffrey and Lutz, op. cit., pp. 75–77.

where associations have been denied standing even though each individual member could demonstrate a sufficient personal interest to obtain standing.[42] In marked contrast, the citizen suit provisions of numerous U.S. environmental and health and safety statutes[43] explicitly authorize actions by public interest groups against the administrative agencies. Even in the absence of such provisions, the Supreme Court has affirmed that "an organization whose members are injured may represent those members in a proceeding for judicial review."[44] In sum, U.S. law erects the lowest entry barriers against both associations and individuals wishing to challenge administrative decisions in court.

Suits to Compel Administrative Action

The issues of reviewability and standing arise with special force in lawsuits brought to compel administrative action. To begin with, plaintiffs in such suits must show that the inaction they complain of amounts to a breach of law. Moreover, the power of the courts to order performance can be invoked, as a rule, only by persons to whom the statutory duty is owed and who are aggrieved by the administration's failure to perform. In spite of these legal obstacles, environmental groups in the United States have frequently succeeded in obtaining court-ordered action on toxic substances. Comparable cases are essentially unknown in the three European countries. The developments in the United States reflect a convergence of interests between Congress and the courts that has led to an extraordinary expansion of judicial authority at the expense of administrative autonomy.

In reviewing cases of administrative inaction, federal courts have drawn general authority from the APA section on scope of review, which authorizes them to "compel agency action unlawfully withheld or unreasonably delayed."[45] This provision has been broadly construed as permitting judicial intervention even under a statute like the National Environmental Policy Act, which does not explicitly provide for enforcement by the courts. The courts have been similarly liberal in deciding what constitutes an unlawful withholding or unreasonable delay. For example, in agreeing to review the secretary of agriculture's failure to cancel certain pesticide registrations, the D.C. Circuit Court of Appeals observed that "when administrative inaction has precisely the same impact on the rights of the parties as a denial of relief, an agency

---

[42] Rehbinder, op. cit., p. 44.

[43] Among the federal statutes that include specific citizen suit provisions are the Clean Air Act of 1970, the Federal Water Pollution Control Act of 1972, the Noise Control Act of 1972, and the Toxic Substances Control Act of 1976.

[44] *Sierra Club v. Morton,* 405 U.S. at 739.

[45] 5 U.S.C. §706.

cannot preclude judicial review by casting its decision in the form of inaction rather than in the form of an order denying relief."[46] The federal courts have thus affirmed their willingness to serve as watchdogs over the administrative agencies in cases of inaction as well as unlawful action.

That Congress approves the activist self-image of the courts is clearly borne out by the judicial review and citizen suit provisions of American environmental and health and safety statutes. By specifying precise rule-making obligations, often with associated timetables, these laws create a schedule of legal duties which courts are authorized to enforce. Citizen suit provisions extend the right to seek judicial intervention to virtually any individual or public interest group. The entire legal framework so heavily favors judicial control that lawsuits even become a precondition to agency action. For administrators faced with painful regulatory choices, lawsuits function as a convenient go-ahead signal, absolving them of the responsibility for deciding to act.[47]

In the three European legal systems, one rarely encounters a conjunction of two factors that strongly encourage judicial activism against noncomplying agencies in the United States—relaxed standing requirements for public interest groups and a clear statutory definition of agency responsibilities. The importance of the first factor is self-evident. Few private individuals have the resources or the inclination to mount legal challenges against reluctant governmental agencies. In the United States, activist public interest organizations have been responsible for most successful lawsuits to compel regulation. The second factor is equally significant, for, without it, activist groups, however committed they are to enforcing the law, have no secure legal basis for invoking the power of the courts.

In both France and Britain, where standing is not a serious problem for public interest groups, the vague, general, and discretionary formulation of public duties in chemical control legislation makes it well-nigh impossible for such groups to argue that agency inaction amounts to a breach of a legal obligation. For example, the laws do not typically specify time periods within which agencies are required to act or safety standards against which the adequacy of their performance can be measured. Nor do they provide many examples of nondiscretionary duties that government officials can be ordered to perform.[48] The conferral of wide discretion on implementing officials ousts

---

[46] *EDF v. Hardin,* 428 F. 2d at 1099.

[47] For a suggestion that EPA, at least, has welcomed such intervention in the past, see R. Jeffrey Smith, "Toxic Substances: EPA and OSHA Are Reluctant Regulators," *Science,* 203, no. 4375 (1979), 28–32.

[48] See chapter 3 for a general discussion of this point. It is instructive to consider in this context a New Zealand mandamus action in which an environmental group was denied standing to compel a public board to prevent the use of harmful chemicals. *Environmental*

judicial control more effectively than any positive language excluding re-view.[49] In Germany, citizens wishing to sue administrative officials or agencies for nonfeasance face even greater difficulty. Such lawsuits are barred both by the rigid standing rules of German law[50] and by the fact that in Germany, as in France and Britain, chemical control legislation seldom states the obligations of public officials in mandatory, judicially enforceable terms.

Though one can rightly question the efficacy of judicial supervision in the European administrative process, it should be recalled that massive regulatory delays of the kind that plague U.S. administrative agencies occur less frequently in Europe. German regulators, for example, often succeed in drafting implementing regulations within the time that elapses between the enactment of a statute and its effective date. This efficiency is due in large measure to the relative simplicity of European rule-making procedures. But whatever the explanation, from the standpoint of the individual citizen or the public interest group, the timely issuance of regulations partially compensates for the more limited right to sue for enforcement in the courts.

Scope of Review

Once an administrative decision is properly before the courts, the judicial inclination to examine it critically varies considerably across the four countries. Some fundamental principles concerning the scope of judicial review are common to all four legal systems. Errors of law, for example, are fully reviewable everywhere. There are important differences, however, in the extent to which courts reexamine administrative findings of fact or inquire into agency rule-making procedures. As we see below, these differences reflect the widely divergent views held by American and European judges about the credibility and finality of technologically complex administrative decisions.

Judicial Review of Facts

In contrast to the common law courts, the administrative courts of France and Germany enjoy an essentially unrestricted right to reexamine the factual

---

Defence Society, Inc., v. Agricultural Chemicals Board [1973] 2 NZLR 758. Although the case was decided on the standing issue, one commentator has noted that the board in question had discretionary power and no specific duty (Wade, op. cit., p. 611, n. 4).

[49] Wade, op. cit., p. 720.

[50] For mandamus actions, the standing requirements may be slightly more relaxed than in other contexts. In particular, the "protective law theory" is applicable not to determine the threshold issue of standing, but only when the matter is considered on the merits. See Rehbinder, op. cit., p. 42. The basic standing question for the courts in a mandamus action is "whether the plaintiff is entitled to demand implementation of the action which the agency has either refused or failed to take" (pp. 44–45).

and legal bases of challenged administrative decisions. A close inquiry into the actual practice of the courts, however, reveals a blurring of this apparently straightforward difference between the two legal systems.

In French law, even acts committed to the absolute discretion of an administrator may be controlled by the courts to ensure that no errors of fact or law have been committed.[51] In reviewing administrative decisions, courts are empowered not only to interpret relevant statutes and apply general legal principles, but also to reassess the underlying facts in light of the governing law. In cases involving scientific or technical evidence, however, the Conseil d'Etat has indicated that it will not exercise its authority to review administrative determinations of fact.[52] For example, the court has refused to review findings as to whether a hair lotion was poisonous[53] or whether a wine deserved the classification "appellation contrôlée."[54]

In principle, German administrative courts also have the authority to carry out a de novo review of disputed administrative findings. They may summon their own witnesses, take testimony, and reach independent factual conclusions. Both legal commentators and the courts in Germany have consistently stated that technical matters are fully reviewable, even in areas of high scientific uncertainty.[55] To hold otherwise would be equivalent to carving out a sphere of unreviewable discretion within the regulatory process, a result that would be inconsistent with the doctrine of complete reviewability for all administrative decisions impinging on individual rights.[56]

Though the German courts have been very careful not to relinquish their theoretical right to review administrative fact finding, in practice they are prepared to let the regulatory agencies have the final say on factual questions relevant to chemical control. In a well-known case arising under the Pollution

---

[51] Brown and Garner, op. cit., p. 136.

[52] Ibid., p. 138. The other important category involves policing decisions, such as actions against foreigners.

[53] *Société Toni* (C.E., April 27, 1951).

[54] *Syndicat Agricole de Lalande-de-Pomerol* (C.E., October 4, 1960).

[55] See, for example, Rüdiger Breuer, "Die Rechtliche Bedeutung der Verwaltungsvorschriften nach 48 BImSchG im Genehmigungsverfahren," *DVBl.* 1978, pp. 28–37. A slightly different position has been advanced by Hermann Ule. While Ule, too, recognizes that technical questions are, in principle, subject to judicial review, he would deny the courts the right to reverse the judgment of the administration in borderline cases where the facts lend themselves to no single, certain interpretation. See Ule, "Unbestimmte Begriffe und Ermessen in Umweltschutzrecht," *DVBl.* 1973, pp. 756–63; "Die Bindung der Verwaltungsgerichte an die Immissionswerte der TA Luft," *Betriebs-Berater*, 10 (1976), 446–47.

[56] Accordingly, German legal scholarship has generally held that in interpreting indefinite legal terms (unbestimmte Rechtsbegriffe), the administration enjoys no automatic room for exercise of discretion (Beurteilungsspielraum). See, for example, Breuer, op. cit., pp. 32–34; Ernst K. Pakuscher, "The Use of Discretion in German Law," *University of Chicago Law Review*, 44, no. 1 (1976), 94–109.

Control Act,[57] the Federal Administrative Court held that it is unnecessary for a reviewing court to hear independent expert testimony if the administrative agency has already consulted a representative body of experts in the course of standard setting. The standards developed by the agency in this case were recognized as a kind of "anticipated expert opinion"[58] that the courts could not improve on through further factual inquiry. Judicial restraint in this case was a consequence of the court's familiarity with the administrative standard-setting process and its recognition that a new round of fact finding would add nothing to the record built up by the agency.

Anglo-American law has historically followed the rule that administrative findings of fact fall outside the scope of judicial control. The theoretical separation between "law" and "fact," however, has long been a source of scholarly unease, and facts are never completely excluded from review by either British or American courts. The former, for example, freely assert control over "jurisdictional facts," since errors concerning such facts would place the administration outside its lawful jurisdiction.[59] British courts are also prepared to consider the adequacy of evidence supporting a factual determination and to invalidate findings resting on "no evidence."[60] Nevertheless, review of facts in Britain is limited both by habits of judicial restraint and, as a practical matter, by the absence in the administrative process of a requirement to produce transcripts or a written record of decision making.[61] Moreover, British courts are reluctant to authorize extensive public scrutiny of matters that can be regarded as governmental "policy." In one recent decision, the term *policy* was used to shield a manual of methodology from public criticism, even though objectors challenged the government's methodological approach.[62]

The American administrative process exposes the factual basis for agency action to a far more exhaustive review. The APA provides a statutory basis for the review of both adjudicatory decisions and agency policies of more general application. In reviewing decisions of the latter type ("legislative" decisions), courts are permitted to set aside actions that are "arbitrary, capricious, an abuse of discretion, or otherwise not in accordance with law."[63] To determine whether an agency has acted in an arbitrary or capricious manner,

[57] BVerwG, *DVBl.* 1978, pp. 591–98 (Voerde case).

[58] Ibid., p. 594.

[59] Schwartz and Wade, op. cit., pp. 236–37; Wade, op. cit., pp. 249–52; S. A. de Smith, *Judicial Review of Administrative Action* (London: Stevens and Sons, 1973), pp. 120–22.

[60] Schwartz and Wade, op. cit., pp. 238–40; Wade, op. cit., pp. 274–81.

[61] It has been pointed out that this need not prove an insurmountable obstacle for the courts, since it is possible to receive testimony through affidavits if necessary in the course of judicial review. Schwartz and Wade, op. cit., p. 240.

[62] *Bushell v. Secretary of State for the Environment* [1980] 3 W.L.R. 22.

[63] 5 U.S.C. §706.

the APA authorizes the courts to review the whole record or any portions that are cited by any party to the proceedings.

Federal courts in the United States have found it difficult to define the "arbitrary and capricious" standard in operational terms. The problem is particularly acute when the "facts" in question fall at the "frontiers of scientific knowledge." In such cases the agency is dealing less with conventional facts than with "normative conflicts, projections from imperfect data, experiments and simulations, educated predictions, differing assessments of possible risks, and the like."[64] A record consisting of elements such as these cannot be subjected to the standards of adequacy and substantiality developed by the courts for less speculative types of evidence.

Faced with these difficulties, American courts could have taken the easy course of bowing to agency expertise and accepting the administrator's determinations of risk. Instead, led by the D.C. Court of Appeals, the federal courts have chosen to review such determinations rigorously, even in rapidly changing areas of scientific knowledge. As articulated by the late Judge Harold Leventhal of the D.C. Court of Appeals, the prevalent doctrine of review calls on the courts to ensure that the agency has taken a "hard look" at the facts before it and that it has engaged in "reasoned decision-making."[65] To this end, the courts are prepared to demand considerable detail and rigor in the agency's substantive record: "Assumptions must be spelled out, inconsistencies explained, methodologies disclosed, contradictory evidence rebutted, record references solidly grounded, guesswork eliminated and conclusions supported 'in a manner capable of judicial understanding.' "[66] Moreover, to ascertain whether the agency has met its obligations, the court itself must undertake a "searching inquiry" into the factual record, steeping itself in the relevant technical issues. A conscientious inquiry along these lines comes close to the full de novo review permitted in French and German administrative law. The readiness of the U.S. courts to engage in this strenuous exercise reveals a far less deferential attitude toward administrators than has been displayed by the courts in the three European countries.

Judicial Enforcement of Procedural Rights

Lawsuits based on alleged violations of administrative procedure require the courts to balance two dissimilar kinds of interests. In each case the

[64] *Amoco Oil Co. v. EPA,* 501 F. 2d 722, 735 (D.C. Cir., 1974).

[65] Harold Leventhal, "Environmental Decisionmaking and the Role of the Courts," *University of Pennsylvania Law Review,* 122, no. 3 (1974), 511–12; *Greater Boston TV v. FCC,* 444 F. 2d 841 (D.C. Cir., 1970); *International Harvester Co. v. Ruckelshaus,* 478 F. 2d 615 (D.C. Cir., 1973); *Ethyl Corp. v. EPA,* 541 F. 2d 1, 68–69 (D.C. Cir., 1976) (separate statement).

[66] William H. Rodgers, Jr., "A Hard Look at Vermont Yankee: Environmental Law under Close Scrutiny," *Georgetown Law Journal,* 67, no. 3 (1979), 706 (footnote omitted).

complainant's claim to be heard before a decision is taken must be weighed against the administrative agency's interest in an orderly and efficient rule-making process. In reviewing "adjudicatory" administrative decisions, where the interests of individuals or small groups are at stake, courts in all four countries agree that the plaintiff's rights take precedence over the interests of the administrative agency. The rights of individuals are frequently recognized even in the absence of statutory procedural requirements. Concepts such as "due process," "natural justice," or "general legal principles" are then invoked to safeguard the individual's right to an administrative hearing. The interests of the regulatory agencies weigh more heavily when the proceedings are of the "legislative" type. In such cases courts are reluctant on the whole to recognize procedural rights beyond those established by the legislature and the agencies themselves. Only the U.S. courts have shown an inclination to depart from this position.

Judicial enforcement of procedural claims arising from proceedings of a legislative nature appears weakest in Germany. Although errors in administrative procedure can provide partial grounds for invalidating agency action, court orders are rarely based on procedural deficiencies alone. As a threshold matter, German law does not tolerate suits based solely on alleged procedural violations.[67] The issue of procedural error can only be raised following a final agency action and by an individual whose rights are adversely affected. Even then, courts may disregard the procedural complaint altogether if the error did not keep the plaintiff from seeking relief on the merits, or if correct procedures would not have led to a different result.

For German courts, then, even the violation of a statutory right to participate in administrative proceedings is an insufficient reason for striking down the subsequent regulatory decision. This anomaly is usually explained with reference to the limited function served by judicial review. The purpose of an administrative hearing is to collect all information relevant to a decision,[68] but judicial review only safeguards the substantive rights of individuals. Courts have no interest in the overall legality or rationality of administrative decision making except to the extent that the decision adversely affects individual rights. This reasoning allows the German courts to go along with a legal regime in which individuals who are entitled to participate in the rule-making process may be powerless to vindicate their procedural claims in court.

In the other three countries, the individual's power to bring a procedural complaint before the courts is not as severely restricted as it is in Germany.

---

[67] Rehbinder, op. cit., p. 43.

[68] This has been confirmed in a decision of the Federal Administrative Court, BVerwG, *DVBl.* 1973, p. 217. But this function tends to be imperfectly performed in many administrative proceedings. See Rehbinder, op. cit., p. 40.

But the readiness of the courts to intervene in procedural matters depends very much on the legal status of the procedures in question. It is difficult, if not impossible, in all three countries to obtain review on procedural grounds unless the administration has violated procedures mandated by law. Cross-national differences in the amount of procedural litigation are thus chiefly due to the fact that some countries use legally compulsory administrative procedures more widely than do other countries.

Although British regulators view consultation as an indispensable element of the administrative process, there is no legal right to be consulted except that conferred by statute.[69] If a statute does not mandate consultation, the courts will not extend the theory of natural justice far enough to read such a requirement into the law. In a representative case under the Solicitors Act of 1957,[70] a member of a solicitors' association requested the court to delay the issuance of a draft order concerning fee scales until the agency consulted more extensively with those affected by the order. In refusing this request, the presiding judge commented, "I do not know of any implied right to be consulted or make objections, any principle upon which the courts may enjoin the legislative process at the suit of those who contend that insufficient time for consultation and consideration has been given."[71] Natural justice did not support the association's claim to be heard in this case since the proposed order was legislative, not adjudicatory, in character.

In France, recent legislation granting environmental associations standing in civil litigation has not, on the whole, broadened the right of such groups to participate in governmental decision making.[72] Under the 1976 Law on the Protection of Nature, for example, associations enjoy no automatic right to participate.[73] The decision to consult approved associations under this law remains discretionary with public officials, and their failure to consult a particular group cannot justify a legal complaint. On the other hand, a violation of the statutory criteria and procedures for granting approval to such groups can be appealed to the administrative courts.[74]

Starting in the mid-1960s, the U.S. federal courts engaged in a more active

[69] Wade, op. cit., p. 482.

[70] *Bates v. Lord Hailsham* [1972] 1 W.L.R. 1373.

[71] Ibid., p. 1378.

[72] One commentator has suggested that the new legislation may even have the effect of reducing citizen participation by limiting it to officially approved groups. Prieur, op. cit., p. 72.

[73] The law provides that approved associations be called on "to participate in the actions of public bodies having as their object the protection of nature and the environment." It is understood that the decision to call on an association to participate rests with the public authorities.

[74] See Michel Despax, "Défense de l'environnement et métamorphose du droit français des associations," *Environmental Policy and Law*, 3, no. 3/4 (1977), 150.

reshaping of agency procedures than would be judicially condoned in any of the other three countries. In a move spearheaded by the D.C. Court of Appeals, U.S. courts began to scrutinize the procedural as well as the factual basis for challenged rules, especially in cases involving complex scientific and technical questions, and to remand agency decisions if the procedures were deemed inadequate for dealing with the issues.[75] The underlying assumption was that the biases of the agencies and their technical experts had to be counteracted through procedures that would subject their views to the fullest possible public airing and testing. While the courts were careful not to specify what procedures the agencies should follow, the practical consequence of their decisions was a proliferation of "hybrid" procedures containing some but not all elements of adjudicatory hearings, such as cross-examination on significant issues.

This judicially sponsored creativity in the procedural field was checked by the Supreme Court in *Vermont Yankee Nuclear Power Corp. v. Natural Resources Defense Council.*[76] The opinion struck down in decisive terms the practice of judicially "correcting" perceived deficiencies in agency procedure without any support in the governing laws. The Supreme Court made it plain that due process could be invoked to justify additional procedures only under extraordinary circumstances.[77] In all other cases, administrative agencies should be held only to procedures specified by their enabling statutes or the APA.

In spite of its strong language, *Vermont Yankee* did not cut off the power of the courts to demand more rigorous rule-making procedures from the agencies. Scientifically or technically grounded decisions may still be remanded for inadequacies in the supporting record. On remand, the agency may be forced to adopt supplementary procedures in order to fill the gaps in the evidence discerned by the reviewing court. As Justice William Rehnquist observed: "If the agency is compelled to support the rule which it ultimately develops with the type of record produced only with a full adjudicatory hearing, it simply will have no choice but to conduct a full adjudicatory hearing prior to promulgating every rule."[78] This statement has been interpreted by one commentator as almost an open invitation for federal judges "to conclude that APA procedures are insufficient and must be supplemented."[79]

---

[75] See David L. Bazelon, "Risk and Responsibility," *Science,* 205, no. 4403 (1979), 822–23; *Ethyl Corp. v. EPA,* 541 F. 2d 1, 66–68 (D.C. Cir., 1976) (Bazelon, J., concurring); *Natural Resources Defense Council, Inc., v. U.S. Nuclear Regulatory Commission,* 547 F. 2d 633, 643–46, 655–57 (D.C. Cir., 1976).

[76] 435 U.S. 519 (1978).

[77] Ibid., p. 542.

[78] Ibid., pp. 547–48.

[79] Richard Stewart, "Vermont Yankee and the Evolution of Administrative Procedure," *Harvard Law Review,* 91, no. 8 (1978), 1816.

Summary

In defining the scope of judicial review, U.S. courts have shown less deference to the administrative agencies than have their European counterparts. American federal judges are prepared to look more critically at the substantive basis of regulatory decisions than are the administrative courts of France and Germany, although there are no legal restrictions on the power of the latter to reexamine administrative findings of fact. American courts also exert considerable indirect influence on the procedures of federal regulatory agencies. They show few signs of relaxing their searching inquiry into the administrative record, however detailed or technical it may be.[80] In turn, the knowledge that their decisions may be remanded for inadequacies in the record holds the agencies to a high standard of procedural formality.

The aggressive posture adopted by the U.S. courts toward the regulatory agencies is consistent with attitudes expressed by Congress in the environmental legislation of the 1970s. These laws, unlike their European analogues, not only define a multitude of substantive and procedural obligations for the agencies, but pave the way to greater judicial involvement by broadening the rights of private plaintiffs to sue federal regulators. The legislature's interest in subjecting agency decisions to judicial review, as well as the courts' own liberal construction of their powers, are symptomatic of a political environment that places extraordinary value on the individual's right to be heard and acknowledged in public regulatory proceedings. The Europeans, in contrast, give priority to the formation of a stable political consensus on regulatory matters. Legislative practice and judicial doctrine in Europe work together to protect such accommodations against legal challenge, even though this requires a curtailment of the individual citizen's right to initiate lawsuits in the public interest. The differing amounts of litigation surrounding chemical control decisions in Europe and the United States reflect these different political philosophies.

Courts and Carcinogens: The U.S. Experience

The record of carcinogen regulation in America shows how commonplace judicial review has become in the administrative process. The list of toxic chemicals brought to the attention of the federal courts includes some of the

---

[80] See, for example, the Supreme Court's intensive review of the facts in the decision overturning OSHA's occupational safety and health standard for benzene. *Industrial Union Department, AFL-CIO v. American Petroleum Institute*, 448 U.S. 607 (1980). Justice Marshall, in dissent, characterized the plurality opinion as "extraordinarily arrogant," because "the plurality presumes to make its own factual findings with respect to a variety of issues relating to carcinogen regulation" (p. 695).

most widely recognized human carcinogens (asbestos, vinyl chloride, DES) as well as substances whose effects on human health are less certain (aldrin, dieldrin, 2,4,5-T, formaldehyde). Reviewing the major issues raised in these proceedings moves us toward a fuller understanding of the role played by the U.S. courts in chemical regulation. It also permits a critical evaluation of the contribution courts can make to the resolution of scientific controversy in administrative rule making.

Until 1970 the Food, Drug, and Cosmetic Act was the principal statute under which the federal government regulated carcinogens. Potentially carcinogenic food additives and animal drugs could be regulated under the act's general safety provisions[81] or under the more specific prohibition of the Delaney clause. In sporadic litigation the courts generally supported FDA's attempts to ban chemicals on the basis of experimental evidence of carcinogenicity. Thus in 1966 a federal court upheld FDA's decision that a pellet containing DES for implantation in poultry was "unsafe" on the basis of evidence that "DES is definitely a cause of cancer in animals, at least an inciter of incipient cancer in man, and possibly a cause of cancer in man."[82]

The 1972 amendments to the Federal Insecticide, Fungicide, and Rodenticide Act led to a series of lawsuits by environmental groups against EPA demanding stricter controls on pesticides suspected of causing cancer. At about the same time, the passage of the Occupational Safety and Health Act led to the regulation of a number of suspected carcinogens and to ensuing legal challenges, primarily at the initiative of the regulated industries. As a result, the federal courts, with the D.C. Court of Appeals again in the forefront, were required to review exhaustively the procedures used by the federal agencies to resolve scientific and legal uncertainties in the regulation of carcinogens.

A notable consequence of this litigation was to draw wholehearted support from the courts for treating carcinogens more restrictively than other toxic substances. Although not legally applicable to pesticides or workplace chemicals, the Delaney clause was construed as a general mandate favoring strict regulation of carcinogens. The D.C. Court of Appeals observed in a 1971 decision that "the [Delaney] Amendment does . . . indicate the magnitude of Congressional concern about the hazards created by carcinogenic chemicals, and places a heavy burden on any administrative officer to explain the basis for his decision to permit the continued use of a chemical known to produce

---

[81] Indeed, prior to the enactment of the 1958 Food Additives Amendment, a letter from HEW Assistant Secretary Elliot Richardson to the House Interstate and Foreign Commerce Committee indicated that in the department's view the addition of the Delaney clause did not change the meaning of the bill. See Charles W. Dunn, ed., *Legislative Record of 1958 Food Additives Amendment to Federal Food, Drug, and Cosmetic Act* (New York: Commerce Clearing House, 1958), p. 40.

[82] *Bell v. Goddard*, 366 F. 2d 177, 182 (7th Cir., 1966).

cancer in experimental animals."[83] Later decisions reviewing the regulation of aldrin/dieldrin,[84] Red Dye No. 2,[85] and PCBs[86] also stressed the unique danger to public health posed by carcinogens.

In these and related cases, the courts developed, in effect, a double standard of review for carcinogen regulation. On the one hand, the judges readily accepted positive agency determinations of carcinogenicity. They reasoned that such decisions are usually made at the "frontiers of scientific knowledge."[87] They are, to a significant degree, policy judgments rather than findings of fact, and they are therefore entitled to great judicial deference.[88] On the other hand, the courts looked with considerable suspicion at decisions not to regulate, emphasizing the "heavy burden" on administrative agencies to justify inaction. For example, EPA's "one sentence discussion" of the carcinogenicity issue was held inappropriate in a case reviewing the agency's failure to suspend the registrations of aldrin and dieldrin.[89] The take-home lesson for the agencies seemed to be that it was safer to err on the side of overregulation than on the side of underregulation.

As regards the scientific basis for controlling carcinogens, the courts approved many of the principles that agencies like EPA, FDA, and OSHA developed for dealing with gaps and uncertainties in the available information. Several decisions condoned the practice of regulating potential carcinogens on the strength of positive data from animal experiments, without corroborating human epidemiological evidence. In reviewing EPA's suspension order for aldrin/dieldrin, the D.C. Court of Appeals noted that "the long latency period of carcinogens . . . hinders epidemiological research, and the ethical problems of conducting cancer research on human beings are too obvious to merit discussion. Although extrapolation of data from mice to men may be quantitatively imprecise, it is sufficient to establish a 'substantial likelihood' that harm will result."[90] The principle of extrapolating from animal results to humans was also upheld in judicial decisions concerning such substances as ethyleneimine,[91] Red Dye No. 2,[92] and heptachlor/chlordane.[93]

Another controversial issue on which the courts generally sided with the

---

[83] *EDF v. Ruckelshaus*, 439 F. 2d 584, 596, n. 41 (D.C. Cir., 1971).

[84] *EDF v. EPA*, 465 F. 2d 528 (D.C. Cir., 1972).

[85] *Certified Color Manufacturers Ass'n v. Mathews*, 543 F. 2d (D.C. Cir., 1976).

[86] *EDF v. EPA*, 598 F. 2d 62 (D.C. Cir., 1978).

[87] *Industrial Union Department, AFL-CIO v. Hodgson*, 499 F. 2d 467, 474 (D.C. Cir., 1974).

[88] See, for example, *Lead Industries Ass'n, Inc. v. EPA*, 14 ERC 1906, 1916 (D.C. Cir., 1980) and cases cited therein.

[89] *EDF v. EPA*, 465 F. 2d at 537.

[90] *EDF v. EPA*, 510 F. 2d 1292, 1299 (D.C. Cir., 1975).

[91] *Synthetic Organic Chemical Manufacturers Ass'n v. Brennan*, 503 F. 2d 1155 (3d Cir., 1974).

[92] *Certified Color Manufacturers Ass'n v. Mathews*, 543 F. 2d 284 (D.C. Cir., 1976).

[93] *EDF v. EPA*, 548 F. 2d 998 (D.C. Cir., 1976).

administrative agencies was the question of safe levels of exposure to carcinogens. In the aldrin/dieldrin case cited above, the court approved the EPA administrator's view that no safe thresholds can be established for carcinogens as a practical matter: "This is due in part to the irreversibility and long latency period of carcinogens. [W]here the matter involved is as sensitive and fright-laden as cancer, and the statute places a burden on the registrant to establish the safety of his product, we shall not, assuming a substantial showing of danger, require the Administrator to make impossible proofs."[94] In an even more sweeping endorsement of the agency's scientific reasoning, the D.C. Court of Appeals upheld EPA's use of seventeen principles for evaluating the carcinogenicity of heptachlor and chlordane. The court stated that "EPA's specific enunciation of its underlying analytic principles, derived from its experience in the area, yields meaningful notice and dialogue, enhances the administrative process and furthers reasoned decision making."[95] Judicial approval in this case was based partly on respect for the agency's expertise and partly on the court's assessment that EPA had complied with the norms of good administrative practice. Ironically, the "cancer principles" failed to win support from the chemical industry and many members of the scientific community.[96]

The major question presented to the courts in the pesticide cases was the appropriateness of the agency's classification of a substance as a carcinogen. In the context of occupational safety and health, the issue has more often been the degree and method of control than the finding of a carcinogenic hazard. But in this context, as well, the courts have generally upheld the agency's decisions, at least when they have been issued a final standards.[97] There have been no systematic differences in the judicial evaluation of agency risk assessments for pesticides and workplace chemicals.

The relatively untroubled pattern of cooperation between the courts and the agencies on positive regulatory decisions was upset by the Supreme Court's 1980 decision on the OSHA benzene standard.[98] A divided court

---

[94] 510 F. 2d at 1298.

[95] 548 F. 2d at 1007.

[96] For a comprehensive history of these developments, see Nathan J. Karch, "Explicit Criteria and Principles for Identifying Carcinogens: A Focus of Controversy at the Environmental Protection Agency," in NAS/NRC, *Decision Making in the Environmental Protection Agency,* vol. 2a (Washington, D.C.: NAS, 1977), pp. 119–206.

[97] The courts have proved more critical in their review of emergency temporary standards issued by OSHA. The Court of Appeals for the Fifth Circuit issued a temporary restraining order against the proposed emergency standard of 1 ppm for benzene on May 19, 1977. See also *Dry Color Manufacturers Ass'n v. U.S. Department of Labor,* 486 F. 2d 98 (3d Cir., 1973) (holding that conditions necessary for issuance of an emergency temporary standard for fourteen chemical carcinogens had not been met).

[98] *Industrial Union Department, AFL-CIO v. American Petroleum Institute,* 448 U.S. 607 (1980).

struck down OSHA's decision to reduce the applicable exposure limit from 10 ppm (parts per million) to 1 ppm.[99] Although five justices agreed that the standard should be set aside, they were unable to agree on a rationale for doing so. A plurality of the members held that the Secretary of Labor had failed to comply with what they saw as an essential requirement of the OSH Act. The Secretary should have made a finding, implicitly mandated by sections 3(8) and 6(b)(5) of the law, that a "significant risk" to worker health existed at the 10 ppm exposure limit and that this would be reduced by changing the standard to 1 ppm.[100]

The benzene decision is problematic for students of judicial-administrative relationships because it can be interpreted in two radically different ways. The more conservative reading holds that the case merely reaffirms traditional judicial standards for reviewing agency decisions, whether or not they are based on uncertain scientific information. This reading is favored by former OSHA officials, who suggest that the agency met with a setback in regulating benzene largely because of its own carelessness and arrogance. Reassured by past successes, OSHA neither presented a clear scientific rationale in support of the new standard nor made the minimal showing of risk and economic feasibility that it had made in previous cases involving carcinogens.[101] In refusing to endorse the 1 ppm standard, the Supreme Court was simply reminding OSHA that such practices were unacceptable. Even "pro-health" agencies must meet basic standards of responsibility when they regulate in the public interest.

This interpretation of the benzene decision is consistent with the plurality's demand that OSHA demonstrate the existence of a "significant risk" at the 10 ppm exposure standard and show that a more stringent standard was "reasonably necessary" to protect worker health. The courts have long insisted that regulatory power should not be invoked to correct trifling or *de minimis* abuses, including negligible risks to public health.[102] The court was also on firm ground in questioning the clarity and sufficiency of OSHA's scientific arguments. During the standard-setting process, OSHA was forced to repudiate some of the epidemiological evidence supporting the new standard. A majority of the justices were not persuaded that OSHA had articulated a

---

[99] The effect of the decision was to leave in place the federal occupational safety and health standard of 10 ppm that had been in effect since 1971.

[100] 448 U.S. at 642.

[101] Interviews, Washington, D.C., December 5, 1980, and April 24, 1981.

[102] See, for example, the position adopted by the D.C. Circuit in *Monsanto v. Kennedy*, 613 F. 2d 947 (D.C. Cir., 1979). Reviewing FDA's regulation of acrylonitrile in that case, Judge Leventhal held that the Commissioner must find that a substance migrates into food in more than insignificant amounts before he undertakes to regulate it. See also *U.S. v. Lexington Mill & Elevator Co.*, 232 U.S. 399 (1914).

convincing alternate rationale for the tighter standard. As Justice Lewis Powell observed in his concurring opinion:

> In my view, the question is whether OSHA successfully carried its burden on the basis of record evidence. That question in turn reduces to two principal issues. First, is there substantial evidence supporting OSHA's determination that available quantification techniques are too imprecise to permit a reasonable numerical estimate of risks? If not, then OSHA has failed to show that its regulation rests on the "best available evidence." Second, is OSHA's finding of significant risks at current exposure levels supported by substantial evidence? If not, then OSHA has failed to show that the new regulation is reasonably necessary to provide safe and healthful workplaces.[103]

By agreeing to invalidate the benzene standard, Justice Powell appeared merely to be reasserting the well-established requirement that agencies explain the reasons for their actions clearly, completely, and "in a manner capable of judicial understanding."[104]

Another reading of the benzene case is more troublesome for agencies regulating at the frontiers of scientific knowledge. The plurality opinion took OSHA to task for using "assumptions," rather than "findings" or "evidence," to support its conclusion that lowering the permissible exposure limit from 10 ppm to 1 ppm would reduce the risk of leukemia. Taken at face value, this criticism seems to undermine some of the basic doctrines developed in earlier cases concerning carcinogens:[105] that, given the scientific uncertainties involved in regulating these substances, agencies cannot sharply distinguish between "fact" and "policy" or "assumption" and "evidence," and that reviewing courts cannot meaningfully apply to such decisions a stricter standard of review than that traditionally applied to policy determinations.[106]

---

[103] 448 U.S. at 667.

[104] See discussion accompanying nn. 65, 66.

[105] Justice Marshall reviewed some of these doctrines in his dissenting opinion: "The plurality is insensitive to three factors which, in my view, make judicial review of occupational safety and health standards under the substantial evidence test particularly difficult. First, the issues often reach a high level of technical complexity. In such circumstances the courts are required to immerse themselves in matters to which they are unaccustomed by training or experience. Second, the factual issues are frequently not subject to any definitive resolution. Often the factual finger points, it does not conclude. Causal connections and theoretical extrapolations may be uncertain. Third, when the question involves determination of the acceptable level of risk, the ultimate decision must necessarily be based on considerations of policy as well as empirically verifiable facts. Factual determinations can at most define the risk in some statistical way; the judgment whether the risk is tolerable cannot be based solely on a resolution of the facts" (citations omitted). 448 U.S. at 704–5.

[106] On the falling together of the "substantial evidence" and "arbitrary and capricious" standards of review in areas of technical complexity and uncertainty, see *Lead Industries*

There are indications that the plurality in the benzene case did not intend to review carcinogen regulation according to more stringent standards than were already in effect. For example, the opinion approvingly cited lower court decisions giving "OSHA some leeway where its findings must be made on the frontiers of scientific knowledge."[107] Yet at least one subsequent decision—a reversal of the Consumer Product Safety Commission's proposed ban on urea-formaldehyde foam insulation[108]—suggests that lower courts may treat the benzene case as an injunction to scrutinize the evidentiary basis for carcinogen regulation much more intensely than before. Such a development not only will increase the differences between American and European judicial review, but will exacerbate the already highly adversarial relationship between courts and agencies in the United States.

While U.S. courts have devoted more attention than courts in other countries to the technical and policy issues involved in regulating carcinogens, some of these questions have also been addressed by the German administrative courts in a different procedural context. As stated earlier, standards for toxic substances are usually immune from challenge in Germany because the mere promulgation of a standard does not affect individual rights. On the other hand, standards may be indirectly attacked when the administration approves construction of a potentially harmful facility that complies with applicable pollution control standards. In one such case,[109] the plaintiff alleged that the issuance of a construction permit to an epoxide-manufacturing facility infringed on his rights, since the carcinogens and mutagens emitted from this facility could injure his health both on their own and in synergism with other substances already present in the environment. In upholding the plaintiff's cause of action, the Lüneburg administrative court agreed that potentially carcinogenic emissions present special problems for risk assessment and regulatory policy.[110]

For the most part, however, the court deferred to the expertise of the established scientific and governmental bodies to a much greater extent than could be expected in the United States. In the case of one specifically identified pollutant (1-chloro-2,3-epoxy-propane), the court accepted as

---

Ass'n, Inc. v. EPA, 647 F. 2d 1130, 1146, n. 29 (D.C. Cir., 1980); Associated Industries of New York State, Inc., v. U.S. Department of Labor, 487 F. 2d 342, 349–50 (2d Cir., 1973); Kenneth C. Davis, *Administrative Law Treatise,* 2d ed. (San Diego: K. C. Davis Publishing Co., 1978), vol. 1, pp. 467–68 (discussing standard of review under the 1977 Clean Air Act Amendment); Antonin Scalia and Frank Goodman, "Procedural Aspects of the Consumer Product Safety Act," *UCLA Law Review,* 20, no. 1 (1973), 935, n. 138.

[107] 448 U.S. at 656.

[108] *Gulf South Insulation v. U.S. Consumer Product Safety Commission,* 701 F. 2d 1137 (1983).

[109] OVG Lüneburg, *Gewerbe Archiv* 1980/6, pp. 203–8.

[110] Ibid., pp. 204–5.

prima facie evidence of carcinogenicity the listing of the substance as a carcinogen by the DFG commission on hazardous substances in the workplace. The court also accepted the commission's view that even very low concentrations of carcinogens may present a risk to health. The court then left it to the administrative agency to demonstrate either that the risk of cancer was practically nonexistent or that emission levels for the named pollutant were being kept "as low as possible" in compliance with the governing statute.

Conclusion

The absence of chemical-related litigation in France and Britain and the infrequency of such lawsuits in Germany must be explained partly in light of factors that lie outside the preserve of law. It is intriguing, for example, that regulated industries in the European countries rarely sue governmental agencies, although they face many fewer legal impediments than do public interest groups. The reasons have to do with social, political, and cultural considerations, some of which are difficult to document. Thus, German officials allege that industry is unwilling to litigate unfavorable regulations because of the negative publicity surrounding lawsuits. What can be easily verified, however, is that all three European governments go to considerable lengths to protect the accommodations they reach with industry, using the institutional and procedural devices described in chapters 2–4. For example, significant prior consultation with industry (Britain, France, and Germany), voluntary safety requirements (Britain), and low reliance on ambient workplace standards (Britain and France) can all be regarded as "pro-industry" practices that reduce the probability of litigation. After winning most of what can be won during administrative deliberations, industry stands to gain little more from taking the agencies to court.

The analysis of judicial review in this chapter reveals an additional basis for differences in U.S. and European litigation patterns. Though there are significant similarities in the law of judicial review across the four countries, the U.S. courts, often acting in partnership with the legislature, have consistently interpreted the relevant legal principles in ways that enhance their power to supervise the administrative agencies. To begin with, the public enjoys much more liberal access to the courts in the United States than in Europe. Public interest associations that would be completely barred from litigation in Germany, and at least restricted in Britain and France, can sue with relative ease in the United States pursuant to specific statutes and judicially defined standing rules. The comparatively clear definition of public responsibilities in U.S. law also offers plaintiffs unique opportunities to challenge administrative inaction.

After accepting jurisdiction, U.S. courts aggressively review the substantive arguments advanced by the regulatory agencies. This practice markedly distinguishes American reviewing techniques from those of all three European countries, although in principle the French and German administrative courts also enjoy unlimited power to reexamine the facts underlying agency decisions. The availability of a written record considerably enhances the power of American courts to scrutinize the substantive basis for agency decisions. In turn, judicial activism in remanding decisions for inadequacies in the record pushes the American agencies to greater precautionary formality in the preparation and presentation of their scientific and technical arguments.

The record of judicial review in the specific context of U.S. carcinogen regulation suggests that intense supervision by the courts has brought the agencies a number of benefits along with the disadvantages of delay and uncertainty. By and large, the standard of review has been deferential. The courts have repeatedly asserted that administrative judgments on uncertain scientific issues should be treated as policy decisions and respected accordingly. Even the Supreme Court's decision in the benzene case can be read as an isolated act of exasperation, a response to unusual provocation by the agency, rather than a sweeping realignment of judicial-administrative relationships.

Yet the current malaise affecting federal regulatory policy leads us to conclude that judicial approval has not shielded the agencies very effectively against charges of overreaching and excess. To some extent, the judicial process itself can be blamed for this failure. The federal judiciary has attracted growing criticism from Congress and the public for intruding too deeply into social policy making. To the extent that the courts are perceived as imposing an authoritarian or antidemocratic rule on the country, their power to confer legitimacy on the administrative agencies is understandably weakened.

As a technique for resolving conflicts over social regulation, judicial review leaves much to be desired. Intermittent lawsuits expose the fragility of the consensus embodied in American environmental or health and safety statutes, but they provide no mechanism for creating lasting political accord. In interpreting ambiguous legal mandates, such as the "feasibility" standard of the OSH Act, the courts are at best able to provide a plausible reading of the law as it applies to a particular set of facts. They lack the institutional, political, and even moral capacity to construct accommodations between regulators and regulated interests that extend beyond specific disputes. As a result, adjudication focuses attention on the vulnerable legal or scientific position of the administrative agencies without eliminating any of the larger conflicts surrounding social regulation. Restoring confidence in the regulatory agencies requires a sustained political endeavor for which the courts cannot and should not be held exclusively responsible.[111]

[111] Given the nature of legislative politics in the United States (see chapter 3), it is improbable that Congress will exercise such guidance in the future through more careful drafting of regulatory statutes. For the same reason, Justice Rehnquist's resurrection of the nondelegation doctrine in the benzene case, 448 U.S. at 671–88, is likely to prove more an artifact of judicial reasoning than an incentive for renewed assumption of policy-making responsibilities by Congress. Reforms tending to legitimate administrative actions are more likely to occur in the sphere of institutional innovation than in the domain of legislative draftsmanship. (See further discussion of this point in chapter 12.)

6

The Development of
the Scientific Base

The history of governmental attempts to control the harmful effects of chemicals on human health and the environment is intimately linked to the scientific community's progress in identifying, measuring, and understanding the nature of chemical toxicity. Increased knowledge and methodological advances in the use of animal tests, in vitro tests, and epidemiology have been particularly important in fashioning the scope and nature of the public role in controlling carcinogens. It is to be expected that further clarification of the science underlying risk assessment will have a significant impact on how public authorities handle the regulation of these substances in the future.

At first glance, the scientific parameters of chemical control policy would seem to offer few rewards as a focus of cross-national analysis. Science is perhaps the most universalistic force in modern society, governed by strongly consensual norms and methodologies that transcend geography and culture.[1]

---

[1] The role of science as a force of change in society is the subject of a vast body of literature. For an introduction, see Daniel Bell, *The Coming of Post-Industrial Society* (New York: Basic Books, 1973); Talcott Parsons, *Societies: Evolutionary and Comparative Perspectives* (Englewood Cliffs, N.J.: Prentice-Hall, 1966); Alain Touraine, *The Post-Industrial Society* (New York: Random House, 1971); I. Spiegel-Rösing and D. de Solla Price, eds., *Science, Technology, and Society: A Cross-Disciplinary Perspective* (Beverly Hills, Calif.: Sage, 1976). For a review of the literature comparing science and public policy in different countries, see Ronald Brickman, "The Comparative Political Analysis of Science and Technology," Review Essay, *Comparative Politics,* 13, no. 4 (July 1981), 479–96.

Its role in chemical control policy would appear to be uniformly powerful, overriding many of the institutional and procedural factors that give national regulatory approaches their individuality.

The three chapters that follow, however, reveal considerable differentiation in the relationship of science and public policy across the four countries. In a surprising number of ways, the generation and utilization of policy-relevant scientific information are themselves functions of different national processes and circumstances. In the end, science is seen to be less a force of policy convergence than a showcase of the particular political needs and dynamics of each country.

The analysis begins at the grass-roots level. This chapter examines within each country the evolution of the scientific disciplines most directly related to carcinogenic risk evaluation and assesses their impact on the regulatory capabilities and decisions of the four governments. It also analyzes the role that each government plays in stimulating and directing research on chemical carcinogenesis. The level of public R & D investments, the priority allocated to the analysis of specific carcinogenic hazards or to more general scientific questions, the linkages between R & D policy and the regulatory agenda—all these are matters that clarify the public role in identifying and controlling cancer-causing substances and help account for the observed similarities and differences in national regulatory approaches.

Development of the Research System

Scientific activity in fields most closely associated with research on chemical carcinogenesis and safety evaluation has followed, as one might expect, a broadly parallel intellectual development in the four countries. The exceptionally efficient networks of communication in international science have served to diffuse scientific discoveries rapidly across national borders and have created an expanding pool of common knowledge to which individual scientists from the four countries have made important contributions. In turn, the parallel development of the underlying science of chemical risk evaluation has given national authorities similar access to new ideas and techniques that bear on their regulatory responsibilities. Tests for mutagenicity, for example, made their appearance in testing protocols at roughly the same time in each nation.

But if the intellectual foundations of chemical carcinogenesis research are broadly international, the institutional context in which such research is carried out and its specific focus vary from one country to the other. For a variety of reasons—the disciplinary structure of universities, the presence of exceptional scientific talents in certain areas, the support or neglect of science funding agencies, and even the vagaries of local scientific fashion—the study of chemical carcinogenesis has a varying history in each national context.

Before the environmental causes of cancer became a matter of intense public concern, cancer epidemiology was not a well-established field of inquiry in any of the four countries. Despite a prestigious history dating back to the eighteenth century,[2] the field has suffered from inherent methodological difficulties and the tenuous status of epidemiology as a biomedical research speciality. Perhaps its most solid institutional foundation is in Britain, where both governmental and philanthropic organizations have long provided financial support. British cancer epidemiology has been dominated since the 1950s by Sir Richard Doll and his collaborators at Oxford University.[3] Epidemiology in France, however, has been impeded by an unfavorable career structure in medical research. Since the field is not accorded a separate section in the all-important University Consultative Committee, which acts on academic recruitment and promotion, few university scientists seek professional rewards in the area, and teaching is limited.[4] Epidemiology has had a similarly sparse following in Germany; most contemporary studies of cancer demography have been conducted either by industry or by the German Cancer Research Center in Heidelberg.[5]

In the United States, epidemiology has developed primarily in schools of public health. Until the 1920s, when it began to take on a more academic cast, the field was oriented toward the practical goals of public hygiene and disease prevention.[6] The number of trained specialists has always been low (fewer than fifty received doctorates in the field in 1975), reflecting the paucity of training centers and the greater prestige and material rewards traditionally associated with clinical specialization.[7]

---

[2] For the history of cancer epidemiology, see G. Peck and I. Ariel, "A Half-Century of Effort to Control Cancer," *International Abstracts of Surgery,* 100, no. 4 (April 1955), 309–543; David S. Lilienfeld and Abraham M. Lilienfeld, "Epidemiology: A Retrospective Study," *American Journal of Epidemiology,* 106, no. 6 (1977), 445–59; and Abraham M. Lilienfeld, ed., *Times, Places, and Persons* (Baltimore: Johns Hopkins University Press, 1980).

[3] For information on the work of this group, see Imperial Cancer Research Fund, *Scientific Report,* London, 1979.

[4] Catherine Sceautres, "L'épidémiologie n'est plus ce qu'elle était . . . ," *La Recherche,* 11, no. 110 (April 1980), 486–93. Most French studies on cancer epidemiology are published in *Revue épidémiologique de la santé publique.*

[5] Based on the survey of IARC, "Directory of On-Going Research in Cancer Epidemiology 1980," IARC Scientific Publications no. 35, Lyon, 1980.

[6] "The Epidemiologic Tradition," *Public Health Reports,* 94, no. 3 (May–June 1979), 203–9; C. E. A. Winslow et al., *The History of American Epidemiology* (St. Louis: C. V. Mosby, 1952).

[7] Roger Detels, "The Need for Epidemiologists," *Journal of the American Medical Association,* 242, no. 15 (October 12, 1979), 1644–46.

Some indication of the relative level of research activity in cancer epidemiology across the four countries is provided by international bibliographies.[8] A summary of work by the World Health Organization, published in 1963 and covering the period from 1946 through 1960, listed 20 studies conducted in the United States, 7 in West Germany, 2 in France, and 6 in the United Kingdom. A more recent survey by IARC listed 28 studies underway in German institutions, 20 in France (other than those undertaken by IARC in Lyon), 141 in the United Kingdom, and 373 in the United States.[9]

The institutional problems of general toxicology and experimental chemical carcinogenesis are of a different order.[10] Neither field has developed a distinct institutional identity in any of the four countries. In Germany, toxicology has long been a minor branch of pharmacology, located within medical schools. In 1975 there were only fourteen senior-level positions in toxicology at German universities, where an estimated three scientists a year were completing training in the field.[11] As in other countries, however, experimental work on chemical carcinogenesis in Germany is also performed outside university departments of toxicology, in such locales as the German Cancer Research Center, the Institute of Aerobiology of the Frauenhofer Society, and university departments of environmental research, industrial medicine, and public hygiene.[12]

French research on chemical carcinogenesis was for years dominated by the figure of Antoine Lacassagne, whose studies focused on the carcinogenic properties of benzene compounds, nitrosamines, and fluorenes, and the inhibitory and promotional effects of estrogens and other compounds.[13] After his retirement, the field went into a period of decline, as French cancer research followed the international trend toward work in fundamental molecular biology and therapy. Some research activity in cancer cause and prevention was sustained at the cancer research center in Villejuif and at the Institut Curie. As an academic discipline, French toxicology developed

---

[8] WHO, *Bibliography on the Epidemiology of Cancer* (Geneva: WHO, 1963).

[9] IARC, op. cit.

[10] For a general history of chemical carcinogenesis research, see M. M. Coombs, "Chemical Carcinogenesis: A View at the End of the First Half-Century," *Journal of Pathology*, 130 (1980), 117–46; I. Berenblum, *Science vs. Cancer* (London: Sigma, 1946); James A. Miller, "Carcinogenesis by Chemicals: An Overview—G. H. A. Clowes Memorial Lecture," *Cancer Research*, 30, no. 3 (March 1970), 559–73.

[11] DFG, *Toxicology,* DFG Memorandum (Boppard: Harald Boldt, 1980).

[12] For a survey, see UBA, *Umweltrelevante Krebsforschung in der Bundesrepublik Deutschland* (Berlin: UBA, 1979).

[13] Joseph C. Arcos, "French Research on Chemical Carcinogenesis in the Last Quarter Century with Special Reference to the Contributions of A. Lacassagne and N. P. Buu-Hoi," in Paul O. P. Ts'o and Joseph A. Di Paolo, eds., *Chemical Carcinogenesis,* pt. a (New York: Marcel Dekker, 1974), pp. 5–58.

mostly in medical schools, although with fewer ties to pharmacology than in Germany.

British studies on experimental carcinogenesis in the interwar period included the pioneering work of Kennaway and Hieger on tumor induction as well as studies on the chemical constitution and activity of the carcinogenic agent; attempts were also made to correlate carcinogenic activity with chemical structure.[14] After the war, attention shifted to the properties of cells and tissues and the nature of their reactions to carcinogens. In 1947 the Medical Research Council (MRC) established the Toxicological Research Unit under the direction of J. M. Barnes, the leading toxicologist of the period. The laboratory has investigated the carcinogenic properties of nitroso-compounds and mycotoxins, among other substances, but today it does not specialize in carcinogenesis analysis. Aside from related work in a few other MRC laboratories, in the British Industrial Biological Research Association (BIBRA), and in a small number of university laboratories, experimental chemical carcinogenesis, and toxicology more generally, has had little following among British scientists.[15]

Training of toxicologists in the United States takes place primarily in medical schools, where toxicology is commonly treated as a subdiscipline of pharmacology, in colleges of veterinary medicine, and, more recently, in schools of environmental health science. Many scientists now engaged in toxicological research, and more specifically in chemical carcinogenesis and safety evaluation, have moved into the area laterally from other fields, such as pathology and biochemistry.[16] The heterogeneity and ill-defined boundaries of the discipline are illustrated by the fact that no professional organization represented the field as a whole until the Society of Toxicology was founded in 1961, and even today there are at least fourteen national societies which claim to represent toxicology or one of its subfields.[17]

Toxicologists in the United States are now engaged in a vigorous debate about the discipline's professional and scientific status and the adequacy of training programs to meet both the growing demand for skilled manpower and emerging scientific challenges. Although the conflict is detectable in other countries as well, the field in the United States appears especially torn be-

---

[14] Imperial Cancer Research Fund, *Fifty Years of Cancer Research,* Supplement to Forty-Ninth Annual Report (London: Imperial Cancer Research Fund, 1952).

[15] MRC Toxicology Unit, "Current Research," March 1979; interviews with scientists at BIBRA, HSE, MRC and in industry, London, 1980.

[16] Frederick W. Oehme, "The Development of Toxicology as a Veterinary Discipline in the United States," *Clinical Toxicology,* 3, no. 2 (June 1970), 211–20; Christopher O. Schonwalder, "NIEHS Holds Toxicology Training Symposium," *Veterinary and Human Toxicology,* 23, no. 2 (April 1981), 110–22.

[17] *Clinical Toxicology,* 10, no. 2 (1977), 261–64.

tween the desire for professional consolidation and autonomy arising largely in response to external demands and the increasing reliance on neighboring disciplines to address more fundamental questions about toxicological processes.[18]

Compared to research on chemical carcinogenesis in the three European countries, the field in the United States has benefited from longstanding and generous governmental support. In this way, it was able to overcome some of the institutional obstacles that hindered its development elsewhere. The environmental cancer section of the National Cancer Institute, under the direction of William Hueper from 1948 to 1964, was particularly instrumental in stimulating research on occupational and environmental agents in cancer formation.[19] Other NCI laboratories, notably those of pathology and biology, now probe related questions on the histopathologic features of tumors in various laboratory animals and organ systems, the development of carcinogenic models, tumor transplantation, and carcinogenic metabolism.[20] As discussed below, NCI has also sponsored a large carcinogens-testing program.

Thanks largely to NCI's intramural and extramural programs, research and testing in experimental toxicology related to chemical carcinogenesis in the United States currently overwhelms that of any other country. A 1978 IARC survey of carcinogenicity testing on animals, for example, relying on country reports of studies at various levels of completion, uncovered 14 separate studies undertaken at French institutions, 78 in the United Kingdom, 162 in West Germany, and over 670 in the United States.[21]

A more recent entrant to the scientific fields underlying chemical risk assessment is the study of mutagenesis.[22] Of particular regulatory interest is the development of in vitro tests for mutagenicity that can be used more rapidly and inexpensively than animal bioassays to predict a substance's potential carcinogenicity. An early landmark was the work begun in 1964 by Bruce Ames and his colleagues, whose basic research on the molecular biology of

[18] See Schonwalder, op. cit.; John Autian, "Are We Getting Too Many Voices for Toxicology?" *Veterinary and Human Toxicology,* 21, no. 2 (April 1979), 127; William J. Hayes, Jr., "The Discipline of Toxicology: Its Future in Training and Research," *Toxicology and Applied Pharmacology,* 25 (August 1973), 502–6.

[19] See, in particular, the landmark work of W. C. Hueper, *Occupational Tumors and Allied Diseases* (Springfield, Ill.: Thomas, 1942); also Philippe Shubik, "Environmental Carcinogenesis: Priorities and Perspective," in Myron A. Mehlman et al., *New Concepts in Safety Evaluation,* pt. 2 (New York: John Wiley, 1979), pp. 1–10.

[20] Umberto Saffiotti, "Carcinogenesis, 1957–77: Notes for a Historical Review," *Journal of the National Cancer Institute,* 59, no. 2 (supplement) (August 1977), 617–22.

[21] IARC, "Information Bulletin on the Survey of Chemicals Being Tested for Carcinogenicity," no. 7, Lyon, January 1978.

[22] For the development of this field, see Lionel A. Poirier and Frederick J. de Serres, "Initial National Cancer Institute Studies on Mutagenesis as a Prescreen for Chemical Carcinogens: An Appraisal," *Journal of the National Cancer Institute,* 62, no. 4 (April 1979), 919–26.

the salmonella bacteria led to the development of a test system for detecting mutagens that could be used as a valid predictor of carcinogenesis.[23] Intense research activity during the 1970s has produced more than one hundred different "short-term" tests, most of them assaying for mutagenicity. By 1979 results had been published on over twenty-six hundred chemicals using the salmonella/Ames test alone.[24]

As far as can be determined, the scientific communities of the four countries have participated in this burgeoning field at levels comparable to their efforts in more traditional areas of chemical carcinogenesis research. A 1979 German survey identified nineteen academic scientists working in the area, and a similar inquiry in France revealed fifteen research teams in governmental and academic institutions. In Britain, the level of interest appears somewhat higher than that in long-term research on animals.[25]

In view of the economic incentives to develop reliable and inexpensive alternatives to long-term animal tests, the chemical industry has followed developments closely and has itself invested large sums in mutagenicity research. Imperial Chemical Industries (ICI) in Britain, for example, was instrumental in launching one of the most ambitious efforts to date to assess the ability of short-term tests to distinguish correctly between carcinogens and noncarcinogens. Initially funded by the U.K. Medical Research Council under commission from the Health and Safety Executive, the project was later expanded to an international collaborative effort coordinated by the U.S. National Institute of Environmental Health Sciences (NIEHS). By 1979 some sixty-five private and public investigators from thirteen countries (including the United States, Britain, and West Germany) had subjected forty-two chemicals, including fourteen pairs of carcinogens and noncarcinogens, under blind conditions to thirty-five different assay systems.[26]

The Research System and Regulatory Policy

The preceding review indicates a broadly parallel intellectual development across the four countries in scientific fields most relevant to chemical control

[23] Bruce N. Ames, "Identifying Environmental Chemicals Causing Mutations and Cancer," *Science,* 204 (May 11, 1979), 587–93.

[24] Monica Hollstein and Joyce McCann, "Short-Term Tests for Carcinogens and Mutagens," *Mutation Research,* 65 (1979), 133–226.

[25] For an overview of current British work on mutagenesis and other short-term tests, see "Chemical Carcinogenesis: Predictive Value of Carcinogenicity Studies" (Papers presented at a symposium at the University of Surrey, Guildford, August 1979), in *British Journal of Cancer,* 41, no. 3 (March 1980), 489–508. A U.S. survey in 1980 found forty-seven mutagenicity testing laboratories. See NIEHS, "Mutagenicity Testing Laboratories in the U.S.," April 1980.

[26] Poirier and de Serres, op. cit.; Frederick de Serres and John Ashby, eds., *Evaluation of Short-Term Tests for Carcinogens: Report of the International Collaborative Program* (Amsterdam: Elsevier/North Holland, 1981).

policy, but also points to some disparities in institutional strengths and affiliations. The question is how these varying levels and focuses of scientific activity bear on the regulatory activities of the four governments. Although cause and effect cannot be established with precision, the development of carcinogen control policies does reflect to some degree the distinctive character, capabilities, and conceptions of national research systems. Often this impact derives from differences in prevailing scientific opinion which emerge around technical issues not yet subject to international consensus. This matter is discussed at length in chapter 8, which examines areas of scientific uncertainty in carcinogenic risk assessment and the debates that these have engendered in different national settings. Here we assess the impact of the more institutional features of national research systems on the development of regulatory programs.

One such impact is the constraint on regulatory momentum imposed by a shortage of specialists in critical areas of inquiry. All four governments have found that their regulatory objectives far outstrip the availability of qualified scientists and technicians. To implement the French chemicals law, for example, public officials estimated the need for at least a 40 percent increase in the country's testing capability.[27] A workshop on manpower held in the United States in 1977 calculated that one thousand more toxicologists would be needed by universities, government, and industry by 1979, and that an additional two hundred each year would be required over the next five to ten years.[28] A U.S. survey on epidemiology training revealed that the current rate of degrees awarded was sufficient to meet only 10 percent of the need for personnel with the doctorate and 30 percent of the need for those with the master's degree.[29] Although the U.S. government has long supported these disciplines through research and training grants, it was no more successful than its European counterparts in anticipating the rise in demand.

This manpower shortage has various effects on regulatory policy. It impedes the development of public R & D programs that serve regulatory goals. It sets upper limits on the amount of testing which public officials can reasonably ask of industry. By creating an imbalance between supply and demand, it increases costs and creates downward pressures on scientific quality. The

---

[27] Assemblée Nationale, Commission de la Production et des Echanges, "Rapport," *Journal Officiel,* Documents Annexe no. 2870, 1977, p. 83.

[28] Conservation Foundation, "Training Scientists for Future Toxic Substances Problems," Washington, D.C., 1977.

[29] Detels, op. cit. See also *Wall Street Journal,* April 14, 1981. For a discussion of toxicology training programs in Europe, see W. N. Aldridge and C. Schlatter, "Training and Education in Toxicology," *Archives of Toxicology,* 45 (1980), 249–56.

latter problem has been most visible in the United States, where examples of sloppy and even fraudulent testing have been uncovered.[30]

In Europe, the fewer numbers of bonafide scientific specialists are most conspicuous in the restricted pool of scientists available to serve as policy advisers. (Those playing a public role are invariably a small subset of practicing scientists in any country.) Partly for this reason, some scientists in Europe have gained extraordinary personal influence over governmental policy. Dietrich Henschler, the director of the Institute of Toxicology at the University of Würzburg, for example, has for years played a central role in setting toxic concentration limits in the workplace via the chairmanship of the DFG commission involved in the matter. The case of René Truhaut in France is even more exceptional. This dominant figure of French safety evaluation has served on the most important science advisory committees in all four regulatory areas, and he is typically the French delegate to the major scientific committees at the international level. When a new evaluation committee was created to implement the 1977 chemicals law, Truhaut was not just made a member, he was also appointed "senior scientific adviser" to the Ministry of the Environment.

The smaller pool of recognized experts in the European countries also means that intellectual and institutional backgrounds are likely to be similar.[31] This in turn makes opposing views on scientific issues less likely to be articulated than they are in the United States, where the large numbers of recognized experts engaging in policy debates no doubt reflect in part the multiple and relatively open channels of recruitment and training in American science. As noted above, in the United States, disciplines of environmental health have developed in a wide variety of institutional settings (public health schools, land-grant veterinarian schools, departments of statistics) that tend to attract students of diverse social origins. In Europe, the same fields are more closely tied to medical faculties, whose students come predominantly from the middle classes and whose internal organization concentrates scholarly recognition on a handful of top scientists.

These same factors help to explain the greater difficulties that European scientific communities have in producing individuals, such as Irving Selikoff, Samuel Epstein, and Peter Infante in the United States, who enjoy a public forum in which to articulate strong safety-oriented positions bolstered with credible scientific credentials. When the General and Municipal Workers' Union (GMWU) in Britain wanted to present a firmer scientific argument for

---

[30] See "Tighter Controls on Toxics Testing," *Chemical Week,* August 24, 1983, and *Science,* June 10, 1983.

[31] For an analysis of how differing national contexts bear on scientific research, see Stuart S. Blume, *Toward a Political Sociology of Science* (New York: Free Press, 1974).

stricter regulation of workplace carcinogens, for example, it could do no better than to call on Epstein, one of the most active scientist-advocates in the United States. Another union, the Association of Scientific, Technical, and Managerial Staffs (ASTMS), had difficulty recruiting qualified British experts to review its cancer-policy position paper.[32]

Nevertheless, it takes only two scientists to advocate opposing stands on a scientific or regulatory matter, and even in a tightly knit regulatory system like the French, rival *patrons* may find themselves on different sides of a regulatory issue. A rare public glimpse of such a debate occurred in the case of amaranth (Red Dye No. 2). Both the joint Food and Agricultural Organization/World Health Organization committee on food additives, on which Truhaut served since 1956, and the European Community scientific committee on food nutrition, which he chairs, gave amaranth an acceptable daily intake (ADI) level and thus implicit approval. Gounelle de Pontanel, the president of the food committee of the Académie de Médecine and the section on food hygiene and nutrition of the Conseil Supérieur de l'Hygiène Publique, both of which are obligatorily consulted on food-additive decisions, has well-known views on the necessity of regulatory stringency with respect to additives, particularly colors.[33] In the academy discussions, Gounelle de Pontanel recommended a complete ban on the substance, or at least its restriction in France to the lowest usage compatible with the European Community directive. Truhaut, an invited participant in the debate, defended the less stringent stands of the FAO/WHO and EC committees, on the grounds that the FDA results "did not permit, on a scientific basis, the conclusion that amaranth is harmful," and that any effective ban in France could therefore not be justified solely on the toxicological evidence.[34] (In both the academy recommendation and the final ministerial decision, the views of Gounelle de Pontanel prevailed.) While the importance of such differences of opinion among experts in the French regulatory setting cannot be underestimated, the contained nature of the debate provides a striking contrast to the pitched battles that typically develop among American scientists over similar issues (see chapter 8).

Research Policy

None of the four governments under review confines its role to receiving passively knowledge that emerges spontaneously from national and interna-

---

[32] Interviews, London, July 1980.

[33] H. Gounelle de Pontanel et al., "Réticences de l'hygiéniste vis-à-vis des colorants utilisés en technologie alimentaire," *Annales de l'Académie Nationale de Médecine,* Session of April 22, 1975, pp. 318–22.

[34] *Annales de l'Académie Nationale de Médecine,* Session of June 15, 1977, pp. 572–76.

tional scientific communities. The level of scientific effort in carcinogenesis research and its intellectual orientation are shaped in large part by governmental funding policies and priorities. Indeed, public investments in research on the mechanisms, identification, and control of carcinogens must be considered an integral part of a government's policy to substantiate and abate the threat of cancer from chemical substances. The following analysis reveals several important differences in the level, orientation, and priorities of public R & D programs related to regulation—differences that both derive from and reinforce the countries' distinctive approaches to chemical control.

Research Programs of Regulatory Agencies

In all four countries, governmental sponsorship of research related to the regulation of chemicals is shared between the R & D programs that are under the direct guidance of regulatory agencies and those efforts supported by more general science-promotion agencies that do not have regulatory responsibilities. These two branches of regulatory R & D are less easily distinguishable in the United States than they are in the European countries, simply because the U.S. government supports a broad spectrum of basic and applied work in both. In Europe, the research efforts of the regulatory agencies and their affiliated technical institutes tend to be small in scale and confined to short-term, highly specific inquiries that seldom involve substantial experimental or exploratory work. European science agencies, in turn, have concentrated on fundamental research in chemical carcinogenesis and related fields and have eschewed the large testing and applied research programs that figure so prominently in the work of the National Cancer Institute and other federal science centers.

By European standards, the R & D efforts of U.S. regulatory agencies are quite impressive. In fiscal year 1984, EPA's research budget totaled some $246 million (up from $129 million in FY 1983, but still smaller than during the Carter administration). The same year, FDA spent over 20 percent of its budget, or $74 million, on research, with nearly one-third of the amount allocated to the agency's own research facility, the National Center for Toxicological Research. OSHA's research is in principle carried out by the National Institute for Occupational Safety and Health, a part of the Centers of Disease Control within the Department of Health and Human Services. NIOSH's 1983 research budget came to almost $50 million.[35]

All of these programs devote a substantial part of their resources to research on toxic chemicals, including basic toxicology research, human

---

[35] NTP, *Fiscal Year 1983 Annual Plan,* NTP 82–119, January 1983.

epidemiology, testing, and methods development. In FY 1983, for example, 25 percent of EPA's total R & D budget was used for this purpose, while corresponding figures were 37 percent in FDA and 5 percent in NIOSH. Total federal expenditures on research and testing related to chemical toxicology in 1983 came to $343 million.[36]

The testing component of these programs is of particular interest because of its potentially direct impact on the regulatory agenda. Among the three agencies, the Food and Drug Administration demonstrates perhaps most effectively the use of research as an integral part of regulatory strategy. The agency's intramural program related to food additives stresses the health effects resulting from long-term, low-level exposure, the study of biological processes in animals to enable better extrapolation to man, and the development of improved testing methods and protocols. The testing program concentrates on substances having no clear industrial sponsorship, such as food contaminants and GRAS substances, and substances for which information is needed beyond that which industry supplies. In 1980 FDA listed 112 substances undergoing some form of toxicological testing, including several for chronic toxicity and carcinogenicity, such as gentian violet, sulfamethazine, and carrageenan. Epidemiological studies were underway for PCBs, methylmercury, and ochratoxin.[37]

Whether or not these efforts incite a regulatory response clearly depends on many factors besides the nature of the results obtained. But FDA's long-standing interest in saccharin illustrates the pivotal role that R & D results can play in agency decision making. As early as 1948, FDA scientists undertook a one-generation rat-feeding experiment on saccharin, with inconclusive results. Preliminary findings of a later study, together with a parallel investigation by an independent laboratory, prompted the agency in 1972 to change the artificial sweetener's classification from a GRAS substance to the "interim" category. While the studies showed a significantly high incidence of bladder tumors, assessments by the National Academy of Sciences and others raised doubts about the results, evoking the possibility that the carcinogenic activity was due to an impurity. As a result, FDA did not take further regulatory action and suspended additional research pending the results of a Canadian study designed to clarify the purity issue. After these became available, FDA in 1977 proposed a ban on saccharin, a measure subsequently prevented by congressional action. More recently, the agency has sponsored additional chronic toxicity and DNA repair studies and has collaborated with NCI on an epidemiological study on the relationship between saccharin consumption and bladder cancer incidence.[38]

---

[36] NTP, op. cit.
[37] See ibid.; and FDA, *Bureau of Foods Research Plan,* 1980.
[38] See OTA, *Cancer Testing Technology and Saccharin* (Washington, D.C.: GPO, 1977);

FDA's research on nitrite developed somewhat differently, but it demonstrates just as forcefully the potential impact of an agency R & D initiative. Concerned about the health effects of nitrosamines in food produced by the interaction of water and morpholine when morpholine is used as an anticorrosive agent in boilers, FDA asked Paul Newberne of M.I.T. to undertake a study using three species of animals and various levels of nitrites and amines. The investigation, begun in 1971, demonstrated that the separate administration of nitrite and amines produced the same effects as preformed nitrosomorpholine, prompting the industry to suspend use of the anticorrosive substance. As a byproduct of the study, it was found that one group of rats ingesting nitrite alone showed a significant increase in leukemia, with or without lymphomas. This led FDA to contract with Newberne in 1974 to design another study using only nitrites. As with saccharin, the agency initiated rule-making proceedings following the first review of the results, only to become embroiled in an intense scientific controversy over the validity of the study and the interpretation of the findings.[39]

One FDA-sponsored scientific investigation having more general significance to carcinogens control is the ED 01 or "megamouse" study. The project was designed to clarify the problem of extrapolating the likelihood of cancer at low exposure levels (for reasons of cost, experimental animals in bioassays are typically exposed at much higher levels). By using larger numbers of animals, FDA scientists provided new information about low-dose responses, although they were unable to establish experimentally the dose-response curve down to zero dose.[40]

NIOSH's institutional separation from OSHA has proved to be an impediment in funneling the former's research efforts into the regulatory process. In effect, the two agencies tend to pursue their objectives independently, and coordinated research programs have been few.[41] NIOSH's own research is conceived largely to provide scientific support to the preparation of criteria documents, that is, compilations of hazard, exposure, and technical information accompanied by recommended standards. The institute's attention to carcinogens increased throughout the 1970s, so that by FY 1980, approximately $6 million, or 16 percent of its research budget, was devoted to cancer research.[42] NIOSH initially selected toxic agents for its research and stan-

Reginald W. Rhein, Jr., and Larry Marion, *The Saccharin Controversy* (New York: Monarch Press, 1977).

[39] GAO, "Does Nitrite Cause Cancer? Concerns about Validity of FDA-Sponsored Study Delay Answer," Washington, D.C.: January 31, 1980; interview with Paul Newberne, Ithaca, N.Y., February 1981.

[40] House Committee on Appropriations, *Hearings on Agriculture, Rural Development, and Related Agencies: Appropriations for 1982*, pt. 4A, 97th Cong., 2d sess., pp. 137–38.

[41] Interview with a former OSHA official, Washington, D.C., April 1981.

[42] NIOSH, "Program Plans by Program Areas FY 1980," October 1979, p. xii.

dard-developing activities on the basis of the population at risk and relative toxicity, as determined by subjective evaluations of a panel of experts. In 1976, the agency revised its priority-setting procedures to give more weight to whole industries, occupations, chemical classes, and industrial processes, to seek views from a wider array of groups and institutions, and to allow for longer-term information gathering and research.[43] Despite these changes, the institute was still criticized for its failure to coordinate with OSHA's regulatory agenda and for the diversion of its limited funds away from long-term research and toward the issuing of bibliographic documents having little practical relevance.[44]

Although EPA spends several million dollars each year on research related to toxic chemical control, its testing program on specific chemical hazards is relatively small. The agency focuses on the human health effects of exposures to pollutants through various pathways and on the development and validation of alternative test methods.[45] The agency's own Health Effects Research Laboratory has done some carcinogenicity testing on such substances as arsenic, chlorophenols, chloroform, and haloethers. Since 1978, EPA has also collaborated with the National Cancer Institute on projects of mutual interest.[46]

In contrast to the situation in the United States, few regulatory agencies in Europe have sizeable research programs, and where such capacity exists, research on chemical carcinogenesis has not been particularly favored. One of the larger general programs is that of Britain's Health and Safety Executive, which in 1978 spent some £100 million, or 22 percent of its total budget, on research.[47] Most of these funds are spent on accident research, safety engineering studies, and analytical methods. Work on carcinogenesis takes the form of field surveys of workers who are exposed to selected substances (asbestos, lead, vinyl chloride, acrylonitrile) or who are employed in hazard-

---

[43] James L. Perkins and Vernon E. Rose, "Occupational Health Priorities for Health Standards: The Current NIOSH Approach," *American Journal of Public Health*, 69, no. 5 (May 1979), 444–48.

[44] M. Donald Whorton and David H. Wegman, "Occupational Health Standards: What Are the Priorities?" *American Journal of Public Health*, 69, no. 5 (May 1979), 433–34; "Finklea Quits as Chief of Occupational Health Institute," *Science*, 199 (January 27, 1978), 408.

[45] EPA, "Research Outlook, 1979," February 1979, p. 8.

[46] NCI, "Annual Report on National Cancer Institute and Environmental Protection Agency Projects," February 1980. Projects have included the development of a data base on chemicals that have been identified in human tissues and fluids, experimental studies (in vivo analysis of UV-B induced photooxidations, chloroform in drinking water, aromatic amines, and benzidene compounds), methodology (particularly evaluation of the transformation screening assay and genetic toxicology bioassays), and epidemiology (hexachlorobenzene, nonferrous smelting, geographical studies, and the development of national mortality data bases for environmental epidemiology).

[47] HSE, *Health and Safety Research, 1978* (London: HMSO, 1979).

ous industries (rubber and cable making, foundries). A small amount of experimental work, such as that on asbestos in the late 1970s, is commissioned from outside research institutes.[48] Unlike the situation in the United States, where agencies with large R & D budgets can pursue lines of inquiry that are relatively distant from their immediate regulatory aims, HSE's research program on toxic chemicals appears to be tightly controlled by its regulatory agenda. Regulatory decisions, in turn, are often delayed while the agency awaits confirmatory results.[49]

In the food safety area, Britain's Ministry of Agriculture, Fisheries, and Food relies almost exclusively on industry to provide the scientific information it needs. Some research of a more fundamental nature on food toxicology is performed under MAFF financing by the British Industrial Biological Research Association.[50] MAFF and the Department of the Environment also initiate occasional surveys to determine population exposure to a variety of potentially toxic compounds, including some heavy metals and pesticide residues.[51] MAFF's research program in pesticides, linked to that of the Agricultural Research Council, is strongly oriented to efficacy and crop productivity.[52]

French ministries responsible for regulating carcinogens and other toxic chemicals have demonstrated little interest in sponsoring research or testing related to their policy goals. In the early 1970s, the environmental ministry's research program included a component on the contamination of the biological chain, focusing on ecotoxocological effects of heavy metals, chlorinated pesticides, and aflatoxins.[53] But no research activity has originated within the division responsible for implementing the chemicals law. Although a large research capability exists in the agricultural ministry in the form of the National Institute of Agricultural Research (Institut National de la Recherche Agronomique, INRA), the toxic properties of pesticides have been given scant attention.

Something of an exception to the general French pattern is the National Institute of Research and Safety, the research and information arm of both the Ministry of Labor in the area of worker safety and of the quasi-public insurance fund for occupational accidents and sickness. A division of chemistry

[48] HSE, *Employment Medical Advisory Service Report, 1977–78* (London: HMSO, 1979).

[49] Ibid., and various HSE annual reports, 1974–1978.

[50] BIBRA, "Annual Report, 1979"; interview, Carshalton, August 1980.

[51] These include surveys of cadmium in food and the vinyl chloride content of polyvinyl chloride in contact with food (various reports prepared by MAFF and published by HMSO).

[52] Royal Commission on Environmental Pollution, *Agriculture and Pollution*, 7th report (London: HMSO, 1979), p. 84.

[53] *Rapport d'activités du Conseil de la Recherche Scientifique et Technique sur l'Environnement, 1974–1975* (Paris: La Documentation Française, 1976).

and toxicology is included in the institute's laboratory facilities at Nancy. Its work is oriented toward sampling and analysis, but recently the division has developed a limited capability for short-term testing and epidemiological studies.[54]

In Germany, some research is carried out in each of the four technical support agencies serving the regulatory programs of the federal ministries (see chapter 4). The Federal Environmental Agency administers the R & D programs of the Federal Ministry of the Interior and also initiates its own research and monitoring activities. UBA has devoted a fair share of its research program to studies on toxic chemicals and environmental effects and to serve in the development of criteria for control.

Other German technical institutes have given chemical safety research less attention. An affiliate of the Federal Health Office, the Max von Pettenkofer Institute, undertakes analytical work and some laboratory research on food and pesticides.[55] Projects relating to chemical carcinogenesis initiated by BGA or the health ministry have centered on the detection of nitrosamines and mycotoxins in food.[56] The Federal Biological Research Center for Agriculture and Forestry (Biologische Bundesanstalt für Land- und Forstwirtschaft) plays a central role in the pesticide-licensing procedure, but its research program is on a small scale and is focused on efficacy and analytical methods. A few projects related to carcinogenic risk (nitrites in meat and the detection and persistence of chemicals in soil) have been undertaken in other agricultural research institutes. Like worker safety programs in France and Britain, the Federal Institute for Occupational Safety and Accident Research (Bundesanstalt für Arbeitsschutz und Unfallforschung) has stressed accident research over the investigation of chronic health hazards, although it has financed a limited amount of work by external scientists on the development of testing methods.

In sum, American and European agencies administering regulatory programs show a marked contrast in their willingness to support R & D as an integral part of their implementation strategies. The greater interest of EPA, FDA, and OSHA's research arm, NIOSH, in sponsoring scientific work is particularly evident with respect to exploratory research on carcinogenicity and other long-term chemical hazards. As a rule, European agencies and their affiliated technical institutes engage in limited testing and focus more exclusively on exposure and monitoring studies of hazards that are already controlled or undergoing regulatory scrutiny.

---

[54]"Dix ans d'INRS," *Travail et sécurité,* December 1978; INRS, "Programme d'activité 1978–79, études et recherches," September 1978; interviews, INRS, Nancy, France, June 1980.

[55]Bundesministerium für Forschung und Technologie, *Fünfter Forschungsbericht der Bundesregierung* (Bonn: BMFT, 1975), p. 274.

[56]UBA, op. cit.

Research for Regulation in Science-Promotion Agencies

In the research programs of science-promotion agencies that bear on chemical carcinogenesis, there exists a similar disparity in American and European practices. In the United States, these agencies, led by the National Institutes of Health (NIH), have given relatively lavish support to carcinogenesis research and related fields, and a significant proportion of their funding goes to testing particular compounds. In the European countries, research on cancer causation has received less support, both absolutely and relative to other research interests. Moreover, testing is virtually ignored by these agencies.

The National Cancer Institute has long been the paramount organization for research on chemical carcinogenesis in the world. Since its formation in 1937, NCI has devoted a significant portion of its resources to cancer causation. Formal programs in the area were established in 1961 and again in 1968; after 1971, the field further profited from the funds that flowed into cancer research following passage of the National Cancer Act.[57] This effort was not enough, however, to satisfy many in Congress and others responding to the public's increased sensitivity to the environmental causes of cancer. In 1978, NCI was mandated by law to intensify its program on the occupational and environmental origins of cancer and its prevention.[58] In the next two years, NCI funds for research into physical, chemical, and environmental cancer causes and mechanisms jumped 43 percent, compared to a 15 percent increase in the total institute budget.[59] In recent years, NCI initiated carcinogenicity tests at the rate of thirty to forty-five annually; by the end of 1980, its series of published bioassay results numbered over two hundred.[60]

NCI came under frequent criticism for its administration of the carcinogenicity testing program. A 1976 GAO report found that "in view of NCI's fiscal constraints and the universe of untested chemicals, some of the chemicals tested for carcinogenicity are of questionable priority because their produc-

[57] See Richard A. Rettig, *Cancer Crusade* (Princeton: Princeton University Press, 1977); Senate Committee on Labor and Public Welfare, *National Program for the Conquest of Cancer* (Washington, D.C.: GPO, 1971).

[58] House Committee on Interstate and Foreign Commerce, Subcommittee on Health and the Environment, *Hearings on Biomedical Research and Research Training Amendments of 1978,* 95th Cong., 2d sess., Serial no. 95–109, March 1–3, 1978 (Washington, D.C.: GPO, 1978).

[59] Statement by Vincent T. De Vita, acting director of NCI, before the House Committee on Interstate and Foreign Commerce, Subcommittee on Health and the Environment, *Hearings on Health Research Act of 1980,* 96th Cong., 2d sess., February 21, 25, 29, and March 3, 1980 (Washington, D.C.: GPO, 1980), p. 346.

[60] DHEW, Public Health Service, and NTP, "Review of Current DHEW Research Relating to Toxicology," FY 1980; NTP, "Carcinogenesis Testing Program, Chemicals on Standard Protocol," July 17, 1981.

tion or use is limited and the public exposure is minimal."[61] These criticisms prompted the institute to replace the informal assessments of its internal staff with a more formal selection procedure that relies more on external expertise and on explicit evaluation criteria, summarized as follows:[62]

Stage 1 Qualifying Criteria	*Stage 2* Selection Criteria	*Stage 3* Recommendation
1. The chemical is not currently on test in NCI's Bioassay Program or other testing programs 2. There are no adequate carcinogenicity bioassay results from thorough testing of the chemical 3. There is evidence of potential exposure based on (a) annual U.S. consumption $\geq$ 4.5 × 10 grams or (b) evidence of exposure from environmental occurrence	1. Exposure information –Commercial availability (production, imports, exports) –Use pattern (intermediate or dispersive, range of applicatons) –Human exposure (based on national hazard data bases) –Environmental occurrence (data as available on presence and persistence in various milieus) –Regulatory status (limits imposed by federal standards for estimating human exposure) 2. Evidence for carcinogenic activity and relative importance –Human data –Animal data –Short-term tests –Metabolism –Structure/activity relationships 3. Other considerations –Input from regulatory agencies –Research interest –Substitute chemicals for regulated chemicals – . . .	Select/Reject –Major reason –Priority

[61] GAO, "Federal Efforts to Protect the Public from Cancer-Causing Chemicals Are Not Very Effective," Washington, D.C., June 16, 1976, p. 28.

[62] "Who Chooses Chemicals for Testing?" *Science,* 201 (September 29, 1978), 1202. The list is adapted from internal NCI documents.

The agency has also come under attack for its management of contracts with outside laboratories, which do virtually all of NCI's testing.[63]

In recent years, NCI has augmented its activities in cancer epidemiology. The Field Studies and Statistics Program, with branches in biometry, clinical epidemiology, and environmental epidemiology, had a budget in 1980 of nearly $30 million. A major component is the Surveillance, Epidemiology, and End Results (SEER) project, which obtains cancer incidence and survival data through eleven cancer registries in different geographical areas, covering about 10 percent of the total U.S. population. Because of inherent methodological limitations—and possibly because the program has come under less intense political scrutiny—NCI's epidemiological work is not guided by a systematic selection process but, rather, responds to the predilections of its own staff or to the proposals of external scientists.[64]

While NCI has by far been the dominant federal sponsor of R & D on chemical carcinogenesis, other important contributions have been made by the National Institute of Environmental Health Sciences, sister institution to NCI in the National Institutes of Health. As part of its wide-ranging program studying hazards to human health and the environment, NIEHS has stressed the study of effects of low levels of environmental chemicals over long periods of exposure and environmental mutagenesis and the development of test systems.[65]

Greater public attention to chemical safety evaluation and the rapid development of toxicological research in federal agencies led the secretary of the Department of Health, Education, and Welfare to establish in November 1978 the National Toxicology Program. The objective was to coordinate toxicological research, particularly its more applied components, among several DHEW agencies (NCI, NIEHS, NIOSH, and FDA), to accelerate federal activity in the testing of toxic substances, and to develop and validate test protocols appropriate for regulatory needs. Since its creation, NTP has acted to combine traditional testing with the investigation of a wider range of toxicological mechanisms and effects, including studies in neurobehavioral, immunological, and reproductive toxicology. It has also introduced more systematic use of short-term tests to screen chemicals for chronic effects, gradually reducing the number of chemicals subjected to chronic testing.[66]

[63] GAO, "The National Cancer Institute Has a Shortage of Qualified Scientists for Its Carcinogenesis Testing Program," Washington, D.C., March 30, 1979; "Hatch Batters NCI with Straus Case . . . ," *Science,* 212 (June 19, 1981), 1366–67.

[64] DHEW, NCI, "Report of the Field Studies and Statistics Program," FY 1980, NIH Publication no. 81–2311, 1981.

[65] NIEHS, "Research Programs, 1976–1977," NIH Publication no. 77–1130, 1977; DHEW, Public Health Service, and NTP, op. cit., pp. 26–39.

[66] See DHEW, Public Health Service, and NTP, op. cit.; and NTP; *Fiscal Year 1984 Annual*

The research programs of European science agencies do not have the applied dimension found in U.S. programs. But all three European governments
have recently given official recognition to the need for increased effort in
chemical toxicology and related fields and have taken steps to reinforce their
capabilities in more fundamental areas of research. In France, for example,
the National Institute of Health and Medical Research (Institut National de la
Santé et de la Recherche Médicale, INSERM) has increased support for
epidemiology, targeting research on digestive cancer. The Institut de Radium
has stressed quantitative methods and in vitro test methods. Other science
agencies followed suit,[67] in fulfillment of the government's 1977 decision to
give a high priority to research on ecological and health effects, particularly
those of a long-term nature, and to food toxicology.[68]

In Britain, the Medical Research Council supports work in fields related to
carcinogenicity in five of its own laboratories.[69] Following a general reform of
British science policy in the early 1970s, part of MRC's resources come under
the control of other governmental departments to meet practical policy
needs.[70] But in the area of health effects research, at least, the reform has
brought few apparent changes. Although the Department of Health and Social
Security (DHSS) is a major funder of MRC research, officials most closely
involved with the hazard-assessment activities of that department concede
that they exert little influence over MRC activities.[71] In reviewing the progress
of a similar kind of policy arrangement, a joint committee of the agricultural
ministry and the Agricultural Research Council in 1977 deplored the low level
of food-related R & D and recommended specifically that research on food
toxicology and testing methods be reinforced.[72]

In Germany, the Deutsche Forschungsgemeinschaft plays a central role in
the support of the natural, biomedical, and engineering sciences and the
humanities. Besides funding unsolicited proposals, the DFG devotes about
one-half of its budget to priority programs, some of which are related to the

---

Plan (Washington, D.C.: DHHS, 1984). In FY 1983, NCI's chemical testing program was
transferred integrally to NIEHS, which has taken the lead role in administering the National
Toxicology Program.

[67] See *Projet de loi de finances, document annexe, La recherche scientifique et technique
en France,* 1975, 1976, 1977, 1978, 1979.

[68] Délégation Générale à la Recherche Scientifique et Technique, *Schéma directeur de la
recherche* (Paris: La Documentation Française, 1977).

[69] European Medical Research Councils, *Collaborative Research in Toxicology* (Stock-
holm: Goteborgs offsetryckeri, 1976); MRC, *Annual Report, 1977–78* (London: HMSO,
1978).

[70] See Philip Gummett, *Scientists in Whitehall* (Manchester: Manchester University Press,
1980), for a description of these reforms.

[71] Interviews, DHSS, London, July 1980.

[72] Joint Consultative Organization for Research and Development in Agriculture and Food,
Third Report, 1976–1977 (London: HMSO, 1977), p. 77, and preceding reports.

organization's role as governmental adviser (see chapter 7). These have included programs on occupational health hazards, on toxicity mechanisms of foreign substances, and on the analysis of n-nitroso compounds. Other programs give preferential support to specialized institutes, including those in the fields of teratology, general cancer research, and cell membrance research, or provide start-up funding to such interdisciplinary centers as the Central Laboratory of Mutagenic Testing.[73] Another research body, the Max-Planck Gesellschaft, supports mostly basic research through the maintenance of its own specialized laboratories, including those in molecular genetics and cell biology. In contrast, the Frauenhofer Gesellschaft, an association financed by grants from government, donations, and industry contracts, has a more applied mission. Among its twenty-three laboratories, the Institute for Aerobiology has taken the lead in toxicology, with a staff of about one hundred involved in research on asbestos, cadmium, and diesel fuel emissions, among other topics.[74] Finally, the Federal Ministry for Research and Technology has played an important role in implementing the government's overall R & D priority programs, which included, under the Social Democrat government in the late 1970s, the areas of health, nutrition, environmental engineering, and the "humanization of the working environment"—all of which helped to infuse new funds into research of general relevance to the control of hazardous chemicals.[75]

Contrasting Uses of R & D in Regulation: Toward an Explanation

All three European governments, in sum, have followed the American lead in increasing their support for research into chemical carcinogenesis, cancer epidemiology, and toxicology, and into health and environmental protection generally. In the long term, many of their programs may yield important results that will bear on regulatory responsibilities or otherwise reduce the incidence of cancer. But the governments of Britain, France, and Germany have stopped far short of developing, whether under the auspices of regula-

[73]DFG, *DFG Programme und Projekte, 1979*, and *DFG Tätigkeitsbericht, 1979* (Bonn: DFG, 1979).

[74]*International Environmental Law Reporter,* November 7, 1979. The institute announced a sizeable expansion to meet the expected rise in demand through implementation of the Chemicals Law.

[75]Bundesministerium für Forschung und Technologie, *Sixth Report of the Federal Government on Research* (Bonn: BMFT, 1980). In 1980 the ministry announced a collaborative program with NCI. See Steven J. Fitzsimmons, "International Science and Technology Arrangements in the Federal Republic of Germany and the European Common Market: Recent Developments and the Potential for Future Collaboration with the United States," Report to NSF, Abt Associates, Cambridge, Mass., October 1981.

tory agencies or of research agencies, a comprehensive R & D effort tied to immediate regulatory needs. In particular, all have refrained from launching a systematic testing program on carcinogenesis and other chronic effects.

This significant contrast to American practices reflects, at bottom, a different conception of public regulatory responsibility and the proper role of public-sponsored R & D in meeting social goals. At least throughout the 1970s, the dominant view in the United States was that major threats are still apt to be discovered in the thousands of substances that have not yet been thoroughly studied, that such discoveries are not likely to be made spontaneously and in a timely and reliable manner by undirected science or industry, and that current methods and knowledge provide an adequate, albeit imperfect, indication of risk. The dominant European conception sees the relationship of carcinogens research and regulation in a quite different light. This view holds that investments in carcinogenic testing and many other kinds of safety evaluation research cannot always be justified as a research policy decision, since current methodologies and approaches do not yield results whose contribution to the advancement of knowledge is commensurate with their cost. As a regulatory policy decision, in turn, such investments are often unwarranted, either because results are too uncertain to permit their systematic incorporation in safety evaluation, or because their financing is not regarded as the proper responsibility of government.

For the most part, these contrasting conceptions do not originate within the research system itself. Scientists in Europe and the United States tend to follow similar instincts and interests. Many European scientists, for example, express reluctance to embark on an ambitious and expensive testing program as long as the underlying assumptions and methodologies of carcinogenic risk assessment remain uncertain. But such views have also been voiced in the United States. Joshua Lederberg, a former member of the National Cancer Advisory Board, has stated that "the one or two or three hundred million dollars a year that we're now spending on routine animal tests are almost worthless from the point of view of standard-setting."[76] He has advocated less immediately practical work and more fundamental research in comparative toxicology in order to make better predictions about the effects of animal carcinogenicity in man. In the United States, such opinions have helped to broaden research programs into the mechanisms and conditions of carcinogenic activity. But in Europe, they tend to reinforce the reluctance of scientists and administrators to embark on a program of toxicological data accumulation. (They do not, however, preclude the examination of testing results when these are generated under other auspices.)

A large part of the explanation for these varying outcomes lies in the

[76] Joshua Lederberg, "A Challenge for Toxologists," *Chemical and Engineering News,* March 2, 1981.

institutional context that links scientists to political processes, including the nature of political control over R & D policy. The institutional history of NCI strongly indicates that it would not have developed a carcinogenicity testing and research program on the scale it has without the persistent prodding of U.S. legislators, for whom cancer research has long been a popular mission. When the quest for a cancer cure proved more elusive than envisaged and public opinion became alarmed about environmental causes in the mid-1970s, the dynamics of American science policy making quickly translated these factors into a reordering of NCI priorities.

But in Europe, science policy is aligned more closely with the spontaneous and slow-moving reorientations within the scientific community itself, with political control, especially from the legislature, playing much less of a role in setting research objectives. As noted earlier, the European scientific community has never accorded a high priority to experimental toxicology, and work on chemical carcinogenesis has not been favored in cancer research programs. European scientists show in particular a marked disinclination to engage in routine cancer testing.[77] One prominent toxicologist in Britain, for example, commented that a shift in his government's funding toward safety testing would be strongly resisted and, if effected, would result in the departure of many from the field.[78] Meeting such resistance from their primary constituency and little countervailing pressure from their political overseers, European R & D agencies have been able to maintain and even increase support for general programs of environmental health research without having to give these programs a strong applied dimension.

The relative availability of resources helps to reinforce these contrasting research orientations. Scientists everywhere are especially opposed to applied work when funds must be taken from more challenging fundamental research. Operating on more limited budgets than the comparatively well-heeled NIH network or U.S. regulatory agencies, European scientists and administrators feel that large-scale testing is beyond their means. These attitudes are consistent with the widespread belief that testing, when indispensable for regulatory purposes, should be the responsibility of private industry having a commercial interest in the substance. Accordingly, the European governmental role in testing is largely confined to studying the health effects of substances, such as mycotoxins, that have no apparent industrial sponsor, a criterion that is not especially prominent in the American selection process.[79]

---

[77] Even NCI has had difficulty staffing its bioassay program because of its limited appeal to the scientific community. See GAO, "Federal Efforts."

[78] Interview, August 1980.

[79] The question arises whether European industry is performing, either in response to governmental demands or on its own initiative, more testing than American industry per-

These variable practices in R & D policy go hand in hand with the differences in priority, first noted in chapter 2, placed by the four governments on old and new chemical substances in general and on carcinogens in particular. Just as American lawmakers and administrators tend to take a comprehensive view of the potential for harm of all chemicals and have singled out for special attention those that can cause cancer, so they have deployed a significant portion of their R & D resources to identify and measure the magnitude of carcinogenic risk stemming from a large universe of candidate substances. European authorities, in contrast, have from the start reduced the scope of their regulatory objectives, devoting most of their attention to new chemicals and new chemical uses, and have seldom given carcinogens special priority. Defining their responsibility for protecting the public in less global terms, these officials appear to perceive less justification for spending large sums to determine the extent of the cancer threat from the thousands of chemicals in common usage.[80]

Less oriented toward the detection or elucidation of chemical hazards, environmental R & D programs in Europe give relatively more attention to the search for better technological controls, analytical methods, and monitoring devices. In effect, these research efforts either assist industry in making its activities and developments less dangerous or improve the detection and monitoring of harm. European programs of public R & D, in other words, tend to document the extent of industry's transgressions and to help alleviate them, while U.S. programs are conceived more to increase the store of knowledge that may eventually be used—subject to prevailing political winds—to substantiate the government's case for taking regulatory action. The orientation of public R & D is thus another reflection of the contrast in the relationship of government and industry that differentiates European and American approaches to regulation in general.

Finally, one cannot overlook the possibility that European governments carry a lighter burden in funding policy-relevant R & D simply because the U.S. government is doing so much of the work for them. The American government, with its considerable expenditures on chemical hazards research, clearly subsidizes the public risk assessment activities of the rest of

---

forms. In the absence of hard data, no firm answer can be given. But it is clear that European industry has not followed the lead of U.S. industry in establishing collaborative testing centers such as the Chemical Industry Institute of Toxicology (CIIT), founded in 1974 by thirty-five American firms with an initial investment of $14 million. CMA also sponsors cooperative testing, unlike its European counterparts. Despite some joint work by the larger European firms (for example, for Maltoni's work on vinyl chloride and more recent work on ethylene oxide), the larger effort of U.S. companies may reflect a greater need to anticipate, with scientific evidence in hand, regulatory action against high-volume existing chemicals.

[80] Among the three European governments, the Germans have expressed the strongest interest in a more intensive research effort on existing chemical hazards.

the world. The use of American-sponsored studies has become commonplace in the regulatory processes of the three European governments over the past several years. Although European scientists and administrators do not always reach the same conclusions about the significance of the findings (see chapter 8), they are well aware of their dependency on American hazard assessment data, particularly data on existing substances. Since American authorities presumably believe that they reap their own sufficient rewards from their investments, the situation presents a classic case of the "free rider" phenomenon—even if many Europeans, not anxious to hear bad news, may sometimes be unwilling passengers (see chapter 11).

Research and Regulatory Outcomes

The preceding analysis argued that, for reasons having mainly to do with institutional context, the production of the scientific base for regulation in the United States and in the European countries takes on quite different dimensions and forms. The question now becomes: To what extent and how are these clear contrasts in the role of public R & D affecting actual regulatory strategies and outcomes? We shall argue that cross-national differences in impact are not nearly as great as the observed cross-national differences in R & D policy would suggest.

In the United States, the large sums and presumably large hopes invested in public research on chemical carcinogenesis have not produced a similarly large effect on regulatory outcomes. There are surprisingly few instances where results from the extensive federal testing programs have exerted a decisive influence on the regulatory agenda. A more typical outcome is for research results to enter the general pool of scientific knowledge and remain in relative obscurity until the study is seized on by a concerned public or draws official attention on other grounds.[81] Even a cursory comparison of the many known or suspected carcinogens studied by NCI, NIOSH, or the regulatory agencies themselves with the amount of actual regulatory output indicates how far apart are the worlds of public research and public regulation.[82]

---

[81] See Devra Lee Davis et al., "Basic Science Forcing Laws and Regulatory Case Studies: Kepone, DBCP, Halothane, Hexane, and Carbaryl" (Washington, D.C.: Environmental Law Institute, 1980).

[82] The regulatory history of DBCP (Dibromochloropropane) provides a revealing case study of this pattern. Following some evidence of toxic effects accumulated in the 1950s and 1960s, NCI selected DBCP for carcinogenicity testing in 1968. The first results were published in 1973, indicating carcinogenic potential, but the effects of the chemical on fertility were not emphasized. FDA, EPA, and OSHA, each having potential jurisdiction over the chemical in different kinds of exposure, did not take action until EPA targeted the substance for RPAR review in 1976. Only after the alert in August 1977 by the Occidental Chemical Company that DBCP induced sterility in workers did EPA and OSHA take concrete preven-

There are several reasons for this lack of impact. Few studies, particularly long-term animal bioassays, provide conclusive evidence of the existence and magnitude of risk. They can usually be cited to show as much the need for additional research as the need for immediate regulatory action. Those instances (saccharin, nitrites, Love Canal, and formaldehyde are recent examples) where regulators have taken action on the basis of preliminary or questionable scientific results, only to come under intense political fire or be overruled in the courts, have reinforced the cautious incorporation of R & D findings into decision making.[83]

More broadly, the relevance of R & D programs to regulation falls victim to the vast and complex difficulties inherent to both R & D and regulation. In view of the large number of potential candidates for assessment and the multiple parameters of testing systems, even the NCI/NTP program can appear small in scale. On the control side, as observed in previous chapters, the efforts of U.S. regulatory agencies to address the problems of carcinogens have been handicapped by the intrinsic uncertainties of hazard assessment, the magnitude of the task, and a thicket of procedural requirements. When programs of public research and public regulation are overloaded by their respective assignments, the likely points of effective intersection become few indeed.

Additional constraints are institutional in nature. Different constituency and oversight pressures on the scientific agencies limit their responsiveness to the research demands of regulators. Research institutions of all kinds, but particularly those within a governmental bureaucracy, tend to build up program inertia that limits their adaptability to shifting regulatory needs. Moreover, research projects generally operate on a different timetable from that of regulatory processes. It takes three to five years, for example, to conduct an animal bioassay and evaluate its results. While decision making on a chemical hazard can take at least that long, the critical points where knowledge is most useful do not always coincide with the availability of results.

---

tive measures. See Francine Pollack, "Federal Regulation of Toxic Substances: The Case of DBCP" (Master's thesis, Department of Technology and Human Affairs, Washington University, St. Louis, Missouri, 1979). For other case studies, see Robert W. Crandell and Lester B. Lave, eds., *The Scientific Basis of Health and Safety Regulation* (Washington, D.C.: Brookings Institution, 1981), and Davis et al., op. cit. A more recent example is ethylene dibromide. See *Washington Post,* February 14, 1984.

[83]Once the agency decides to intervene—often in response to an external crisis or to political pressure—and seeks scientific backing for its actions, however, the instrumental value of R & D can gain considerably. Much of the R & D program of EPA is directed to filling in scientific and technical gaps pertaining to proposed standards and crisis situations. However, this highly focused and pragmatic work creates other problems, notably quality control and planning deficiencies. See George E. Brown, Jr., and Radford Byerly, Jr., "Research in EPA: A Congressional Point of View," *Science,* 211, (March 27, 1981), 1385–90.

Finally, regulatory authorities typically exercise considerable discretion in how they interpret and act on scientific information. If the scientific basis of regulatory action is clearly established, the relevance of a directed program of testing and research, and the regulatory impact of the results, are enhanced. The Delaney clause, for example, provided a straightforward justification for FDA's initiation of rule-making proceedings on saccharin and nitrites. Similarly, full implementation of OSHA's generic policy on occupational carcinogens would have implied a more rationally targeted R & D program having increased relevance to decision making. But as long as there are no explicit guidelines that translate the arrays of scientific evidence into various regulatory responses, the relationship of research and regulation is apt to remain indirect and tentative.

Many of the same factors impeding an effective linkage between R & D and regulation are found in the European countries, with even greater consequences. The R & D programs of European regulatory agencies are less well developed than those of the United States, while those of research-promotion agencies are more insulated both from these departments and from political control. There is a greater disinclination in Europe to formulate generic policy principles that tie regulatory action to varying arrays of scientific evidence (see chapter 2). Much public-sponsored work addresses fundamental scientific questions that have no immediate relevance to the discovery or abatement of public health hazards. The limited research funds of European regulators tend to be deployed on highly focused inquiries to clarify the effects of substances that typically are already candidates for regulatory action.

In sum, the U.S. government spends vast amounts to generate new scientific information about potential carcinogenic hazards, but this information has had limited impact on the national regulatory agenda, at least in the short term. European governments invest much smaller sums overall and devote proportionally more to fundamental areas of research that have little immediate bearing on regulatory goals. They also have access to American data when they need it. In both settings, the policy relevance of research findings often depends on whether the examined substance becomes a regulatory issue on other grounds. As a result, public-supported R & D by itself, despite great differences in levels and orientation between the United States and the three European countries, does not produce a similar divergence in regulatory performances.

Conclusion

This chapter has demonstrated the importance of distinctive national institutions and political processes where it was least expected: in the development of the scientific base of chemical risk assessment and control. While the strongly international character of scientific knowledge exerts an undeniable universalistic influence on national policies, the actual role of research in support of regulation is subject to considerable differentiation. Longstanding traditions that tie relevant fields of inquiry to different institutions and social milieus tell part of the story. But even more important are the particular needs, dynamics, and priorities of each government that fix the level and nature of sponsored research and define its uses in the regulatory arena.

Political processes in the United States produce a strong demand for scientific information in support of regulatory goals, a demand that has been met by the scientific community at considerable cost to taxpayers. But the same U.S. processes that stimulate information are less adept at exploiting it. The European governments do not show a comparable need or inclination to generate policy-relevant data. There, the public production of science tends to take on the colors of the cautious, highly incremental approach that characterizes European toxic chemicals policy in general.

7

Expertise and Decision Making

Government programs designed to control cancer-causing chemicals and other toxic substances raise complex questions that fall outside the usual areas of competence of public administrators. No government, for example, wants to regulate chemicals unless they show a high potential for inflicting harm to humans and the environment. But in many cases the evidence of harm is sketchy, based on studies of variable design and quality, and subject to interpretation according to changing assumptions and analytical judgments that are beyond the grasp of the untutored. Similarly, the effectiveness and cost of alternative control measures are difficult to estimate, and their appropriate design and application often depend on the knowledge of specialists. To aid them in dealing with such matters, regulators necessarily seek guidance from those with the requisite scientific, technical, and professional expertise.

The universal requirement for specialized knowledge in the regulation of chemicals and other advanced technologies has raised fears that the power of public decision will shift from politically accountable authorities to those who best comprehend the nature of the hazards and the means for their control.[1] The analysis presented in this chapter paints a more intricate picture. Far from paving the way to power for a corps of like-minded technocrats, the

---

[1] See David Elliot and Ruth Elliot, *The Control of Technology* (London: Wykeham, 1976), and Langdon Winner, *Autonomous Technology: Technics-out-of-Control as a Theme in Political Thought* (Cambridge, Mass.: MIT Press, 1977).

inescapably technical component of toxic chemical regulation has given rise to remarkably diverse uses of expertise across programs and countries. Governments vary in their inclination to rely on expertise generally, and on various kinds of experts specifically, in their programs of toxic chemical control. They draw experts into their regulatory processes through different institutional means, and they juxtapose in different ways the views of scientists and other professionals with the articulation of more partisan interests.

Governmental choices along these dimensions reveal a great deal about the orientation and guiding philosophy of their regulatory programs. Their choices help shape the political debate surrounding chemical control and raise fundamental questions about the legitimacy and rationality of state action. This chapter examines how different configurations of expertise and decision making affect both the regulatory programs and the regulatory politics of the four countries. It also traces the origins of these different configurations to deeper political requirements and institutional needs peculiar to each country.

The Variable Acquisition of Expertise

The governments of France, Britain, West Germany, and the United States rely on three principal mechanisms for acquiring relevant expertise: internal agency staff supplemented by outside consultants under contract or by affiliated technical institutes; standing advisory committees; and other external sources such as professional societies and scientific academies. With a view toward identifying distinctive national patterns, the following sections examine the role of each mechanism in supplying regulatory authorities with technical information and advice.

Internal Resources

Regulatory agencies in the United States have developed large staffs of technically trained personnel to perform much of their chemical risk assessment work. The day-to-day evaluation of food additive hazards, for example, is the responsibility of the toxicology division of FDA's Bureau of Foods.[2] In the case of suspected carcinogens, other officials from inside FDA are brought in to form the Cancer Data Review Committee. A similar arrangement is found at EPA: the large numbers of toxicologists and other specialists within the Office of Pesticides and Toxic Substances are complemented by the

---

[2] Interview, FDA, Washington, D.C., November 1980. Also, GAO, "Does Nitrite Cause Cancer? Concerns about Validity of FDA-Sponsored Study Delay Answer," Washington, D.C., January 31, 1980.

agency-wide Carcinogen Assessment Group (CAG), formed in 1976 to review the evidence of carcinogenicity of chemicals considered for rule making under most EPA-administered statutes.

OSHA diverges from the pattern in that its principal source of expertise, as defined by the OSH Act, is the National Institute for Occupational Safety and Health. In addition to its research activities, NIOSH reviews data on suspected hazardous substances and makes recommendations for health and safety standards to OSHA. Criticized in its early years for its slow pace in issuing these criteria documents, the agency accelerated its program in the late 1970s; by 1978 it had proposed over one hundred occupational health standards covering more than two hundred substances, including many suspected carcinogens.[3] But NIOSH's tenuous relations with its client agency have limited the impact of its recommendations. Relatively few have been acted on, and in several cases where OSHA did take action, the proposed or promulgated standard varied from the NIOSH recommendation, often in the direction of greater leniency.[4] In recent years, OSHA has taken steps to increase its own corps of technical experts.

U.S. regulatory agencies have also built up impressive staffs trained in law, economic analysis, and planning. Lawyers have been a fixture of the newer agencies of social regulation since their creation, and a legal perspective remains prominent even at low administrative levels and at early stages of rule making. The development of an internal capability in economic analysis accelerated significantly in the mid-1970s. All three U.S. agencies now have bureaus that specialize in the economic evaluation of proposed or current regulatory measures. There are also special planning, management, and policy evaluation offices within each agency. These bureaus assist in developing goal-setting criteria and program strategies, promoting organizational efficiency, and evaluating the effectiveness of operating procedures and control measures.

Complementing the extensive expertise within the agencies is the contractual use of external consultants. In all specialized areas of relevance, U.S. agencies contract for studies and analysis from private consulting firms and other outside sources. A typical example is the contract issued by EPA in 1979 to Management Analysis, Inc., to devise a comprehensive planning approach and implementation schedule for TSCA. In the more scientific and

---

[3] James L. Perkins and Vernon E. Rose, "Occupational Health Priorities for Health Standards: The Current NIOSH Approach," *American Journal of Public Health,* 69, no. 5 (May 1979), 444–48.

[4] M. Donald Whorton and David H. Wegman, "Occupational Health Standards: What Are the Priorities?" *American Journal of Public Health,* 69, no. 5 (May 1979), 433–34; John Mendeloff, *Regulating Safety: An Economic and Political Analysis of Safety and Health Policy* (Cambridge, Mass.: MIT Press, 1979), p. 60.

technical areas, EPA's Carcinogen Assessment Group, NIOSH, and FDA have all used outside sources for preliminary risk assessments and literature searches. In 1980 alone, EPA's Office of Pesticides and Toxic Substances spent over $10 million on outside contracts covering such diverse topics as asbestos control options, chemical scoring procedures, assessment methods for toxicity tests, and environmental fate analysis.[5]

These contingents of technical experts at the reach of the agencies are such a familiar feature of U.S. regulation that their presence would not be worth acknowledging but for their almost complete absence in Europe. The three European countries show much less inclination to build up internal resources in specialized expertise. The only resident scientific staff of any size providing essential services of risk assessment is Britain's Employment Medical Advisory Service (EMAS). This corps of approximately one hundred and fifty health professionals traditionally manned the regional inspectorates of occupational medicine, and now constitutes the primary reservoir of scientific expertise for the Health and Safety Executive.[6] Dominated by industrial physicians, EMAS still specializes in clinical observations and field studies of worker injury and sickness. Until recently, it had limited expertise in the assessment of chemical risk based on experimental evidence; before 1981, for example, no staff member had had professional training in toxicology.[7]

Moreover, European regulatory bureaus do not attempt to complement their resident experts by hiring consultants. As noted in chapter 6, many European agencies do sponsor a limited amount of external research on the more technical aspects of chemical control or on the hazardous properties of targeted substances.[8] But these studies hardly match the scope and dimensions of work contracted out in the United States.

A more prevalent mode of acquiring scientific and technical expertise in Europe, particularly in Germany, is through affiliated technical institutes. Although attached to ministries with regulatory authority, these institutes typically enjoy a measure of administrative independence; they rarely make final decisions or issue rules (see chapter 4). Of the four German institutes,

---

[5] EPA, Science Advisory Board, Toxic Substances Subcommittee, internal documents.

[6] HSE, *Employment Medical Advisory Service Report, 1977–78* (London: HMSO, 1979).

[7] Interview at HSE, London, August 1980. At that time, one staff member was undergoing training in the area; HSE's capability in safety evaluation has increased to implement the chemicals notification scheme.

[8] A list of studies undertaken by private organizations for French public agencies shows that, among the three ministries of interest here, the environmental ministry made most extensive use of such arrangements. Most of the studies appear to be more in the nature of technical research not having immediate instrumental relevance to regulatory programs. "Liste des organismes à caractère privé ayant effectué au cours de l'année 1975 pour le compte de l'administration des études de quelque nature que ce soit," Paris, Imprimerie Nationale, 1976.

BGA has the best capability for chemical risk assessment, providing opinions on human health hazards to both the food additives and the pesticides regulatory programs. The role of BGA's sister institute in the area of occupational health, BAU, is less developed, owing to its more recent creation and the longstanding role of the DFG commission on hazardous substances in the workplace.

The only technical institute of a similar kind serving French programs is the Institut National de Recherche et de Sécurité, whose work in chemical risk assessment expanded following passage of the 1976 worker safety law. INRS receives and analyzes the notification files submitted to the Ministry of Labor under this law and can make regulatory recommendations.[9] A similar but more limited function is performed in Britain by the Harpenden Laboratory in the context of the voluntary pesticide clearance scheme. The small staff of this unit oversees the preliminary testing and data submissions of industry prior to their review by the competent advisory committees.[10]

Contrasts between American and European practices are even more apparent in legal and economic analysis and planning. Legal staffs in France and Britain are usually found in department-wide juridical services, and their role is confined to the final review of proposed regulations for their conformity to authorizing statutes and to standard rules of presentation. For the more important decrees in France, the Conseil d'Etat undertakes a thorough legal examination (see chapter 5). Only in Germany does the presence of legally trained civil servants in the regulatory agencies approach the levels encountered in the United States.[11] The capabilities of European agencies for economic analysis, planning, and evaluation are uniformly negligible.

With respect to other relevant technical fields, including environmental and safety engineering, food analysis, and pesticide use and monitoring, national patterns are less distinctive. What role experts in these fields have in decision making is largely a function of agency career tracks and institutional arrangements which bring field inspectors and safety technicians into positions of authority and influence at the policy-making level. In most cases, career paths are separate, although many agencies have developed mechanisms for receiving feedback from their field operatives. In Britain's Health and Safety Executive, however, an unusually large number of top administrators have risen from the ranks of the inspectorates. A similar pattern is found in the French Service of Fraud Repression and Quality Control which issues regulations on food additives and other consumer goods. Of a total staff of 1,167 in 1979, 721

[9] Interviews, INRS, Nancy, France, June 1980, and internal INRS documents.
[10] Interviews, Harpenden Laboratory, Harpenden, England, August 1980.
[11] The important role of lawyers in German public administration is noted by David P. Conradt, *The German Polity* (New York: Longman, 1978), pp. 165–68.

were inspectors and another 230 were laboratory analysts. Almost all section heads in the central office had backgrounds as one or the other.[12] In the United States, both safety engineers and occupational health specialists have been well represented on the OSHA staff.[13]

Standing Advisory Committees

Besides developing their internal staffs, hiring external consultants, and relying on affiliated technical institutes, the four governments make variable use of standing advisory committees to fulfill their needs for expert analysis. In the sixteen regulatory programs of interest here, eighteen committees play a regular advisory role. All of them have relatively stable memberships, are composed of individuals who are not regular employees of the regulating agency, and intervene more or less continuously in the assessment and control of toxic chemicals. But beyond these commonalities, there are noteworthy differences in composition, role, and influence.

With respect to composition, the eighteen committees fall roughly into four categories (see Table 1). Interdepartmental committees are composed exclusively or primarily of public officials representing other ministries and services. A second type of committee relies on independent scientists from universities or other health and scientific organizations which are not directly tied to either private interests or the regulating agency. A third type draws members from interest groups, including industry and, less systematically, public interest groups and labor. Finally, there is a category that includes committees having a more mixed composition (see Table 2).

The influence of these committees on policy is more difficult to characterize. Influence depends, essentially, on three factors: the scope of involvement (i.e., how much of the regulatory agenda is channeled through the committee), mandate (on those matters treated, the breadth of analysis and the type of output), and impact (the likelihood that committee outputs become official policy). According to these criteria, certain committees must be judged very powerful indeed.[14] They review nearly all agency programs and proposals, typically enjoy the power of initiation and unrestricted purview,

---

[12]Ministère de l'Agriculture, Direction de la Qualité, "Rapport annuel, 1979," Paris.

[13]See Steven Kelman, "Occupational Safety and Health Administration," in James Q. Wilson, ed., *The Politics of Regulation* (New York: Basic Books, 1980), pp. 236–66.

[14]The analysis of committee role and influence is based primarily on interview data. Public officials who participated on or provided administrative support to each committee were questioned about the committee's role and the likelihood that its opinions would become official policy. In most cases, several committee members were interviewed, and the opinions of other concerned parties ascertained. Documentary materials were examined for U.S. committees and, as available, for the European committees.

Composition of standing advisory committees

	Interdepartmental	Independent scientists	Interest-representation	Mixed
United States				
Food additives				
Pesticides		FIFRA Scientific Advisory Panel		
Industrial chemicals	ITC	Toxic Substances Subcommittee/Science Advisory Board	ATSAC	
Occupational health			NACOSH	
Great Britain				
Food additives		Committee on the Toxicity of Chemicals		FACC
Pesticides		Scientific Subcommittee/ACP		ACP
Industrial chemicals			ACTS	
Occupational health			ACTS	
France				
Food additives		Académie de Médecine		CSHP
Pesticides	Comité d'Homologation			Pesticides-Toxicity; Pesticides-Products
Industrial chemicals				Comité d'Evaluation de l'Ecotoxicité des Substances Chimiques
Occupational health			Comité des Substances/CSPRP	
West Germany				
Food additives				
Pesticides				
Industrial chemicals			AGA	Expert Committee
Occupational health				DFG Committee

and almost always see their recommendations adopted by their official sponsors. Three of the British committees (FACC, ACTS, and ACP) fall into this category, as does the French Comité d'Homologation des Produits Antiparasitaires à Usage Agricole et des Produits Assimilés (Authorization Committee for Agricultural Pesticides and Related Products). Having a similar impact but a shared responsibility are the two committees advising the German government on occupational health hazards.

Other committees perform more of a "gate-keeper" function. The terms of reference are usually confined to risk assessment and do not extend to standard setting. But these committees are often pivotal in determining which substances are taken up for possible regulatory action, and most can request additional testing data from industry. Included in this group are the French Comité d'Etude de la Toxicité, which reviews the safety of pesticide products before final recommendation by the authorization committee (only substances approved by the first are considered by the second), the Scientific Subcommittee of Britain's ACP, the toxicity committee advising the British FACC on food additives, and the Interagency Testing Committee, which selects chemicals for priority testing under TSCA. Another kind of committee is more properly termed a "precedent setter." Its voice is usually far from determining, yet regulators often find its recommendations politically difficult to ignore or overturn. In this category are the French CSHP in the context of food-additive regulation and the FIFRA Scientific Advisory Panel in the United States.

Finally, the role of some expert committees is either highly unpredictable or consistently marginal. With neither the effective authority nor the unquestioned prestige of the others, these sources of scientific advice often serve as political footballs; they are consulted as a tactical device by regulatory authorities either to divert political pressure or to delay taking unpalatable action, respectfully listened to without significant follow-up, cited only when their proffered opinions confirm preconceived positions, or ignored altogether. The EPA Administrator's Toxic Substances Advisory Committee (ATSAC), the Toxic Substances Subcommittee of the EPA Science Advisory Board, the National Advisory Committee on Occupational Safety and Health (NACOSH), the French Académie de Médecine, and the Comité des Substances Dangereuses (Dangerous Substances Committee) advising the French Ministry of Labor appear to fall into this category.

Viewing the constellation of advisory committees in these terms, it is possible to discern the outlines of consistent national preferences. Among the four countries, the French, followed by the British, show the strongest tendency toward interdepartmental consultation; their committees, especially the more influential ones, give prominent representation to public officials from outside the regulatory agency. Interest group participation is much more typical in

TABLE 2.
Membership of "interest-representation" and "mixed" committees

	Total number	Public officials	Industry	Public interest/ unions	Academics/ medical	Other
United States						
ATSAC	16	3 (3L)	4	3	5	1
NACOSH	12	1 (1L)	4	3	4	0
Great Britain						
ACTS	4	2 (2L)	6	4	2	0
FACC	15	2 (1L,1C)	6	1	6	0
ACP	24	14 (3L,11C)	0	0	9	1
France						
Comité des Substances/CSPRP	21	7 (7C)	5	5	2	2
CSHP	89	26 (14L,7C,5S)	6	3	46	8
Pesticides-Toxicity	30	15 (10C,5S)	4	1	9	1
Pesticides-Products	57	33 (2L,11C,20S)	15	1	5	3
Comité d'Evaluation de l'Ecotoxicité	49	29 (3L,11C,15S)	9	2	9	0
West Germany						
AGA	22	4 (4L)	9	2	2	5
DFG Committee	37	0 (4L)	14	0	19	4
Pesticides Expert Committee	—				—	—

Key: C = central agency administrators; L = local authorities, enforcement officers; S = public laboratory scientists. Industry group includes scientists working in industrial laboratories and users as well as manufacturers. "Other" column includes health, safety, and other professionals, private consultants, and those unclassified for lack of information. Composition as of 1980 (NACOSH, 1981).
Compiled from miscellaneous official documents.

European committees than in American committees, and such pluralistic forums in Europe are generally far more powerful than bodies of similar composition in the United States. Committees dominated by independent scientists are found in both the United States and Europe, but in Europe they are invariably seconded, in the same regulatory program, by another committee having a more "political" composition. In all four countries, interest group participation is most common and balanced in the area of occupational health, and least common and balanced in the area of pesticide control. Across the four regulatory sectors, British regulators seem to show the strongest deference to the opinions of their respective advisory bodies, while advisory committees in the United States are weakest on the whole.

Other Sources of Expertise

As observed in chapters 2 and 4, the United States has relied on mechanisms other than advisory committees to allow industry, public interest groups, governmental scientists, and others the opportunity to comment on relevant scientific and technical issues. The most prominent device is the administrative hearing, whereby the regulatory authority organizes inquiries on proposed rules or other issues and initiatives. In Europe, such proceedings are much less common. Only in the area of food additives has Germany relied on administrative hearings rather than on a standing advisory committee to receive the views of concerned parties on proposed regulations.[15]

The British government, in turn, has a well-known tradition of convening ad hoc commissions of inquiry on selected issues, and the practice has spilled over into toxic chemical policy. HSE, for example, organized a special panel to examine the hazards and means of control of asbestos. A more far-reaching inquiry was undertaken in the early 1970s by the Robens Committee, whose report played an influential role in the reorganization of British health and safety policy. In the United States, OSHA made a practice of organizing ad hoc advisory committees to review some of its earlier proposed standards, including the set of standards on occupational carcinogens issued in 1974. FDA has also convened, on occasion, ad hoc panels of outside experts to examine the health effects of selected additives. A more episodic and general role in toxic chemical policy has been played by high-level governmental commissions on environmental policy, which all four governments created around 1970.[16]

---

[15]This is less the exception than it appears. The hearing is a de facto standing committee, since the same private representatives tend to reappear.

[16]These are the Council on Environmental Quality in the United States, which was instrumental in developing policy that ultimately led to TSCA; the Council of Experts on Environ-

Scientific and professional societies are called on for advice most consistently in the United States and Germany. The National Academy of Sciences (NAS) in the United States and the Deutsche Forschungsgemeinschaft in the Federal Republic of Germany are the leading examples. Although they have different organizations, institutional status, and functions (NAS is an honorary scientific society, while the DFG dispenses public research funds), both give advice to their respective governments on a wide range of scientific and technical issues.

Most of NAS's considerable output of policy advice issues from the affiliated National Research Council (NRC), whose panels and commissions give large representation to experts drawn from outside the ranks of elected academy members. Over the years, NAS/NRC has addressed many issues that bear on the regulation of carcinogens and other toxic chemicals.[17] Its studies were launched either on the academy's own initiative or under contract to the government. Although the resulting reports often go beyond the strict limits of verifiable scientific analysis and make prescriptive judgments, those pertaining to carcinogens control show no consistent regulatory philosophy. No doubt this is due in part to the ad hoc, decentralized manner in which the panels are convened.

DFG commissions are less responsive to specific governmental requests and more concerned with defining the "state of the art" on general scientific and technical issues. DFG commissions pertinent to chemical safety include a panel on the testing of foreign substances in food and another on the analysis of plant protection materials.[18] The DFG commission on hazardous substances in the workplace enjoys an unusually direct and regular influence over official policy by setting recommended tolerance levels for toxic substances and listing carcinogens on a regular basis.

In Germany and the United States, and to a lesser extent in the other

mental Questions (Rat von Sachverständigen für Umweltfragen) in Germany, which, besides issuing two general reports on environmental policy, raised questions about the draft German Chemicals Law; the Royal Commission on Environmental Pollution in the United Kingdom, whose reports have occasionally addressed toxic chemical issues; and the Haut Comité de l'Environnement in France, which, among the three European commissions, appears least publicly visible and influential.

[17] NAS/NRC reports of relevance include a 1959 report on the evaluation of carcinogenic hazards from food additives, and several assessments of the hazards associated with specific substances (red dye no. 2, cyclamates, saccharin, chlordane, kepone, mirex, agent orange, benzene, arsenic, etc.). More recently, the organization has studied mutagenic risk, nitrites, and procedures of chemical selection for NTP. In 1976 NAS began publication of a nine-volume analysis of decision making in EPA. See NAS/NRC, *Decision Making in the Environmental Protection Agency*, vols. 1–9 (Washington, D.C.: NAS, 1976–77). Volume 7 covers the area of pesticides.

[18] DFG, *Tätigkeitsbericht* (Bonn: DFG, 1978), p. 142.

countries, professional societies have intervened on specific aspects of chemical regulation. The Association of German Engineers (Verein Deutscher Ingenieure), the German Committee on Standards (Deutscher Normenausschuss), and the technical inspection associations exercise important technical responsibilities. In the United States, a prominent voice in the field of occupational health has for years been the private American Conference of Governmental Industrial Hygienists (ACGIH). Created in 1938 by a group of federal, state, and local employees and associations as an unofficial body in order to avoid the restrictions and pressures placed on governmental agencies, ACGIH issued its first list of threshold limit values (TLVs) in 1946.[19] The ACGIH lists, periodically revised, have come to have considerable influence in the United States and abroad; for example, they are regularly published as recommendations by the British and French worker protection services. Shortly after its creation, OSHA promulgated many of ACGIH's values into law, and some of these remain in effect.[20] Mention can also be made of the Federation of American Societies for Experimental Biology (FASEB), which, at FDA's request, reviews the safety of substances "generally regarded as safe."

Impact on Regulatory Policy and Politics

Our review of the sources and mechanisms of expert intervention in toxic chemical regulation reveals some recurring and noteworthy national practices. U.S. regulatory institutions show greater recourse to expertise of all types. Parallel to their observed tendency to spend large sums on research, U.S. agencies show a strong inclination to build up their resources in expert analysis through civil service recruitment and by engaging the services of outside consultants. Official sources of expertise in the European countries are more typically concentrated in standing advisory committees, although affiliated or internal technical services play an important role in Germany and in worker safety programs elsewhere. Compared to similar bodies in the United States, European advisory structures and other institutionalized sources of analysis outside the regulatory agencies tend to enjoy a more influential, comprehensive, and continuous voice in decision making. The British make fullest use of standing committees and ad hoc commissions of inquiry, while German authorities show particular deference to established professional and scientific organizations.

---

[19] Edward J. Calabrese, *Methodological Approaches to Deriving Environmental and Occupational Health Standards* (New York: John Wiley and Sons, 1978), pp. 214–18.
[20] Ibid., p. 220.

The identification of these national patterns encourages two paths of inquiry: What consequences do they have for regulatory policy and politics? And what leads governments to adopt one format over another? In this and the following sections, we examine first the policy implications and then the origins of the variable uses of expertise in regulation.

Expertise and Policy Choice

Different kinds of experts clearly do not intervene in the regulatory process in the same way or with the same perspectives. They bring with them different methods of analysis, particular conceptions of what is important and worthy of emphasis, and often divergent views on the "right" way to proceed.[21] Accordingly, the design and outcomes of regulatory programs can be influenced by which experts play central roles and which are relegated to the sidelines. The contrasting uses of different kinds of experts in chemical control programs across the four countries establish a framework for exploring policy impacts.

A comparison of worker safety programs offers a particularly fruitful starting point. According to one scholar, the ideology of the occupational safety and health professionals who dominate OSHA's staff is the most important determinant of agency decision making.[22] Through selective recruitment into the profession, subsequent socialization, and the prevailing system of career rewards, industrial physicians and hygienists tend to equate performance with protection. A professional orientation placing the highest value on the reduction of risk to workers will favor stricter standards and more enforceable control instruments over less stringent or uncertain directives. In comparing OSHA with the Swedish agency of worker protection, Steven Kelman attributes the similarity of adopted standards to the presence of like-minded professionals on each staff.[23]

Extending the analysis to France, Britain, and West Germany, however, one finds a less clear-cut pattern. In France, for example, industrial physicians and hygienists play a central role in worker health policy. But unlike similar professionals in the United States, where strict numerical standards setting limits of tolerated exposure are the preferred control measure, the French have stressed the obligatory provision of medical care and surveil-

---

[21] For general discussion, see Duncan Macrae, Jr., "Technical Communities and Political Choice," *Minerva,* 14, no. 2 (Summer 1976), 169–90.

[22] Kelman, op. cit.

[23] See Steven Kelman, *Regulating America, Regulating Sweden: A Comparative Study of Occupational Safety and Health Policy* (Cambridge, Mass.: MIT Press, 1981), pp. 54–62.

lance of workers. According to some observers, French industrial health specialists have actually hindered the use of threshold limit values as a control measure, as this would reduce their status and influence relative to safety engineers and work inspectors.[24]

The same situation does not arise in Britain, where the medical professionals of EMAS share policy-making influence in HSE with those having backgrounds in the technical inspectorates. This arrangement has given EMAS a less comprehensive role in standard setting than that played by its French or American counterparts, and its influence centers more on risk assessment. In this area, however, EMAS's strength in industrial medicine has probably affected organizational strategy in other ways. Its clinical focus and lack of expertise in experimental toxicology are in line with its parent agency's tendency to downgrade carcinogenic risk identification and assessment in favor of other health effects and safety issues. EMAS's professional orientation also conforms to the agency's strong reliance on workplace health statistics and clinical observations, rather than laboratory studies, in its research programs and hazard evaluations.

In Germany, the more recent build-up of occupational medicine in the worker health program has not given industrial physicians the same leverage over policy that they enjoy elsewhere. Unlike in the British and French programs, the internal weaknesses of the German labor ministry in relevant expertise have long been compensated for by reliance on an external source, in the form of the DFG committee on workplace hazards, whose familiarity with the nuances of chemical risk assessment has in turn helped to give carcinogens an official prominence that they lack elsewhere in Europe.

The role of safety engineers in OSHA has been similarly linked to a preference for engineering controls over personal protective equipment as a means to limit exposure.[25] Protective equipment, although usually cheaper than engineering controls, causes worker discomfort and is more difficult to inspect in monitoring compliance. Moreover, according to this interpretation, its use runs counter to the professional image of the safety engineer.[26] But the argument receives little support in the three European countries. There, personal protective equipment and hygienic practices figure prominently as required control measures, but the policy-making role of safety engineers and other technically trained personnel appears, if anything, even greater than it is in OSHA.

---

[24] This point was made by an official in the French labor ministry (interview, Paris, July 1980). See also M. C. Amoudrou, "La notion de valeur limite de concentration," Note no. 928–77–74, INRS, Paris, 1974.

[25] Kelman, "Occupational Safety."

[26] Ibid., p. 252.

In his review of OSHA up to 1976, Nicholas Ashford argues that the higher number of safety-oriented compliance officers, compared to industrial hygienists, on the agency staff (759 compared to 174 in 1975) contributed to a "safety bias" in agency orientation.[27] If such a bias can be observed in the relative number of safety and health standards issued during the agency's early years, the emphasis noticeably shifted after 1976. The agency's preoccupation with health hazards from 1977 on was most evident in its efforts to formulate a comprehensive policy for occupational carcinogens. An important factor in this shift was no doubt the professional background of Eula Bingham, assistant secretary of labor for occupational safety and health during the Carter administration and a former professor of environmental health.

In Britain's HSE and the French agency handling food additive regulations, there is further evidence of the policy influence of technical specialists. In the British case, the significant policy-making role of former inspectors, who have intimate acquaintance with plant operations and compliance difficulties, has no doubt reinforced the agency's choice of best practicable technology as a preferred control instrument, an overriding concern with compliance feasibility, an avoidance of strict, obligatory standards in favor of flexible recommendations that can be negotiated with individual firms, and a predilection for phasing in requirements.

In the case of the French Service of Fraud Repression, the dominating role of the technical corps is seen both in agency style and in the substance of rules. In-house expertise lies in the technicalities of enforcement, forcing the service to rely exclusively on external advisory committees (CSHP and the pesticide toxicity committee) for the evaluation of risk. The role of the central staff in this situation, like that of the pesticide registration and chemical notification authorities in France, remains essentially administrative. Within the agency itself, there are no professionals capable of handling the subtleties of hazard assessment and tracking the international scientific literature on existing chemicals; the prevailing perspective is one of routinely processing new industry applications. Largely oriented toward monitoring product quality, the service also shows a preference for the drafting of regulatory statutes whose technical specificity facilitates the enforcement efforts of its inspectors and laboratory technicians.[28]

The role of legal expertise in the regulatory programs of the four countries largely derives from the variable status of law and the courts. Legally trained

---

[27] Nicholas A. Ashford, *Crisis in the Workplace* (Cambridge, Mass.: MIT Press, 1976), pp. 460–62.

[28] See M. Belot, "Problèmes internes de contrôle des additifs," Service de la Repression des Fraudes et du Contrôle de la Qualité, Centre National des Stages de Formation et de Perfectionnement, Cycle d'Etude sur les Additifs, Strasbourg, France, November 30–December 4, 1970.

specialists everywhere are responsible for making laws and regulations conform to broader constitutional and legal requirements. The question is whether their relative presence or absence in centers of decision making has a detectable impact on other policy choices. According to some analysts, the American penchant for the "command-and-control" approach to regulation—that is, the setting of precise, obligatory standards and detailed procedures covering every contingency—reflects the prominence of lawyers at every stage in U.S. regulatory policy making.[29] The argument receives some cross-national support in that West Germany, where lawyers are similarly visible in public administration, most closely matches the United States in its preference for numerical standards and precise rules.

Other factors, however, limit the persuasiveness of the argument. Just as the heavy recruitment of lawyers in the United States responds to the extensive needs of federal regulatory agencies to establish the legality of their actions, so does the "command-and-control" approach to regulation facilitate the agency's efforts to delimit and justify its regulatory role. In other words, both the presence of lawyers and a legalistic approach to regulation derive, at least in part, from the same underlying cause: the constitutional basis of the American (and, to a lesser extent, the German) policy that relies on law to bind the separate branches of government and to define the federal government's role vis-à-vis the states and private citizens. Lawrence Bacow cites other reasons for the approach in the United States: the public's demand for immediate action, the American tendency to believe in technological fixes amenable to legal prescription, and compliance costs that are less visible in standard-setting than they are in taxes and other incentives.[30]

The analysis of the regulatory impact of economic expertise must be even more one-sided since, as we have seen, it is only in the United States that such skills have regularly been brought to bear on decision making. In this case, the actual policy influence of economists remains somewhat conjectural. By gathering and synthesizing relevant information for decision makers, economic studies have undoubtedly proved useful in many instances. But high-quality data are in short supply, and their interpretation often depends critically on unproven or controversial assumptions such as the economic value of good health or the value of the discount rate.[31] These limitations, which often are more transparent to the layman than are deficiencies in scientific assessments of risk, help to undermine the credibility of results. The

[29] See, for example, Lawrence S. Bacow, *Bargaining for Job Safety and Health* (Cambridge, Mass.: MIT Press, 1980).

[30] Ibid.

[31] See Peter Self, *Econocrats and the Policy Process: The Politics and Philosophy of Cost-Benefit Analysis* (Boulder, Colo.: Westview Press, 1977); and Michael S. Baram, "Cost-Benefit Analysis: An Inadequate Basis for Health, Safety, and Environmental Regulatory Decisionmaking," *Ecology Law Quarterly*, 8 (1980), 473–531.

impact of economic analysis is also constrained by the fact that American regulatory policy usually stops short of indicating specific economic thresholds to trigger regulatory responses. In the absence of such guideposts, U.S. authorities must show only that economic costs and benefits have been considered and that benefits are in some reasonable relationship to costs. They need not demonstrate that their actions are dictated by the figures. Despite these limitations, the increasing importance given to the weighing of costs and benefits in U.S. regulation has undoubtedly enhanced the policy influence of those who master the only available calculus for reducing disparate and far-ranging impacts of risk and benefit to a single evaluative framework.

In Europe, the need for information and input of an economic nature has not produced the same demand for those with analytical qualifications. As observed in previous chapters, assessments of the economic impact of proposed regulatory measures tend to be ad hoc, implicit, narrow, and unsystematic. They are provided through means other than formal economic analyses: informal discussions between regulators and industry, consultation with governmental departments handling economic or industrial affairs, and representation of economic interests on advisory committees. But this more casual approach to incorporating economic factors in decision making has not, from all appearances, reduced their importance to final regulatory outcomes. If anything, the approach is more influential in that it does not strive to cloak the assumptions and interests implicit in such analyses in the mantle of rationalistic objectivity.

The impact of management planning and evaluation on regulatory processes and decisions is similarly difficult to characterize. While the United States has deployed far greater resources to achieve a coherent organization and management of its regulatory programs, it is also in the United States that agencies are most persistently criticized for deficiencies in this regard.[32] From a cross-national perspective, the interesting point is not the impact of such analysis in the United States but the ostensibly greater need for it in the first place.

In summary, the relative prominence of one type of expert or another in regulatory processes does exert some influence on policy choice. The impact is most noticeable in the setting of priorities and in the choice of control instruments. With respect to priorities, the dominant role of clinically oriented professionals in some of the worker protection services seems to hinder a more aggressive policy on carcinogen identification and assessment and tends to foster a wait-and-see stance with respect to existing chemical

[32] See, for example, GAO, "EPA Is Slow to Carry Out Its Responsibility to Control Harmful Chemicals," Washington, D.C., GPO, 1980; GAO, "Delays and Unresolved Issues Plague New Pesticide Protection Programs," Washington, D.C., GPO, 1980.

hazards. More generally, the lack of an internal agency capability in long-term risk assessment, when not compensated for by an external source having influential input into decision making, veers regulatory attention away from a continuous and exploratory analysis of human health hazards and toward a narrower and more passive posture. With respect to the choice of control instrument, the relative prominence of technical, legal, and enforcement specialists in agency headquarters is often reflected in the development of control measures that enhance the professional inclinations and areas of competence of these specialists.

Both the types of experts consulted and the institutional channels through which their advice is obtained underlie several of the cross-national differences in regulatory procedures first observed in chapter 2. The heavy reliance on internal sources of expertise and on formally commissioned studies by outside organizations under agency direction is a clear corollary to the tendency of U.S. agencies to provide a fully documented and reasoned public justification for their regulatory actions. As economic analysis became more important as a basis of decision making, U.S. agencies expanded their internal capabilities and increased their contractual arrangements with outside firms to provide these inputs. The extensive recruitment of lawyers in the United States attests to the continued importance of law as the sinew of political authority and to litigation as the privileged means of resolving disputes. In all these respects, the special nature of U.S. regulatory processes creates special demands for expertise that European processes can largely forego.

Expertise and Regulatory Politics

The policy roles of experts have become on occasion the focus of controversy and criticism. The most typical complaint is that official purveyors of technical advice are overly biased toward a particular policy orientation or partisan interest. EMAS, for example, has come under increasing attack by some of the more vocal British unions not only for the level of its efforts to uncover chemical hazards but also for deficiencies in its data-gathering and analytical methods. One union accused the service of contriving with a chemical producer to suppress data on the health effects of certain chemical substances.[33] The National Union of Agricultural and Allied Workers led a similar attack on the Advisory Committee on Pesticides, charging that its members from academia and the civil service hold "shared assumptions" with the industry interests they are charged with overseeing.[34] Elsewhere, union

---

[33] *European Chemical News,* June 30, 1980; interviews with trade union officials in the London area, July–August 1980.

[34] Interview with trade union official, London, July 1980.

leaders and public interest groups have expressed reservations about the orientation of such institutions as the National Academy of Sciences, the American Conference of Governmental Industrial Hygienists, and the DFG committee on workplace hazards.[35]

Not all charges of bias come from the advocates of stricter controls, however. In the past, the U.S. chemical industry has expressed concern that official sources of scientific expertise are too closely linked with the regulating agencies and are thus susceptible to the regulatory impulses and philosophies of public officials. The American Industrial Health Council (AIHC), speaking for a group of chemical manufacturers, has promoted the creation of a science panel that would be located within government but separate from the regulatory agencies as the best assurance that scientific inputs will be of the requisite quality and free of conflicts of interest. According to the council, "In the development of carcinogen and other federal chronic health control policies, scientific determinations should be made separate from regulatory considerations and such determinations, assessing the most probable human risks, should be made by the best scientists available following a review of all relevant data."[36] The idea of a single risk assessment panel that would have sole responsibility for assigning risks to chemicals that come under regulatory scrutiny by all federal agencies has also received attention in Congress.[37] More recently, AIHC has advocated the creation of independent peer review panels that would be attached to specific programs.

The Food Safety Council, a group composed largely of industrialists, has promoted a similar restructuring of advisory input into food-safety decision making. The council wants an expert committee that is "appropriately representative" to be given the task of setting general standards of "unacceptable risk" and "minimum benefit" and allowed to report directly to Congress.[38] A separate committee would resolve conflicts between risks and benefits in difficult cases. In the area of pesticide policy, American industry has gener-

---

[35]The strongest criticism of CSHP we heard came from an official in the French industry ministry, who thought the committee insufficiently attentive to economic factors. The British committees, in turn, are viewed with some skepticism by some environmentalists and union officials, who feel they reflect industrial concerns too much. (Interviews in Paris and London, Summer 1980.)

[36]AIHC, "AIHC Proposal for a Science Panel," Scarsdale, N.Y., March 26, 1980. Some leaders of public interest groups have also criticized the scientific staffs of some U.S. agencies (interviews 1980–81), but more on grounds of professional competence.

[37]House Committee on Agriculture, Subcommittee on Department Operations, Research, and Foreign Agriculture, *Hearing on National Science Council Act,* 97th Cong., 1st sess., June 23, 1981; H.R. 3976, Central Board of Scientific Risk Assessment Act of 1983, 98th Cong., 1st sess. The NAS has endorsed a similar proposal in its report, *Risk Assessment in the Federal Government: Managing the Process* (Washington, D.C.: National Academy Press, 1983).

[38]Food Safety Council, *Principles and Processes for Making Food Safety Decisions* (Washington, D.C.: Food Safety Council, 1980).

ally been supportive of the work of the FIFRA Scientific Advisory Panel, the most influential committee of nongovernmental experts serving any of the four areas of U.S. regulation. The National Agricultural Chemicals Association (NACA) has even proposed that the policy role of the FIFRA panel be enlarged.[39]

Judging by the relative absence of similar suggestions in Europe, it seems that chemical industries there are more comfortable with current sources and channels of official expertise. Several reasons can be advanced to account for this relative complacency. In Europe, as previously noted, the preferred mechanism for acquiring expertise is the standing advisory committee, a format that typically puts industrial experts in permanent and close contact with their academic and governmental counterparts. The participatory formats favored in the United States do not give American industry representatives the same opportunities for a meeting of minds. Similarity in outlook among public sector and private sector scientists in Europe is also fostered by the relatively smaller and more homogeneous research communities in these countries. Risk assessment practices that are firmly entrenched in Europe but less common in the United States, in particular the case-by-case approach to evaluation and a cautious use of incomplete data, generally dovetail with industry's preferences on both sides of the Atlantic. Moreover, at least through the 1970s, governmental scientists in Europe tended to advance less adventurous, safety-oriented views on controversial issues of toxic chemical evaluation than have similar officials in the United States (see chapter 8).

The tableau of official expertise facing the European chemical industries is not trouble-free, however. Some industry spokesmen in Germany and France, for example, have expressed concern that the advisory structures serving the newer programs of industrial chemical notification may be driven by ever-larger appetites for information and testing results before they reach a firm opinion. For the older European programs, this danger seems to have been averted by the close association between industrial petitioners and official advisers.[40]

Another kind of political debate concerns the types of analysis granted entry into the decision-making process. In the United States, this debate has centered in recent years on the relevance and validity of economic analysis in support of regulatory decisions. The chemical industry, among other business interests, has aggressively promoted the increased use of cost-benefit analysis and its variants.[41] Representatives of public interest groups, in contrast, have

[39] Position papers provided by the NACA, Washington, D.C., November 1980; *New York Times,* November 13, 1980.

[40] Interviews with industrialists and trade association representatives in France and Germany, Summer 1980.

[41] See, for example, Etcyl H. Blair and Fred D. Hoerger, "Risk/Benefit Analysis as Viewed

raised many questions about the value of these techniques.[42] The reasons for these divergent positions are not difficult to discern. Economic analysis uses methods of reasoning familiar to businessmen. It relies largely on data that only industry can provide. It tends to enhance the weight of quantifiable indicators of short-term, direct economic effects relative to "quality of life" consequences that are often indirect, long-term, and unquantifiable. It is apt to emphasize economic efficiency relative to other values as a policy guidepost. More extensive use of economic impact analysis—besides further delaying the rule-making process—could lead to the selection of fewer regulatory targets than would be the case if agendas were set on the basis of risk alone and could minimize the perceived significance of a particular hazard by relating it to a larger spectrum of other risks and consequences.[43] As one might expect, the political debate over the value and limitations of cost-benefit analysis intensified as the technique gained in visibility and use; in the late 1970s, its role occupied center stage in American regulatory polemics.

The value of legal analysis and planning expertise has been somewhat less controversial in the U.S. regulatory context. As a rule, public interest groups most active in toxic chemical regulation have championed a regulatory approach that prescribes in detail the respective obligations of industry and the agencies to meet publicly defined health and environmental goals. They have promoted the adoption of explicit procedural guarantees of public participation and administrative openness. But American industry, on the whole, has not taken the opposite tack and pressed for policy changes that would undermine the legalistic approach and thereby diminish the policy role of lawyers and the courts. The reasons for this stance may include industry's unfamiliarity with alternative regulatory approaches, the benefits it also derives from procedural complexity and legal challenge, and the traditionally dominant role of lawyers in handling industry's relations with government.

The use of planning expertise in U.S. regulatory programs has also escaped serious polemics. Since management planning is concerned, above all, with

by the Chemical Industry," in E. Cuyler Hammond and Irving J. Selikoff, eds., *Public Control of Environmental Health Hazards,* Annals of the New York Academy of Sciences, vol. 329 (1979), pp. 253–63.

[42] See Mark J. Green and Norman Waitzman, "Business War on the Law: An Analysis of the Benefits of Federal Health/Safety Enforcement," Corporate Accountability Research Group, Washington, D.C., 1979; and Mark J. Green, "Cost-Benefit Analysis as a Mirage," in Timothy B. Clark, Marvin H. Kosters, and James C. Miller III, eds., *Reforming Regulation* (Washington, D.C.: American Enterprise Institute, 1980), pp. 113–16.

[43] For a more extensive treatment of the role of economic thinking in regulation, see Steven Kelman, *What Price Incentives?* (Boston: Auburn House, 1981).

organizational efficiency, it can be (and has been) marshalled to serve the interests of both those who press for tighter rules and those who advocate their relaxation or elimination.

The strong American penchant for expert analysis of all types has given rise to another criticism, once again having no parallel in the European countries. Several observers have called U.S. regulatory agencies to task for their tendency to "overanalyze," to identify and peruse every study on and facet of a scientific issue. A GAO report on EPA's test rule program under TSCA stated that agency policy was to review 95 percent of all published material on a chemical, going back as far as thirty to fifty years, and to explore all possible health and environmental effects.[44] According to the Administrator's Toxic Substances Advisory Committee, such a "search for perfection in a proposed rule is not only unnecessary from a scientific standpoint, but it actually frustrates the accomplishment of the Act's objectives."[45]

American practices in this regard contrast sharply with European procedures. In one year, for example, the French Pesticide Authorization Committee, meeting just five times, examined 1,546 applications that involved minimal staff preparation and analysis. The toxicity committee serving the same program examined in the same year 33 files on new products or new uses.[46] The Ecotoxicity Evaluation Committee, charged with reviewing the notifications of new industrial chemicals for the environmental ministry, was expected to process without difficulty between 50 and 100 files a year. Clearly, French procedures, like the German and British, do not require the kind of thorough, heavily documented risk assessments that have come to characterize American evaluations. Whether or not this practice comes at the expense of professional rigor cannot be ascertained with the evidence at hand. But at least in terms of their credibility in the eyes of competent national observers, official European assessments appear no less consistent, coherent, or scientifically reasoned than those arrived at following U.S. procedures.[47]

What is most striking when the nature of the political debate surrounding the relationship of expertise to regulation in the four countries is reviewed is

[44] GAO, "EPA Is Slow."

[45] EPA, ATSAC, "Four-Year Report on the Implementation of the Toxic Substance Control Act," November 17, 1980. The EPA administration, in reply, defended this practice in order to reduce the grounds of subsequent challenge. See EPA, "Response to the ATSAC Four-Year Report on TSCA Implementation," November 18, 1980.

[46] Ministère de l'Agriculture, Direction de la Qualité, "Rapport annuel, 1978," Paris.

[47] When a regulatory matter becomes controversial in Europe—when, in other words, the probability and political costs of making a "wrong" decision increase—European officials also show more inclination to bolster their position with analytical and scientific underpinnings. This has occurred, for example, in both Germany and the United Kingdom with respect to both asbestos and 2,4,5-T. In each case, public controversy was countered by the official publication of well-documented scientific reports.

the absence of challenge to the role of experts per se. The focus of controversy has been on which experts are consulted and how they are consulted—but that experts have a legitimate role to play seems everywhere acknowledged. The finding is at odds with the argument against technocratic decision making, which holds that those who have specialized skills and knowledge will come to exert undue influence at the expense of elected or politically accountable authorities.

The reasons the fears of technocracy have not done more to mobilize dissent in the comparative politics of chemical regulation must be differentiated according to the peculiar way expertise merges with political processes in each of the four countries. In the United States, all parties intensely engaged in the regulatory debate can be relatively complacent about the policy role of experts because the American political process is structured to demonstrate that decisions ultimately rest with political authority. With well-developed capabilities to counter the arguments of opponents and multiple opportunities for exerting pressure, U.S. interests quickly learn that expertise is a vehicle, rather than a substitute, for political persuasion. The overriding issue in the American context is not whether expertise detracts from political processes, but how it is harnessed and steered to serve some political interests over others. Suggestions for reform, such as the creation of an independent science panel, do reflect at one level a deep and perhaps uniquely American faith in the ability of science to provide rational answers to regulatory problems. But they also reflect the hope of some proponents that such changes will reorient official expert analysis more favorably toward particular objectives and viewpoints.

In the European countries, the fears of technocracy are dampened for entirely different reasons. Since the requirements for both expert opinion and political input are typically met through a representative advisory committee often playing a determining role in decision making, the most powerful European interest groups have little basis for calling the legitimacy of advisory channels into question. Even in those instances where committees are composed of "experts" per se (i.e., scientists who have no affiliation to a particular interest), one finds a complementary forum where more partisan viewpoints can be articulated.

Insofar as European channels of expertise are legitimated by their association with affected interests, one could expect that this legitimacy would be eroded whenever concerned private groups are excluded or underrepresented. This occurred, for example, in the case of the British Advisory Committee on Pesticides, whose anomalous composition in the British context gave unions powerful ammunition to contest its role and opinions. Union challenges to EMAS also reflect the frustration of labor, which seeks more influence over HSE policy on toxic chemicals. Elsewhere, the fewer inroads, compared to those made by labor, of consumer and environmental associations on official committees (see Table 2) have not, from all appearances, seriously undermined legitimacy. This is in part attributable to the generally lower credibility of these groups as political forces on the European scene, their relative inattention to issues of chemical regulation, or an organizational strategy that de-emphasizes participation on official bodies (see chapter 10).

In sum, specialized analysis, and those who can provide it, play a pivotal but variable role in the overall functioning and political dynamics of the four regulatory systems. Since different kinds of experts and institutional arrangements have detectable impact on regulatory philosophies and decisions, the policy choices defining the role of experts become themselves a focus of political conflict. Since the United States makes the most extensive use of all kinds of expertise and provides the most thorough support for its regulatory actions through formal analytical argumentation, it is also in this country where the value and credibility of various kinds and means of analytical input are most heatedly debated. In Europe, the regulatory role of expertise rarely takes on the same political overtones. Expert analysis of relevance is already provided or sanctioned by the most powerful parties to the regulatory debate, and its more extensive use or acquisition from other sources is usually regarded as unnecessary.

Preconditions of the Variable Uses of Expertise

The observed diversity in the ways expertise is brought into regulatory processes does not lend itself to simple explanation. Some choices are no doubt circumstantial and do not reflect any deeper political or institutional pattern of significance. Other factors, such as an ingrained respect for professionalism and science, derive from largely unfathomable cultural attitudes. Falling in between, however, are distinctive features of political organization and tradition that predispose the four governments toward particular configurations of expertise in their chemical control programs. This final section examines three such underlying features.

The Political Vulnerability of Decision Makers

The unusually fragmented division of political authority within the U.S. government puts administrators in an exceptionally vulnerable position. Compared to regulatory authorities in Europe, those assuming responsibility for chemical control decisions in the United States act in the knowledge that whatever their final judgment, they are apt to come under criticism and challenge. As delineated in previous chapters, these challenges come from Congress, the courts, or the political hierarchy of the executive branch—all of whom, under pressure from private interests, are able to overturn decisions or otherwise cause discomfort to the regulator. The openness of American decision making and the extensive use of adversarial proceedings increase the likelihood that any perceived weakness in the administrator's case will be fully exploited.

This high degree of political vulnerability leads American regulators to behave in distinctive ways. In particular, it encourages the use of expert analysis in reaching and justifying regulatory decisions. Lacking sufficient stature to take a binding action that would be accepted by all interests, U.S. officials must seek another basis of action and defense. One of their few alternatives is to find refuge in objective scientific analysis and professional consensus. Indeed, science, or expertise more generally, is such a necessary adjunct to the exercise of regulatory authority that decision makers cannot afford to distance themselves from it. Agencies must be capable of fending off attack from all quarters, using every scientific, economic, technical, or legal argument at their disposal. The agency staff itself, reinforced by hired consultants, becomes the primary reservoir of information and expertise on which intervention is based. One of the agency's most essential and time-consuming functions is to generate, assimilate, and package information in order to provide the strongest analytical foundation for its decision making.

Since different kinds of experts provide different kinds of rationales, the relative need for one or the other can shift according to prevailing political circumstances. At the beginning of the environmental decade, when the public demanded immediate action on health and environmental hazards and newly formed agencies were pressed to establish a firm record of performance, legal analysts, seconded by health professionals, held sway. From the mid-1970s through the early 1980s, however, a variety of developments, including inflation and recession, a more effective political strategy of industry (see chapter 9), and changes in political leadership, raised the political demand for economic analysis. Given the special relationship between expertise and decision making in the U.S. context, these political shifts were quickly reflected in new recruitment patterns on agency staffs and in contractual arrangements with outside firms.

European authorities, operating in a climate of considerably greater security, have less need to anchor their decisions in rationalistic arguments and scientific evidence. Decisions are negotiated through channels of interest group consultation where political, scientific, and economic inputs can mingle with no apparent contradiction. As a result, European regulators have little incentive to bolster the technical competence of their immediate staffs or to accompany their actions with elaborate analytical argumentation. In the same way, they can adjust to changing political realities without having to call on different kinds of experts to provide a compatible rationale.

The Role of the Civil Service

Longstanding differences in the role and status of the civil service reinforce the effects of institutional context on the acquisition of expertise. Historically, the American bureaucracy has had lower prestige and a more tenuous reputation for professionalism than the bureaucracies of the European countries. In the early years of the Republic, resistance to an established central authority helped to keep the civil service in the unenviable position of the hapless object in a political spoils system. A series of reforms designed to bring greater professional integrity into public service has not entirely dispelled the public's perception that the civil service, when it is not the mere pawn of its current political masters, performs—with considerable inefficiency—functions that are either useless or perversely meddlesome and is guided by little more than bureaucratic imperatives of self-perpetuation and aggrandizement. These perceptions are periodically reinforced by the rhetoric of politicians, many of whom find it expedient to channel the strong antigovernment strain in American political culture away from their own shortcomings.

This negative view of the bureaucracy has had the somewhat paradoxical effect of helping to bring into the civil service scientists and other experts whose qualifications can escape the taint of opportunism or incompetence. As early as the 1800s, individuals with desirable technical skills were the first to enter public administration on the strength of their abilities rather than their political affiliations; as a result, "the scientific services were the first to be developed on a nonpartisan and efficient basis."[48] In a development that paralleled the movement of technically trained personnel into management positions in the emerging private corporations,[49] many of these scientists and engineers rose to the highest ranks of appointed officialdom. Following these precedents, the reform of the civil service in the latter part of the century stressed individual merit and specialized training in recruitment and promotion. To this day, scientific training has proved to be no obstacle to attaining entry and prominence in U.S. public administration, and technical knowledge is accorded special deference in the performance of regulatory functions.

The situation is far different in the European countries. There, the legiti-

[48] Don K. Price, *Government of Science* (New York: New York University Press, 1954), pp. 1–31.
[49] See David Noble, *America by Design* (New York: Knopf, 1977).

macy of central authority been established through centuries of political tradition; indeed, perhaps more than any other institution, the stable, professional bureaucracy is identified with the "state" and the public interest. While training and routes of entry vary from one country to another (in France, the elite technical schools provide the "high road" into governmental service, while in Britain a comparable function is performed by the more humanistic-oriented universities of Oxford and Cambridge),[50] all three bureaucracies are dominated by general administrators whose authority resides more in their office and in their educational and social backgrounds than in their technical competence per se.

The effects of these varying traditions are observable in national programs of chemical control. In the United States, scientists and other experts have had easy access into the civil service and into high-level appointment, and no incompatibility is seen between technical and administrative functions. In the European bureaucracies, however, the traditional dominance of generalists has impeded the assumption of high-level responsibility by those who possess technical qualifications alone. In areas where specialized knowledge is indispensable, as in chemical regulation, institutional devices were found that supplemented rather than displaced the less formalized skills of generalists. These devices included committees made up of external, part-time advisers—the dominant format in France and Britain, where the motivation to limit administrative costs appears especially strong—and separate or subordinate technical support services, which are found in all four programs in Germany and in worker health and safety programs elsewhere.

The Association of Interest Groups in Policy Making

Another factor that has influenced how different governments conceptualize and institutionalize their needs for expert judgment in chemical regulation has to do with a more general tendency to bring major private groups into the actual process of governmental decision making. In Europe, this trend is indicated by such institutional innovations as the National Economic Development Council, the Conciliation and Arbitration Council, and the Manpower Services Commission in Britain, the Konziertierte Aktion in Germany, and the Conseil Economique et Social and various planning commissions in France. All of these bodies are policy-making or high-powered consultative mechanisms that associate business and labor with government.

Several scholars have seen a link between this development and the grow-

---

[50] See Ezra N. Suleiman, "The Myth of Technical Expertise," *Comparative Politics*, 10, no. 1 (October 1977), 137–58, for France; Philip Gummett, *Scientists in Whitehall* (Manchester: Manchester University Press, 1980), pp. 67–90, for Britain.

ing activism of Western governments, particularly in economic affairs.[51] In their view, the introduction of basic economic changes that characterize advanced capitalism, including industrial concentration and international competition, have rendered inadequate and obsolete both the traditional laissez-faire stance of government and the confinement of pressure group activity to the narrow defense of group interests. In order to legitimize their expanded role and maintain social harmony in this new economic context, public authorities have given major private interests an unprecedented, institutionalized voice in policy formulation and implementation.

For a variety of reasons, however, this "neocorporatist" trend has found less fertile soil in the United States. There, the dominant political philosophy has been liberal pluralism, whereby the appropriateness of governmental action is gauged primarily by reference to the competitive interplay of group demands.[52] The proper role of the state is not to impose its own notions of the public good, but to act as an arbiter, assuring that all claims made by individuals and groups are heard and considered, and that no group is given privileged access or the opportunity to gain ascendancy over others.

The involvement of affected interests in frameworks of chemical control, as documented in this chapter, thus reflects broader trends in the relationship between private and public spheres and impinges directly on the provision of expertise. Private interests in Europe have been intimately involved in the expansion of state authority in areas of chemical regulation, readily joining administrators in the quest for acceptable, well-informed solutions. This privileged access has not been granted to all interests, however—only to those whose claim to be a party to the "social contract" is unquestioned. Once admitted, these representatives can assume the status of "experts" without having to limit their interventions to the strictly objective.

In the United States, liberal pluralism has given birth to multiple provisions designed to give all groups the opportunity to express their demands. But the same philosophy has helped to prevent the formation of influential representative councils that would give certain groups privileged access and enhance the dangers of agency capture. As a result, external sources of expert advice that are not hired surrogates of the agency staff are kept at a distance: either they do little more than serve as a sounding board for agency actions or purely partisan viewpoints (NACOSH, ATSAC), or they must appear to conform to irreproachable standards of neutral scientific opinion (NAS, the

---

[51] For an introduction to this debate, see the series of articles edited by Philippe C. Schmitter under the title "Corporatism and Policy-Making in Contemporary Western Europe," *Comparative Political Studies,* 10, no. 1 (April 1977), entire issue.

[52] Charles W. Anderson, "Political Design and the Representation of Interests," in Schmitter, op. cit., pp. 127–51.

FIFRA Scientific Advisory Panel, and the Toxic Substances Subcommittee of the EPA Science Advisory Board).[53]

Conclusion: The Political Functions of Expertise

This chapter has examined the role that different experts play in the chemical regulatory processes of the four countries and the institutional arrangements through which specialists articulate and apply their analytical judgments. The considerable variation uncovered has been analyzed in terms of both its impact on regulatory policy and politics and its origins in underlying political organization and behavior. At the least, the analysis shows that national approaches to using expertise in chemical control are hardly uniform. Experts everywhere have gained access to the inner circles of decision making; their presence is virtually inevitable when the state assumes responsibility for chemical control. But this access has not been a Trojan horse for the imposition of universal scientific imperatives on political decision making. On the contrary, the policy role of experts has given rise to a complex array of arrangements that reflect the particular institutional needs of governments and that distinctively color their overall approach to regulation.

A more thorough assessment of the impact of expert judgment on chemical control policy must await examination of the several substantive issues in risk assessment that divide technical communities—an assignment reserved for the following chapter. At this point, however, it is possible to conclude that experts do more than simply provide their respective governments with technical skills and recondite analysis. They provide them in some fashion with plausible justification for taking authoritative action. The ways in which this is done has less to do with the variable needs of public authorities for expert opinion than it has to do with their special needs for legitimation and political support.

As Max Weber and others have observed, reason (or science), co-optation, and hierarchical authority are alternative means, short of the use of force, to exert control over others.[54] The four governments use all three means in their program of chemical regulation, but the relative weight given to each varies considerably. As a rule, Europeans rely more on the traditional authority of the state and on the inclusion of affected interests in decision making; science

[53] See Nicholas A. Ashford, "Advisory Committees in OSHA and EPA: Their Use in Regulatory Decisionmaking," *Science, Technology, and Human Values*, 9, issue 1 (Winter 1984), 72–82, for a characterization of the role of advisory committees in U.S. regulation.

[54] Aaron Wildavsky, *Speaking Truth to Power: The Art and Craft of Policy Analysis* (Boston: Little, Brown, 1979); Richard N. L. Andrews, "Values Analysis in Environmental Policy," *Policy Studies Journal*, 9, no. 3 (Winter 1980), 369–78.

is used to support rather than to displace these as a source of authority. (It is worth noting that the Germans seem to accord more deference to science itself, while the French rely somewhat more on hierarchy; the British are less consistent across programs.) But for historical and institutional reasons, American regulators are largely deprived of the legitimizing advantages of co-optation and unquestioned hierarchical authority. They therefore turn to scientific argumentation and other forms of analysis that point the way to defensible solutions and that can provide, as protection against inevitable external pressures, a rationalistic veneer to political decision making.

In the American political system, however, no source of authority is ever too great to go unchallenged. As we shall see in the next chapter, the American regulatory context provides the ideal hot-house atmosphere for the flowering of debate on virtually every weakness in the analytical rationale for or against a regulatory action. Just as the organization and processes of U.S. government lead the regulating agencies to bolster their positions with science, they also undermine science's potential for conferring legitimacy. The result is a fundamental structural conflict in the regulatory uses of expertise that serves as a powerful destabilizing force in American policy making for toxic chemical control.

8

The Politics of Scientific Uncertainty

The regulation of toxic substances offers unusually fertile ground for studying the impact of politics on the evaluation of scientific information. The process of identifying carcinogens, in particular, is fraught with uncertainties that can only be bridged through the exercise of combined scientific and political judgment. Despite decades of well-funded research, the etiology of cancer remains imperfectly understood. There is energetic debate about the role various environmental factors play in causing cancer. Since the disease does not ordinarily appear for ten or twenty years following exposure, epidemiological evidence linking cancer to specific causative agents is often scanty or inconclusive. Secondary indicators, such as positive carcinogenesis bioassays using laboratory animals, provide the only practical basis for estimating the risk of exposure to most potential carcinogens. But the assumptions underlying animal experimentation and the principles for extrapolating laboratory results to humans also remain controversial.

Though public officials and scientists in the four countries agree about the nature of the issues left unresolved by science, there is no meeting of the minds about what assumptions should control regulatory decisions when the evidence is inconclusive. Disagreements persist not only across national lines, but also among administrators, experts, and interest groups within a single country. As this chapter illustrates, these uncertainties make it possible for proponents and opponents of regulation to interpret the scientific basis for cancer risk assessment in ways that advance their particular policy objectives. The picture that emerges is a complex one. Differences of opinion on scientific issues are most clearly aligned with political ideology in the United States. Both industry and public interest groups have tried to develop coherent packages of theory, data, and inference to support their case for or against stricter control of carcinogens. At the other extreme, French scientific debate concerning carcinogens has been restricted to closed professional and policy circles, and private interest groups have not seized on expert disagreements for political advantage. Germany, too, has been fairly successful in protecting scientific debate from overt political influence, whereas in Britain there are signs that the traditionally clear distinctions between scientific and political process are beginning to break down.

Our description and analysis of these divergences is organized around three major issues: the interpretation of epidemiological evidence, the identification of carcinogens through laboratory experiments, and risk assessment. Under these headings, we describe the positions adopted by affected interest groups and public authorities in each country. We then briefly assess the impact of politics on scientific debate in one specific instance of decision making: the regulation of the herbicide 2,4,5-T. The chapter concludes by examining the institutional and procedural factors that promote aggressive political manipulation of scientific uncertainty in some countries.

Interpreting Epidemiological Evidence:
The Occupational Cancer Debate

Western scientists have known for more than two hundred years that environmental factors can play a part in inducing human cancer. However, the idea that environmentally caused cancer can be prevented by precautionary government regulation is of much more recent vintage. In 1964 an authoritative report of the World Health Organization called attention to the preventable aspects of the disease:

> The potential scope of cancer prevention is limited by the proportion of human cancers in which extrinsic factors are responsible. These include all environmental carcinogens (whether already identified or not) as well as "modifying factors" that favour neoplasia of apparently intrinsic origin (e.g., hormonal imbalances, dietary deficiencies, and metabolic defects). The types of cancer that are thus influenced, directly or indirectly, by extrinsic factors include many tumours . . . which, collectively, account for more than three-quarters of human cancers. It would seem, therefore, that the majority of cancer is potentially preventable.[1]

---

[1]WHO, *Prevention of Cancer,* Technical Report Series no. 276 (Geneva: WHO, 1964), p. 4.

Twenty years ago, when cancer treatment technologies were in their infancy and a cure for cancer was only a distant vision, this pronouncement held out hope for preventive action through regulation of the "extrinsic factors" responsible for cancer or through voluntary changes in personal habits.

Many of the external factors implicated in human cancer causation, including alcohol and tobacco consumption, diet, and patterns of sexual behavior, relate to personal choices of lifestyle and, thus, do not easily lend themselves to governmental control. There are also several categories of carcinogenic agents to which people may be involuntarily or unknowingly exposed. These include food additives, cosmetics, household products, and industrial chemicals and processes. Public regulation of carcinogens necessarily focuses on the category of "environmental," rather than "lifestyle," factors.

The increasing political pressure to regulate chemicals in recent years has tended to overemphasize the role of involuntary environmental exposures in cancer causation.[2] Lacking detailed scientific knowledge, some policy makers have at times mistakenly attributed all environmentally induced cancer to man-made chemicals. An extract from a debate in the German Bundestag illustrates this confusion:

> *Dr. Gruhl:*   Research in the United States has come to the conclusion that 60 percent of cancer incidence is to be attributed to chemical substances.
>
> *Riesenhuber:*   No, "to all environmental factors" is what the study says!
>
> *Dr. Gruhl:*   We do not have to argue about how much it is exactly. I mention it only as an indication.
>
> *Riesenhuber:*   But please cite correctly![3]

For the most part, however, politicians and policy makers recognize that chemicals represent only one of many environmental factors implicated in human carcinogenesis, and their inquiries have turned toward establishing the specific contribution of toxic substances to overall cancer incidence. Much of this effort has been directed toward ascertaining the impact of occupational exposure to carcinogens. Attempts to estimate the risk of occupational cancer have stirred up the greatest public controversy in the United States.

From the available mass of epidemiological research on cancer in the workplace, American labor organizations and the chemical industry have constructed radically different positions about the importance of occupational

---

[2] The original author of the estimate that about two-thirds of all cancers are environmentally caused, John Higginson, founding director of IARC, has called attention to what he sees as a widespread misinterpretation of his earlier observations. See "Cancer and Environment: Higginson Speaks Out," *Science,* 205, no. 4413 (1979), 1363–66.

[3] Deutscher Bundestag, Plenarprotokoll 8/225, Bonn, June 25, 1970, pp. 18192–93.

exposure to carcinogens. In general, unions and environmentalists have seized on assertions by some epidemiologists that, even after correcting for the effects of smoking and aging, cancer rates for the U.S. population as a whole are rising. These groups also point to notable increases in certain site-specific cancers as evidence of the growing impact of chemical pollution on public health. Adherents of these views predict that cancer rates will continue to rise as the effects of present exposure to environmental carcinogens gradually become apparent. The chemical industry, by contrast, sides with experts who see no significant gains in the cancer rate after adjusting for smoking and old age.

An unpublished report prepared in 1978 by the U.S. government strongly supported the view that occupational exposure is a major cause of cancer and that the impact of such exposure has been seriously underestimated in the past. It was written by well-known scientists[4] from three federal research institutions: the National Cancer Institute, the National Institute of Environmental Health Sciences, and the National Institute for Occupational Safety and Health.[5] Their analysis suggested that estimates that 20 percent of cancer is caused by occupational exposure "appear . . . reasonable, and may even be conservative."[6] Looking to the future, moreover, the report found "nothing in the gross cancer statistics for the U.S. population which is inconsistent with the hypothesis that up to 20–40 percent of all cancers are (or will be in the next several decades) attributable to occupational factors."[7]

These findings contrast sharply with estimates that occupational exposure accounts for no more than 1 to 5 percent of all cancers among industrial workers,[8] a view that was authoritatively presented in a study carried out on

---

[4]The following ten contributors were listed on the title page: K. Bridbord (NIOSH), P. Decoufle (NCI), J. Fraumeni (NCI), D. Hoel (NIEHS), R. N. Hoover (NCI), D. Rall (NIEHS, director), U. Saffiotti (NCI), M. Schneiderman (NCI), A. Upton (NCI, director), N. Day (NCI, IARC).

[5]NCI-NIEHS-NIOSH, "Estimates of the Fraction of Cancer in the United States Related to Occupational Factors," Washington, D.C., September 15, 1978.

[6]Ibid., p. 1.

[7]Ibid., p. 22.

[8]See, for example, J. Higginson, "Present Trends in Cancer Epidemiology," *Proceedings of the Canadian Cancer Congress,* 8 (1969), 40–75; J. Higginson and C. S. Muir, "The Role of Epidemiology in Elucidating the Importance of Environmental Factors in Human Cancer," *Cancer Detection and Prevention,* 1 (1976), 79–105; E. L. Wynder and G. B. Gori, "Contribution of the Environment to Cancer Incidence: An Epidemiological Exercise," Guest Editorial, *Journal of the National Cancer Institute,* 58 (1977), 825–32. The percentage of occupationally induced cancer was estimated at less than 15 percent for men and 5 percent for women by P. Cole, "Cancer and Occupation: Status and Needs of Epidemiologic Research," *Cancer,* 39 (1977), 1788–91. R. Preussmann of the German Cancer Research Center (DKFZ) has estimated that occupational exposure accounts for 1 percent of cancers in Germany. See *Umwelt,* 72 (1979), 2.

behalf of the U.S. Office of Technology Assessment by Sir Richard Doll and Richard Peto of Britain's highly regarded Imperial Cancer Research Fund.[9] Instead of focusing on individual hazardous substances, as did the authors of the 1978 NCI-NIEHS-NIOSH "estimates paper," Doll and Peto assessed the contribution of occupational factors to cancer at specific sites in the body. By using this technique, they arrived at "an estimate of approximately 4 percent with an acceptable range from 2 to 10 percent"[10] for cancers attributable to occupational exposure.

Within the scientific community, the U.S. "estimates paper" met with vociferous and widespread criticism. An editorial in *Science* dismissed the report as "flimsy."[11] Reaction in Britain was even more pronounced: Sir Richard Doll condemned the report as "scientific nonsense,"[12] and the medical journal *Lancet* commented that "it is sad to see such a fragile report under such distinguished names."[13] But in spite of these extremely negative appraisals, the "estimates paper" acquired a life of its own as a political document. The debate it generated in scientific circles provided crucial rallying points for the opposing interests involved in carcinogen regulation, particularly in the United States, where the publication of the report created a powerful rationale for OSHA's decision to develop a generic cancer policy.

The American Industrial Health Council, a task force representing some one hundred and forty chemical companies and eighty trade associations, sharply attacked the report's scientific merit.[14] In AIHC's view, the authors of the "estimates paper" were guilty of "multiple counting," that is, attributing a single case of cancer to several different chemicals.[15] AIHC claimed that projections for the future were vastly exaggerated through use of antiquated epidemiological data from studies carried out at exposure levels far higher

---

[9] Richard Doll and Richard Peto, "The Causes of Cancer: Quantitative Estimates of Avoidable Risks of Cancer in the United States Today," *Journal of the National Cancer Institute*, 66 (1981), 1191–1308.

[10] OTA, *Assessment of Technologies for Determining Cancer Risks from the Environment* (Washington, D.C.: GPO, 1981), p. 88.

[11] Philip Abelson, "Cancer: Opportunism and Opportunity," *Science*, 206, no. 4414 (1979), 11.

[12] Ibid.

[13] Ibid.

[14] AIHC, "Reply to Paper Prepared by National Cancer Institute (NCI), National Institute of Environmental Health Sciences (NIEHS) and National Institute for Occupational Safety and Health (NIOSH) on 'Estimates of the Fraction of Cancer in the United States Related to Occupational Factors'," Washington, D.C., October 1978. Further, AIHC, "Post-Hearing Brief re OSHA Generic Cancer Policy," October 23, 1978, pp. 19–35; Statement on S. 1080, submitted to Senate Judiciary Committee, Subcommittee on Regulatory Reform, May 15, 1981, Attachment 3, no. 11.

[15] See AIHC "Post-Hearing Brief," pp. 21–24. Also, interview at AIHC, Scarsdale, N.Y., June 25, 1981.

than are now encountered in the chemical industry. AIHC also questioned the report's scientific credibility on the grounds that it was neither published nor circulated for peer review and that most of the authors eventually dissociated themselves from the paper's strongest claims.

At the same time, the "estimates paper" continued to win approving citations from sources outside industry. Samuel Epstein, a scientist widely known for his insistence on stricter governmental control of carcinogens, endorsed the report in his book *The Politics of Cancer*.[16] President Carter's Toxic Substances Strategy Committee accepted the paper with minor qualifications.[17] TSSC noted that a study commissioned by AIHC itself used somewhat different assumptions to reach an estimate of 10 to 33 percent for cancers possibly related to occupational exposure.[18] In promulgating its generic policy on carcinogens in 1980, OSHA also endorsed the study.[19]

U.S. labor and environmental groups at first expressed unqualified support for the "estimates paper" and the government's overall response to it. However, as the dust settled and the Reagan administration began to unfold its own policy toward carcinogens, these groups partially modified their initial positions. Many advocates of regulation admit, at least privately, that the NCI-NIEHS-NIOSH report was more a political than a scientific statement about risk. But they also claim that all such probabilistic estimates are politically colored. It is even suggested, for example, that the highly influential Doll-Peto study was written from an overtly antiregulatory viewpoint and thus should be discounted as a basis for policy making.

The debate about the dimensions of the occupational cancer problem quickly spilled over to Britain, engaging a somewhat different cast of actors. Unlike U.S. regulatory authorities, British governmental agencies refrained from taking a public stance on the dispute. Instead, the trade unions and the chemical industry took up the scientific arguments advanced by their counterparts in the United States. Two of Britain's most influential trade unions urged stricter controls on occupational carcinogens, underscoring the apparently increasing rate of cancer and emphasizing linkages between cancer and chemicals in the environment. In a position paper on cancer prevention, the General and Municipal Workers' Union,[20] Britain's second largest trade un-

---

[16] Samuel S. Epstein, *The Politics of Cancer,* rev. ed. (New York: Anchor Press, 1981), p. 18.

[17] TSSC, *Toxic Chemicals and Public Protection* (Washington, D.C.: GPO, 1980), pp. 153–60.

[18] Ibid., p. 160, citing R. A. Stallones and T. Downs, "A Critical Overview of: Estimates of the Fraction of Cancer in the United States Related to Occupational Factors" (Manuscript provided by AIHC).

[19] 45 *FR* 5032, January 22, 1980.

[20] GMWU, "A Preliminary Cancer Prevention Programme" (undated). The document consists of a two-page programmatic statement followed by tables showing cancer incidence

ion, downplayed the significance of individual lifestyles. For example, the paper did not mention tobacco smoke or diet as preventable causes of cancer.

In early 1980, the Association of Scientific, Technical, and Managerial Staffs, Britain's major union of white-collar and scientific workers, published a longer and more sophisticated document on "The Prevention of Occupational Cancer." Like the GMWU paper, the ASTMS document underplayed the role of lifestyle and accorded greater prominence to environmental causes of cancer: "It is the striking geographical variations in cancer incidence that have led epidemiologists to attribute 70 to 90 percent of cancers to environmental factors—background radiation, naturally occurring plant and fungal carcinogens, chemical and industrial carcinogens polluting air, water, food, the workplace, home and community."[21] While admitting that personal habits may be implicated in cancer incidence, the ASTMS report suggested that their role is often exaggerated and that further research is required to assess their impact accurately. With respect to occupational cancer, ASTMS endorsed both the methodology and the conclusions of the NCI-NIEHS-NIOSH report. Criticisms of the U.S. paper were set aside as primarily political. ASTMS asserted, "Despite the frenzy they created, the committee's estimates stand intact."

The British chemical industry's reaction to the ASTMS document followed a path similar to AIHC's in the United States. J. Keir Howard, medical adviser to the Chemical Industries Association (CIA), responded with a chapter-by-chapter critique,[22] predictably dwelling on the union's questionable scientific assumptions. It challenged ASTMS's easy acceptance of the U.S. occupational cancer estimates and provided a lengthy rebuttal to the NCI-NIEHS-NIOSH report. The CIA rejoinder also criticized ASTMS's exclusive reliance on Epstein's analysis of particular occupational carcinogens, citing conflicting data from numerous other authorities.

Unlike AIHC in the United States, CIA openly accused the unions of playing politics with the occupational cancer issue. The first paragraph of the CIA review characterized the ASTMS document as a call to "political action" aimed at altering the existing relations between employers and employees and destroying the impartiality of scientific debate:

> While attempts to bring about an effective debate on the issue of occupational cancer are to be welcomed, it is essential that these are factual, balanced and objective. The ASTMS document fails on these counts at a

---

and mortality rates in Britain and chemicals and industrial processes associated with cancer induction.

[21] ASTMS Health and Safety Policy Series, no. 3, London, February 1980.

[22] J. Keir Howard, "The Prevention of Occupational Cancer: An ASTMS Policy Document—A Review," CIA Background Paper, June 1980.

number of points. In [their] overwhelming desire to press [their] arguments, the authors are guilty of distortions of fact, of using language colored by emotion and of making fallacious judgments.

In private, CIA representatives carried their critique even further, suggesting that ASTMS's real political agenda had more to do with increasing the association's membership than with health and safety.[23] ASTMS, in CIA's view, simply seized on the emotional issue of occupational cancer in a drive to mobilize traditionally "nonunion-minded" white-collar employees.

These accusations seem superficially at odds with the American chemical industry's effort to keep the cancer policy debate within a dispassionate scientific framework. But at a deeper level, industry's political objectives in the two countries were quite similar. By focusing on the scientific weakness of federal carcinogen policies, including the 1978 "estimates paper," AIHC hoped to generate support for significant institutional change: the transfer of decision-making authority to a scientific panel that would be more attentive to the needs of industry (see chapter 7). In the British case, on the other hand, CIA wanted to preserve the status quo: a regulatory process traditionally dominated by scientists. By denigrating not only ASTMS's scientific credibility but also its political motives, CIA wished to end the public debate on occupational cancer, restoring policy making to the established control of experts. Though AIHC's interests favored institutional change and CIA's favored continuity, both industry associations were committed to a strategy that would strengthen the role of scientists in the policy system.

In contrast to the situation in Britain and the United States, the occupational cancer issue aroused little public controversy in France or Germany. In 1981 the Deutsche Forschungsgemeinschaft published a study of occupational cancer which estimated that up to 25 percent of cancers among industrial workers may be due to exposure in the workplace. This finding, of course, was significantly more conservative than the U.S. report's claim that 20 to 40 percent of *all* cancers are occupationally induced. The introduction to the German study took pains to distance itself from the U.S. "estimates paper" and endorsed Sir Richard Doll's observation that industrial pollutants are unlikely to be "responsible for any substantial proportion of the total cancer hazard."[24] Even the relatively modest claims of the DFG report were challenged by the German chemical industry. However, the dispute did not unfold into major proportions, no doubt because the Bonn government showed no inclination to use the report as a catalyst for significant policy change.

[23] Interview, CIA, London, July 3, 1980.
[24] DFG, *Berufskrebsstudie* (Bonn: DFG, 1981), p. 24.

The Identification of Potential Carcinogens

A persistent source of uncertainty in the regulation of carcinogens is the use of laboratory test systems to identify potential carcinogens and to assess their effects on human health. The use of mutagenicity tests to detect potential carcinogens is one issue on which scientists differ. Comparisons among the four countries also reveal considerable expert disagreement about the methodology and interpretation of cancer bioassays. This section looks at these scientific conflicts and identifies the different assumptions used by government officials, political subgroups, and scientists themselves to overcome the uncertainties.

Short-Term Tests

Short-term methods for detecting chemical mutagens are a comparatively recent addition to the roster of scientific techniques for identifying carcinogens. Their acceptance by regulatory agencies in all four countries reflects a consensus that mutagenic activity provides a probable marker for potential carcinogenicity. Interest in these tests has been spurred by the clear economic advantages they offer over traditional bioassays involving tumor induction in laboratory animals. For the present, however, it is generally agreed that short-term tests are not a substitute for, but are a useful addition to, results obtained through epidemiological studies or animal experiments.[25]

Nevertheless, two aspects of the use of short-term tests have given rise to differences of opinion among those responsible for regulating carcinogens. The first, and less significant, concerns the number of tests that should be carried out in order to obtain a reliable indication of the presence or absence of carcinogenic risk. U.S. scientific and regulatory agencies, for the most part, advocate a "battery" of up to a dozen short-term tests in order to minimize the false negative and false positive results obtained from individual tests. The National Toxicology Program, for example, initiated a three-phase mutagenicity testing program in which candidate chemicals are successively subjected to assays using bacterial systems, cultured mammalian cells, and, finally, in vivo animal systems.[26]

In Europe, debate on an appropriate strategy for mutagenicity testing was partly preempted by the 1979 EC directive on chemical notification, the Sixth Amendment, which prescribes a "step-sequence" approach to chemical test-

---

[25] See OSHA generic cancer policy, 45 *FR* 5161–62; IRLG proposed carcinogenic risk assessment guidelines, 44 *FR* 39869–70, July 6, 1979.

[26] NTP, "1980 Annual Plan," Washington, D.C., November 1979, pp. 23–39.

ing and assessment. The directive calls for two tests, one bacteriological and one nonbacteriological, to be performed as part of the "base set" for new chemicals.[27] Two additional verification tests are required for chemicals that are selected for more intensive screening.[28] The Sixth Amendment's testing scheme does not, however, preclude member states from developing independent guidelines on the use of mutagenicity assays. A different approach was taken, for example, by the Committee on Mutagenicity of Chemicals in Britain's Department of Health and Social Security. The committee recommended a "basic package" of four tests that are functionally selected to demonstrate a variety of possible mutagenic properties.[29]

Because of their potential economic impact, national and international decisions concerning short-term testing are inescapably influenced by political considerations. The EC's decision to prescribe only two mutagenicity tests for the "base set," for example, represented a victory for cost-cutting arguments over proposals to minimize the number of false negatives. Nonetheless, questions about the number and types of short-term screening tests have been treated in all four countries as technical matters to be decided by expert committees and research institutions.

Interpreting results of short-term tests has generated considerably more public controversy than the question of number, especially when positive indications of mutagenicity are not supported by evidence of carcinogenicity from other test systems. To date, debate on this issue has taken place primarily in the context of U.S. regulatory proceedings on carcinogens. One of the first attempts to regulate chemicals on the basis of positive short-term tests occurred in 1976, when the Environmental Defense Fund (EDF) petitioned the Consumer Product Safety Commission to require cautionary labeling on clothing treated with the flame-retardant chemical Tris.[30] Although Ames test results indicated that Tris was a mutagen, CPSC withheld regulatory action until the National Cancer Institute reported preliminary positive results from a bioassay on Tris.[31] This precedent was followed by other federal agencies, so it became clear that toxic substances would not be regulated solely on the basis of short-term tests.

While the agencies agree that more than positive mutagenicity assays should be required to regulate a chemical as a carcinogen, how much more remains a question. Widely divergent views surfaced during OSHA's hearings

[27] Council directive, 79/831/EEC, Annex VII.

[28] Ibid., Annex VIII.

[29] DHSS Committee on Mutagenicity of Chemicals in Food, Consumer Products and the Environment, *Guidelines for the Testing of Chemicals for Mutagenicity* (London: HMSO, 1981), pp. 53–54.

[30] See 42 *FR* 28060, June 1, 1977.

[31] "Ames Replies to ICI Toxicologists," *European Chemical News*, 32, no. 830 (1978), 23.

on its proposed cancer policy. Some environmentalists resolutely maintained that positive evidence from one or more short-term tests should trigger regulation, even without convincing support from other sources.[32] At the other extreme, some witnesses for industry argued that no significance should be attached to these tests until they are more thoroughly validated.

The agency ultimately adopted a pragmatic compromise along lines suggested by David Rall, director of NIEHS:

> There is no question that positive results in short-term tests add to the confidence that one would have in a single positive animal test. This is not to say that these short-term tests are *equivalent* to lifetime bioassays in rodents: it merely reflects the fact that most carcinogens give positive results in short-term tests. Hence, if there is any reluctance to accept the result of a single animal bioassay, positive results in short-term tests would add sufficient evidence to overcome this reluctance. Certainly, it seems reasonable to use them in this way rather than to demand a second lifetime test in a rodent, which would be lengthy and expensive.[33]

Acting on this opinion, OSHA decided as a matter of policy that positive results from one well-conducted bioassay and one well-validated short-term test would suffice for classifying a chemical as a Category I (high-risk) toxic substance.[34] A report issued by IRLG in 1979 agreed that positive responses in short-term tests are "suggestive of a carcinogenic hazard," even when the substance has shown only negative responses in some animal bioassays.[35]

Animal Assays

For more than a century, scientists have espoused the view that studies of cancer in animals can enhance our understanding of the disease in humans. In the last few decades, this hypothesis has found a practical application as regulatory agencies have turned to animal experimentation in their effort to identify chemicals presenting a risk of cancer to humans. Statements issued during this period by the International Union against Cancer (IUAC), IARC, and several U.S. research institutions established the principle that any substance inducing cancer in test animals should be regarded at least as a potential human carcinogen.[36] This proposition derived empirical support from the

---

[32] *45 FR* 5161.
[33] Ibid.
[34] Ibid., p. 5284.
[35] *42 FR* 39870.
[36] See, for example, IUAC, Proceedings of Symposium on Potential Cancer Hazards from Chemical Additives and Contaminants in Foodstuffs, *Acta Union Internationale contre le Cancer*, 13 (1957), 179–363; IARC, *Evaluation of Carcinogenic Risk of Chemicals to Man*,

observation that most known and suspected human carcinogens also produce malignancies in test animals. One review of eighty-two chemicals for which some epidemiological evidence of carcinogenicity existed indicated that, with the exception of arsenic, all were carcinogenic in animals.[37]

Nevertheless, the attempt to draw regulatory implications from the results of animal testing remains problematic. Extrapolations from animal to human for specific chemicals give rise to a host of expert disagreements about the adequacy of the experimental design, the presumed metabolic pathways followed in humans and test animals, the evaluation of different types of neoplasms, and the relevance of tumors induced at very high doses.

The Search for "Cancer Principles" in the United States   In the course of promulgating its generic regulations on occupational carcinogens, OSHA compiled a lengthy record of opposing views on the interpretation of animal data.[38] EPA's regulation of the organochlorine pesticides in the early seventies generated an equally extensive, though less organized and issue-oriented, record.[39] When the two records are placed together, a sharply resolved picture emerges of the diverse scientific stands taken by chemical manufacturers, environmentalists, labor groups, and federal research institutes. The thrust of U.S. policy in the late 1970s was to abstract from these divergent positions a set of general principles which would facilitate the regulation of all carcinogens.

Widely used in agriculture since the mid-1940s, chlorinated hydrocarbon pesticides were seriously targeted for regulatory action only around 1970, when environmental activists, disturbed by the persistence of these chemicals, first took their case to EPA. But the effort to restrict these pesticides faltered until new evidence from animal experiments revealed that they might be carcinogens.[40] EPA was then faced with what by now is a familiar dilemma: Should substances of proven benefit to society and of high economic worth be

---

IARC Monographs, vol. 1 (Lyon: IARC, 1972); NAS/NRC, *Principles for Evaluating Chemicals in the Environment* (Washington, D.C.: NAS, 1975).

[37] Thomas H. Maugh, "Chemical Carcinogens: The Scientific Basis for Regulation," *Science,* 201, no. 4362 (1978), 1200–1201.

[38] The whole record consisted of more than two hundred and fifty thousand pages and was summarized in the introduction to OSHA's generic cancer policy regulations, 45 *FR* 5001–5282 (1980).

[39] Major scientific questions concerning carcinogen regulation were raised in EPA's suspension and cancellation proceedings on DDT, aldrin/dieldrin, heptachlor/chlordane, and Mirex. Together, these proceedings covered a period from about 1970 to 1976.

[40] Although regulatory debate in the United States focused on their potential carcinogenicity, these substances have not been regarded as carcinogens in any of the three European countries, where they have been regulated primarily because of their persistence in the environment.

withdrawn from the market solely on the basis of experimental evidence of carcinogenicity? The agency's actions raised troublesome scientific questions that have recurred in many later proceedings.[41]

Chemical manufacturers challenged EPA's reliance on positive carcinogenesis results obtained in certain mammalian test systems, particularly some commonly used mouse strains.[42] It was argued that the high spontaneous tumor incidence observed at sites such as the liver rendered these animals unsuitable for cancer testing. These arguments were further elaborated during the OSHA hearings.[43] AIHC contended, for example, that animals with a high incidence of spontaneous tumors are inherently suspect in cancer research because they increase the likelihood of false negatives. To guard against such errors, AIHC suggested that positive results should be obtained in at least two mammalian species before a substance is classified in a high-risk category. As a general matter, the U.S. regulatory agencies refused to go along with AIHC's suggestions. Instead, EPA, OSHA, and IRLG all affirmed that positive results in a single adequately designed and conducted animal bioassay are sufficient grounds for treating a substance as a suspect human carcinogen and assigning it the highest regulatory priority. Though all these agencies emphasized the need for judgment and caution in interpreting animal results, none agreed to make systematic distinctions between bioassays in certain rodent species and other mammalian systems.

Regardless of their political affiliation, scientists generally agree that the practicalities of cancer research make it imperative to test laboratory animals at much higher doses than the expected levels of human exposure. To detect excess risk at low doses, it would be necessary to use unmanageably large numbers of animals, making such experiments prohibitively expensive. NCI guidelines on rodent bioassays[44] approve the practice of testing at the maximum tolerated dose (MTD) and at two lower dose levels. The MTD is defined as the highest dose administered during a chronic study "that can be predicted not to alter the treated animal's longevity from toxic effects other than carcinogenicity."[45] For any tested substance and species of test animal, establishing the MTD involves making a prediction, and experts may differ, or even err, in their judgments. If the MTD is wrongly determined, the test animals

[41] The scientific debate at EPA has been ably described by Nathan J. Karch, "Explicit Criteria and Principles for Identifying Carcinogens: A Focus of Controversy at the Environmental Protection Agency," in NAS/NRC, *Decision Making in the Environmental Protection Agency*, vol. 2a (Washington, D.C.: NAS, 1977), pp. 119–206.

[42] Ibid., pp. 86–88.

[43] 45 *FR* 5068–78.

[44] J. M. Sontag, N. P. Page, U. Saffiotti, *Guidelines for Carcinogen Bioassays in Small Rodents*, NCI Carcinogenesis Technical Report, series 1 (Washington, D.C.: GPO, 1976).

[45] 45 *FR* 5084.

may die too soon or suffer other adverse health effects that cast doubt on the results of the experiment.

The use and interpretation of high-dose tests gained public notoriety in the United States following FDA's unsuccessful attempt to ban saccharin in 1977. Popular misconceptions were fueled by an FDA press announcement that the proposed ban was based on a test in which rats had consumed the equivalent of the saccharin contained in 800 cans of diet soda.[46] Sensing that the time was ripe, opponents of the technique went public with their arguments that chemicals administered at the MTD interfere in various ways with the body's natural detoxification mechanisms and induce cancers that would not be observed at lower doses. An impressive list of experts representing the chemical industry presented testimony to this effect during OSHA's cancer policy proceedings.[47] OSHA concluded, however, that in the absence of truly substantial counterevidence,[48] it would continue to rely on data from bioassays at "any level of exposure or dose."

Decisions such as these were among the packages of general "principles" or "policies" developed by EPA and OSHA for dealing with the uncertainties involved in carcinogenicity testing. The impetus for these developments came primarily from lawyers and administrators rather than from scientists. Officials in both agencies hoped that such rules would provide firm guidelines for evaluating toxicological data and speed up regulatory proceedings on individual substances. A key objective was to decide in advance the answers to the scientific questions that seemed to recur when either agency tried to regulate a suspected carcinogen.[49] But, given the magnitude and complexity of the task, it is not altogether surprising that these efforts met with only dubious success. After several years of trying to get scientists to agree on its cancer principles, EPA was forced to give up the attempt and to publish much more flexible "guidelines" for risk assessment.[50] Subsequently, IRLG attempted to develop a more extensive set of guidelines for interdepartmental use,[51] but these efforts came to a halt when the Reagan administration took office.

OSHA's failure was even more dramatic. Carrying the idea of "cancer principles" to its logical conclusion, the agency tried to develop an explicit system of rules to bridge every uncertainty in the risk assessment process. But the procedures OSHA used were much more successful in illuminating the areas of uncertainty and disagreement than in pressing the parties toward

[46] See Reginald W. Rhein, Jr., and Larry Marion, *The Saccharin Controversy* (New York: Monarch Press, 1977), pp. 4–5.

[47] 45 *FR* 5088.

[48] Ibid., p. 5093.

[49] See OSHA's explanation for the generic cancer policy at 42 *FR* 54154 (1977).

[50] EPA, "Health Risk and Economic Impact Assessments of Suspected Carcinogens," 41 *FR* 21402 (1976).

[51] IRLG, "Scientific Bases for Identification of Potential Carcinogens," 41 *FR* 21401 (1976).

a policy consensus. On many crucial points, the scientific adversaries testifying before OSHA were so far apart that it was difficult, if not impossible, to find a middle ground. The course eventually adopted by the agency was often an uneasy, even unscientific, compromise. OSHA's proposal for interpreting high-dose animal experiments illustrates the point.

As noted above, OSHA decided that positive animal tests should be treated as grounds for regulatory intervention regardless of the dose at which malignancies were induced. Yet the agency was reluctant to reject outright the chemical industry's contention that cancer at such high doses may be caused by "metabolic overloading" or other functional disturbances that would not occur at lower doses. Accordingly, OSHA agreed to consider evidence of such special causal mechanisms if it met certain rigid criteria of quality.[52] In effect, these "minimum" standards were designed as exclusionary rules. Under the guise of fairness and flexibility, OSHA actually determined that evidence of metabolic disorders at high doses should never take precedence over positive bioassay results.

Understandably, the chemical industry refused to live with a policy that subtly discriminated against the evidence most favorable to its position. AIHC accused OSHA of oversimplifying complex scientific issues through a "checklist" or "cookbook" approach that was neither good science nor good policy.[53] The cancer policy was soon mired in litigation and renegotiation, and the Reagan administration made it clear that it would not be enforced without substantial revision.[54]

The European View of Animal Testing   There is a night-and-day difference in the degree of public attention directed at the uncertainties of cancer testing in the United States and Europe. Yet the problem of interpreting cancer bioassays is equally acute in Europe, since all three European countries recognize animal tests as important indicators of carcinogenicity. Through interviews with scientists and public officials, and from reports of occasional well-publicized controversies, it is possible to construct a picture of the positions taken by European authorities on the role of animal data in regulating carcinogens. These differ in many respects from the policies endorsed by regulatory agencies in the United States.

As we noted in chapter 6, experimental toxicology in Germany has attracted a small but steady stream of eminent practitioners over the years. In contrast, epidemiology has been relatively neglected in terms of financial and institutional support. Accordingly, German toxicologists today work in a re-

---

[52] 45 *FR* 5093–94.
[53] Interview, AIHC, Scarsdale, N.Y., June 25, 1981.
[54] Partly in response to litigation initiated by AIHC, OSHA undertook a comprehensive review of the generic cancer policy. See *Washington Post,* January 6, 1982, p. A21.

search system that is more hospitable to identifying carcinogens through animal experiments than through human epidemiological studies. In keeping with common scientific practice, German cancer researchers have never sought to formulate general principles for interpreting animal bioassays, even though many of them are engaged in evaluating such data for use by policy makers. These scientists view with considerable skepticism both the scientific and the policy principles underlying the U.S. effort to develop generic rules for evaluating animal experiments.

German toxicologists grant that a chemical may be classified as a carcinogen on the basis of animal evidence alone, but they emphasize the need to review each case on its own merits. One expert at the German Cancer Research Center (Deutsches Krebsforschungszentrum, DKFZ) spoke cautiously of the "minimum" conditions under which an animal carcinogen should be treated as a threat to human health.[55] In his view, such a relationship can be assumed only when three criteria are satisfied: (1) there is a clear dose-response relationship; (2) positive results are obtained in more than one animal species; (3) the dose at which a tumorigenic response is observed stands in a "reasonable" relationship to the expected level of human exposure, for example, in a ratio of 100:1.[56] U.S. agencies at the time were viewing positive evidence from a single well-designed animal assay as sufficient for classifying a chemical as a suspected human carcinogen.

Dietrich Henschler, chairman of the influential committee that establishes TLVs for toxic substances in the workplace, confirmed that the appropriateness of an experimental dose is viewed rather differently in Germany and the United States.[57] While endorsing the concept of the MTD, Henschler indicated that German toxicologists determine this dosage by more rigorous techniques than were proposed by NCI. Thus, a German MTD determination involves three months of observation, rather than four weeks, and more animals than required by the NCI guidelines. Henschler attributes these differences to dissimilarities in the disciplinary background of German and American scientists engaged in experimental cancer research. German toxicology has strong ties to analytical chemistry and is more "process oriented" in its study of the effects of chemicals on organisms. NCI, on the other hand, has been dominated by "pure pathologists," who, in Henschler's opinion, adopt something like a black-box approach to carcinogenesis, focusing more on end points than on intermediate physiological processes.

On the whole, German authorities appear more reluctant than U.S. officials to intervene on the strength of experimental evidence alone—unless the

---

[55] Interview, DKFZ, Heidelberg, July 15, 1981.
[56] These views were represented as being shared by most German scientists concerned with carcinogenesis research. This interviewee drew an explicit contrast with the United States, stating that "there are no Sam Epsteins" in Germany.
[57] Interview, Würzburg, July 17, 1981.

findings are incontrovertible. It is difficult to find public statements to this effect by governmental authorities. However, in evaluating the teratogenicity of 2,4,5-T, the Federal Biological Research Center stated that "proof of the teratogenic effect of a pesticide observed in an animal experiment does not by itself require a general ban or stringent restrictions on its use."[58] Presumably BBA and its sister technical agencies adopt a similar position with respect to animal evidence of carcinogenicity.

Like German experts, British regulators and their scientific advisers are opposed to the idea of a generic cancer policy, believing that toxic substances must be evaluated individually on the basis of all the available evidence. The proceedings on aldrin and dieldrin in Britain revealed additional disagreements with the American approach to interpreting animal tests. Although EPA had found these pesticides to be carcinogenic, British authorities in MAFF concluded on the basis of the same studies that they did not present a risk of cancer.[59] One possible explanation for this outcome is that scientists in the two countries were using different standards of proof to measure carcinogenicity. But this is probably an overstatement. The real differences between the two countries lay in the treatment of uncertainty by those responsible for deciding how much risk the public should bear. Faced with inconclusive scientific evidence, EPA decided *as a matter of policy* to regulate aldrin and dieldrin as if they were known human carcinogens. Scientific advisers to the British government, on the other hand, argued successfully that the evidence was too inconclusive to justify such a restrictive policy choice.

Read in this way, the aldrin/dieldrin case suggests that British agencies generally require more definite evidence of carcinogenicity before initiating regulatory action than do their American equivalents. Several additional bits of evidence support this conjecture. In a review of the safety of 2,4,5-T, the Advisory Committee on Pesticides pointed out that interpretations of animal data should take into account not only the relationship between dose and body weight, but also physiological and metabolic differences between the tested animals and humans.[60] According to one senior scientist who is familiar with both governmental and industrial views on cancer research, testing at the MTD is seen in Britain as "a bit unrealistic," since high doses can interfere with metabolism.[61] In his view, testing should be carried out at more dose

---

[58] See Egmont R. Koch and Fritz Vahrenholt, *Seveso ist überall* (Frankfurt: Fischer Verlag, 1980), p. 188.

[59] For a comparative exploration of the reasons for these divergent outcomes, see Brendan Gillespie et al., "Carcinogenic Risk Assessment in the United States and Great Britain: The Case of Aldrin/Dieldrin," *Social Studies of Science*, 9, no. 3 (1979), 265–301.

[60] ACP, *Further Review of the Safety for Use in the U.K. of the Herbicide 2,4,5-T* (London: HMSO, 1980), p. 14.

[61] Interview, Albright and Wilson, Ltd., London, July 3, 1980.

levels than recommended by NCI. HSE, he indicated, would require positive evidence from experiments with two animal species—"for a start"—before entering a substance on a list of recognized carcinogens.

Questions about the conduct and interpretation of cancer bioassays were propelled into the British political arena in the early 1980s through the debate between ASTMS and the CIA on occupational cancer. As on the issue of epidemiological evidence, the union borrowed its major scientific arguments from U.S. authorities. Industry responded with views more in line with the opinions of British regulators and scientific advisers. ASTMS, for example, voiced wholehearted support for NCI's animal-testing guidelines.[62] In contrast, CIA's critique emphasized the uncertain value of animal data, citing complicating factors such as species variability and high spontaneous tumor incidence in inbred laboratory strains.[63]

Public discussion of the uncertainties inherent in cancer testing is more muted in France than in Germany or Britain. But to the extent that French views on relevant scientific issues can be deduced from secondary sources, they differ little, if at all, from the positions adopted by other European regulators. Thus, France shares with the two other countries a commitment to case-by-case decision making, and there is little sympathy in France for the idea of generic cancer principles. In France, as in Britain, regulators treat carcinogenicity as just one toxic effect among others. In principle, however, French scientists approve the use of animal experiments to evaluate the carcinogenicity of environmental chemicals. This is clear, for example, in the writings of René Truhaut, who recommends the selection of animal species that have metabolic properties similar to human metabolic properties. He urges a close collaboration between epidemiologists and experimental toxicologists to improve the selection of test systems.[64]

Assessing the Risk of Cancer

Negative and Positive Evidence

Assessing the risk to human health from exposure to carcinogens requires regulatory agencies to evaluate both positive and negative evidence from a variety of sources: human epidemiological studies, short-term tests for mutagenicity, and long-term animal bioassays. Frequently, the results from these different areas do not point conclusively in one direction, and regulators must

[62] ASTMS, op. cit., pp. 26–28.
[63] Howard, op. cit., p. 12.
[64] R. Truhaut, "The Problem of Permissible Limits of Potentially Toxic Substances in the Working and General Environment of Modern Man," in F. Coulston and F. Korte, eds., *Environmental Quality and Safety*, vol. 2 (Stuttgart: Georg Thieme Verlag, 1973), p. 147.

decide how much weight to attach to each category of evidence. In its generic cancer policy, OSHA made a rare attempt to develop principles for dealing with conflicting data about carcinogenicity. The agency proposed, as a general rule, that positive results from either human or animal studies should supersede negative epidemiological evidence. Nonpositive epidemiological data would be considered only if they met certain minimum criteria concerning the duration and design of the study.[65] As in the case of metabolic disorders at high doses, these criteria were all but impossible to meet, given the state of the art in epidemiological research. It appeared again that OSHA was using the cancer policy as a filter to exclude a troublesome category of evidence.

Interestingly, neither OSHA nor the other U.S. agencies seemed interested in establishing comparable criteria for screening *positive* epidemiological studies, though British regulators, with their more demanding attitude toward positive evidence, seemed to be moving in this direction. In its 1980 review of 2,4,5-T, Britain's ACP discussed the problem:

> There is no short cut to establishing linkages of this kind. The essential preliminaries are to demonstrate that the mother was exposed to the environmental agent concerned at a meaningful level and . . . at a relevant time of foetal development. This time factor is especially important with a substance like 2,4,5-T which, unlike dioxin, is excreted fairly rapidly from the body, i.e., exposure may therefore not occur at the time when the affected tissue or organ of the foetus is developing.[66]

In America, comparable methodological critiques were seldom advanced, at least before 1980, as grounds for dismissing seemingly positive epidemiological correlations.

Classifying Carcinogens

Regulatory agencies in both Europe and the United States have used qualitative criteria—usually the nature, amount, and reliability of the evidence—to classify carcinogens in different risk categories. OSHA's generic policy defined two categories of "potential occupational carcinogens."[67] Category I consisted of substances for which there was either direct human evidence of carcinogenicity or evidence from a bioassay in a single mammalian species that was supported by scientifically evaluated results from another source. If there was no evidence, or only suggestive evidence, in concordance with a positive bioassay, the candidate substance was placed in Category II. The classification scheme entailed certain automatic consequences. For example,

[65] 45 *FR* 5059–60.
[66] ACP, op. cit., p. 13.
[67] 45 *FR* 5284.

the 1980 regulations required that permissible exposure limits for substances in Category I should be set "as low as feasible" and should be achieved primarily through engineering and work practice controls.[68] These provisions reflected OSHA's judgment that positive results from a single well-designed and well-conducted bioassay were a sufficient basis for stringent regulation.

One of EPA's earliest initiatives during the Reagan administration was to develop a classification scheme that would not treat all animal carcinogens as though they presented an equally high risk to humans. Top agency officials proposed that evidence of genotoxicity be used as an additional basis for sorting carcinogens into greater and lesser risk categories. Under this proposal, nongenotoxic compounds were to be treated relatively leniently for regulatory purposes, even if they appeared to be animal carcinogens. For example, EPA indicated that it might be appropriate to assume a safe threshold of exposure for these substances. This radical shift from prior governmental policy was severely criticized by scientists outside the agency. Under investigation by a House subcommittee, EPA was eventually forced to withdraw the controversial proposal.[69]

A quite different system of categorization is employed by the German committee responsible for evaluating hazardous substances in the workplace. In the German scheme, the highest-risk category consists only of those substances "capable of inducing malignant tumors as shown through experience with humans." The second category is reserved for substances that have proved "unmistakably carcinogenic" in animal experimentation. A third category includes all additional substances and materials "for which a considerable carcinogenic potential can be suspected" but which require further study. These categories reflect the dominant German view that animal carcinogens should not automatically be regarded as threatening to humans. This conservatism no doubt explains why it has been unnecessary for German scientists to use additional explicit criteria, such as genotoxicity, to distinguish among subgroups of animal carcinogens.

The German classification criteria represent, at bottom, a variant of the principles underlying IARC's three-part categorization of carcinogenic substances. IARC designates these three categories as follows: "carcinogenic for humans" (Group 1), "probably carcinogenic for humans" (Group 2), and those that "could not be classified as to their carcinogenicity for humans" (Group 3).[70] The International Labor Organization (ILO) also lists carcinogens "on the basis of their estimated potential for inducing cancer

[68] Ibid., p. 5286.
[69] Eliot Marshall, "Revisions in Cancer Policy," *Science* 220, no. 4592 (1983), pp. 36–37.
[70] IARC, *IARC Monographs on the Evaluation of the Carcinogenic Risk of Chemicals to Humans,* IARC Monographs Supplement 1 (Lyon: IARC, 1979).

in working populations."[71] But ILO experts have not identified the criteria they use to assign carcinogens to different categories.

As in the United States, the classification of carcinogens in Germany carries predetermined regulatory consequences. For substances in the two highest-risk groups, the Federal Ministry of Labor, with the advice of its expert committee on hazardous substances, establishes permissible ambient concentrations.[72] Other regulations, including reporting, medical surveillance, and personal safety requirements, are developed in part by the ministry and in part by the insurance association for the chemical industry. In contrast, substances in the third risk category are not automatically channeled into the standard-setting process.

Not surprisingly, the chemical industry in both the United States and Europe has rejected OSHA's approach to classifying carcinogens in favor of the more cautious approach favored in Germany. The European Chemical Industry Ecology and Toxicology Centre (ECETOC), a multinational European trade association, has proposed a classification scheme based on criteria similar to those endorsed by the Henschler committee.[73] ECETOC distinguishes between "proven" and "putative" human carcinogens, the latter defined as substances that cause "malignant neoplasms in adequate animal experimentation, under exposure conditions which correspond to those in man." A "questionable" human carcinogen is one for which there is only suggestive evidence of carcinogenicity, from observations either in man or in animals. Similar positions were advanced in the United States by ACGIH and other representatives of the chemical industry.[74] On the other hand, the French chemical industry opposed the introduction of any kind of "risk index," perhaps out of fear that such a scheme would encourage bureaucrats to stray beyond case-by-case processing of chemical notifications. All these developments have been overtaken to some degree by the growing demand for quantitative risk assessment, which many chemical companies now regard as the only reasonable way to establish relative risk.

Finding a Safe "Threshold"

The idea that no safe threshold can be established for exposure to carcinogens not only pervades the international scientific literature, but has left deep

---

[71] ILO, *Occupational Cancer: Prevention and Control,* Occupational Safety and Health Series no. 39 (Geneva: ILO, 1977), pp. 10–12, 27–28.

[72] See BMAS, Anhang II der Verordnung über gefährliche Arbeitsstoffe vom 29. Juli 1980, Anlagenband zum BGBl. 1, no. 42, August 2, 1980, pp. 257–63.

[73] ECETOC, *A Contribution to the Strategy for the Identification and Control of Occupational Carcinogens,* Monograph no. 2 (Brussels: ECETOC, 1980).

[74] See, for example, Peter B. Hutt, "Unresolved Issues in the Conflict between Individual Freedom and Government Control of Food Safety," *Food Drug Cosmetic Law Journal,* 33, no. 10 (1978), 577.

imprints in the chemical control policies of all four countries, most notably in the Delaney clause of the U.S. Food, Drug, and Cosmetic Act. During the 1970s, U.S. agencies on several occasions reviewed the evidence that thresholds or no-effect levels (NOELs) may exist for some carcinogens. Each time, the incompleteness of the data and the apparent variations in individual and species susceptibility led them to reaffirm that, for policy purposes, no safe threshold should be assumed for any carcinogen. An interagency consensus to this effect was expressed in IRLG's guidelines on assessing carcinogenic risk: "Since threshold doses for carcinogenesis have not been established, a prudent approach from a safety standpoint is to assume that any dose may induce or promote carcinogenesis."[75] Adoption of the no-threshold hypothesis explains the relative willingness of U.S. agencies to ban or severely curtail the use of carcinogenic products, as well as their preference for rigid engineering controls, to some extent irrespective of cost. Of course, such practices are also consistent with statutory mandates that place a heavy premium on public health, even if they do not require complete elimination of risk.[76]

German scientific advisory committees appear to be as wedded to the no-threshold principle as are U.S. regulatory agencies. Indeed, the DFG commission on hazardous substances in the workplace refuses to set tolerance levels for carcinogens because there are no scientifically validated methods of calculating such thresholds. This leaves the federal labor ministry free to set exposure standards for carcinogens at any level it regards as economically and technically feasible. AGA, the ministry's standing expert committee, provides a multipartite forum for establishing the so-called "technical guiding concentrations" (TRKs) for carcinogens. The entire process neatly separates the scientific phase of risk assessment from the political phase of determining how to control risk.

It is also the accepted view among French experts that there are at present no practical methods for establishing threshold doses for carcinogens.[77] French regulatory policy is consistent with this position. INRS, the Ministry of Labor's main technical agency, has generally refrained from adopting TLVs for occupational carcinogens. INRS argues not only that individual responses to such agents are unpredictable, but that exposure standards for

---

[75] 44 *FR* 39872.

[76] See, for example, the Supreme Court's discussion of the OSH Act's safety standard in *American Textile Manufacturers Inst., Inc., v. Donovan*, 49 *U.S. Law Week* 4720, June 16, 1981 (cotton dust case).

[77] R. Truhaut, "Can Permissible Levels of Carcinogenic Compounds in the Environment Be Envisaged?" *Ecotoxicology and Environmental Safety*, 1 (1977), 31–37; IARC, *An Overview of the Problem of Thresholds for Chemical Carcinogens*, IARC Scientific Publications, vol. 74, no. 25 (Lyon: IARC, 1979), pp. 191–202.

individual substances are inadequate to protect workers against cumulative or synergistic impacts.[78] Given the uncertainties of carcinogen regulation, French officials are reluctant to establish TLVs that could give workers a misleading sense of security. Instead, the French strategy for regulating carcinogens in the workplace is to combine strict medical monitoring with reporting and personal hygiene requirements.

British regulators and scientific advisers are decidedly more favorably disposed to the threshold concept, even for carcinogens, than are their counterparts in the other countries. This position squares with official British disinclination to treat carcinogenicity any differently from other forms of toxicity. Regulatory analysis in Britain relies heavily on such concepts as ADIs and NOELs. For example, in evaluating the risks of exposure to 2,4,5-T, ACP paid particular attention to the NOEL of 3 mg/kg of body weight established by a WHO/FAO expert committee for the most sensitive animal species exposed to the herbicide.[79] More generally, ACP's Scientific Subcommittee regards pesticide residue levels below 1 ppm as essentially harmless for all classes of compounds.[80] In the area of worker safety and health, an HSE Guidance Note proposed a method of determining a "practical threshold of neoplastic response" while conceding that "precisely defined" thresholds cannot be attained.[81]

Though British theory and practice on thresholds has had some support in international scientific circles,[82] the weight of contrary opinion ensured that the issue would be featured in the occupational cancer debate between ASTMS and the chemical industry. Predictably, the union endorsed the no-threshold hypothesis and took the government to task for continuing to reject it. But ASTMS stated its position cautiously. While the cancer-policy document posited that "there is no known safe level of exposure" to carcinogens, it also indicated that mechanisms such as DNA repair preclude any simple generalization about the nonexistence of thresholds.[83] CIA's attack was unex-

---

[78] A. Rébière, "La Protection des travailleurs contre les substances et préparations dangereuses," Ministry of Labor, Paris, June 24, 1980; INRS, "La Notion de valeur limite de concentration," Note no. 928–77–74, 1974; idem, "Valeurs limites de concentration des substances toxiques dans l'air," Note no. 884–74–74, 1974.

[79] ACP, op. cit., p. 14.

[80] Interview, London, July 31, 1980.

[81] HSE Guidance Note EH15, Appendix A (1978).

[82] It appears that the concept of a threshold for carcinogens is more widely accepted for purposes of food safety regulation that in other sectors of chemical control. In particular, there may be a difference of opinion on the threshold issue between WHO's Food Additives Committee and the experts on chemical carcinogenesis at IARC. Interview, WHO, Geneva, July 3, 1980.

[83] ASTMS, op. cit., pp. 1, 22–23, 49–50.

pectedly vehement and was aimed at destroying the union's scientific credibility:

> ASTMS is firmly wedded to the "no threshold" concept, which does not stand up to scientific scrutiny, and to uncritical adoption of the proposals of the U.S. regulators. Indeed, the arguments adopted are essentially a rehash of the old OSHA and EPA cliches used to support their generic cancer policies. In taking this line ASTMS is copying one of the fundamental errors of the American proposals.[84]

More clearly than any other single issue, the question of thresholds highlights the dilemmas and the opportunities for manipulation that confront administrators in areas of high scientific uncertainty. Faced with the need to make enforceable decisions, agencies in all four countries found ways of getting around the strict implications of the no-threshold concept, but in each case the result was an unstable compromise. In the United States and Britain, regulators tried to keep their scientific assumptions and their policy decisions consistent, but their strategies were diametrically opposed. U.S. agencies at first presumed no safe thresholds and attempted to reduce exposure to carcinogens as far as technologically possible. But their actions were denounced by industry, the courts, and the public as unduly restrictive and insensitive to socioeconomic costs. Later, EPA's proposal that nongenotoxic compounds be presumed to have thresholds also foundered, this time because independent experts questioned the scientific validity of such an approach. British authorities, on the other hand, have always maintained that there is scientific support for thresholds and directed their attention to finding NOELs, even for suspected carcinogens. However, the bitter union-industry confrontations over occupational cancer attest to the incomplete political success of this approach.

The two continental European countries avoided direct political conflict on the threshold question, but they did so through an effective separation of scientific and regulatory decision making. In Germany, risk assessment and standard setting for occupational carcinogens are entrusted to different committees, one purely scientific, the other overtly political. The latter has been able to incorporate cost considerations, and even the concept of a "no-effect level,"[85] into its standard setting without openly challenging the validity of the no-threshold hypothesis. France, too, has effectively sidestepped the issue by refusing, in most cases, to adopt numerical exposure standards that suggest the existence of safe thresholds for carcinogens or other toxic substances.

---

[84] Howard, op. cit., p. 18.
[85] Interview, Federal Ministry of Labor, Bonn, August 12, 1980.

Quantifying Risk

Until the early 1980s, regulatory agencies in the four countries displayed a rare unanimity in agreeing that it was premature to insist on quantitative assessments of carcinogenic risk. Based on its detailed review of currently available methodologies, OSHA concluded: "The uncertainties involved in extrapolating from high-dose animal experiments to predict low-dose risks to humans are far too large at present to justify using the estimates for quantitative risk-benefit analyses."[86] The agency proposed a more limited use of quantitative risk analysis to establish the relative risks associated with different carcinogens and to estimate the degree of risk reduction that might be achieved through regulatory action.

European scientific advisers appeared unwilling to go even this far. In Germany, the Henschler commission analyzes the risk of occupational cancer in qualitative, not quantitative, terms. In France, Truhaut has called attention to the limits on quantitative risk assessment caused by the dearth of dose-response data at low exposure levels. British scientists, as well, suggest that it is still too early for quantitative analysis of carcinogenic risk; not enough is known about metabolism, for example, to permit precise comparison of animal and human carcinogenic responses.

More recently, predictive models for estimating the risk of cancer at low doses have gained greater official acceptance, particularly in the United States, where regulators now view quantitative risk assessment as an indispensable, if not wholly reliable, instrument for public decision making. Even those who are dubious about the numerical exactitude of risk estimates see the assessment process as a valuable technique for laying out policy alternatives and explaining the scientific basis for administrative decisions. The arguments favoring risk assessment are, in short, very similar to those advanced in support of cost-benefit analysis in the 1970s. Whether risk assessment will prove the ultimate instrument for rationalizing policy and constraining administrative discretion in the United States remains to be seen. Given the extraordinary political coloration of science in the U.S. regulatory process, skepticism about such an outcome is justifiable.

Science and Politics: The 2,4,5-T Controversy

Though the degree of interaction between science and politics differs greatly among the four countries, it is not immediately clear what impact, if any, this has on the regulation of carcinogens. In this section, we examine one actual

---

[86] 45 *FR* 5200.

case, the regulation of the herbicide 2,4,5-T, and compare the outcomes in Europe and the United States. The case illustrates how regulatory procedure interacts with science to produce different assessments of risk. Yet it also suggests that, in the case of genuinely controversial products, political pressure ultimately overwhelms scientific evaluations and forces similar outcomes in very different policy-making environments.

Trichlorophenoxyacetic acid, commonly known as 2,4,5-T, is the active ingredient in a variety of herbicides used to control broad-leaved weedy growth in forests, range, and pasture lands, and along rights of way. An impurity called 2,3,7,8-tetrachlorodibenzo-*p*-dioxin (TCDD) is generated during the chemical synthesis of 2,4,5-T. TCDD is recognized as one of the most potent man-made toxins currently known.[87] Many countries strictly control the level of dioxin in commercial 2,4,5-T preparations.[88] Both 2,4,5-T and TCDD are suspected of causing a variety of genotoxic effects, including cancer and foetal abnormalities.

During the Vietnam War, the U.S. Army's massive use of the defoliant Agent Orange, an equal mixture of 2,4,5-T and 2,4-D heavily contaminated with TCDD, produced a flood of health complaints from the Vietnamese population and U.S. soldiers who came in contact with the compound. In 1976 dioxin became a household word in Europe when a chemical factory in Seveso, Italy, exploded, releasing a cloud of TCDD and necessitating the evacuation of nearby villages. The political legacy of these events was to intensify public demand for stricter regulation of 2,4,5-T in many industrial countries, including three of the four compared in this book. Only in France did governmental action to limit the dioxin content of 2,4,5-T and to ban its aerial application arouse little political discussion or public scientific debate.

In the United States, 2,4,5-T was one of the earliest agrochemicals regulated by EPA. The use of the herbicide on all food crops except rice was eliminated in 1970 after an announcement was made by the president's science adviser that laboratory tests had linked 2,4,5-T with birth defects in animals.[89] Further action was stalled, however, because EPA did not have sufficient quantitative evidence of human exposure to link the growing body of animal data to reported health effects. The gaps in the chain of evidence

---

[87] Huff et al., op. cit., p. 222.

[88] A regulation limiting the dioxin content of commercial 2,4,5-T to 0.1 mg/kg has been in effect in the United States since 1971. British and German authorities have also applied the same standard for many years to domestic formulations and imports, but in 1980 Britain announced that new analytical techniques had made it possible to lower the standard further, to 0.01 mg/kg.

[89] The following account is based on Sarah L. Hartman, "Case History of 2,4,5-T Regulation," *Congressional Record*, 96th Cong., 1st sess., November 29, 1979, pp. H 11394–H 11395.

seemed to be filled when EPA carried out the so-called Alsea II study, an epidemiological analysis purporting to find a strong correlation between 2,4,5-T spraying in Oregon's Alsea basin and peaks in the local miscarriage rate over a six-year period. Invoking its emergency powers, EPA immediately suspended the registration of 2,4,5-T for use on forests and rights of way.[90] This decision survived a court challenge by Dow Chemical, the leading U.S. manufacturer of the herbicide.[91]

The remaining uses of 2,4,5-T continued to be reviewed under EPA's usual RPAR process. The agency's Scientific Advisory Panel eventually concluded that the available data, including the disputed Alsea II study, supplied no evidence of an immediate or substantial threat to human health or the environment. The panel recommended against cancellation of the herbicide's use on rice and range lands. Subsequently, the agency and the manufacturers of 2,4,5-T entered into negotiations with the object of reaching an out-of-court settlement. In 1983, however, Dow requested EPA to cancel all its registrations for 2,4,5-T on the ground that its profits from the chemical were not high enough to offset the legal and administrative costs of defending its safety.[92]

Though 2,4,5-T has been an object of scientific and regulatory concern in Germany for some time, it rose to prominence on the political agenda through the complexities of federal-state politics. In 1973 a group of thirty German academics published a general statement of concern about the use of herbicides in the Federal Republic and expressed specific reservations about the continued application of 2,4,5-T.[93] This document was taken up a few years later by Diether Deneke, the agriculture minister for Northrhine-Westphalia, to justify his campaign against the aerial spraying of 2,4,5-T over large tracts of privately owned forest land in his state. Failing to win an injunction against the landowner, Deneke took his case to the public through an official report on the negative toxicological effects of 2,4,5-T. The federal government, which had officially approved the use of 2,4,5-T, could not ignore this challenge. In 1978, the Federal Biological Research Center published a review of the substance, upholding its continued use under existing regulations.[94]

This holding action by federal bureaucrats proved unstable. In 1981, 2,4,5-T made its appearance on the national political agenda when Social Democratic members of parliament recommended discontinuation of its use in Germany.[95] Their recommendation forced the Federal Health Office into an

[90] 44 *FR* 15874, March 1979.
[91] *Dow Chemical Co. v. Blum*, 469 F. Supp. 892 (E.D. Mich., 1979).
[92] See *Chemical and Engineering News*, October 24, 1983, p. 5.
[93] See Koch and Vahrenholt, op. cit., pp. 184–89.
[94] BBA, *Stellungnahme zur Anwendung von 2,4,5-T bei der Unkrautbekämpfung im Forst*, Heft 181 (Berlin: BBA, 1978).
[95] *BNA International Environment Reporter*, August 12, 1981, p. 973.

extraordinary new round of consultation with a group of experts from government, industry, and the labor unions.[96]

In Britain, 2,4,5-T resurfaced as a live regulatory issue in 1979 and 1980 largely through efforts by the National Union of Agricultural and Allied Workers (NUAAW) to get the substance banned. The union's strategy was more clearly oriented toward the news media and less conscientiously focused on scientific questions than were the actions of 2,4,5-T critics in Germany and the United States. For example, the union's manifesto "The 2,4,5-T Dossier—Not One Minute Longer," issued in March 1980, recounted a series of health injuries, including miscarriages and birth defects, allegedly caused by exposure to 2,4,5-T. The documentation made no pretense of methodological exactitude. It was intended to raise the emotional pitch of the debate, not to provide a balanced, scientific account of the chemical's effects on human health.

The NUAAW attack drew a quick response from British regulatory authorities. Having reviewed 2,4,5-T as recently as March 1979, ACP issued another, significantly more detailed, report on the herbicide in December 1980. As noted above, the document placed great weight on the nonpositive epidemiological evidence and stressed the methodological weaknesses of the apparently positive Alsea II study. It also emphasized the need to look at human exposure levels in making risk estimates and concluded that the evidence pointed to virtually no risk at very low levels of exposure. In sum, ACP dismissed NUAAW's case as scientifically unconvincing and regrettably sensational.

Although NUAAW lost the scientific battle against ACP, it fared better in the larger political war. The union convinced several large employers to stop using 2,4,5-T and persuaded the Trades Union Congress (TUC) to call for a ban on the substance. The union also demanded the transfer of pesticide regulatory activities to a more representative forum than ACP.[97] ACP's credibility was damaged by the disclosure that 2,4,5-T use in Britain vastly exceeded the level estimated in the committee's 1979 report.[98] The committee eventually acknowledged that additional precautions, such as new codes of practice or expanded education and training programs, might be required to protect agricultural workers adequately against 2,4,5-T.[99]

Several interesting points emerge from this comparison. First, whatever

---

[96] Interview, Pesticide Industry Association (Industrieverband Pflanzenschutz und Schädlingsbekämpfungsmittel, IPS), Frankfurt, July 17, 1981.

[97] See John Mathews, "Unions Press for Herbicide Ban," *New Scientist,* 85, no. 1195 (1980), 558–60.

[98] See "2,4,5-T Cover-up by MAFF," *Ecologist,* 10, no. 6/7 (1980), 249; Lawrence McGinty, "Select a Chemical," *New Scientist,* 87, no. 1213 (1980), 434.

[99] ACP, op. cit., p. 17.

their position about the regulatory significance of animal tests, none of the governmental agencies acted against 2,4,5-T solely on the basis of laboratory results. Even in the United States, where regulators attach most weight to animal data, a partial ban was issued only after apparent fetotoxic effects were observed in human beings. Second, in spite of accumulating laboratory data on both 2,4,5-T and TCDD, no scientific advisory panel either in the United States or in Europe recommended a complete withdrawal of 2,4,5-T herbicides from the market. Nevertheless, EPA undertook to ban certain uses of the substance. This suggests that in the U.S. regulatory system, risk assessment by independent scientists may determine the political outcome less conclusively than in the European systems. Yet in all three countries the unresolved scientific questions about 2,4,5-T generated enough public controversy to render the scientific aspect of regulatory decision making almost superfluous. Whether regulation was relaxed or stringent, 2,4,5-T eventually succumbed to an irreversible public conviction that the substance is too unsafe to use in the human environment.

Conclusion

Scientific uncertainty and political maneuvering are inextricably bound up in the regulation of carcinogens, but the intensity of political response to scientific disputes varies enormously from one country to another. Several factors are responsible for the divergences we have described in this chapter: the structure of administrative decision making, the role of expertise in policy making, the character of interest group politics, and the history of the scientific research system.

The national research traditions discussed in chapter 6 supply one part of the explanation. As an old and respected branch of British science, epidemiology exercises an influence on British policy making that is unmatched in France and Germany, where, as we have seen, epidemiological research still lacks secure institutional foundations. The scientific debate about occupational cancer has thus been conducted largely in a two-country arena, with the older, more experienced British epidemiological school holding out for a more conservative reading of positive studies, and a more critical evaluation of nonpositive results, than is required by American agencies and their scientific advisers.

In contrast, the strength of statistical analysis and mathematical modeling in the United States has permitted a greater reliance on animal studies than regulators could contemplate before the 1970s. This development has held out special promise for British trade unions, which see in American experiments and risk assessment methodologies an independent scientific basis for challenging British epidemiology's strong hold on health and safety policy. The absence of a language barrier facilitates the transfer of policy from American regulatory agencies to British interest groups. Voluminous American records are instantly accessible to potential users such as ASTMS in Britain, whereas French and German associations often come upon them later and in less comprehensible form.

In the end, however, it is necessary to turn to institutional and procedural factors to explain the far greater polarization of the scientific debate surrounding carcinogens in the United States than in the European countries. The detailed and partisan discussion of scientific questions in the United States is an inevitable product of a regulatory process that favors strong adversarial presentation of the issues to be considered by decision makers. The U.S. policy process encourages expert witnesses to appear as advocates of particular policies, thereby creating the impression that science itself is not objective, but a servant of political interests. This contributes to the view, widely held in the United States, that regulation involves largely "transscientific" questions "which can be asked of science and yet which cannot be answered by science."[100]

Curiously, industry's real antagonists in the United States have not always been labor and environmental groups, but governmental scientists and agency staffs. Environmentalists undoubtedly served as catalysts in bringing carcinogens to the center of the regulatory stage in the 1970s. The Environmental Defense Fund, for example, pressured EPA to control the chlorinated hydrocarbon pesticides and, as a consequence, to develop its cancer principles. In later administrative proceedings, however, the important battle lines were drawn between scientists testifying on behalf of the chemical industry, on the one hand, and governmental experts such as Umberto Saffiotti of NCI, David Rall of NIEHS, and Peter Infante of OSHA, on the other. Choices between conflicting scientific positions were eventually made by agency staffs in accordance with their perceived statutory missions. As a rule, their decisions gave greater weight to the views of scientists from public sector research institutions than to the claims of industry's expert witnesses. During the Reagan years, governmental scientists adopted a much more quiescent posture with respect to regulatory issues. But their earlier strong stands continued to provide ammunition for critics of the Reagan administration's efforts to develop a more industry-oriented cancer policy.

On the surface, scientific debate is less politically colored in Europe than in the United States. One reason is that in all three European countries, a large share of health and safety policy is developed by pluralistic or elite expert groups. Both kinds of advisory bodies are committed to resolving disputes

---

[100] Alvin M. Weinberg, "Science and Trans-Science," *Minerva*, 10, no. 2 (1972), 209.

internally rather than opening them up for public discussion. For example, the influential DFG commission on hazardous substances in the workplace, not to be confused with AGA, acts unanimously on all issues before it and makes no provision for minority opinions. The multipartite expert committees provide an even more effective forum for opposing interest groups to iron out their disagreements in private.

Looking across the spectrum of issues involved in carcinogen regulation, it is apparent that Germany and France have been more successful in containing controversy than the United States and Britain. Yet scientists in the first two countries have adopted less conservative positions with respect to the use of animal data and the no-threshold concept than their counterparts in Britain. One explanation for the relative lack of conflict is the more widespread use of pluralistic negotiating bodies in France and Germany than even in Britain, let alone the United States. Since labor, industry, and consumer groups are well represented in such forums, policy decisions cannot be reached without multilateral compromise. A second reason for success is the relatively clean separation of scientific assessment and political decision making in the regulatory frameworks of both countries. Particularly in the area of carcinogen regulation, the ability to maintain scientific support for the no-threshold hypothesis without following through on its draconian policy consequences has protected German and French regulators from the kinds of attacks leveled against OSHA and EPA. However, given the American regulators' need to rationalize policy decisions in scientific terms (see chapters 2 and 7), such a separation appears all but impossible in the United States.

9

The Chemical Industry: Regulatory Challenges and Adaptive Strategies

The influence of industry on regulatory policy has long been debated by political actors and by scholars. Much of the early American work on the subject argued that, with time, all regulated industries succeeded both in "capturing" would-be regulators and in manipulating the regulatory process in ways that served their interests.[1] In Europe, too, while scholars have been less attentive to specific regulatory issues, the power of industry to mold governmental policy has been a constant theme of radical groups and parties on the left which have often viewed nationalization as the only appropriate corrective. However, more recent studies of the social regulation of the 1960s and 1970s, regulation undertaken with newly designed tools and procedures, have claimed that industry influences have been curbed and that public interest groups and dedicated public officials have been successful in ensuring that regulatory agencies remain faithful to their legislative mandates.[2] Indeed,

---

[1] See, for example, Marver Bernstein, *Regulating Business by Independent Commission* (Princeton: Princeton University Press, 1955); Gabriel Kolko, *Railroads and Regulation, 1877–1916* (Princeton: Princeton University Press, 1965); and George J. Stigler, "The Theory of Economic Regulation," *Bell Journal of Economics and Management Science*, no. 2 (Spring 1971), pp. 3–21.

[2] See Paul Sabatier, "Social Movements and Regulatory Agencies: Toward a More Adequate—and Less Pessimistic—Theory of 'Clientele Capture'," *Policy Sciences*, 6, no. 3 (1975), 301–42. See also Paul J. Quick, *Industry Influence in Federal Regulatory Agencies* (Princeton: Princeton University Press, 1981).

American industry spokesmen in the 1970s, discussing the issue of chemical control, gave the impression that affected firms had little or no impact on policy-making decisions. While much less talk of this sort is heard in the American political climate of the 1980s, it is clear that industry seldom defines and dictates the outcomes of regulatory debates.

Our purpose in this chapter is to try to evaluate the impact of industry on the regulatory process of chemical control in each of the four countries. The position we take is between the extremes of inevitable "capture," on the one hand, and industry impotence, on the other. Targeted firms have most certainly experienced a growing regulatory burden over the past two decades, yet they have been remarkably successful in assuring that these new obligations have had only modest impact on industrial performance by arguing effectively for standards that are economically reasonable and technologically practicable and by insisting on a manageable pace of implementation. What is most striking in the analysis that follows is that, while firms faced similar regulatory challenges in the four countries and set similar goals to address those challenges, they adopted very different strategies to do so. And, further, those varied strategies produced roughly similar results for firms in each of the four countries, though the costs of American and European approaches differed sharply. In view of our general theme (elaborated in chapters 3–5) that institutional arrangements define how the regulatory game is played in each country, the varied industry responses are not surprising. That no one national industry seems to have a particular advantage in shaping regulatory outcomes is also consistent with our finding of cross-national policy convergence.

The Chemical Industry

Unlike much of the "social" regulation of the 1960s and 1970s, which aims at a large and diffuse group of industries and, according to one author, accounts for diminished industry influence,[3] efforts to control hazardous substances have focused almost exclusively on the chemical industry. Other sectors that use chemical products or produce other hazardous materials are subject to

---

[3] James Q. Wilson, "The Politics of Regulation," in James Q. Wilson, ed., *The Politics of Regulation* (New York: Basic Books, 1980). Wilson argues that many of these issues are characterized by what he calls *majoritarian* politics, wherein social benefits and costs are widely distributed: "Interest groups have little incentive to form around such issues because no small, definable segment of society . . . can expect to capture a disproportionate share of the benefits or avoid a disproportionate share of the burdens" (p. 367). Much of this reasoning regarding interest group behavior was developed in Mancur Olson, *The Logic of Collective Action* (Cambridge: Harvard University Press, 1965).

some of these regulatory controls, but the chemical industry has been hit hardest, and chemical firms and trade associations have been the principal opponents of governmental intervention.

Prior to the 1970s, government regulation of chemical substances was limited to food additives, pesticides, and drugs, with some attention given to workplace exposures and to plant siting and construction. For some specialized firms, like pharmaceuticals, regulations have had important consequences for company performance over the past twenty years, but for the average large and widely diversified chemical concern, regulated products were but a small proportion of company sales. However, greater scrutiny of workplace hazards, mandatory premarket notification of new chemicals, and growing concern about toxic wastes in the 1970s made regulatory politics a part of every firm's policy agenda.

The challenges of regulation might have been more easily met if the industry did not already face serious difficulties that threatened to end a postwar record of tremendous growth and profit.[4] Heavy dependence on petroleum feedstocks raised problems of price and supply after the oil crisis of 1973–74, and the subsequent recession left the industry with declining sales, surplus capacity, and falling profits. The Europeans were burdened with buy-back or compensation deals that had been concluded with Eastern Europe in the late 1960s. By the mid 1970s, Eastern bloc countries were exporting low-priced fertilizers, synthetic rubber, and other basic chemicals into Western markets. Moreover, the worldwide glut in chemicals was likely to worsen in the 1980s, when Middle Eastern and other third-world producers were expected to begin exporting chemical products. Perhaps most disturbing was the talk of "maturity" in chemicals, the suggestion that the postwar boom in the sector was ending and that growth levels typical of other industries should be anticipated. For an industry driven by rapid innovation and technological change and accustomed to growth levels double those of other industries and booming international trade and investment, the 1970s were sobering years indeed.

Into this economic environment, governments introduced new regulations. Already burdened by the problems of several flagging industrial sectors, national leaders were understandably uneasy about further disrupting the performance of the postwar success story, and such official sensitivity was undoubtedly an asset to chemical leaders in their dialogue with government about the form and extent of intervention. The distinctive features of the modern chemical industry—its diversity, its reliance on innovation and tech-

---

[4]Much of the material on the development of the chemical industry is taken from Thomas L. Ilgen, "'Better Living through Chemistry': The Chemical Industry in the World Economy," *International Organization*, 36 (Fall 1983), 647–80.

nological change, and its international orientation—give us important clues to its response to the regulatory challenges of the 1970s.[5]

The Challenges of Regulation

Regulations in all four countries have imposed two related obligations on industry that are linked to the control of hazardous substances. The first, derived from each country's acceptance of the "polluter pays principle," requires that manufacturers pay for the control or elimination of unacceptable exposures associated with chemical production or use. The second, following from the same principle, indicates that producers of certain groups of chemicals, notably food additives and pesticides, demonstrate that their products are safe for use prior to marketing. Reducing exposures has meant changes in product design or use or in the design and construction of engineering controls or other protective devices for use in the work environment. Assuring that substances are safe has led to the generation of scientific information through an expanded program of chemical testing.

Industry spokesmen argue that these obligations raise a number of serious issues that will affect the future of their firms. First, they worry that regulation will significantly raise the production costs of chemicals already on the market. To limit such costs, industry spokesmen have battled hard for flexibility in the achievement of workplace standards, preferring the use of protective equipment to the more costly engineering controls. Moreover, they have consistently resisted efforts to require testing of old chemicals, which absorbs research energies and shaves profit margins. Firms have also argued for limits on data requirements and record-keeping obligations.

Second, industry leaders are concerned that regulation will result in lower levels and changed patterns of innovation, the lifeblood of the industry.[6] Test-

[5]The absence of cross-national work on regulatory policy is often lamented by American scholars but has seldom resulted in new studies. Notable exceptions are Henry G. Grabowski et al., "Estimating the Effects of Regulation on Innovation: An International Comparative Analysis of the Pharmaceutical Industry," *Journal of Law and Economics*, 21, no. 1 (April 1978), 133–65, and Steven Kelman, *Regulating America, Regulating Sweden: A Comparative Study of Occupational Safety and Health Policy* (Cambridge, Mass.: MIT Press, 1981). For an examination of the control of hazardous chemicals in Canada against the backdrop of U.S. and British regulatory policy, see Thomas L. Ilgen, "Between Europe and America, Ottawa and the Provinces: Regulating Toxic Substances in Canada," *Canadian Public Policy* (forthcoming).

[6]The literature on the impact of toxic chemical regulation on innovation is much less developed, though it is growing rapidly. Foster D. Snell, Inc., "A Study of the Potential Economic Impacts of the Proposed Toxic Substances Control Act (TSCA)," (unpublished paper) examined a number of expected consequences: (1) increased industry concentration;

ing requirements raise the costs of bringing new products to the market, encouraging firms to concentrate on making existing products better and producing them more efficiently rather than sinking funds into risky new ventures. Moreover, it is argued that regulation discourages innovation in small-volume chemicals, where expected returns are not sufficient to offset testing costs. Testing is also disproportionately burdensome for small, highly innovative chemical firms, which lack the resources to mount a sophisticated screening program.[7] Weaken the incentives to innovate, so the industry argues, and you will transform chemicals into just another "mature" or declining industry.

To justify their fears, chemical leaders cite the impact of regulation on innovation in pesticides and drugs in the United States.[8] For both, the cost of

---

(2) increased costs of specialized, low-volume new substances; (3) wasting of patent time, and (4) test marketing in other countries. See also Nicholas Ashford and George R. Heaton, "The Effects of Health and Environmental Regulation on Technological Change in the Chemical Industry: Theory and Evidence," in Christopher T. Hill, ed., *Federal Regulation and Chemical Innovation,* American Chemical Society Symposium Series, no. 109 (1979); "Effects of Regulations on Innovation Problems," *Chemical and Engineering News,* September 18, 1978, pp. 21–22; J. C. Ivestine, *The Impact of Environmental Protection Regulation on Research and Development in the International Chemical Industry* (Washington, D.C.: NSF, May 1978); James P. Meagher, "Another Man's Poison," *Barrons,* September 5, 1977, pp. 11–13; Glenn E. Schweitzer, "Regulation and Innovation: Short-Term Adjustments and Long-Term Impacts," Program on Science, Technology, and Society, Cornell University, September 1, 1978.

[7] For the views of the small chemical company, see Elmer Fike, "The Small Company and TSCA," *Toxic Substances Journal,* 2 no. 1 (Summer 1980), pp. 103–11.

[8] For an excellent review of the current state of the pesticide industry, see Theodore Eichers, "The Farm Pesticide Industry," United States Department of Agriculture, Agriculture Economic Report no. 461 (September 1980). See also J. D. Riggleman, "Perspective on Costs of Regulation" (Presidential Address at the 33d Annual Meeting of the Northeastern Weed Science Society, Boston, January 3, 1979), and Dale J. Menkhaus, "The Effects of Environmental Legislation on the Structure of the Pesticide Industry: A Simulation Study" (Ph.D. diss., Purdue University, December 1973). The literature on the impact of regulation on drug innovation is extensive, and only a portion of it is cited here. Much of the work has been done by associates of the American Enterprise Institute, an organization with a long-standing interest in documenting the impact of regulation on the performance of the American economy. See, particularly, Martin Bailey, "Research and Development Costs and Returns: The United States Pharmaceutical Industry," *Journal of Political Economy,* 80 (January–February 1971), 70–85; Joseph Cooper, *Regulation, Economics, and Pharmaceutical Innovation* (Washington, D.C.: American University, 1976); Henry G. Grabowski, *Drug Regulation and Innovation* (Washington, D.C.: American Enterprise Institute, 1976); R. Helms, ed., *Drug Development and Marketing* (Washington, D.C.: American Enterprise Institute, 1975) especially articles by Clymer and Lasagna and Wardell; David Schwartzman, *Innovation in the Pharmaceutical Industry* (Baltimore: Johns Hopkins University Press, 1976); Sam Peltzman, *Regulation of Pharmaceutical Innovation* (Washington, D.C.: American Enterprise Institute, 1975); UN Centre on Transnational Corporation, *Transnational Corporations and the Pharmaceutical Industry* (New York: United Nations, 1979). These studies focus on the costs of regulation. For a critique and an accounting of the

introducing new substances has risen sharply and the number of new products marketed has dropped significantly.[9] By the 1970s, innovation had become the domain of large firms, which focused principally on big payoff products: pesticides for large-volume crops and drugs for widespread diseases.[10] Cross-national studies of pharmaceutical firms also indicate shifts in R & D strategies.[11] In growing numbers, American firms have taken research and development facilities to Europe, particularly Britain, where test requirements are less onerous and new products are more rapidly approved.[12] Those who dispute the claims of chemical leaders point to the "maturity" of both industries rather than to regulatory effects to account for the decline in innovation.[13] Even so, the evidence points to a greater slowdown in the introduction of new products in the United States than in Europe.[14]

---

benefits of regulation, see James Jondrow, "A Measure of the Monetary Benefits and Costs to Consumers of the Regulation of Prescription Drug Effectiveness" (Ph.D. diss., University of Wisconsin, 1972), and Thomas McGuire, Richard Nelson, and Thomas Spavins, "An Evaluation of Consumer Protection Legislation: The 1962 Drug Amendments—A Comment," *Journal of Political Economy*, 83 (May–June 1975), 655–62.

[9] For a number of reasons, most of which the industry would like to tie to regulation, the cost of marketing new pesticide products has been growing rapidly. The costs of developing one new crop protectant in the United States increased from $195 million in 1956 to $915 million in 1970 (Riggleman, op. cit.). Between 1967–1970 and 1977–78, research and development costs in the industry as a whole increased 400 percent, while the number of new products registered dropped from ten to two per annum. The number of new chemicals screened annually in 1967–1970 was 6,500, compared to 84,000 in 1977–78. The average time it took to get a product registered from this initial screening increased from 68 months in 1967–70 to 110 months in 1977–78. Sixty-five percent of expenditures for research and development in 1977 went for developing new products; 35 percent went for protecting and expanding existing registrations (Eichers, op. cit.). Students of the drug industry have traced the impact of the 1962 amendments to the Food, Drug, and Cosmetics Act which specified that marketed drugs must be shown not only to be safe but also to be effective. By the early 1970s, Peltzman argued that the costs of marketing a new drug had doubled and that the number of new drugs marketed had been reduced by one-half. See *The Regulation of Pharmaceutical Innovation: The 1962 Amendments* (Washington, D.C.: American Enterprise Institute, 1974). Schwartzman showed that the time required to get FDA marketing approval had reduced the effective patent life of a new drug from 13.9 years (between 1966 and 1969) to 12.4 years (between 1970 and 1973) (Schwartzman, op. cit., p. 180).

[10] For pesticides, see Eichers, op. cit., pp. 21–22, and Menkhaus, op. cit. For drugs, see Henry Grabowski and John Vernon, "Structural Effects of Regulation in the Drug Industry," in Robert Masson, ed., *Essays on Industrial Organization in Honor of Joe Bain* (Cambridge, Mass.: Ballinger, 1976); Lewis H. Sarett, "FDA Regulations and Their Influence on Future R and D," *Research Management*, 17, no. 2 (March 1974), 18–20; and Peltzman, op. cit.

[11] Grabowski and Vernon, op. cit.

[12] Louis Lasagna and William M. Wardell, "The Rate of New Drug Discovery," in Helms, op. cit., pp. 155–64; David Schwartzman, *The Expected Return from Pharmaceutical Research* (Washington, D.C.: American Enterprise Institute, 1975); UN, *Transnational Corporations and the Pharmaceutical Industry* (New York: UN, 1979); and Harold Clymer, "The Economic and Regulatory Climate: U.S. and Overseas Trends," in Helms, op. cit.

[13] UN, op. cit., pp. 6–7.

[14] See Henry Grabowski, John M. Vernon, and Lacy G. Thomas, "The Effects of Regula-

The need for governmental authorities to review company test data raises delicate problems of confidentiality, or the protection of trade secrets. Seemingly unimportant data in the hands of regulators may provide important assistance to knowledgeable competitors. An inability to protect confidentiality rapidly diminishes the returns from innovation. In part, problems of confidentiality can be remedied by limiting testing requirements and the kinds of data that are passed along to governmental authorities. But by and large the means of protecting trade secrets depend on the relationships between regulator and regulated. Where strong trust prevails, informal assurances may be sufficient. Where suspicion exists, industry will seek formal procedures to routinize the handling of confidential information. Despite company concerns, the experiences of drug and pesticide regulation suggest that problems of confidentiality can be worked out to industry's satisfaction.

A fourth problem derives from the international character of chemical production and marketing and the fact that differences in regulations can raise important nontariff barriers to trade and investment.[15] Nonuniform testing protocols complicate the procedures firms must follow before placing their products in different markets. Stringent use restrictions exclude some products altogether, and varying rules on exposure levels in the workplace may necessitate the design of different manufacturing processes for foreign plants.

Some firms have responded to potential barriers to trade and investment by pushing for the harmonization of divergent national policies, coordinating their efforts through international trade associations, and pressing for consensus in the EC, the OECD, and various United Nations agencies. Others have lobbied their own governments to export national policy through the international harmonization process, that is, to protect and extend advantages that

---

tory Policy on the Incentives to Innovation: An International Comparative Analysis," in Samuel A. Mitchell and Emery A. Link, eds., *Impact of Public Policy on Drug Innovation and Pricing* (Washington, D.C.: American University, 1976), pp. 47–82, and Clymer, op. cit. In comparing the United States and Britain, Grabowski, Vernon, and Thomas conclude that research and development productivity dropped off precipitously in both countries in the 1960s compared to the 1950s, but while the drop was sixfold in the United States, it was only threefold in Britain. In a broader comparison, Clymer finds that research and development in the U.S. pharmaceutical industry is growing much more slowly than it is in other countries. EC funds now exceed those of the United States, and Japan spends 75 percent of the funds committed in the United States, although it has a much smaller domestic base. Worldwide introductions of new chemicals were down 28 percent between 1961 and 1973, but American introductions were down 53 percent. While the United States accounted for one-fifth of all new products in the 1950s, it accounted for only one-sixth of new products in the 1970s. The declining home market position has also hurt American drug exports, which have declined by one-third since 1950 as a percentage of total exports.

[15] Ingo Walter, "Non-Tariff Barriers and the Control of Chemicals" (Paper prepared for OECD Environment Directorate, October 1979). See also, "Will Toxic Substances Laws Be Trade Barriers?" *Chemical Week*, March 7, 1979, pp. 39–40.

the industry enjoys at home. Still others have used harmonization to pressure their own national government to rid its domestic arrangements of provisions unfavorable to the industry.

Chemical firms are bothered by all four of these regulatory problems, although different industries frequently rank the effect of the four problems differently. As a result, industry energies are seldom focused on identical issues. Moreover, the efforts of firms to cope with one or two of these regulatory challenges may actually complicate their management of others. Exceptional success in limiting test requirements in a particular country, for example, may disrupt delicately laid plans for harmonization. Firms that are determined to facilitate harmonization may be willing to tolerate more stringent regulations at home in order to bring domestic rules in line with those of trading partners. Successful harmonization, which depends on effective channels of information exchange, may complicate problems of confidentiality.

Industry Responses

Confronted with generally similar regulatory problems, industries in the four countries have responded with widely varied strategies. Yet each industry has met with comparably satisfying results in moderating production costs, protecting the potential for innovation, assuring confidentiality, and achieving a significant measure of cross-national harmonization. British firms have cultivated a relationship with governmental regulators that emphasizes informal consultation and the development of reasonable, practical, and flexible regulations. Success with this approach at home has encouraged industry spokesmen to push for its extension abroad through international negotiations. The powerful German industry has developed a cooperative but formal relationship with German regulators, resulting in rules that are precisely formulated and inflexibly implemented. The Germans, too, have promoted adoption of their national approach abroad. French chemical firms have pursued a strategy of apparent acceptance and adaptation, accepting the role of the state as chemical regulator and concentrating on ways to adapt to that fact. By contrast, American industry has chosen a strategy of active resistance to all governmental efforts to regulate hazardous chemicals. Moreover, unlike the Germans and the British, American managers have used the process of harmonization to restrain rather than promote the approach preferred by regulators at home.

Differences in approach grow from deeply rooted traditions of government-industry relations unique to each country and from the industry's particular history, organization, and economic strength. But, most importantly, differences in strategy grow from the special features of each country's regulatory system and the recognition by chemical firms that influence is maximized by exploiting every opportunity presented by the prevailing "rules of the game."

Britain

The chemical industry has had a long and successful history in Britain.[16] As the first modern chemical industry, it supplied inorganic chemicals to the British textile industry in the early stages of the industrial revolution. When German producers of organic dyes threatened its leadership role in the late nineteenth and early twentieth centuries, the British chemical industry utilized technological know-how and an active strategy of mergers to sustain itself when other early British industries could no longer keep pace. The most ambitious merger, in 1926, yielded Imperial Chemical Industries, a giant firm that soon came to dominate the sector in Britain.[17] ICI remains today a highly innovative, diversified, and truly international firm, accounting for 25 percent of all British chemical production. Several smaller but competitive firms (British Petroleum, Albright and Wilson, Courtaulds) complement the activities of ICI, contributing to what has been a most prosperous part of the British economy. Chemical firms have recorded steady growth in production, stable employment, trade surpluses, and healthy profit margins, enabling them to remain modern and innovative. Moreover, the discovery of North Sea oil in the early 1970s promised a bright future in petrochemicals. This unusual success has won the industry many friends in high places.

For these and other reasons, including the strategic importance of chemicals in time of war, relations between the government and the chemical industry have always been close. Ties have also been facilitated by the professionalism of the British civil service and the preference of public officials for personal and informal relations with private interests and groups.[18] Officers of leading firms, as well as representatives of the Chemical Industries Association, the industry's trade association, maintain close relations with officials at the Department of Trade and Industry, the Health and

---

[16] Literature on the history of the British chemical industry is extensive. See Archibald Clow and Nan L. Clow, *The Chemical Revolution: A Contribution to Social Technology* (London: Batchworth Press, 1952); D. W. F. Hardie, *A History of the Modern British Chemical Industry* (Oxford: Pergamon Press, 1966); and T. I. Williams, *The Chemical Industry* (London: Penguin Books, 1953).

[17] The best history of ICI is William J. Reader, *Imperial Chemical Industries: A History* (London: Oxford University Press, 1970).

[18] Much has been written about the strengths and weaknesses of the British civil service. See, for example, R. Brown and D. Steel, *The Administrative Process in Britain* (London: Methuen, 1979), and Henry Parris, *Constitutional Bureaucracy: The Development of British Central Administration since the Eighteenth Century* (London: George Allen and Unwin, 1969).

Safety Executive, and the Department of the Environment (DOE). Informality is the preferred way of conducting regulatory business in Britain; a legacy of trust and good feelings has permitted the tackling of tough policy problems in a spirit of accommodation rather than confrontation.

Since 1945, government-industry relations in Britain generally have been consistent with the pattern observed in chemicals. Starting with a tradition of economic liberalism that discouraged government intervention in economic affairs, the British have increasingly adopted a "mixed economy" model. Political leaders have experimented with the public ownership of selected industries and have evolved a unique approach to economic planning that is administered by the National Economic Development Office.[19] The continuing difficulties in British industrial performance gave considerable impetus to experimentation, particularly when similar planning efforts seemed to be promoting industrial revival and modernization in France.

Economic planning in Britain is of special interest both because it affected chemicals directly and because some instruments used in it were later incorporated into health and safety legislation. The approach, as contrasted with more direct state intervention in France and elsewhere, gave government the role of facilitator rather than director of economic activity.[20] It institutionalized a tripartite process of cooperation in which representatives of business, government, and labor meet and discuss common problems. Government's role is to improve the environment for making business decisions, not to make those decisions itself. Tripartite working parties were formed for several sectors of the chemical industry, and they have met regularly to discuss current problems and prospects.[21] Most agree that the work of these groups has been of limited assistance to industrial performance, but close personal relations encouraged by these meetings have made easier the task of toxic substances control.

While the planning exercise affirmed the British preference for informality

---

[19]There is an extensive literature on government-industry relations in Britain. See, for example, Andrew Shonfield, *Modern Capitalism: The Changing Balance of Public and Private Power* (New York: Oxford University Press, 1965), chap. 6; Stephen Blank, *Industry and Government in Britain: The Federation of British Industries in Politics, 1945–1965* (Lexington, Mass.: Lexington Books, 1973); Trevor Smith, "Great Britain," in Raymond Vernon, ed., *Big Business and the State* (Cambridge: Harvard University Press, 1974), pp. 87–104; and Stephen Young, *Intervention in the Mixed Economy: The Evolution of British Industrial Policy, 1964–1972* (London: Croom Helm, 1974).

[20]For discussions of British planning, see Shonfield, op. cit., chap. 6; E. E. Hagen and S. F. T. White, *Great Britain: Quiet Revolution in Planning* (Syracuse: Syracuse University Press, 1966); and Trevor Smith, "Britain," in Jack Hayward and Michael Watson, eds., *Politics, Planning, and Public Policy* (Cambridge: Cambridge University Press, 1975), pp. 111–27.

[21]Interviews at National Economic Development Office and Department of Industry, London, January and June 1980.

and flexibility in addressing policy problems, this form of public-sector/private-sector accommodation had already been tested in the regulatory arena with the adoption in 1957 of the Pesticide Safety Precaution Scheme to assure the safety of new pest control products. The PSPS prescribes ongoing discussions between industry and government prior to the marketing of any new pesticides; the discussions culminate not in registration or legal approval but in an informal agreement specifying whether and under what conditions the product may be manufactured and used. While the scheme is voluntary and operates without statutory authority, industry has been a willing and cooperative participant. Individual firms might have entertained thoughts of acting otherwise, but the industry trade association, the British Agrochemical Association (BAA), has pressed for conformity.

In Britain, regulation by informal cooperation benefits industry in several ways. Because participation is limited to representatives of "legitimate" interests, company spokesmen are assured significant input. Industry's influence in informal discussions is further strengthened by the technical character of many regulatory issues and the industry's knowledge of such issues in contrast to the limited expertise held by labor or environmental groups.[22] Technical know-how also makes it easier for industry representatives to communicate with the various expert advisory committees that exert considerable influence over regulatory outcomes.

Industry also benefits from a process that allows accommodation and agreement to be reached out of public view. Confidential negotiations are likely to permit greater industry control over the information and documentation that is introduced, and they also discourage the public posturing that frequently hardens interest group positions and prevents acceptable compromise.

Finally, industry benefits from British regulators' preference for pragmatism and flexibility in addressing chemical hazards. This approach calls for chemicals to be assessed and controlled substance by substance rather than generically, and for test requirements to be tailored to the needs of particular chemicals, thereby minimizing unnecessary and costly testing.[23] Pragmatism also generally argues against outright bans or drastic reductions in usage and in favor of reducing production incrementally and imposing restrictions gradually.

Concepts like "reasonable" and "practicable" sum up British regulatory

---

[22] Interviews at ICI, London, June 1980; the Confederation of British Industry, London, June 1980; and HSE, London, January and June 1980.

[23] The advantages of flexibility were cited repeatedly by spokesmen for both government and industry. Interviews at HSE, the Department of Environment, ICI, and the CIA, London, June 1980.

philosophy, a philosophy generally shared by industry. Britain's historic emphasis on voluntary compliance rather than legal enforcement permits industry to meet the burdens of regulation by entertaining more options.[24] As one industry spokesman put it, if British chemicals must abide some form of governmental intervention for regulatory purposes, they could hardly design something superior to the existing approach.[25]

Two developments, however, threaten to alter the British process in ways that would be detrimental to industrial interests. First, international discussions aimed at the harmonization of national policies have underscored the fact that the informality and flexibility of the British approach is increasingly out of step with policies adopted elsewhere. In the words of one individual at CIA, the British have been "swimming upstream" for flexibility, even though it is "the sensible way versus the Code Napoléon."[26] While British industry is not opposed to harmonization—indeed, British manufacturers are as worried about barriers to trade as anyone—it is concerned that harmonization could bring additional regulatory burdens. In negotiations for a European-wide premarket notification scheme, British officials and industry spokesmen repeatedly found themselves outnumbered, battling for a flexible approach to hazard assessment against those who advocated a checklist of test requirements.

The second challenge has come from several British labor unions that have broken with the tripartite bargaining process and have taken their cases concerning specific health hazards to the public and the press. A case in point is the effort by NUAAW, the agricultural farm workers' union, to ban 2,4,5-T (see chapter 8). The union's highly public and emotional campaign drew a heated response from industry, represented primarily by BAA, which characterized the debate as a conflict between objective scientific assessment and decision making by the media.[27] A reexamination of the issue by ACP reaffirmed the governmental position, but industry spokesmen were not optimistic about the prospects for a return to more limited public debate in the future. The challenge brought by ASTMS and GMWU on the issue of occupational carcinogens (discussed in chapter 8) is an even more politically charged issue because of the range of scientific uncertainties invoked and the number of chemicals under scrutiny. In time, the airing of scientific debates may erode public confidence in existing arrangements, and the formal and public requirements of international harmonization may undermine mutual trust between industry and government.

[24] Interview at ICI, London, June 1980.
[25] Interview at the CIA, London, June 1980.
[26] Interview at the CIA, London, June 1980.
[27] Interview at BAA, London, June 1980.

West Germany

The Germans, like the British, have enjoyed a long history of industrial leadership and commercial success in chemicals. Prominence was first achieved in the late nineteenth century on the strength of academic knowledge of organic chemistry and an industrial ability to synthesize and market organic dyes for use in the textile industry.[28] By 1900, German dyestuffs accounted for 80 to 90 percent of world production. Rationalization and merger in the 1920s resulted in the creation of I. G. Farben, the chemical giant that dominated the industry in the interwar years and whose services to the Third Reich during World War II are well known.[29] In an effort to rid Germany of any undue concentration of power, the Allies divided I. G. Farben into four separate companies: BASF (Badische), Bayer, Hoechst, and Hulls. Nevertheless, BASF, Bayer, and Hoechst still account for about 80 percent of German chemical production. The Germans have also regained their position as a leading exporter of chemicals and rank only behind the United States and Japan among OECD countries in total chemical production. The "Big Three" German firms rank among the largest in the world and are the prototype of today's chemical giants: broadly diversified, highly innovative, and fully internationalized. Chemicals are one of a small group of industries that share much of the credit for German postwar economic successes. Substantial investments in research and development (4 to 5 percent of sales) have resulted in a steady stream of new products, keeping these firms competitive at home and facilitating their penetration of new markets abroad.

As in Britain, the general character of government-industry relations in Germany offers a good starting point for explaining regulatory strategy. The German state has long been in the business of industrial development—its involvement reached a peak during the interwar years—but the close and trusting relationship between civil servants and industrialists that evolved in Britain never developed in Germany.[30] In the years of reconstruction after World War II, greater distance between government and industry was en-

[28] See the chapters on Germany in L. F. Haber, *The Chemical Industry in the Nineteenth Century* (Oxford: Oxford University Press, 1955).

[29] Joseph Borkin, *The Crime and Punishment of I. G. Farben* (New York: Free Press, 1978).

[30] Industry-state relations in Germany have generated considerable interest since the 1930s. See, for example, Alexander Gerschenkron, *Bread and Democracy in Germany* (New York: Fertig, 1966); Karl Hardach, *The Political Economy of Germany in the Twentieth Century* (Berkeley and Los Angeles: University of California Press, 1980); Henry Wallich, *Mainsprings of the German Revival* (New Haven: Yale University Press, 1955); George Kuster, "Germany," in Vernon, op. cit.; Michael Kreile, "West Germany: The Dynamics of Expansion," in Peter J. Katzenstein, ed., *Between Power and Plenty: Foreign Economic Policies of Advanced Industrialized States* (Madison: University of Wisconsin Press, 1978), pp. 191–224.

couraged by Allied, and particularly American, occupiers, a pattern elaborated in the concept of a "social market" economy (soziale Marktwirtschaft).[31] According to this view, government undertook numerous social obligations but left economic processes primarily to marketplace forces. In operation, the "social market" economy has required regular discussion between industry and government, since social programs and economic developments are closely related, but communication has remained at arm's length, assuming a more formal and structured character than the dialogue in Britain. The successful recovery of the German economy and continuing prosperity in the 1960s and 1970s provided little impetus to experiment with economic planning.

In the formulation of a national environmental policy in the early 1970s, the Germans raised this practice of formal discussion and consultation to the status of an organizing principle (Kooperationsprinzip), and regular cooperation among specified interest groups is a requirement for the development of toxic substance regulations. While both the Germans and the British stress cooperation between affected parties and the government, the formal distance implied in German regulatory procedures results in somewhat different behavior by German firms.

As their first line of defense, German industrialists argued that intervention in chemicals was simply unnecessary.[32] Managers pointed to thirty years of self-regulation, during which new products were carefully screened and workers were protected from chemical hazards. The preference for self-regulation also grew from the knowledge that, once involved, German officials tended to demand "legislative perfectionism" (Gesetzgebungsperfektionismus).[33] Unlike their British counterparts, renowned for their flexibility and pragmatism, German regulators have acquired a reputation for statutory precision and faithful execution of regulatory requirements. The powerful German Chemical Industry Association (Verband der Chemischen Industrie, VCI) criticizes German environmental laws as the strictest in the world precisely because regulators are so conscientious in their implementation.[34]

In the mid-1970s, when it became obvious that self-regulation was no

---

[31] For an interesting discussion of the evolution of the social market economy, see Edwin Hartrich, *The Fourth and Richest Reich: How the Germans Conquered the Postwar World* (New York: Macmillan, 1980).

[32] Virtually all industry statements begin with this assumption. For example, see Bundesverband der Deutschen Industrie (BDI), *Jahresbericht, 1979–1980* (Cologne: BDI, 1980), pp. 153–60; BDI, *Umweltschutz und Industrielle Entwicklung in der Bundesrepublik Deutschland* (Cologne: BDI, 1980); and VCI, *Jahresbericht, 1978–1979* (Frankfurt: VCI, 1979), pp. 47–62.

[33] VCI, op. cit., pp. 8–9.

[34] Ibid.

longer a viable strategy regarding the broad range of industrial chemicals, industry adopted new tactics. The passage of premarket notification legislation in the United States and France ensured a German legislative response.[35] However, German firms preferred intervention of a very different sort from that favored by British industry. Where the latter pressed for broad enabling legislation and flexible implementation, German chemical manufacturers were more comfortable with detailed and precisely worded legislation that spelled out industry's obligations clearly and limited the discretion of German bureaucrats.[36] In negotiations leading to the passage of the German Chemicals Act in 1980, for example, industry argued for the so-called *Stufenplan* (step-sequence plan), which linked testing to production quantities and permitted firms to predict accurately the costs of testing.[37] Chemical leaders also battled hard for the exclusion of existing substances from notification and testing requirements, fearful that zealous bureaucrats would quickly demand unreasonably costly testing programs.

At odds with the predictability preferred by German industry is the uncertainty that is inherent in chemical risk assessment. As British firms are fond of pointing out, neither a standard set of tests nor the tying of test requirements to production levels makes sense scientifically. Test standardization ensures that many unnecessary tests will be performed and increases the likelihood that others, critical for assessing a product's safety, will be avoided. Not surprisingly, the draft legislation, reflecting the industry's point of view, drew precisely this criticism from German scientists.

German chemical leaders are probably more concerned about regulation's impact on innovation than any of their European competitors.[38] Of special concern is the expected negative impact on highly innovative sectors of the industry, such as organic dyestuffs, which produce new products in small volume. It is argued that the anticipated regulatory costs have already had an impact on German dyestuffs by giving rise to new industries in East Asia, where regulations are less stringent. Clearly, the burdens of regulation fall more heavily on small than large firms, and small firms are an important source of innovation in high value-added specialty chemicals, a range of products that is increasingly crucial to the continuing competitiveness of the German industry.[39]

[35] Interview at Hoechst, Frankfurt, June 1980.

[36] See Klaus Weissermel, "Die Kontinuitat der Chemischen Forschung Sichern," *Chemie Fortschritt* (March 1979).

[37] Interviews at Hoechst, BASF, VCI, Frankfurt, and Ludwigshafen, June 1980.

[38] Interviews at VCI, Hoechst, BASF, Frankfurt, and Ludwigshafen, June 1980. We did learn of one empirical study under contract from the Umweltbundesamt on the likely impact of the German Chemicals Act on innovation in the chemical industry. It is being conducted by Professor Schulze, a chemical engineer at the Technical University of Berlin.

[39] Chemical testing by industry in Germany is conducted almost exclusively in-house by

Of greatest concern to German firms, however, is the proliferation of incompatible chemical control schemes abroad and the barriers these may create for international trade. With more than 50 percent of their foreign sales going to EC countries and another 10 percent to the United States, German firms have worked hard for cross-national harmonization. On the issue of premarket notification, German industry leaders sought European agreement in the negotiation of the EC's Sixth Amendment prior to the passage of national legislation. This strategy not only gave German officials greater flexibility in international negotiations, which increased the chances for agreement, but also served to contain the debate over the national law in ways that were compatible with industry interests. Harmonization serves as a means not only to export the German regulatory approach to others, but also to limit what overzealous German bureaucrats might try to impose at home. The "Big Three" have coordinated their international efforts through VCI. Knowledgeable representatives of the association work closely with the German national delegations to the EC, OECD, and other international institutions.[40] VCI leadership was also behind the early growth and development of CEFIC, the European-wide chemical trade association that coordinates chemical industry interests vis-à-vis the EC on a broad spectrum of issues.[41]

In the end, the German industry's response to governmental intervention for chemical control derives principally from the highly legalistic political culture in which it must operate. In stark contrast with their British competitors, German firms can only feel confident that their interests are protected if the rights and duties of public officials and private actors are formally elaborated in law. Yet, the arm's-length relationship between industrialist and bureaucrat has proved a cooperative one because both share a deep concern for the economic future of chemical production and chemical exports in Germany and both recognize the need to define a reasonable accommodation regarding the regulatory burden.

France

The chemical industry in France has charted a course different from those followed in Britain and Germany.[42] Through most of the twentieth century, the

---

the largest chemical firms. To date, there are no laboratories jointly financed by a number of chemical firms such as the Chemical Industry Institute of Toxicology in the United States, nor is there a network of independent facilities where smaller firms could go to have tests conducted for them. At the European level, forty firms have sponsored the formation of ECETOC, a cooperative venture that can provide scientific information for member firms. Participation thus far has been limited primarily to large firms.

[40] Interviews at VCI and Hoechst, Frankfurt, June 1980, and CEFIC, Brussels, January and June 1980.

[41] Interviews at CEFIC, Brussels, January and June 1980.

[42] For a good brief review of French chemical development, see Jean-Claude Achille, "A

French have preferred to be self-sufficient rather than internationally competitive in chemicals, forgoing the rationalizations and mergers following World War I that produced internationally competitive firms elsewhere and concentrating instead on servicing the domestic market. As a result, French chemicals entered the 1960s with an abundance of small and inefficient family-owned firms that were locked together by a complicated network of joint ventures which had been forged to give the industry some of the benefits of scale.

It took the formation of the European Community and exposure to foreign competition in the late 1950s to crack the wall of protectionism and to begin the painful process of restructuring and rationalization. The first objective was to build several internationally competitive firms through consolidation and merger. Rhône-Poulenc and Péchiney Ugine Kuhlman (PUK) were the beneficiaries of state-encouraged mergers in the private sector. ATO-Chimie, CdF-Chimie, and Entreprise Minière et Chimique (EMC) were the products of merger in the public sector. By 1977, these five firms accounted for 33 percent of French chemical production. Second, the state and the firms together sought to disentangle the complicated and largely inefficient joint ventures and to devise market-sharing schemes to prevent unnecessary competition. This rationalization was largely complete by the late 1970s.[43]

The French government also sought to boost the fortunes of the industry by expanding productive capacity, but its efforts were dealt a serious blow in the early 1970s, when feedstock prices soared and the subsequent recession left much of the new capacity standing idle. A rationalization scheme that had built scale but not depth and diversity left some large firms particularly exposed. The socialist government's decision in the early 1980s to nationalize the remaining large chemical firms and to embark on an even more ambitious restructuring is but the most recent example of a growing governmental presence in the industry.[44]

All of French industry has grown accustomed to state intervention.[45] In the

---

Survey of the French Chemical Industry," *Chemistry and Industry,* November 18, 1978, pp. 855–60. For a more comprehensive history, see John G. Smith, *The Origins and Early Development of the Heavy Chemical Industry in France* (New York: Clarendon Press, 1979).

[43] For a more thorough discussion of this rationalization legacy, see Ilgen, "Better Living," pp. 662–66.

[44] See "French Chemical Industry Completes Massive Restructuring," *Chemical and Engineering News,* April 2, 1984, pp. 22–25.

[45] On the importance of French administration, see Ezra N. Suleiman, *Politics, Power, and Bureaucracy in France: The Administrative Elite* (Princeton: Princeton University Press, 1974), and Michel Crozier, *The Bureaucratic Phenomenon* (Chicago: University of Chicago Press, 1967). On French industry, see Henry Ehrman, *Organized Business in France* (Princeton: Princeton University Press, 1957).

first decades of industrialization, the state played a paternal role, protecting family-owned firms from their more competitive foreign rivals with quotas and high tariffs. To meet foreign competition in the liberal international economy after World War II, the French embraced the idea of a national economic plan and established a large planning bureaucracy to devise five-year blueprints for modernization.[46]

Industry's response to intervention has varied according to the government's plans for the moment. Individual family-owned firms benefited enormously from the early protection they received, even if the long-term effects were harmful to French industry in international competition. Postwar rationalization benefited some firms and was ruinous to others. Even when mergers promised to expand the size of their firms, some company officials resisted the burdens of unprofitable or declining subsidiaries.

Regardless of how individual interests are affected, it is undeniable that the state is a formidable presence in the French economy, one that industries must learn to accommodate if they hope to prosper. The question in France has never been whether the state has a legitimate role to play in industry affairs, a question that is vigorously debated in the United States, but, rather, how to react to the state's role to gain best advantage. Industry regularly reacts to governmental plans and directions rather than designing plans of its own. Initiative is presumed to rest with the state.

Not unexpectedly, this pattern of state-industry relations colors the French government's approach to chemical control. In this light, regulation has been much more an intragovernmental matter than the negotiated arrangement between the state and the private sector typically found in Britain and West Germany. For example, the French state acted in considerable autonomy in developing both the 1977 Act on the Control of Chemical Products and the 1976 Prevention of Accidents in the Workplace Act. What little discussion did take place between industry and government in the drafting of these laws only confirms the government's control over the proceedings. Chemical leaders were given little personal access to governmental deliberations and were represented indirectly and not very successfully by the Ministry of Industry,

---

[46]On the changing role of the state in the economy in the postwar period, see Charles-Albert Michalet, "France," in Vernon, op. cit., pp. 105–25, and John Sheahan, *Promotion and Control of Industry in France* (Berkeley and Los Angeles: University of California Press, 1977). There is an abundance of literature on the experience of French planning. See, for example, Stephen Cohen, *Modern Capitalist Planning* (Cambridge: Harvard University Press, 1969); Jean-Jacques Bonnaud, "Planning and Industry in France," in Hayward and Watson, op. cit., pp. 93–110; John H. McArthur and Bruce R. Scott, *Industrial Planning in France* (Boston: Harvard University, Division of Research, Graduate School of Business Administration, 1969); and Yves Ullmo, "France: The National Context," in Hayward and Watson, op. cit., pp. 22–51.

the sector's principal spokesman within the bureaucracy. Unlike the German VCI, the French Chemical Industry Association (Union des Industries Chimiques, UIC), a weak federation of sixty-five smaller associations, played but a small role in the regulatory debate.

French bureaucrats regularly maintain a measure of aloofness from both public interest groups and industry, calling on the latter only when they are in need of technical information. Chimie et Ecologie, a consulting group of industrialists and scientists organized by UIC to provide technical expertise to the Ministry of the Environment, has been unable to develop an effective working relationship with government officials.[47] Indeed, in deliberations leading to the passage of the Chemical Law, one member claimed that the government never even revealed a draft text of the proposed statute during all of the informal meetings.[48] Or, as summed up by one UIC official, "[these discussions] went quite well when there were no disagreements," otherwise, "they didn't listen to us."[49] When discussions with government did take place, they were almost always about technical matters and seldom about the shape and conduct of policy.[50]

The chemical industry's relations with the ministries charged with regulatory duties raised special difficulties. Relations with the Ministry of the Environment had never been close, and those with the Ministry of Labor posed even greater problems, staffed as it is by work inspectors and physicians who are sympathetic to the objectives of worker protection. Bureaucratic rivalry between the two ministries further complicated the defense of industry interests. One consequence of this rivalry has been that French firms must now submit two separate notification files for new chemical substances. The UIC has had only limited success in coordinating these separate submissions.

If we assess the influence of French chemical manufacturers by the standards applied in the other three countries, we might conclude that they have had little success in defining the contours of regulatory policy. Yet, industry spokesmen remain relatively unconcerned about the threats posed by regulation. Rising costs, a lower rate of innovation, and the loss of trade secrets are sometimes raised by company officials, but these topics are seldom given the urgency they receive, for example, in the United States. Less reliant on exports than either the British or the Germans, French firms have also been less concerned about international harmonization.

The greatest concern about regulation's impact on industry is voiced not by

[47] Interview at Colgate-Palmolive, Paris, June 1980.
[48] Ibid.
[49] Interview at UIC, Paris, June 1980.
[50] Interview at Rhone-Poulenc, Paris, June 1980.

industrial managers but by bureaucrats charged with overseeing the industry's economic fortunes. Officials at the Ministry of Industry argue that chemicals have not received the governmental attention accorded to other sectors and that this has permitted regulation to gain momentum. They maintain that risks are overstated and that regulatory actions are taken simply to appease public opinion.[51] The ministry has also pressed the industry position that France should forgo unilateral action and wait for harmonization within the EC and OECD.[52]

Two explanations can be advanced for the complacency on the part of French industry. The first focuses less on industry's involvement in the formulation of policy and more on the government's record of implementing and enforcing it. In contrast to the situation in Germany, where industry knows that bureaucrats will meticulously adhere to every letter of the law and is insistent that its obligations be specified in advance, industrial leadership in France is more comfortable with broad and comprehensive legislation. They can countenance bureaucrats demonstrating their vigilance in health and environmental matters to the public, secure in the knowledge that implementation will fully consider the impact on industry.

Firms may also anticipate weak enforcement, permitting them to deflect the burdens of regulation by simply ignoring them. Early and fragmentary evidence regarding new chemical notifications under the 1977 chemicals law suggests a pattern of enforcement problems and poor compliance. In place of the anticipated fifty to one hundred notifications, government officials received approximately ten notices in the first year of operation. While several factors may account for this low response, it is clear that French bureaucrats seemed reluctant to hold companies strictly accountable, particularly at a time when other Western governments had not yet put similar schemes in place.

A second and more compelling explanation of industry's passive stance relates to the legacy of state involvement in the economy. French firms are resigned to the presence of government in a wide range of activities and have learned to accommodate that presence more easily and without the fanfare that has accompanied state intervention elsewhere. The best strategy is to accept the new state role and to work quietly to adapt to it. This adaptation is easier in the implementation stage and is facilitated by the state's dual role as regulator and economic manager. For the government to succeed as entrepreneur and economic modernizer, regulatory burdens must remain within reason. The fusion of economic and regulatory roles in the French government is

---

[51] Interviews at the Ministry of Industry, Paris, June 1980.
[52] Ibid.

the chemical industry's best guarantee of moderate regulatory requirements and absolves it of the need for the vigilant persuasion and possible confrontation that are the hallmarks of industrial regulatory behavior elsewhere.

From one perspective, the chemical industry has had little impact on regulatory policy in France; it is more a consumer than a molder of state action. But French industry is not a typical interest group, separate from the French state, in the way industry is in the United States or Britain. Instead, the state itself is a critical part of the chemical sector, and its policy is unavoidably conditioned by industrial perspectives. Taking advantage of this identity of views, French chemical firms have been able to contain regulatory momentum with a minimum of effort.

The United States

The American chemical industry started slowly in the late nineteenth century, and a good part of the twentieth century has been spent catching up.[53] Supply shortages during both world wars provided the incentive for building a viable and independent industry. The cutoff of German dyestuffs during World War I brought federal assistance, followed by congressional tariff protection. The shortfall of natural rubber during World War II resulted in governmental support for development of a synthetic substitute, which in turn laid the foundation for a flourishing postwar petrochemical industry. While the American industry too went through phases of merger and concentration, the enormous domestic market has always allowed competition among a much larger number of fully diversified firms than in any European country. In 1980 thirty-six American firms had chemical sales in excess of $1 billion, compared to fifteen for all of Europe (three in Germany, two in Britain, and two in France). The number of large firms grew in the 1960s and 1970s, when the major oil companies moved extensively into chemicals. While most of the larger firms have expanded abroad, the domestic market has remained their primary focus. Foreign trade and production make up a much smaller part of overall revenues for U.S. companies than for German or British firms. As a result, American chemical leaders have been more concerned about the national, rather than the international, implications of chemical control.

The postwar success of the chemical industry has also failed to attract the

---

[53]The most extensive American industrial history is the six-volume study by William Haynes, *American Chemical Industry* (New York: D. Van Nostrand, 1954). For a concise history, see John F. Henahan, "Two Hundred Years of American Chemicals," *Chemical Week*, February 18, 1976, pp. 25–60. There are also a number of good company histories of DuPont, Dow, and Monsanto.

same political attention that it has in Britain and Germany. In a large and diversified economy, the sector has been one success story among many. In the 1950s and the 1960s, Washington trusted industry to manage its own affairs, a decision reinforced by a legacy of remarkable growth and expansion.

Portions of the industry got a strong foretaste of governmental involvement with the passage of food additive legislation in the late 1950s, the establishment of a registration scheme for pesticides, and the regulation of drugs in the early 1960s. However, it was not until the 1970s that the industry as a whole began to feel the full weight of intervention. In contrast to the view taken by European firms, regulation was viewed by U.S. companies as their chief challenge in the 1970s.[54] Large companies have reorganized to create a new "counterbureaucracy" to collect the necessary data and to prepare the obligatory paperwork.[55] Testing facilities have undergone rapid expansion, most notably when 40 big companies jointly created the Chemical Industry Institute of Toxicology (CIIT) to test large volume chemicals.[56] Considerable resources have been devoted to lobbying and litigation, to underwriting the activities of a myriad of trade associations and to building formidable legal departments.[57]

---

[54]The chemical industry, citing Department of Commerce data, claims to spend more for pollution control than any other U.S. industry ($2.5 billion in 1979, 22 percent of the $11.1 billion spent by industry as a whole). See "Industry Spending on Pollution Control," *Chemecology,* May 1981. Dow Chemical calculates what it regards as the appropriate and the excessive regulatory costs it pays out each year. Total costs increased from $147 million in 1975 to $186 million in 1976 to $268 millioin in 1977, a jump of 82 percent in two years. Excessive costs increased from $50 million in 1975 to $60 million in 1976 to $115 million in 1977. Such figures lead Paul Oreffice of Dow to conclude, "Clearly there are no faster rising costs of business than expenses related to governmental regulations."

[55]One example is the organizational impact on Allied Chemical Company following the Kepone incident. See *New York Times,* January 16, 1980, p. D1. Monsanto and Shell Chemical have also reorganized extensively to address regulatory concerns. The Monsanto response was triggered by the unexpected ban of its acrylonitrile bottle, jointly developed at considerable expense with Coca Cola. Public relations were developed in an attempt to upgrade the industry's image. Monsanto President John Hanley has made a concerted effort to speak out on regulatory issues, and Monsanto has mounted a major public relations campaign to spread the word about Monsanto's activities in this area. CMA has also launched a major media program to upgrade the image of chemicals. The chemical industry occupies a status in the mind of the public similar to that of tobacco companies. See "Cleansing the Chemical Image," *Business Week,* October 8, 1979, p. 73; and "Adversaries or Allies? American Attitudes on Business, Government, and Growth," a survey conducted by Cambridge Reports, Inc., for Union Carbide Corporation, New York, 1980.

[56]For a discussion of CIIT, see "Chemical Firms Try Joint Product Testing," *Industry Week,* February 3, 1975, pp. 22–23. For a broader discussion of the industry's efforts to expand its toxicological facilities, see "Industry's Preemptive Strike against Cancer," *Fortune,* February 13, 1978.

[57]For a discussion of the growth of company offices in Washington and their lobbying

Industry's vigorous and negative response to the expansion of regulation must be viewed beside the broader legacy of public-sector/private-sector relations in the United States. Nowhere have the classical liberal views about the efficacy of a free-market economy and the need to maintain a separation between the public sector and the private sector penetrated so deeply.[58] Early efforts to regulate were not motivated by a desire to introduce new principles of economic organization but, rather, to correct perceived failures in the functioning of the market. The government was to be an arbiter among market forces, not a director of economic activity. Even so, its intrusion has always been controversial—actively debated in advance and then roundly criticized in the event of failure. In an important sense, the role of the state in the economy has never been as fully accepted in the United States as it has been in Europe. Debate over this role is frequently reopened, seldom generating more than a fragile consensus of the sort that is easily undone by a new political climate. Even within industry, views about the proper role of government vary widely. Firms in sectors such as transportation and communications have gained important advantages from particular regulatory arrangements, while most pharmaceutical and pesticide firms have struggled with regulatory burdens.

More recent attacks on a variety of social programs and on the wave of "social" regulation continue to raise fundamental questions about state intervention in the economy across the political spectrum. The American inability to resolve this question once and for all stems from a basic distrust of government accompanied by a fundamental belief that a market system, while not perfect, is the preferable means to meet the needs and desires of free citizens.[59] The shortcomings of the marketplace inevitably bring government into the economy, but government cannot be trusted to do the job right, for reasons of both incompetence and political opportunism. Continuing failures of the market will strengthen the case for expanded governmental activity at times; perceived failures of government encourage a return to the market-

---

efforts, see "Chemical Firms in Washington: Getting Their Point Across," *Chemical and Engineering News,* December 20, 1976, pp. 17–18; and "More Firms Set Up Government Relations Unit," *Chemical and Engineering News,* July 2, 1979, p. 18. For a discussion of chemical trade associations, see "Trade Groups: Voice for Industry in Washington," *Chemical and Engineering News,* December 20, 1976, pp. 12–13. With the growing presence of large oil firms in the chemical sector, the American Petroleum Institute (API) increasingly lends its influence to battles over chemical regulation. It was API that brought suit against OSHA in the benzene case.

[58] See Louis Hartz, *The Liberal Tradition in America* (New York: Harcourt Brace, 1955).

[59] John G. Ruggie, "International Regimes, Transactions, and Change: Embedded Liberalism in the Postwar Economic Order," *International Organization,* 36 (Spring, 1982), 379–415.

place. In Europe, where faith in the market is less pervasive, and faith in and protection by the state are more pronounced, a public-sector/private-sector accommodation is more easily achieved.

The American regulatory process for chemical control, discussed in earlier chapters, reflects this ambivalence about government and the marketplace. The recognition that the market has inadequately protected the public against significant chemical hazards has opened the door to governmental intervention. The concern that government will prove incapable of regulating efficiently or will be co-opted by special interests has in turn resulted in a process structured to give broad industry opportunities for participation in the formulation, implementation, and litigation of policy. It is a process designed to bring marketplace dynamics to the political arena. Interested parties must be willing to invest considerable time and energy to see their interests protected. Moreover, the investment is often unending, since issues are seldom put to rest but are, rather, reassessed in new political environments. The very length of the regulatory debate often advantages industry, endowed as it often is with superior organization and extensive resources.

The changing character of the state-industry relationship and a regulatory process that is structured to play to short-term political forces make the government's role as regulator most unpredictable. Unlike in Britain, where policy grows from close relations between civil servants and powerful private interests, or in Germany, where predictability follows the rule of law, or in France, where regulation tends to follow orderly bureaucratic routine, governmental action in Washington is capable of dramatic swings. The knowledge that government can do unpredictable and significant damage and that loud protest and persistent challenge can make a difference leads to an industrial strategy of active resistance in regulatory affairs.

Political and economic circumstances unique to the U.S. chemical firms also result in a different ranking of regulatory priorities. International harmonization, while potentially useful as a means to bridle the excesses of regulators at home, receives much less attention than it does in Europe. Regulations affecting the marketing of American products in European countries are a minor problem, particularly in view of the success of European firms in achieving acceptable domestic arrangements. U.S. firms thus direct their attention to more pressing problems at home: the costs of testing both new and existing chemicals, growing paperwork burdens, the protection of trade secrets, and the suspected determination of some regulators to achieve a risk-free environment.

The diversity of the American chemical industry, with its many firms of varying sizes and its specialized trade associations, is reflected in its regulatory behavior. Dow Chemical has fought regulation at every opportunity and with all the resources it can muster.[60] DuPont, Union Carbide, and Monsanto have taken a more moderate stance and have sought to develop a reasonable working relationship with governmental officials.[61] Small companies, effectively represented by the Synthetic Organic Chemical Manufacturers Association (SOCMA) and spokesmen such as Elmer Fike of the Fike Chemical Company, have been among the most outspoken critics of regulation's impact on small-volume speciality chemicals.[62] The Chemical Manufacturers Association (CMA), the largest U.S. chemical trade association, has enjoyed a steady rise in influence during the regulatory debates of the 1970s, giving it a prominence that is considerably greater than UIC's in France but less than VCI's in Germany. However, as the representative of many firms with varying interests and styles, CMA frequently has been unable to find a position that represents the whole industry effectively. At these times, individual firms have preferred to plead their own case in Washington.

The American industry's strategy of active resistance can be illustrated by its response to two important regulatory events of the 1970s, the passage and implementation of the Toxic Substances Control Act (TSCA) and the attempt by the Occupational Safety and Health Administration to implement a generic policy on occupational carcinogens.

TSCA was the first American law aimed at the chemical industry as a whole. In the five years of debate prior to the law's enactment in 1976, the industry, relatively naive in the ways of Washington, received an intensive education in regulatory politics.[63] Much of that learning took place after 1975, when the industry resigned itself to the act's passage and organized to ensure that intervention would be manageable.[64] Chemical firms worked hard for selective, as opposed to comprehensive, test requirements, for a limit to the number of existing chemicals to be tested, for the exclusion of research and development chemicals and mixtures of approved substances, and for a

[60] Interviews at Dow Chemical, Washington, January 1981.

[61] Interviews at DuPont, Union Carbide, and Monsanto, Wilmington, Del., New York, N.Y., and Washington, D.C., January 1981.

[62] See Fike, op. cit.

[63] The Manufacturing Chemists Association (MCA later changed its name to CMA) established a Special Committee on Toxic Substances Legislation chaired by Richard Heckert, senior vice-president of DuPont. Heckert's committee was given authority to act for the industry without consultation, but as Heckert admitted, committee members had little idea about how to go about their task: "When I first got into this, I hadn't the foggiest notion of how things are done. There were so many turns in the road it was hard to keep up. The process just wasn't orderly. Sometimes days were spent on things not worth an hour, and sometimes important things were done fast" (see "How They Shaped the Toxic Substances Law," *Chemical Week,* April 27, 1977, p. 52).

[64] Ibid. *Chemical Week* relates how Heckert first tried to lecture Congressman Bob Eckart (D-Texas) on cancer data and the "good deeds" of the industry—with no success. Only when industry came around to the tactic of trading concessions did its influence begin to grow.

minimal package of data submissions for new chemicals prior to manufacturing.

To buttress its case, the industry contracted with Foster D. Snell, Inc., for a study on the economic impact of the proposed legislation. The report estimated overall compliance costs at $300 million to $1.3 billion and predicted that the number of new products would drop 10 to 20 percent in large firms and 75 percent in small companies.[65] It also forecast increased industry concentration, a move of research and development capacity abroad, fewer new low-volume chemicals, and other problems.[66]

When TSCA finally passed, chemical companies, with few exceptions, viewed it as tough but acceptable.[67] The act did convert chemicals into a "regulated industry," but industry efforts to make the law "acceptable" paid off in important ways.[68] The definition of new substances excluded those used for research and development as well as mixtures in which component chemicals were known to be safe. The amount of information required in new chemical notifications met industry conditions regarding confidentiality and record keeping. The number of existing chemicals to be scrutinized annually was set at fifty, down from the three hundred initially proposed. Prior to any action to ban or restrict use, EPA was required to give industry forty-five days notice to rebut the proposed action and then to secure a court injunction before the agency proceeded.[69]

The passage of the law did not end the debate. The industry has taken full advantage of the opportunities provided by the statute to challenge EPA's implementing decisions. In March 1977, EPA published its draft guidelines on

[65] Snell, Inc., op. cit. For a discussion of the study, see "Setting Up for Toxic Substances," *Chemical Week*, February 23, 1977, p. 58.

[66] In addition to the industry studies, a number of other attempts were made to assess the costs of TSCA. An EPA study in 1974 put the costs at between $40 and $45 million; a second EPA study in 1975 increased the estimate to between $78 and $141.5 million; a 1975 GAO report put the annual cost at $100 to $200 million. For a good review of these studies, see George S. Dominguez, *The Business Guide to TOSCA: Effects and Actions* (New York: John Wiley, 1979).

[67] DuPont, Monsanto, and Union Carbide, as well as CMA, endorsed the legislation. Among the steadfast dissenters were Dow Chemical and most small chemical companies, which continued to feel, with justification, that the law would hurt them the most. One indicator of the impact of TSCA is the literature that has appeared to help companies cope with their obligations under the law. George S. Dominguez of Ciba-Geigy has contributed considerably to this literature. See his *Business Guide to TOSCA* and his "Practical Business Effects" (Paper presented at the Executive Enterprise Institute, Washington, D.C., March 1981).

[68] Robert Zener, "The Toxic Substances Control Act: Federal Regulation of Commercial Chemicals," *Business Lawyer*, 32 (July 1977), 1685–1703.

[69] See "A Tough—But Acceptable—Toxic Chemicals Law," *Business Week*, October 25, 1976, p. 102.

the information needed for the inventory of existing substances. The industry complained that these requirements violated the spirit of the law, imposed extraordinary costs of data collection, especially on small firms, and threatened trade secrets.[70] After almost a year of deliberations, EPA issued its final rules for inventory reporting, sticking with its request for volume and site data but devising new procedures to protect confidentiality and to reduce the impact on small firms. A second fight came on the issue of guidelines for notification concerning new chemicals. The early draft brought heated opposition and threats of court action if modifications were not made. The absence of major difficulties with the notification scheme once it was in place suggests that reasonable and workable arrangements have emerged.[71]

The second major challenge came with OSHA's efforts in the late 1970s to

---

[70] Meagher, op. cit.

[71] There were some indications that industry did not fully comprehend the long-term implications of regulation's impact on innovations. Throughout the debate about implementing TSCA, more and more arguments are raised about changing patterns of investment, from offensive investment (the development of new products) to defensive investment (the protection of existing products). See Philip H. Abelson, "Regulation of the Chemical Industry," *Science,* 202 (November 3, 1978), 473, and Jackson R. Browning, "The Hidden Costs of Regulation," *Chemical Week,* March 4, 1981, p. 5. Browning, who heads the unit on Environment, Health, and Safety Affairs at Union Carbide, argues that a growing share of capital investment made by U.S. industry is mandated by law. Since regulation has increased the uncertainty of research and development, regulation has also made it less and less attractive. In Browning's words, "Is it worth investment in R and D when the potential commercial application may lie a decade in the future and across a regulatory minefield?" Abelson, in quoting TSCA directly, reminds us that Congress calls for regulations that are "not to impede unduly or create economic barriers to technological innovation while fulfilling the primary purpose . . . to assure that such innovation and commerce . . . do not present an unreasonable risk."

Evidence of the growing regulatory burden was readily available in the pesticide industry, which was deep in the throes of reexamining the safety of existing products through the RPAR process. In 1978 the industry had twenty-five chemicals constituting between $350 and $500 million in sales going through the process, and chemicals constituting between $650 and $850 million in sales in the pre-RPAR stage. In other words, 20 to 25 percent of the pesticide business was under scrutiny, resulting in a loss of much potential business and contributing to the fact that not a single new pesticide was registered in 1977, even though the industry spent between $200 and $300 million on research and development. See the *Chemical Marketing Reporter,* April 3, 1978, p. 74.

Curiously, there was some new sentiment in industry that TSCA had a "silver lining" and that, if the act was approached correctly, it could actually improve the position and performance of some chemical firms. Remarkably, this view was expressed by Elmer Fike, one of the most adamant opponents of TSCA for its impact on small companies. Fike argued that the small firms' advantage has always been adaptability and that this advantage could be put to use in coping with TSCA. See his "The Small Company and TSCA." See also "Living with the New Regulations," *Modern Plastics,* September 1977, pp. 51–71.

Academic work on the impact on chemical innovation also has begun to appear. See, especially, Hill, op. cit. In "The Effects of Health and Environmental Regulation on Technological Change in the Chemical Industry," Ashford and Heaton argue that regulations properly conceived can be "technology forcing," encouraging creative responses to indus-

develop a generic policy for regulating occupational carcinogens. OSHA's initiative (discussed in chapters 4 and 8) elicited an immediate and strongly negative reaction from industry. Spokesmen were wary of any policy that played on the fears of an "epidemic of cancer" or that could lay the foundation for a larger national cancer policy.[72] The industry mobilized as never before. In late 1977, the major chemical firms created the American Industrial Health Council to fight the policy. AIHC's first objective was to upgrade and coordinate scientific positions. As we observed in chapter 8, industry stressed the scientific uncertainty surrounding several issues relating to carcinogenicity as well as the pitfalls of automatic policy responses when scientific issues remained cloudy.[73] Spokesmen argued that the policy would "freeze science" and deny flexibility in testing. AIHC also called for the establishment of a science panel, independent of the regulatory agency, to make judgments about scientific questions (see chapter 7).[74]

Industry feared that OSHA was pursuing the unobtainable objective of a

---

trial development. They go on to assert that the chemical industry has adapted well to regulations thus far, and then they give recipes for regulatory design that will produce the desired results.

[72] The cancer mentality and movement are carefully explored by Robert Rettig, *Cancer Crusade* (Princeton: Princeton University Press, 1977). See the comments of Ronald Lange of the Synthetic Organic Chemical Manufacturers' Association in *Chemical Week,* October 12, 1977, p. 18. Monte C. Throdahl of Monsanto put it directly in a speech to the Chemical Manufacturers' Association on November 22, 1977: "The way the present carcinogens issue is handled today will ultimately dictate the future not only of the Toxic Substances Act but of regulation and probably the future of our industry."

[73] In the words of one observer, "Never have so many been given so much power to effect so little of value by the regulation of what they understand so meagerly." Attributed to Wardell Harris, Penn State University, and quoted by Monte C. Throdahl, remarks at the Toxics Control Conference of the Government Institutes, Inc., Washington, D.C., December 11, 1979. The AIHC refutation of the "epidemic of cancer" argument and the data to support it can be found in AIHC, "AIHC Recommended Alternatives to OSHA's Generic Carcinogen Proposal," OSHA Docket no. H-090, February 24, 1978, pp. 1–8. DuPont makes much the same argument in its publication, *Occupational Safety and Health: A DuPont Company View* (Wilmington, Del.: DuPont, 1980), pp. 26–28. See also Thomas H. Maagh, "Industry Council Challenges HEW on Cancer in the Workplace," *Science,* 202 (November 10, 1978), 602.

[74] Cf. chapter 7 herein. See also AIHC, "AIHC Proposal for a Science Panel," Washington, D.C., March 18, 1980. The panel would exist to separate the scientific function from the regulatory function in policy decisions. The scientific function is to identify and estimate risk; the regulatory function is to devise methods of risk avoidance. The panel would be established in government but outside any particular agency, and it would be involved through agency referral. It would be composed of fifteen members drawn from different disciplines who would serve three-year terms and would be appointed by an "objective" group of eminent scientists such as NAS. The panel's primary task would be to assess risk on a case-by-case basis, and it would be immune from litigation. A similar proposal was advanced by the Office of Science and Technology Policy in its report "Identification, Characterization, and Control of Potential Human Carcinogens: A Framework for Federal Decision-Making," Washington, D.C., February 1, 1979. It proposed that the panel be under the jurisdiction of the NTP. AIHC endorsed this report.

risk-free society by mandating that all exposures be reduced to the lowest feasible level. It advanced the view that some risk is inevitable and that policy benefits should be based on the assessment of relative risks.[75] The chief task of the proposed science panel would be to conduct quantitative risk assessments. Moreover, OSHA should consider both the costs and the benefits of proposed standards: benefits should be commensurate with the costs of achieving them.[76] AIHC insisted that this consideration did not entail less regard for human health: AIHC is "not advising trading dollars for lives. What we are talking about is making the best use of limited dollars so that society's limited resources can wisely be spent."[77]

Industry again contracted Foster D. Snell, Inc. to assess the economic impact of the OSHA plan. The results, using the most extreme scenario, in which 2,415 substances were regulated, projected $88 billion in capital costs.[78] Industry's case was strengthened by national economic difficulties in the late 1970s and by the general move toward a more cost-effective approach to regulation.

These efforts produced a number of significant changes in the OSHA proposal. In the opinion of industry leadership, "AIHC's efforts contributed to a much more flexible OSHA policy, the group of materials has been markedly narrowed and broad generic approaches have been blunted."[79] More specifically, AIHC convinced OSHA to adopt a priority risk assessment mechanism that met most of industry's criteria for determining the relative risks of identified carcinogens. Some within OSHA were also attracted to the idea of a science panel, but only if it involved governmental employees and

[75] For a good critical discussion of the American ideal of absolute safety at any cost, see Gio Batta Gori, "The Regulation of Carcinogenic Hazards," *Science,* 208 (April 18, 1980), 256–62. Gori sees the all or nothing response of American regulators slowly changing: "Gradually, loftier views are giving way to a realism that expects regulation to improve the quality of life for the living, not merely to extend life expectancy." When absolute safety goes, it becomes "the business of regulators to define tolerable levels of risk" (p. 256). This is a position that industry heartily endorses.

[76] The point is made in AIHC, "AIHC Recommended Alternative to OSHA's Generic Carcinogen Proposal," and idem, "Toward a Sound Public Policy on Carcinogenic Agents: AIHC Comments on Chapters I, VI, VII of the Public Review Draft of the Report to the President by the Toxic Substances Strategy Committee," Washington, D.C., October 15, 1979.

[77] Quoted in *Chemical and Engineering News,* July 3, 1978, pp. 14–15.

[78] See Foster D. Snell, Inc., "Preliminary Estimates of Direct Compliance Costs and Other Economic Effects of OSHA's Generic Carcinogen Proposal on Substance Manufacturing and Using Industries," 1978. For a description of the study, see "Industry Capital Costs Seen Skyrocketing If Generic Carcinogen Plan Goes Through," *Chemical Marketing Reporter,* April 13, 1978, p. 3. In later interviews with us, several industry spokesmen indicated that the industry lost some credibility when it announced these enormous costs. The study was roundly criticized by those on both sides of the regulatory debate.

[79] AIHC, "1980 Report to the Membership," Washington, D.C.

examined a limited range of evidence. Moreover, AIHC was assured that OSHA would consider regulatory measures other than engineering controls, long opposed by industry because of exorbitant costs. All in all, industry was encouraged by these changes but ultimately remained unsatisfied with the results, filing suit against the agency in January 1980.[80]

In both examples, the American chemical industry adopted the same strategy: to protest loudly and resist actively all efforts by government to increase the regulatory burden at every twist and turn of the policy process. A less aggressive posture would permit regulatory proponents to seize the initiative and make an unfavorable swing in policy more probable. The two examples also demonstrate the limited but very real effectiveness of this strategy. Actual regulatory burdens have grown, but they have grown at a slow and manageable rate, a rate not unlike that in Europe.

While American industry has generally met its regulatory objectives, success has come at high cost. Success in the open and adversarial American setting requires effective industry organization and coordination of views, the marshalling of scientific and economic evidence, the education of a skeptical public, and constant vigilance and activity from one end of the policy process to the other. The American reluctance to "decide" an issue also requires that industry always be prepared to renew the fight.

Conclusion: Industrial Impact on the Regulatory Process

The principal lesson of our cross-national analysis of regulatory politics is that the key determinants of strategies for meeting regulatory challenges are the wider patterns of industry-government relations and the narrower features of national regulatory policy making. Informal consultation in Britain, formal cooperation in Germany, acceptance and adaptation in France, and active resistance in the United States are approaches that grow logically from national "rules of the game." As regards the procedural rules for participating in the regulatory debate, industry leaders are rule takers, not rule makers. Even in the pursuit of international harmonization, so important to the Germans and the British, the desire is to export a more congenial national approach, not to impose a new global process. The relative sizes and strengths of various industries only marginally affect these patterns of behavior. The German chemical industry, long a potent force in the national economy, is no

---

[80] The composition and powers of the science panel, the limited use of risk assessment, and the continued emphasis on engineering controls as opposed to performance standards were among the reasons for filing suit. Interview at AIHC; AIHC, "1980 Report to the Membership."

less willing to adapt and play by national rules than are the French or American industries, whose relative economic importance is less.

Further confirmation of this conclusion derives from the behavior of multinational firms in different countries. In each of the countries under study, foreign firms have been quick to adopt the strategies of the domestic industry, frequently employing an employee who is native to the country and who is knowledgeable about domestic regulatory affairs to head their health and safety departments. Perhaps the most striking example comes from the activity of foreign firms in a country outside this study. In Canada, where the proximity to the United States and the overwhelming presence of American firms encourage us to overlook the differences in regulatory approach, American firms are quick to adopt new strategies tailored to the Canadian process, a process that more closely approximates the British than the American design.[81]

At the same time, each chemical industry has been remarkably adept at using existing national processes to its full advantage. British and German firms have taken every opportunity to consult and cooperate, pressing their concerns about economic impact and technical feasibility. U.S. firms have used the multiple channels of access and the procedural complexities of the American system to moderate and modify governmental proposals. French firms have counted on the role of the state as entrepreneur as well as regulator to assure a reasonable regulatory burden. All four industries have been successful, not in preventing regulation altogether, but in making certain that it poses no serious threat to the future of the industry.

Because industry is quick to adapt to and play by the prevailing rules in each country, its activities tend to reaffirm the strengths and weaknesses of each regulatory process that have been identified in preceding chapters. In dealing with the scientific uncertainty endemic to chemical risk assessment, for example, European firms are confident that issues will be managed in a fair-minded way. They have no incentive to upset the tacit consensus that links uncertainty with regulatory caution. American firms, by contrast, have wholeheartedly entered the scientific fray in an attempt to use uncertainty as a means to slow hostile regulatory action or to prevent it altogether. The vigorous reaction of the industry to OSHA's generic cancer policy, a deliberate agency effort to "settle" some scientific issues, is the best example of industry's recognition that to abstain from or concede defeat in the scientific debate in the United States constitutes a significant loss of influence over the process as a whole.

Throughout the book, we have also pointed to the higher costs associated with the design and implementation of regulations for chemical control in the

---

[81] For a discussion of Canada, see Ilgen, "Between Europe and America."

United States compared to their cost in the three European countries. In the United States, costs in time, money, and manpower derive both from the extensive participation of interested parties and from the scientific, legal, and economic argumentation. These costs are borne by industry no less than by other American actors. Industry's willingness to absorb these ever-increasing costs encourages similar behavior among its regulatory opponents and affirms the tendency toward a steady escalation of costs for the process as a whole. While costs for firms vary among the three European countries, they are markedly lower than expenditures made by firms in the United States and have remained relatively constant.

Both the inability of the American process to resolve regulatory issues and the high costs of reaching decisions have contributed to the growing public dissatisfaction with governmental programs of social regulation. American industry has encouraged this declining legitimacy by constantly challenging government's right to intervene as well as the nature of its intervention. Given the ambivalence surrounding the state's proper role, the public is receptive to industry arguments. Deregulation, currently pushed by many politicians, economists, and businessmen, has rapidly gained a following from a public that has come to expect government to perform badly. In Europe, regulation is less under attack, and the role of the state is more fully accepted; industry, accordingly, has no need to take its case to the public or otherwise to undermine the legitimacy of governmental action.

Industry behavior affirms and further contributes to tendencies we have uncovered in other aspects of the regulatory process. Chemical firms consistently use the rules of the game for their own purposes, often at the expense of public objectives. Even in the United States, where the regulatory process has been purposely designed to frustrate the efforts of powerful special interests, chemical leaders have found ways to make manageable the burdens of chemical control.

10

The Advocates of Regulation

This chapter assesses and compares the political behaviors, backgrounds, and policy influence of the three groups that in each country have taken the lead in advocating governmental controls on toxic chemicals: consumer associations, which include food safety issues among their concerns; environmental groups, which have a record of involvement in restraining the use of pesticides and limiting other forms of chemical pollution; and trade unions, whose concerns about toxic chemicals have focused on hazards in the workplace.[1] The analysis fills in several of the remaining blanks in the characterization of national regulatory systems. How have these groups defined their objectives, mobilized their resources, and fashioned their tactics to promote the interests of environmental protection and public safety? Compared to the varied but uniformly successful strategies of national chemical industries, as analyzed in the last chapter, how influential are they in shaping the regulatory policies of their respective governments?

The delineation of the role of these groups in national regulatory politics offers, in addition, an opportunity to address more general questions about comparative interest group behavior. How do groups with variable political resources, such as labor and consumer organizations, behave when they

---

[1] Advocacy groups sometimes involved in chemical control but not examined here include the organic farming/natural foods movement, wildlife sports associations, professional societies, and public interest associations that operate only at the local or regional level.

tackle the same kind of issue? Do organizational priorities and political tactics depend more on features intrinsic to the groups themselves or on the national policy context in which they operate?

In exploring these questions, the analysis uncovers and then explains an apparent anomaly: despite vastly different structures, resources, and strategies of intervention, all these groups manage to exert only limited influence on the shape and pace of regulatory policy in each of the four countries. There is, however, no single factor that accounts for this limited role. Instead, circumstances that are peculiar to each group and to its particular national context combine to make advocacy politics everywhere an important but far from determining voice of policy change.

Players and Strategies

Reflecting the parallel economic and social development of the four countries, organizations now active in promoting chemical safety rose to national prominence at approximately the same times. Environmental groups were created in two waves: older associations, often dating back to the nineteenth century and primarily oriented toward nature conservation and wildlife, have been joined in the past two decades by a newer generation, whose interests focus more on the safety of advanced technologies and on other adverse effects of massive industrialization. Most consumer associations became politically active in the 1950s and 1960s, while organized labor has been a fixture on the national political scene of each country since the nineteenth century.

As intervenors in the national politics of chemical control, all these groups have relatively dispersed memberships and small central staffs. Altogether, the number of activists tracking national policy in the four regulatory areas of interest here is perhaps no more than twenty in each of the European countries and twice that many in the United States. Also, unlike industry, which uses its market-generated income to finance its political activities, most of these groups must rely on the voluntary contributions of their adherents or other financial resources. Only unions, which have a longer history and more economically motivated members, enjoy a measure of financial security. Similarly, union leaderships can exercise more hierarchical control over their members than can leaders of environmental or consumer groups.

As a rule, American public interest groups are more numerous and specialized than their counterparts abroad. In the area of food safety, for example, the most active U.S. groups are the Center for Science in the Public Interest, a small association specializing in food safety issues; the Community Nutrition Institute, which also lobbies on other food-related issues such as hunger and nutrition; and the Health Research Group, a branch of Ralph Nader's network, which is active not only in food safety but also in drugs and occupational health. In each European country, in contrast, typically only one or two national consumer associations are active, and these tend to resemble more the Consumer Federation of American and Consumers Union in their broad-based efforts to promote consumer interests.

Environmental groups follow the same pattern. Such leading American organizations as the Sierra Club, the National Audubon Society, Friends of the Earth, the Environmental Defense Fund, the Natural Resources Defense Council (NRDC), and Environmental Action are all aggressively engaged in chemical control at the national level. But only two German groups, the Bund für Umwelt und Naturschutz Deutschland and the Bundesverband Bürgerinitiativen Umweltschutz, are prominent in the area; although they are nationally organized, their activities are mainly directed toward local and regional issues. Only with the advent of the Green party in the late 1970s did German environmentalism become a more cohesive political force at the federal level. French environmental groups are numerous, fragmented, and politically weak; none has become a noteworthy national champion of the need for chemical control. Three of the more active and visible groups are Amis de la Terre, the Fédération Française des Sociétés de Protection de la Nature (FFSPN), and SOS Environnement. Environmental associations in Britain include the older Council for the Protection of Rural England and the newer activist associations, Friends of the Earth and the Conservation Society.

Chemical workers' unions reflect the organizational features of national labor movements.[2] German chemical workers have the most monolithic organization, with both blue- and white-collar employees belonging to a single union, the Industriegewerkschaft Chemie-Papier-Keramik (IG-Chemie). The union belongs to the sole German labor federation, Deutscher Gewerkschaftsbund (DGB). The French labor movement is the most fragmented; it has four national federations and a separate association for white-collar workers but no umbrella organization representing labor as a whole. Most chemical workers belong to the chemical industry section of either the Confédération Générale du Travail (CGT), which is tied to the French Communist party, or the Confédération Française Démocratique du Travail (CFDT), which is affiliated with the French Socialist party. Chemical workers in the United States, as in France, belong to several competing unions, the

[2]On European labor movements and their political role, see Marguerite Bouvard, *Labor Movements in the Common Market Countries: The Growth of a European Pressure Group* (New York: Praeger, 1972); Jack Barbash, *Trade Unions and National Economic Policy* (Baltimore: Johns Hopkins University Press, 1972); Gerald A. Dorfman, *Government versus Trade Unionism in British Politics since 1968* (Stanford: Hoover Institution Press, 1979); David P. Conradt, *The German Polity* (New York: Longman, 1978).

largest of which are the International Chemical Workers Union; the Oil, Chemical, and Atomic Workers (OCAW); and the Steelworkers. Similarly, in Britain, chemical workers are represented by several unions, most prominently the more white-collar Association of Scientific, Technical, and Managerial Staffs, and the General and Municipal Workers' Union. Both countries, like Germany, have a single labor confederation incorporating most industrial sectors (AFL-CIO in the United States and the Trades Union Congress in Britain). With trends in chemical union memberships following national labor patterns generally, the percentage of unionized workers is higher in Britain and Germany than in France and the United States.

Policy Objectives

Chemical safety is not the exclusive concern of any of these groups. Thus, the priority accorded to chemical control relative to other organizational goals is an important parameter in defining their role in regulatory politics. In this respect, American groups of every type stand out by their sustained attention to the issue. To a far greater extent than in Europe, controlling the hazards of chemical technology looms large in the strategies of American advocates.

The contrast in priority is most noticeable among environmental groups. Many U.S. organizations, led by NRDC and EDF, attach great importance to toxic chemicals and track the issue's development in all relevant regulatory programs. But no major environmental group in Europe has made toxic chemicals a principal rallying cry. Instead, organizational emphasis is placed on the natural habitat or on other technologies, especially nuclear power.[3] These issues reflect a general orientation among European environmentalists to focus on ecological deterioration rather than threats to public health. When specific chemicals such as PCBs, DDT, and other organochlorine pesticides became objects of concern, they were attacked as much for their harmful effects on the biosphere as for their effects on human health. The threat of cancer is notably less prominent as a mobilizing issue.

In turn, the agendas of many European associations give priority to procedural reforms, including the ability to bring suit (in Germany), administrative decentralization (in France), and greater access to information (in all three European countries). American environmental groups, having already acquired by law extensive guarantees of openness and legal access, tend to

---

[3] Favored themes of European environmental movements are developed in their periodicals: *Natur und Umwelt,* published by BUND; *Umweltmagazin* (BBU); *La Baleine* (Amis de la Terre); *Combat Nature* (Associations Ecologiques et de Défense de l'Environnement); etc. Also, interviews with environmental leaders in Bonn, Paris, and London, Summer 1980.

address procedural issues only when these prerogatives are threatened or curtailed. The public availability of industry-supplied information on health effects was a prominent procedural concern of U.S. environmentalists in the early 1980s. American groups also tend to advocate the centralization of environmental decision making at the federal level, where their political resources are most effectively deployed.

Another notable contrast between American and European environmentalists is the specificity of their respective regulatory strategies. Groups in the United States, at least those most involved in toxic chemical regulation, formulate detailed objectives on even the most technical aspects of lawmaking, risk assessment, and administrative implementation. The goals of the environmental movements in Germany and France and, to a lesser extent, Britain are more likely to remain at the level of broad principles aimed at overall environmental enhancement or even the massive restructuring of industrial society. The 1979 NRDC annual report, for example, gives a fairly detailed picture of the current agenda confronting U.S. regulators, noting the organization's efforts to find solutions to such concrete problems as premarket testing guidelines under TSCA.[4] The literature of the French association Amis de la Terre of the same period scarcely mentions that a similar French law was passed and was undergoing implementation; instead, there is an abundance of quasi-philosophical expositions on the various tenets of "ecological democracy."

National consumer groups also show variable interest in toxic chemical hazards. The most prominent British group, the Consumers' Association, gives food safety policy only passing attention, and its occasional pronouncements are usually supportive of the governmental position. During the 1970s, its principal organ, the consumer periodical *Which?*, published testing results on only two substances of relevance, nitrites in ham and products containing asbestos, noting simply in each case that results were within statutory or recommended limits. In contrast, American groups have vigorously pursued tighter controls on a wide range of food additives and contaminants, including saccharin, DES, nitrites, PCBs, aflatoxins, lead, coal-based colors, and acrylonitrile.[5] The three U.S. consumer groups most involved in food safety policy staunchly defend the Delaney clause, but this zero-risk principle is not a prominent objective of any European association.[6]

[4] NRDC, "Annual Report, 1978/79," New York.

[5] Documents of the Community Nutrition Institute, the Health Research Group, and Center for Science in the Public Interest; interviews, Washington, D.C., 1980 and 1981.

[6] Ibid., and interviews with consumer association leaders in Washington, D.C., November 1980 and April 1981.

French and German consumer associations resemble American groups in the relative priority they accord to food safety, but their campaigns are more selective. The Union Française des Consommateurs (UFC) has launched consumer awareness programs on aerosols, asbestos products, food colors and preservatives (amaranth, in particular), hair dyes, and polysterene as a food packaging material.[7] A major campaign in 1980 was directed toward the continued use of DES and other estrogens in veal.[8] The Deutscher Verbraucherschutzverband (DVS) has addressed such issues as CFC-propelled aerosols, lindane and other pesticides, chromium, PCBs, and chemicals added to animal feed. Another German group, the Arbeitsgemeinschaft der Verbraucherverbände (AGV), whose literature is somewhat less polemical and less focused on food safety matters than that of DVS, has taken stands on colors, nitrites, and saccharin.[9]

Among the three types of organizations, chemical workers' unions show the greatest cross-national similarity in their chemical control objectives. For years, worker health and safety was not a top priority of unions, as they founded their political activities on more traditional bread-and-butter concerns and more general political aims. But in recent years, all have raised worker health and safety issues to new prominence. The turning point was the passage of key worker protection statutes in each country. In the period immediately preceding and subsequent to the enactment of the OSH Act and counterpart legislation in Europe, unions took measures to reinforce their staffs, expertise, and programs in the health and safety area. European unions placed initial priority on building up their presence in health and safety matters at the plant level, including the election and training of safety representatives in Britain, the functioning of health and safety committees in Germany and France, and the provision of information on toxic hazards to workers in all three countries.[10] Until recently, and unlike the situation in the United States, European unions have had only limited involvement in standard setting for health hazards; their traditional focus has been workplace safety. Organized labor in all four countries now expresses general satisfaction with

---

[7]*Que Choisir?* is published monthly by UFC, Paris. Another French group, Laboratoire Coopératif, has published articles on a wide range of chemical hazards, particularly food additives and contaminants, in its publication *Bulletin d'information* (Saint Mire), published bimonthly.

[8]*Le Monde,* November 16, 1980.

[9]Publications and internal documents of DVS and AGV; interviews at AGV, Bonn, June 1980.

[10]*Health and Safety at Work,* July 1980, p. 17; P. Auer et al., "'Humanization of Work' between Labor Unions and the State: A Survey of Seven Countries," International Institute for Comparative Social Research, Berlin, February 1980; Confédération Française Démocratique du Travail, *Hygiène et sécurité dans l'entreprise* (Paris: Montholon, 1978).

the legal framework in place but criticizes the pace and stringency of administrative implementation and enforcement.[11]

Among occupational hazards, carcinogens have been accorded high priority by all chemical workers' unions; the same substances, such as vinyl chloride and asbestos, tend to reappear as objects of concern in national campaigns. But beyond consistently pressing OSHA to accelerate its programs, the American labor movement was not the primary impetus for OSHA's generic policy on carcinogens.[12] In Britain, in contrast, a proposal modeled on the OSHA initiative was taken up and heavily promoted by ASTMS in the face of strong industrial opposition and a less than enthusiastic response from most HSE officials (see chapter 8).

Tactics

National public interest and worker associations active in chemical control policy use remarkably different means to attain their objectives. Electoral participation, the most basic means of articulating policy preferences in democratic societies, plays an important role in the national environmental movements of only Germany and France.[13] Efforts to form national ecology parties are less central in ventilating environmental concerns in American politics and are totally absent in Britain. Organized labor, in contrast, has long been affiliated with one or more of the major political parties in all four countries. But the importance of partisan electoral activity in achieving policy objectives varies in organizational strategies. It remains high for British labor, for example, but is less central to U.S. unions. Consumer groups are seldom engaged in electoral activities, although some American consumer groups, like some environmental associations in the United States and Britain, give endorsements and other kinds of support (such as publicizing legislative records) to candidates who champion their cause.

Outside the electoral process, all groups cultivate informal relations with elected legislators. But circumstances peculiar to the groups themselves or to national politics give these ties variable importance in political strategies. The substantial role of the U.S. Congress in regulatory policy making, together with the sensitivity of individual legislators to interest group intervention and the weak ability of the parties to absorb and attenuate political demands,

[11] Interviews with labor representatives in Paris, November 1979 and July 1980; Bonn, July 1980; and London, July and August 1980.

[12] Interview, AFL-CIO, Washington, D.C., November 1980.

[13] The platform of the German "Green party" is contained in *Die Grünen: Das Bundesprogramm* (Cologne: Verlag Die Grünen, n.d.). For France, see Jean-Luc Parodi, "Les écologistes et la tentation politique, ou essai de problématique du mouvement écologiste," *Revue politique et parlementaire,* 81 (January–February 1979).

make legislative lobbying a central and often fruitful activity for all American groups. In Europe, where intervention tends to be mediated by the political parties, the reliance on legislative lobbying depends more on traditional partisan affiliations and the composition of the ruling majority. European labor has ready parliamentary access and influence when its affiliated parties are in the majority, but these ties count for much less when the electoral tide runs against them.

At the implementation stage, interest group participation on deliberative or advisory structures closely linked to regulatory programs is the dominant mode in Europe. As discussed in chapter 7, labor representation on influential committees is common in the area of worker safety, but European environmental and consumer advocates have made fewer inroads. American advocacy groups of all types, in contrast, intervene primarily by formally communicating their views to administrators at critical stages in the rule-making process. Since information and timing are critical, much effort is expended by these groups in perusing official publications, tracking rule making, participating in organized hearings, and petitioning administrators.[14]

The appointment of activists or sympathetic individuals to political or administrative positions is another potential means of intervention. The creation of new governmental services of environmental protection brought into authority everywhere many individuals who were receptive to environmentalists' causes. But prevailing national patterns of civil service recruitment, institutional development, and political appointment make this opportunity less available to European than to American advocates. The more professionalized and stable civil service in European public administration assures considerable continuity in official attitudes and practices, even following changes in political leadership. In the United States, the larger proportion of top agency positions that are subject to political appointment, and the resulting turnover in personnel and policy orientation, became dramatically evident when a number of public interest activists appointed to high-level administrative positions by the Carter administration were subsequently dismissed after the Republican victory in 1980.

The variable role of litigation in the four regulatory settings is similarly reflected in the strategies of advocates. In the United States, the more liberal rules of standing, the range of permissible grounds for bringing suit, and the greater scope of court jurisdiction (see chapter 5) give advocates both the

---

[14] A study by Common Cause, a U.S. public interest group, revealed that contacts of commissioners in independent regulatory commissions, including CPSC, were more frequent by industry than by advocacy groups. (Common Cause, "With Only One Ear," Washington, D.C., August 1977.) This suggests that relations between advocates and government are governed by more formal means of intervention.

opportunity and the incentive to use judicial channels. The specificity of American legislation in the form of obligatory administrative procedures, task agendas, and deadlines—measures that advocates themselves have helped bring into law—provides them with ready-made legal criteria for bringing suit. More vaguely worded statutes and the more restricted role of the courts in Europe largely deprive advocacy groups there of these kinds of legal advantages.[15] But even in the United States, the readiness of advocacy groups to file suit is not uniform. The Environmental Defense Fund, the Natural Resources Defense Council, and the Center for Law and Society make frequent use of legal petitions and suits, and this orientation is reflected in their large contingents of legally trained staff. In the more grass-roots-oriented associations, such as the National Audubon Society and Friends of the Earth, litigation looms less prominently in overall strategy. Legal action by American labor in the worker health area shows a more checkered history, its use reflecting the movement's degree of satisfaction with current OSHA performance and orientation.[16]

Another feature distinguishing many American groups from their European counterparts is the greater use of expert analysis and scientific argumentation in the United States. The most successful alliance of science and interest articulation has been forged by the newer activist groups, particularly EDF, NRDC, the Health Research Group, and the Center for Science in the Public Interest (CSPI). These associations have scientists on their staffs, follow the scientific literature, and benefit from a network of contacts in the academic community.[17] American chemical unions and the AFL-CIO have built up similar capabilities. Some groups undertake original policy analysis and evaluation research; OCAW has even initiated its own scientific studies aimed at clarifying carcinogenic risk.[18]

In the area of toxic chemicals, no European group has developed its resources in scientific expertise to a comparable extent. The U.K. branch of Friends of the Earth has earned a reputation for analytical rigor in its position

---

[15] See Ronald Brickman and Sheila Jasanoff, "Concepts of Risk and Safety in Toxic Substances Regulation: A Comparison of France and the United States," *Policy Studies Journal,* 9, no. 3 (1980), 394–403; for France, see Michel Prieur, "Les tribunaux administratifs, nouveaux défenseurs de l'environnement," *Revue juridique de l'environnement,* 1977, pp. 237–39, and Christian Gabolde, *Les installations classées pour la protection de l'environnement* (Paris: Editions Sirey, 1978).

[16] See Nicholas A. Ashford, *Crisis in the Workplace* (Cambridge, Mass.: MIT Press, 1976), pp. 477–79, for the early period; also, "OSHA: A Ten-Year Success Story," *American Federationist,* July 1980.

[17] Robert Cameron Mitchell, "Since Silent Spring: Science, Technology, and the Environmental Movement in the United States," in H. Skoie, ed., *Scientific Expertise and the Public,* vol. 5 (Oslo: Institute for Studies in Research and Higher Education, 1979), pp. 171–207.

[18] For example, OCAW undertook with NCI an epidemiological study of brain cancer among OCAW members working in Texas oil refineries.

papers, but the organization has not often deployed these skills on issues related to chemical control. Chemical workers' unions in Europe have been making modest efforts to build up their competence in handling the complex scientific issues of chemical regulation.[19] But for the most part, the health and safety staffs of most European labor organizations, never very large in the first place, continue to specialize in workplace organization and accident prevention and have not acquired the internal expertise to deal with chronic health effects. The limited access of European groups to scientific and technical expertise is compounded by the relative dearth of public policy research centers that are active in environmental and public health areas. While U.S. groups benefit from the sophisticated analyses of such institutions as the Conservation Foundation and Resources for the Future, there are few comparable institutions in Europe. One notable exception is the OKO-Institut in Freiburg, Germany, but at least until the public debate leading to passage of the federal chemicals law, the institute had done little work in the area of toxic chemicals.[20]

A large part of the strategy of all these groups is to develop means of communication with their adherents and with the wider public. For most consumer associations, publishing magazines that provide subscribers with product and policy information is the primary means of political intervention.[21] Some environmental groups, such as the German BUND and the French FFSPN, also attach great importance to the publication of their own periodicals, while others, including the British and American branches of Friends of the Earth, rely more on articles placed in the general press. Public demonstrations are also organized by many special interests to demonstrate grass-roots support for particular causes. British groups such as Friends of the Earth appear especially dependent on this tactical device. But few events of this kind specifically address problems of chemical pollution. Chemicals appear to present fewer of the preventive, local, or symbolic features that have helped to draw support for demonstrations organized against other targets, such as industrial siting (few new chemical plants have been built in the four countries in the recent past),[22] nuclear power, highway construction, and military bases.

A comparable grass-roots tactic available to consumer groups is the prod-

---

[19] For France, see "Approche et évaluation du risque toxique," *CFDT Aujourd'hui*, no. 32, n.d.

[20] The OKO-Institut collaborated with NRDC on a comparative study of toxic chemical control policies in the United States, West Germany, and the EC (Work Report of the OKO-Institute, September 1979).

[21] For France, see Luc Bihl, "La Loi no. 78–23 du 10 janvier 1978 sur la protection et l'information du consommateur," *Semaine Juridique*, 52, no. 40 (Doctrine 1978), series 2909.

[22] One successful demonstration against the construction of a chemical plant took place in the Alsatian town of Marckolsheim in 1974.

uct boycott. The French UFC employs this technique as an integral part of its strategy. In 1976 it called for a boycott of food products containing artificial colors, and in 1980 the boycott of veal products was the centerpiece of its campaign against hormones. Nationally organized strikes and other work refusal practices over issues of toxic chemical control, or even health and safety more generally, have been rare in labor efforts in all four countries. The directive of the National Union of Agricultural and Allied Workers to its members employed by the British Forestry Commission, calling for their refusal to use the 2,4,5-T herbicide, and the subsequent general ban by the TUC in February 1980, were exceptional moves in the health and safety politics of labor.

Not all of the efforts of public interest groups and labor are directed toward government. Some groups also attempt to gain direct concessions from management. In the health and safety area, for example, European labor movements have placed higher priority than American labor on negotiating improvements at the plant level. Much of their effort directed to public authorities is designed to obtain through state intervention the legal and institutional backing for such bargaining. With respect to environmental groups, neither the legally oriented associations in the United States (apart from a few experiments in environmental mediation) nor the more radical environmental movements in Europe have developed direct contacts with industry. But while U.S. groups are almost exclusively concerned with public regulatory agendas, the campaigns of European groups, in line with their aims of fundamental social change, do not always bother to differentiate economic and political targets. Many consumer groups, particularly those in Europe, continue to show faith in marketplace forces by concentrating on consumer awareness campaigns. As a rule, then, American advocacy groups of all types focus their strategies more on government than on industry; their campaigns attack the shortcomings of officialdom at least as much as those of industry in protecting the environment and public health.

Impact on Regulatory Policy

Advocacy groups in all four countries, in sum, have joined the battle for chemical control, and in some cases they have deployed considerable resources in this cause. But what have they accomplished? In relatively few instances does their impact appear clear-cut and decisive; where this is the case, the attribution of success may be more a function of the tactic employed than the relative power or influence of the group that used it. Lawsuits, for example, culminate in relatively clear-cut decisions for or against advocated positions. Thus, those American interest groups that have access to this technique enjoy a relatively straightforward indication of their impact. The influence of other groups using other means may be just as great but, exerted through more indirect or diffuse channels, it is more difficult to measure.

Undeniably, U.S. groups pressing for tighter controls have scored some notable successes in court. An early example was EPA's cancellation of the use of DDT following court action initiated by the Environmental Defense Fund. A more recent illustration was NRDC's successful suit against EPA for failure to comply with test rule requirements under section 4 of TSCA. In other cases, just the threat of suit or preliminary court proceedings has prompted or accelerated agency action. This occurred in 1973 and 1974, when suits filed by OCAW and the Health Research Group led OSHA to issue a temporary and then a permanent standard on several carcinogens,[23] and again in 1979, when FDA issued final rules establishing lower tolerances for PCBs in food, pending an EDF lawsuit.[24]

There are other cases, however, in which the litigation route produced no detectable shift in policy, either because the final judicial decision went against the plaintiff or because the case became mired in procedural or technical complications. The same is true for a large number of administrative petitions that have been submitted to the agencies to request action on various issues. Examples include the Health Research Group's petition to OSHA for regulations requiring employers to provide workers with the generic names of chemicals in trade-name products and CSPI's petitioning of FDA to require labeling of ingredients in alcoholic beverages. More successful initiatives of this kind—at least insofar as the petition preceded agency action in the desired direction—include AFL-CIO's original demand that OSHA issue an asbestos standard and EDF's 1979 petition against the use of 2,4,5-T and Silvex. But the success of advocacy groups in using legal channels can be properly assessed only with reference to industry's use of the same procedures. Several industry-initiated suits against the government have gone against the wishes of protection-oriented organizations (see chapter 5).

The effectiveness of legislative lobbying is more difficult to gauge. Typically, more issues are at stake and outcomes take the form of compromises that can mask the relative influence of the forces that produced them. Yet legislative campaigns by some U.S. groups are generally credited with producing a significant impact on lawmaking: examples include labor's somewhat belated defense of OSHA in the face of industry attempts to weaken the law, and environmentalists' efforts to thwart the use of Mirex in fire ant eradication and to achieve passage of the "Superfund" legislation of 1980. Given the substantially different roles played by European parliaments in the

[23] Ashford, op. cit.
[24] Jacqueline Warren, "PCBs: A Status Report," *Environment,* 23, no. 4 (May 1981), 2–4.

lawmaking process, the success of legislative tactics by national groups in France, Britain, and Germany must be assessed on an entirely different scale. Perhaps the most vivid illustration of the direct incorporation of environmental concerns into law at the legislative stage was the modification of the German Chemicals Act to reflect opposition to animal testing by antivivisectionists (see chapter 3).

Where American groups enjoy distinct procedural advantages in litigation and lobbying, many European activists are able to intervene successfully in the policy process via their participation on official advisory boards. As already noted, this institutionalized channel of access benefits labor most, and environmentalists least, among advocacy groups in the three countries. Inclusion gives interest groups regular contact with key public officials and timely knowledge of official plans and industry reactions—privileges that are all the more important in systems where public disclosure of information is not extensive. It also provides an opportunity to introduce new issues on the official agenda and to have a continuous voice in the formulation and adoption of governmental rules and recommendations.

But for several reasons this form of participation does not readily translate into policy influence. First, members representing unions or public interest groups are invariably a minority on official committees. Second, committees have variable influence on policy outcomes (see chapter 7). Third, unions and public interest groups show a varying propensity to take advantage of this means of access. None of the European chemical unions, for example, has been particularly aggressive in using its participatory status to force regulatory agendas or shape decisions, although the British union ASTMS has moved in this direction. On the contrary, participation in these forums appears to engender a commitment to established procedures, a willingness to reach compromise, and an acceptance of outcomes that issue from regular consultative mechanisms. Groups that do not conform to this pattern are viewed with disapprobation by other concerned parties and run the risk of being excluded from or ignored in the inner circle of decision making.[25] Fourth, European advocates are constrained by their limited expertise. Using other channels of influence, U.S. groups that have strength in legal and scientific argumentation have largely overcome this handicap, but like their European counterparts they also have trouble countering the superior resources in expertise of industry.

Ultimately, the political strength of activists derives from their ability to

[25]This was the reaction encountered in industry and governmental circles to the series of initiatives that ASTMS was taking both inside and outside the ACTS forum (interviews in London, Summer 1980). "Confrontationist" tactics by unions are more common in France, but, as discussed in chapter 7, the comparable tripartite committee plays a less central role in decision making in that country.

present themselves as the spokesmen of large constituencies. Their claims are reinforced by a visible manifestation of support at the grass-roots level, which is the essential purpose of demonstrations, letter-writing campaigns, strikes, boycotts, media coverage, and the like. Signs of constituency support are particularly important to counter charges, such as those arising to meet the ASTMS cancer initiative, that organizational leaders are out of touch with the rank and file and are acting on other motives.

The support of a large, regular membership is helpful in this regard, but it is not always sufficient. Both government and industry have a tendency to adjust complacently to the more stable features of their political environments. Public interest groups therefore have every interest in mobilizing the larger public to give themselves an edge. However deplorable in terms of their immediate consequences, environmental disasters such as Seveso, the Flixborough accident, the Kepone disaster, Love Canal, PCB contamination in Michigan, and toxic wastes from Stoltzenberg-Chemie in Hamburg provide unique opportunities to sensitize public opinion, focus political attention, and provoke quantum leaps in policy evolution. Indeed, some observers of French environmental politics have attributed the relative lack of interest group attention and political response to chemical hazards in that country to the absence of similar large-scale crises on French soil.[26]

A more direct and telling indication of public support for environmental and safety causes is electoral behavior. Both of the self-defined ecology parties of France and Germany have done rather well in comparison to other marginal political formations. The German ecologists, following a string of successes in local and regional elections, elected members to the Bundstag in the 1983 parliamentary elections.[27] French ecologists have improved their performance since the presidential candidacy of René Dumont, who in 1974 collected 1.32 percent of the popular vote in the first round. Brice Lalonde, the environmentalist candidate in the 1981 presidential election, won more than one million votes, or 3.87 percent of the total in the first round.[28] In the United States, the Citizen's party presidential ticket of Barry Commoner and Laverne Harris received 0.3 percent of the national vote in the November 1980 election.

The impact of this electoral pressure on national policy is hard to judge. Certainly, it has forced the major parties and candidates to campaign actively for the vote of environmentalist sympathizers, particularly when electoral

[26] The two incidents of chemical pollution receiving greatest press attention in France in recent years were a series of mishaps traced to a plant manufacturing acryloline near Lyon, and water pollution from a titanium dioxide plant in the Seine estuary.

[27] For a short account in English of the electoral performance of the German Green party, see E. Gene Frankland, "Will Germany Go On Green?" *Environmental Action*, February 1981.

[28] See David Gurin, "France: Making Ecology Political and Politics Ecological," *Contemporary Crises*, no. 3 (1979), pp. 149–69.

contests have been as close as they have been in France and Germany in recent years. But whether this has resulted in more than broad rhetorical promises is conjectural. Since toxic chemical control has not been a favored issue in national environmental debates in either country, the impact has probably been greater in other domains (nuclear power in Germany, participation and preservation of wildlife and parklands in France). Moreover, the credibility of the environmental movement as a political force has been somewhat undermined by internal squabbles, the apolitical stance of some associations, and the tendency of some advocacy groups to take radical, uncompromising positions.

In taking a summary look at the impact of advocacy groups on regulatory policies, one must necessarily compare apples and oranges. Clearly, American groups of all types benefit from their multiple opportunities to intervene. They have more opportunities to set and force the regulatory agenda and are able to exert constant pressure on administrators to narrow the implementation gap.[29] When one channel of influence is blocked, for example by the arrival in power of an unsympathetic administration, these groups can readily switch to other tactics and targets to pursue their aims. The evaluation of European groups must be more differentiated. Those admitted to official circles exert quiet and contained influence at the decision-making stage, while those excluded operate through the indirect and diffuse channels of public opinion. The efforts of the latter are more likely to influence the general tenor of national politics than to result in an issue-specific policy response.

The Context of Advocacy Politics

This final section, taking a more analytical bent, explores the broader context of advocacy politics. It addresses two questions: Why do advocacy groups intervene the way they do in the regulatory process? And what accounts for their success or failure? Four factors appear to exert special influence on the patterns of behavior delineated earlier: the receptivity of public opinion, the resources available to each group, organizational ethos, and the policy-making context in which each group fashions its strategy of intervention.

Public Opinion

The available data on public opinion in the four countries suggest a parallel development that has served to sustain at least in general terms the causes

---

[29] Using other cases, W. Solesbury comes to similar conclusions in "Issues and Innovations in Environmental Policy in Britain, West Germany, and California," *Policy Analysis* (Winter 1976), pp. 1–39.

promoted by public interest organizations. Surveys uniformly document the rise of public awareness and sensitivity to environmental and public health concerns during the past decade. A 1976 cross-national poll taken for the European Community, for example, revealed an equally high ranking in European countries of pollution control and consumer protection among issues judged to be important or very important.[30] (There was a somewhat lower ranking of these concerns among British respondents, who were more preoccupied with economic issues at the time.) Surveys in both France and the United States convey the public perception that the chemical industry is a principal contributor to environmental degradation.[31] With respect to the "environmental movement," another EC poll reveals high public support in all three member countries (72 percent in the United Kingdom, 79 percent in Germany, and 81 percent in France gave favorable ratings).[32]

There appears to be, however, some variation in the degree of public alarm over chemical hazards among the four countries. European observers often remark that the level of concern over chemical pollution in general, and carcinogens in particular, is less intense in their countries than in the United States. The American public appears to accord a relatively higher value to health effects than to environmental degradation compared to the inhabitants of France, Germany, and Britain. This relative concern is reflected in the treatment of toxic chemicals in the national media of the four countries.[33] Even fairly obscure developments in the scientific investigation of carcinogenic hazards are apt to be reported in the U.S. media, and in some of the more sensational cases, such as nitrites and caffeine, scientific results have earned the distinction of announcement on the televised evening news. With the exception of major disasters, media coverage of this kind is rare in Europe. Among different kinds of toxic or carcinogenic chemicals, the French media seem to demonstrate greater concern over food additives, while the British are noticeably sanguine in this area. In turn, the British press devotes relatively more space to occupational safety.

These nuances in public concern go hand in hand with the priorities adopted by advocacy groups and with national policy responses. The greater

[30] EC, Commission, *Euro-Barometer*, no. 5, July 1976.

[31] *International Environment Reporter*, June 13, 1979; also, *Les Echos*, June 6, 1979, and "The Public's Attitudes Toward Chemicals, Additives, and Pesticides," Opinion Research Corporation, Princeton, N.J., November 1978.

[32] *Index to International Public Opinion*, 1978–79, EEC s/s 8791, and EC, Commission, *Euro-Barometer*, no. 8, January 1978. A similar question to American respondents elicited an "excellent or pretty good" job rating of environmental protection groups from 57 percent of those polled, and 45 percent gave a similar rating to consumer associations, while organized labor received only 20 percent. *Roper Public Opinion Research Center*, 5, no. 1 (January 1977).

[33] Based on a review of press clippings archives in each of the four countries.

focus in U.S. regulatory policy on carcinogens relative to other toxic effects, for example, is in all likelihood related to the often-observed American "fear of cancer," which finds expression in other spheres of public life (government funding of cancer research and the laetrile phenomenon, for example). It is possible, of course, that the fear of cancer is just as acute among Europeans but is less likely to find expression in political terms. There are other features in American society, including its confrontational politics and investigative media, which promote the dramatization and public activation of these kinds of public fears. American culture, moreover, seems to hold public health more as an absolute good, while attitudes toward environmental protection, since the pastoral ideal gave way to an association of prosperity with industrial development and a tamed frontier in the early nineteenth century, have been marked with more ambivalence. These cultural attitudes may well underlie the pronounced public health dimension that has come to characterize both the politics and policies of U.S. environmental protection.

Resources

Limited staff and financial resources put obvious constraints on organizational strategies and impact. Unions are by far the wealthiest organizations promoting safety regulation, but they spread their resources over a large number of other issues and demands. Environmental groups do not disperse their resources so widely, but at least in Europe their specialization has not always favored serious involvement in toxic substances policy. Resources also constrain the choice of tactics. In the United States, the cost of pursuing a lawsuit to its end can amount to more than five hundred thousand dollars. Unlike large industrial concerns and trade associations, few advocate groups can afford to invest the required sums in litigation or extensive policy analyses and scientific studies. As a result, many are forced to fall back on a more passive or indirect stance of agency monitoring or molding public opinion. In recognition of these financial constraints, the governments of Germany and the United States have made limited efforts to alleviate the cost of public interest intervention; these take the form of, in Germany, subsidies to public interest associations for mass-education campaigns, and, in the United States, financial compensation for participation in certain rule-making proceedings and grants fostering participatory programs. The tax laws of all four countries advantage many groups in their fund-raising efforts and in stretching their limited resources.[34]

---

[34] U.S. tax provisions that confer tax-exempt status on advocacy groups are intended to constrain the legislative lobbying efforts of these groups. There are, however, ways to reduce these constraints, such as the creation of a parallel tax-exempt foundation and the

From a cross-national perspective, the greater size and absolute wealth of American society, plus a tradition of support from foundations and the general public, give many U.S. groups a definite advantage in resources over their European counterparts. A survey of the income in 1976 of the sixteen most prominent national environmental groups indicated total revenues of over $67 million, a level of funding far exceeding that of European environmental movements.[35] But American groups also have correspondingly higher costs, not only in the servicing of larger constituencies but also in intervening in a larger and more complex policy environment. European public interest associations can manage with much less.

Organizational Ethos

Along with financial and political resources, the advocates of regulation enter the political fray with a certain ideological orientation and sense of mission which are tied in part to the circumstances of their creation, to the lessons inherited from past experiences, and to the social composition and perspectives of their adherents. This accumulated baggage sometimes has a decisive influence on group strategy and impact.

Sustained union involvement in the area of occupational health, for example, has come after a long history of battles with management and public authority, and labor's role and achievements in the area have been facilitated, but also somewhat constrained, by its prior successes and failures. For all four labor movements, renewed attention to worker health and safety sprang not only from an increased awareness of long-term health hazards but also from a need to find a new organizational mission in the wake of successes in more traditional spheres. In Europe, it did not prove difficult to extend the principles of tripartite negotiation, comanagement, or worker participation into the health and safety area, as the groundwork for such innovations was laid by a series of more general reforms in labor law and industrial relations evolving over several decades and accelerating in the 1960s and early 1970s. Governmental involvement in labor-management relations in the United States, however, has always been less extensive. When the federal government assumed responsibilities in the worker safety area, the labor movement did not draw on a well-established pattern of negotiation incorporating both public authority and management; instead, labor had always looked to the

---

exercise of some discretion in congressional liaison. See Jeffrey M. Berry, *Lobbying for the People* (Princeton: Princeton University Press, 1979), especially pp. 45–78, and Burton A. Weisbrod, *Public Interest Law* (Berkeley and Los Angeles: University of California Press, 1978).

[35] Mitchell, op. cit., p. 199.

Department of Labor, OSHA's new home, as the principal defender of its interests in the executive branch. Given this background, its strategy from the beginning was geared more to maintaining ascendancy than to negotiating compromises.

In Europe, however, once the unions put procedural reforms behind them, their organizational orientation did not facilitate successful intervention in the complex realm of controlling long-term chemical hazards. Their strength lay rather in the areas of accident prevention and other improvements in working conditions which had long been their traditional interest and which were more amenable to detection and negotiation at the plant level. At the same time, the considerable political power of European labor movements was diffused across the many other issues and policy areas in which the organizations had either acquired an assured voice (Britain and Germany) or aspired to more general political influence (France). This situation helped to relegate health and safety to a somewhat marginal status in organizational strategy, particularly at the federation level. Only in Britain, where chemical worker unions are highly competitive, but not as ideologically differentiated as unions in France, has occupational health been taken up as a primary mobilizing issue.

The organizational weaknesses of American labor, in contrast, have ironically been something of an asset in tackling the problems of chemical hazard control. National leaderships have been less encumbered by a plant-level orientation; more flexible procedures of staff recruitment allowed unions to bring in specialists; and with fewer pretensions to playing a star role in national politics and with fewer opportunities for negotiating other labor issues in governmental forums, American unions could concentrate their political resources on worker safety issues, including the more complex ones, as necessary. As in Britain, rivalries both among and within union leaderships also helped to activate the issue.

Consumer associations rose to prominence at a time when trends in the structure and functioning of modern industrial activity indicated increasing imbalances in the traditional marketplace relationship between consumer and producer. Many still perceive their role above all as a "corrective" to these distortions, in part by helping consumers to discriminate more effectively among services and products and in part by calling for state controls. This conception had led the older consumer associations in particular to focus on their own information services, to stress policy changes designed to increase consumer knowledge (such as labeling requirements), and to place less emphasis than do unions or environmentalists on tactics of direct confrontation and negotiation. Other groups, however, such as UFC in France and the Health Research Group in the United States, were imbued with the spirit of public interest activism that reigned in the 1960s and have adopted more aggressive, policy-oriented tactics and goals.

The organizational ethos of European environmental groups of the newer generation has contributed to their inattention to toxic chemicals as an issue (other issues, such as nuclear power, have been deemed more suitable vehicles), to their lack of interest in administrative implementation, to their ambivalence toward and relative uninvolvement in official decision-making procedures, and to their predilection for grass-roots, obstructionist, and even electoral activities. Taking more the form of social movements than specialized interest groups,[36] many of these formations have guiding philosophies that move them toward antiestablishment positions calling for broad social and economic restructuring and away from tactical opportunities and issues that would compromise either their grass-roots orientation or their ideological purity.

While such currents of thought, and organizations to represent them, are not absent from the American scene, their role in toxic substances control has been overshadowed, if not entirely preempted, by the highly educated policy activists in NRDC, EDF, and other groups whose sophisticated skills and interests are effectively deployed to handle the technicalities and subtleties of policy formulation, implementation, and judicial challenge. Indeed, chemical control, where the problems of conformity of rules and procedures to legislative intent, priority setting, and scientific complexity are particularly acute, provides an almost ideal policy arena for those possessing such skills.

The Policy-Making Context

The comparative politics of toxic substances control offers a vivid refutation of the "demand-response" model of governmental action. When politics is matched to policy in the four countries, the role of interest groups is seen as more the product than the cause of prevailing patterns of policy making. The independent but overlapping powers of the three branches of American government give U.S. groups alternative pressure points to advance their cause and elevate both litigation and lobbying as indispensable components of their strategies. If they are to be effective, American groups are obliged to focus on the details of lawmaking and administrative implementation and to assume the role of congressional and agency watchdog. Moreover, given the tendency of U.S. agencies to rationalize with scientific evidence and analytical argumentation the basis for regulatory action (see chapter 7), American groups have every incentive to acquire the requisite expertise, to argue over technical issues rather than general ideological principles, and to generate new knowl-

[36] See Dorothy Nelkin and Michael Pollak, *The Atom Besieged: Extraparliamentary Dissent in France and Germany* (Cambridge, Mass.: MIT Press, 1981), for an extended analysis of the environmental groups of France and Germany which focus on nuclear power.

edge about hazards and policy impacts. The extensive use of adversarial proceedings, as well as the channeling of political conflict around fragmented points of decision in all three branches, encourage American groups to take unilateral, uncompromising stands (see chapter 8) and to perceive each issue as a separate crusade that is unamenable to more comprehensive political compromises and trade-offs.

In Europe, the different context of decision making has a similarly significant impact on the strategies of advocates. Regulatory systems offer established European interests a voice primarily through participation on standing advisory committees; access acquired in this way tends to preclude intervention through other means. Those most thoroughly assimilated into such forums show a willingness to accept compromise and to negotiate trade-offs over several issues, but they are also dissuaded from taking independent initiatives outside regular consultative channels. Those excluded from or marginally represented in such forums show different behavioral patterns. Many environmentalists in Germany and France have chosen an electoral strategy fashioned around broad-based platforms; environmentalists in Britain and certain groups elsewhere undertake public opinion campaigns that are more issue-specific.

The orientation toward procedural reforms also reflects existing practices in the regulatory process. In general, groups in one country or policy area attempt to gain the advantages of standing and access to information or to officialdom that are standard in another. An interesting exception is the failure of American advocacy groups and of excluded European groups to press for representation on influential advisory bodies. Presumably, American groups believe that they do not need such forums to make themselves heard or to obtain information and concessions from government and industry. A further obstacle to the greater use of consultative formats in the United States is the size and diversity of the American public interest movement, which raises problems of representativeness. In Europe, the reluctance of excluded groups to seek entry into official circles appears often to grow out of a general antiestablishment orientation and fears of co-optation.

In sum, these four features—public opinion, resources, organizational mission, and policy-making context—sustain and shape somewhat different aspects of advocacy group behavior. The impact of public opinion is most diffuse. It has given broad support to the emergence of these groups as forces in the regulatory politics of all four countries and has helped to fashion their relative priority to toxic chemical control. Organizational features intrinsic to the groups themselves, including their self-defined sense of mission and their traditional orientation toward government or the marketplace, have had the greatest impact on the choice of objectives. Features of the national policy-making context and, to a lesser extent, resources, have in turn exerted a powerful influence on the choice of tactics.

Conclusion: The Limits of Advocacy Politics

Advocacy groups perform several functions in the regulatory systems of advanced industrial nations. To a variable degree, they aggregate and express the aspirations of their adherents and seek to effect and defend policy changes in line with those aspirations. They articulate widely held sentiments that otherwise risk being shortchanged in private and public interactions. In a sense, they act as society's conscience in promoting safety and respect for the environment, and, thus, they are an organizational embodiment of values that are shared to some extent by all, including public officials and industrialists. Public interest groups and unions have positioned themselves in the foreground of political battles over chemical control issues, and outcomes depend in many cases on how well they deploy their resources and choose their targets and tactics. The existence and efforts of these associations also serve as useful pretexts for public officials who want to move in the direction of tighter controls but wish to deflect criticism, reprisals, or obstruction of their proposals. They are, in short, a virtually inevitable and indispensable presence in the contemporary politics of social regulation.

But the extent to which these advocacy groups actually determine the shape and outcomes of regulatory programs is another question. A more finely drawn characterization of their role in the control of carcinogens and other toxic chemicals would have to consider them as only one link in a long and intricate chain of actors and circumstances which constitute the regulatory system. Their performance is a function of the organizational choices and the features which are intrinsic to them, but also of the features of policy making, politics, and political culture which characterize the system in which they operate.

Typically, the factors of organizational choice and political context mitigate each other, in ways that reduce the overall effectiveness of advocates in regulatory policy making. On the surface, the resources, array of tactics, priorities, and analytical sophistication of American advocacy groups appear much more impressive and extensive than those of European groups. Yet these advantages can be interpreted and assessed only in relation to the behavior and assets of other key actors in U.S. regulation, specifically industry, political authority, and the scientific community. For example, American groups undoubtedly benefit from the powerful tool of litigation. But industry benefits from the same tool and has often manipulated it to thwart advocates' aims. Similar arguments can be made for the features of openness, multiple access, availability of expertise, civil service appointment, and responsiveness of elected officials to constituency pressures, all of which so singularly distinguish the American regulatory setting from the European. These features do more than simply provide American advocacy groups with diverse and attractive opportunities for intervention—they virtually compel such intervention if advocates are to maintain their visibility and importance in the three-ring circus of American regulatory politics. Full-scale utilization of all available legitimate means of action is all the more necessary in a political system that tends to judge the appropriateness of public policy in terms of the relative strength of the political forces mobilized for or against it.

In looking more closely at the policy roles of different kinds of groups across the four countries, the same pattern emerges: ostensible strategic advantages lose their significance when the larger picture is taken into account. The great political power of British and German labor, compared to other European groups and even to the American labor movement, is offset by a typically low organizational priority to hazardous chemical control. The advantages of regular access to official decision makers in Europe come at the price of adherence to constraining rules of the game. American environmental associations ably maneuver the many levers of influence made available to them. But these pluralistic opportunities also create procedural complexities that, as analyzed in earlier chapters, prevent speedy and definitive regulatory action. Thus, while American environmental groups can force the regulatory agenda, the system as a whole thwarts their ability to translate this advantage into a high rate of favorable governmental output. As for consumer associations, their influence on food safety policy is everywhere limited by the wide range of issues competing for their attention and the lack of a readily mobilized constituency.

Given these compensating circumstances, the comparative politics of advocacy, despite its remarkable diversity, does not add up to a significant force of divergence in regulatory performance, either across sectors or across countries. Interest group political behavior and the policy process intimately affect each other, but with respect to regulatory outcomes, the result is something of a stand-off. The American way of regulation generates a great deal of steam and pressure, while the European approach more successfully diffuses conflict, but both produce in the end a kind of slow-moving equilibrium. Perhaps the most significant difference in the role of advocates is that American groups have to run so much faster to arrive, essentially, at the same place.

It follows that any change in political dynamics, stemming either from strategic revisions on the part of advocacy groups or from modifications in policy process, will not necessarily alter the performance and impact of organized labor and public interest associations. Greater access to information for European groups, a higher priority accorded to chemical control in all four countries, or more consultative forms of participation in the United States are reforms whose effects can be evaluated only after consideration of the changes they induce in the regulatory system as a whole. Given the multiple determinants of a group's strategy and impact and the adaptive capabilities of other actors, such isolated changes may do little to upset the existing order other than redefining the form or forum of political conflict.

The systemic interpretation of advocacy politics cannot be carried too far, however. Public interest groups and unions which have a stake in governmental controls on chemical technology retain at least a marginal independent capacity to move the action, and many probably have a potential for greater policy influence than they currently enjoy. Like others involved in the issues, they are subject to a learning curve, and their success in the future will no doubt depend in part on how well they assimilate the lessons of their past successes and failures.

11

Domestic Policy and International Cooperation

Fewer and fewer areas of public policy in advanced industrial nations are purely domestic in their origins or impact. The interpenetration of modern societies has eroded the ability of national political leaders to govern in disregard of international pressures and consequences. Whether they are affected by formal intergovernmental programs or are responding to the international concerns of domestic interests, public policies increasingly bear the stamp of global interdependence.

Chemical control policies are no exception. At different times and for various reasons, the governments of Britain, France, West Germany, and the United States have sought international solutions to their problems of chemical assessment and control. They have developed a variety of mechanisms to exchange relevant information, narrow policy differences, and reach binding agreements. The business, public interest, and scientific communities have formed their own ties across national borders, using these to affect the pace and nature of intergovernmental cooperation and to further domestic objectives.

For several reasons, the international dimension of chemical control policy, often mentioned in previous chapters, merits close examination. To the extent that international processes, both through the channels of government and through nongovernmental networks, influence the policy objectives, procedures, and decisions of the four governments, they help to account for observed similarities and differences in national regulatory policies. Moreover, the dynamics of international negotiation can reveal the distinctiveness of national policy approaches. By examining the stands taken by national leaders on issues of cross-national policy harmonization, we can better gauge the depth of their commitment to domestic policy preferences and to their individual styles of decision making.

But the relevance of the inquiry goes beyond these immediate analytical objectives. International activities related to toxic chemical control also provide an illuminating case study of how individual states respond to the pressures of interdependence by forgoing domestic policy prerogatives in order to develop mutually compatible norms and common rules.[1] The emergence of such international regimes, according to one developing body of analysis,[2] often depends on the leadership of a single nation which receives disproportionate benefits but also is able to demonstrate the advantages of cooperation to others. In the area of toxic chemical control, as this chapter documents, the dynamics of the process are far more complex. The limited progress in establishing common international regimes of chemical identification, assessment, and control results from a complicated but identifiable pattern of economic, political, and scientific forces operating at both governmental and subgovernmental levels. Although the United States often plays a leadership role in the process, its influence is less deliberate and positive than it is incidental and negative. The formal achievements of international cooperation are an important component of the progress achieved in cross-national policy harmonization. But just as significant are the transnational activities of various actors who, often with diverging motives but converging effect, work toward a spontaneous alignment and parallel evolution of domestic regulatory policies and performances.

---

[1] While the concept of international regime is not a new one, it has received considerable attention recently. See Stephen D. Krasner, ed., "International Regimes," *International Organization* (special issue), 36, no. 2 (Spring 1982), and, particularly, Krasner's lead article, "Structural Causes and Regime Consequences: Regimes as Intervening Variables" (pp. 185–205). For earlier use of the concept, see Richard Cooper, "Prolegomena to the Choice of an International Monetary System," in C. Fred Bergsten and Lawrence Krause, eds., *World Politics and International Economics* (Washington, D.C.: Brookings, 1975); John G. Ruggie, "Collective Goods and Future International Collaboration," *American Political Science Review,* 66 (September 1972); and Robert Keohane and Joseph S. Nye, *Power and Interdependence* (Boston: Little, Brown, 1977).

[2] Perhaps the strongest case for this theory is made by Charles P. Kindleberger, *The World in Depression, 1929–1939* (Berkeley and Los Angeles: University of California Press, 1973). See also Stephen D. Krasner, "State Power and the Structure of International Trade," *World Politics,* 28 (April 1976); Robert Gilpin, *U.S. Power and the Multinational Corporation* (New York: Basic Books, 1975); and Robert O. Keohane, "The Theory of Hegemonic Stability and Changes in International Economic Regimes, 1967–1977," in Ole R. Holsti, Randolph M. Siverson, and Alexander L. George, eds., *Change in the International System* (Boulder, Colo.: Westview Press, 1980), pp. 131–62.

Premarket Notification: Policy Harmonization in the EC

During the late 1970s, the major trading countries of the West intensified considerably their efforts to achieve compatibility in national programs of chemical control. The most conspicuous and successful of these efforts was the attempt to harmonize notification requirements for industrial chemicals introduced to commerce. In September 1979, the member countries of the European Community reached agreement on the so-called Sixth Amendment, which represented a major step forward in assuring a common approach to the screening of new chemicals by the governments of Britain, France, West Germany, and the other EC member countries.[3] The EC agreement became the cornerstone of an expanded effort, including the United States, Canada, and Japan, within the Organization for Economic Cooperation and Development. Within two and a half years, the OECD nations successfully negotiated agreements on test guidelines, standards of laboratory practice, the mutual acceptance of data, and a base set of data requirements in initial notifications. Taken together, these efforts have resulted in the most fully developed international regime to date in the area of hazardous chemical control.

The story behind these achievements is a complicated one of seized opportunities, critical compromises, institutional momentum, and the careful tailoring of objectives to accommodate conflicting interests. Although international officials in both the European Community and the OECD had made preliminary attempts to coordinate national screening programs in the early 1970s, the story more properly begins in 1976, with a unilateral American initiative: the enactment of TSCA. The American law elicited a strong negative reaction from many Europeans, who were disturbed by the statute's sweeping scope and vague language, the broad discretion granted to implementing authorities, and, most alarming of all, its applicability to imported as well as domestically produced substances. To European industrialists, TSCA represented a major threat to their continued access to the lucrative American market. Many European officials, in turn, were irked that they were not consulted prior to the enactment of a statute having such potential significance for international trade in chemicals. In the words of one irate British spokesman:

> I cannot understand the language of the Act. In its wording a chemical substance is not a chemical substance; the environment is not the environment . . . "manufacture" means "import"; in short, everything means everything—including everything else. There also exists international

---

[3]Council directive 79/831/EEC 22 of September 18, 1979, amending for the sixth time directive 67/548/EEC on the approximation . . . , *OJEC*, L259, 10 (1979). The 1967 directive was published in *OJEC*, 196, 234 (1967).

machinery (notably in the OECD)—effective, intelligent, well-serviced machinery—for discussing these subjects, exchanging information, and obtaining advice from individual governments. You have chosen to ignore that machinery. When you know what you want to do, and have something to say to us which we can understand, approach us through proper channels. . . . Until then do not expect the international community to compensate for the defects in your own approach to problems.[4]

Clearly frustrated by their lack of direct leverage in the American political process, European officials sought to counter the real and potential dangers of TSCA by proceeding with the establishment of notification schemes of their own.[5] They realized that their bargaining power over the United States would be furthered by reaching agreement among themselves. The objective was to devise a manageable, European-wide system of new chemical screening that could eventually serve as a model for negotiating standardized requirements covering the major chemical markets. With a long history of involvement in environmental protection and chemical safety and well-established machinery for reaching intergovernmental agreement, the European Community was the logical forum for fashioning the European response to TSCA.

Harmonization within Europe received an added push from a rare congruence of national interests. Although both Britain and West Germany had for some time discussed establishing their own programs of chemical screening, each saw advantages in first reaching agreement at the EC level. With 50 percent of Germany's highly profitable chemical trade going to other EC countries, German businessmen and governmental officials wished to avoid the commercial obstacles that would arise from divergent national requirements. It also made good sense to work out the details of regulatory requirements in an international setting, where trade concerns were paramount and where competing domestic pressures could be more easily circumvented. The British also showed little interest in moving forward with a national plan once EC discussions were on the agenda. The 1972 report of the Robens Committee had proposed a premarket screening program,[6] but no action was taken until the release of an HSE consultative document in June 1977. This statement, however, was less the culmination of an internal policy debate than an outline of Britain's initial negotiating position in Brussels.

Among the EC nations, only France proceeded with enactment of chemical screening legislation prior to Community-level agreement.[7] Passage of the

[4] Remarks of Alan Smith, Washington, D.C., March 22, 1977.

[5] Interview at ICI, London, June 1980.

[6] Report of the Robens Committee, 1970–72, *Safety and Health at Work* (London: HMSO, 1972).

[7] Among non–EC countries, Switzerland passed its Law on Trade in Toxic Substances in 1969 (effective in 1972), and Japan passed its Chemical Substances Control Act in 1973;

French chemicals law in July 1977 reflected in part the desire of French officials to issue a prompt and vigorous response to TSCA. Domestic political concerns were also important. By the mid-1970s, the government felt the need to assuage growing environmentalist pressures, while the fledgling Ministry of the Environment sought to expand its role and prestige through new legislation. Also, French officials hoped that domestic enactment would increase their leverage over EC negotiations.

Discussions within the EC centered on the proposal of the European Commission to establish a common framework for national notification schemes as an amendment to an earlier directive on the classification, packaging, and labeling of dangerous substances. In line with existing EC programs of chemical control (see below), the option of a completely centralized system of new chemical notification administered by the EC bureaucracy was not given serious consideration. Instead, national authorities were to receive and review notifications in their own country, but manufacturers or importers would be required to notify in only one country to gain entry into the entire EC market. The task facing the EC negotiators, then, was to develop common principles, guidelines, and procedures that would minimize divergent national implementation yet satisfy each country's policy objectives and individual styles of regulatory decision making.

Two issues dominated the thirty-six months of negotiations: the extent of exemptions from testing requirements and the degree of flexibility allowed to national authorities in adapting testing requirements to individual chemical substances or classes of substances. Debate on both issues uncovered major differences in national policy preferences, with Germany and Britain taking the most antagonistic positions. The British argued that all new chemicals manufactured or imported in quantities of less than one ton should be exempted from full notification requirements. They also insisted that national authorities be left considerable latitude in setting testing requirements for specific substances.[8] Both positions were in line with the British regulatory philosophy, outlined in previous chapters, which eschews formal legal requirements in favor of flexible, negotiated measures that match the level of clearly demonstrated risk.

The Germans, in contrast, pressed for a predictable and enforceable European-wide scheme that would also provide the framework for an acceptable

---

Sweden (Act on Products Hazardous to Man and the Environment, 1973) and Canada (Environmental Contaminants Act, 1974) followed with similar legislation.

[8] Most of the information on the evolution of the British position prior to international negotiations comes from interviews at HSE. For accounts of the specifics of the early consultative document, see *Chemical Marketing Reporter,* July 4, 1977, p. 5, and *European Chemical News,* June 17, 1977, p. 32.

regulatory program at home.[9] Ministry officials, fully aware of the spotty compliance of some member countries with EC legislation, wanted assurance that the requirements imposed on German industry would be matched by others. German firms, wary of overzealous bureaucrats and the volatility of domestic politics, wanted a full and explicit delineation of their obligations to be defined at the EC level. The solution that satisfied both was the Stufenplan (step-sequence plan), which specified a base set of tests for all newly notified products and further tests as production volumes increased. With this plan, German officials advocated, and spokesmen for industry could accept, a much lower threshold for notification (one hundred kilograms) than the British proposal of one ton.

These disputes impeded progress until 1979, when imminent unilateral implementation of both TSCA and the French law increased the pressure for compromise.[10] In May, the Germans accepted the one-ton threshold advocated by the British, who in turn accepted a modified form of the Stufenplan.[11] The notification package was to contain a base set of tests for all substances produced in excess of one ton annually. Additional testing would become necessary when production volumes reached ten tons per year or a total of fifty tons, and again when they reached one thousand tons per year or a total of five thousand tons. But at British insistence, considerable flexibility was retained at all stages. If the information required was not technically possible to provide or if it appeared unnecessary, notifiers could omit such data with proper justification.[12] The compromise paved the way to final adoption on September 18, 1979.[13]

The Sixth Amendment now stands as the EC's crowning achievement in the area of chemical control. In contrast to other EC programs of chemical regulation, the Sixth Amendment stipulates that manufacturers of new industrial chemicals must face the same initial regulatory hurdles regardless of

---

[9] Most of the information on the evolution of the German position prior to international negotiations comes from interviews at the Ministry of Economics, VCI, and Hoechst, Bonn and Frankfurt, June 1980.

[10] *European Chemical News,* December 22/29, 1978, pp. 28–30.

[11] Ibid., May 28, 1979.

[12] At the ten-ton threshold, the notifier was to perform additional testing only if the national authority decided to require it. It was not to be an automatic obligation. At the one-thousand-ton threshold, the national authority was to be given considerable discretion in designing a program of tests for the notifier to perform.

[13] Several additional disagreements held up passage of the Sixth Amendment in the spring of 1979. Most significantly, the Dutch, under pressure from their environmental lobby, wanted more public access to notified information and a longer interval of governmental review to guarantee more careful scrutiny of submitted data (*European Chemical News,* July 2, 1979).

where in the EC they produce or market their product. In turn, the governments of the ten member countries are presented with a comparable array of data with which to assess potential hazards. Each must admit to its market the substances that have been properly notified in any other member country. Other provisions of the directive impose comparable conditions on the exercise of governmental authority and uniform burdens and guarantees on the notifier, such as standard deadlines and the treatment of confidential information.

Yet the Sixth Amendment still falls short of a fully developed international regime governing the notification of new chemicals. National authorities retain considerable discretion to waive the directive's data requirements in specific cases. They can also demand additional information that they deem necessary for proper hazard evaluation. Both practices open the door to major differences in national implementation. Moreover, the directive does not assure manufacturers that notification in one country grants unconditional access to the markets of others. Files are forwarded to the Commission and to other member governments, which may request additional data through the authority receiving the original notification. More significantly, the Sixth Amendment preserves the right of national authorities to determine, according to their own timetable and criteria (except for labeling and packaging purposes), and subject only to community-level review, if and how a substance is to be controlled.

The first signs of the Sixth Amendment's success in forging a common approach to the notification of new chemical substances came with the enactment of conforming national legislation. By September 1981, the stipulated deadline, most of the member countries had incorporated the provisions of the Sixth Amendment into national law. The German chemicals law, passed in the summer of 1980, followed the EC directive closely in its treatment of exemptions and base set requirements, but went further in calling for limited scrutiny of already marketed substances.[14] The French took a number of administrative actions to bring them into compliance, and in 1982 passed minor amendments to the 1977 law.[15] Britain's HSE issued a revised consultative document on new chemical notification in February 1981.[16] Paralleling the EC directive in most respects, the proposal was noteworthy for the latitude allowed to industry in devising an appropriate test package for notifiable substances. Moreover, testing at higher production levels was not specifically

[14] For early work on the German law, see ibid., p. 6.
[15] For a good discussion of the French law and the process of implementation, see Ministry of Environment, "Ten Questions Concerning Control of Chemicals," May 1979.
[16] *European Chemical News,* February 23, 1981, p. 18, and *International Environmental Reporter,* March 11, 1981, p. 681.

mandated but was left to subsequent negotiation at HSE's discretion. Clearly, British authorities interpreted the data provisions of the Sixth Amendment more as advisory guidelines than as a prescriptive formula.

The effectiveness of the Sixth Amendment in aligning national regulatory policies depends ultimately on the actual implementation of these conforming statutes. By early 1983, all three governments had the basic institutional machinery in place to receive and review notification files, and the commission had published the core inventory of some thirty-four thousand chemicals needed to distinguish new from existing substances. But, as one European official stated in the spring of 1983, "It is far too early to make a full evaluation of any of the systems."[17] In all likelihood, the divergences in regulatory styles and aims which surfaced both in the Brussels negotiations and in subsequent national enactments will continue to characterize the implementation process.

Negotiations in the OECD

Negotiations leading to the Sixth Amendment benefited from a confluence of propitious circumstances: converging national interests, a common external threat, the absence of preexisting, firmly embedded national programs, and the availability of familiar if cumbersome machinery for reaching high-level political compromises. Once the international debate on chemical screening shifted to the Organization for Economic Cooperation and Development, these advantages were less in evidence. OECD's interest in chemical control can be traced to 1971, when the newly created Environment Committee launched the "Sector Group on the Unintended Occurrence of Chemicals in the Environment" to foster common approaches to the treatment of industrial chemicals. The program's work in the early years focused on hazard and economic assessments of specific pollutants.[18] These efforts remained small in scale, however, so that OECD developed neither the expertise nor the collective political momentum that served the EC so well in fashioning a comprehensive agreement on chemical notification systems.

An even more formidable obstacle facing the OECD negotiators was the statutory enactment, on opposite sides of the Atlantic, of two quite different approaches to the screening of new chemical substances.[19] Where the Sixth

[17]R. Lönngren, testimony before the House Committee on Energy and Commerce, Subcommittee on Commerce, Transportation, and Tourism, 98th Cong., 1st sess., April 21, 1983.

[18]OECD, Environment Directorate, "History of the OECD Chemicals Group," Paris, April 1978. An OECD "decision" is regarded as "morally binding" on the governments of its member countries; a "recommendation" entails a weaker political commitment.

[19]For analyses of the similarities and differences between TSCA and the Sixth Amend-

Amendment stipulates the submission of results from a set battery of tests in the initial notification, TSCA gives EPA the discretion to demand results from tests selected on a case-by-case basis, following an examination of the required identifying information and the voluntary test results submitted by the notifier. The European directive also exempts many more substances from notification than does TSCA, and it makes no provision for the testing or regulation of existing chemicals. The Sixth Amendment requires notification ninety days before marketing, while TSCA requires notification forty-five days prior to manufacture (thereby covering intermediates and permitting regulatory intervention earlier in the commercialization process). The two statutes also handle differently such matters as subsequent notifications by manufacturers of the same substance and the treatment of confidential information.

Notwithstanding these difficulties, there were strong commercial incentives to extend the benefits of harmonization to all OECD member countries. The twenty-two member nations of the international organization together account for over 80 percent of world trade in chemicals. Agreement on the basic contours of premarket notification packages would go far to ensure that the previously unfettered commerce in new industrial chemicals would not be impaired by conflicting or discriminatory regulatory controls. American willingness to engage in discussions was also enhanced by the choice of the OECD, an organization in which the United States had long been accustomed to exercising a leadership role, as the forum of negotiations.

The key to success lay in a carefully constructed agenda, one that addressed vital concerns of the participants, yet was practicable in a large multilateral setting.[20] The principal objective was to minimize widely divergent and duplicative data requirements facing chemical manufacturers as they introduce new products into different national markets. To this end, the OECD staff worked first to facilitate the mutual acceptance of test data across national borders based on a consensus on such technical matters as testing guidelines and good laboratory practices. Second, the OECD negotiators sought agreement on a minimum package of data to constitute the initial

---

ment, see George B. Wilkins, "The Sixth Amendment: Toxic Substance Control in the EEC," *Law and Policy in International Business,* 12, no. 2, (1980), 461–500, and George S. Dominguez, "The Sixth Amendment and TSCA: Contrasts in Toxic Substance Identification and Control," *Toxic Substances Journal,* 1, no. 4, (Spring 1980), pp. 349–82. The potential nontariff barriers to trade are discussed by Ingo Walter, "Non-Tariff Barriers and the Control of Chemicals" (Paper prepared for the OECD Environment Directorate, October, 1979), and by Ann Baker Jenkins, "Nontariff Trade Barriers: A Comparison of the Sixth Amendment and TSCA," *Toxic Substances Journal,* 2, no. 1 (Summer 1980), 35–50.

[20] See "Special Programme on the Control of Chemicals" (Background paper prepared by the Chemicals Group, November 7, 1979). Also, *Chemical Marketing Reporter,* November 27, 1978, p. 4.

notification. While not aspiring to the single-market entry provisions of the Sixth Amendment, agreement on both issues would standardize the initial regulatory requirements for new industrial chemicals in all OECD countries.

Progress on the more technical issues was rapid. Expert groups, composed of scientists and technically trained administrators from various countries, worked out standards for relevant test methods (physical/chemical properties, biodegradation, ecotoxicity, long-term toxicity, and short-term toxicity) and for good laboratory practices (GLP). These efforts culminated in a formal agreement, signed by the ministers of the OECD countries in May 1981, to accept in fulfillment of national notification requirements those test results produced in any member country according to the prescribed guidelines.

Agreement on the minimum premarketing data (MPD) set, however, proved more elusive. The concept of a uniform array of test results in the initial notification file was at odds with EPA's authority under TSCA to determine appropriate data needs substance by substance following formal notice of the intent to manufacture. But discussions within the OECD setting during 1979 and 1980 convinced the American and European delegations that these contrasting approaches were reconcilable.[21] A common middle ground was found in the flexibility, established in the Sixth Amendment, to waive or supplement the data requirements of the base set and in the perceived need by EPA to have a benchmark for assessing the adequacy of voluntarily submitted test results. EPA's interest in MPD at this time was further increased by the noticeably sketchy contents of the premanufacture notices (PMNs) that were starting to arrive in the Office of Toxic Substances. The OECD agreement on the MPD, reached informally in May 1980, was seen by EPA officials as a useful means of putting pressure on industry to submit a fuller array of test data. The one remaining hurdle was the lack of explicit authority in TSCA for EPA to issue a generic test rule for new substances. EPA's solution to this difficulty was to publish, in the final hours of the Carter administration, the OECD package as "policy guidance." Having uncertain legal status, the formal notice was intended "to encourage the voluntary development of premanufacture health and environmental health effects test data" by offering the MPD as a "recommended . . . starting point for premanufacture testing."[22]

In early 1981, however, senior EPA officials newly appointed by the Reagan administration announced their opposition to any obligatory testing package for new chemicals reviewed under TSCA, and they objected specifically to the draft language of the OECD agreement on MPD.[23] An eighteen-month stalemate ensued. Finally, in December 1982, the American delegation per-

[21] Interview, former EPA official, May 1983.

[22] 40 *Code of Federal Regulation* 720, January 27, 1981.

[23] See *Chemical Regulation Reporter,* May 1, 1981.

suaded the other participants to weaken the key provision of the agreement through the mere substitution of the word *may* for the word *shall* in the final text, to read: "[I]n Member countries the OECD Minimum Premarketing set of Data *may* be generated or obtained and applied for the purpose of initial assessment of new chemicals" (italics added).[24]

The American government's shift on MPD reflected more than a change in EPA leadership; it also reflected a change in the tactics of the American chemical industry. In the years leading up to the informal agreement of May 1980, industry spokesmen and the leading U.S. trade associations worked closely with their European counterparts in search of an acceptable OECD package. American industry's motive during this period appeared much the same as that of the German chemical industry in supporting the Sixth Amendment: a desire to use an international agreement to rein in domestic regulators. With the long gestation period of TSCA implementation finally coming to an end, the U.S. chemical industry saw advantages in limiting the discretionary authority of an agency that was committed to high standards of public health protection.

The appointment of officials who were likely to be more sympathetic to industry's positions changed these calculations. Although industry spokesmen had earlier expressed their concerns about the compatibility of the MPD approach with TSCA and their fears that EPA's "policy guidance" would be a de facto rule, by the spring of 1981 these reservations turned to outright opposition. In a memorandum to the State Department in April, the Chemical Manufacturers Association detailed its objections: an MPD requirement is illegal under TSCA, and even as a guideline it contradicts the act's underlying philosophy; adoption would disadvantage U.S. industry due to TSCA's broader coverage of new substances; the MPD is itself "neither economically feasible nor scientifically justified" for many substances and fails to take into account the broader contexts of varying national statutes and regulatory systems.[25] What had once seemed to be a useful bulwark against overeager regulators at home now appeared to be an undesirable and unnecessary importation of foreign regulation. The fitting epilogue to this turn of events was, from industry's point of view, the promulgation of a rule by EPA in September 1983 that exempted from full notification requirements most of the same categories of substances that were exempted under the Sixth Amendment. Thus, U.S. industry managed to obtain the most attractive feature of the Sixth Amendment while avoiding all of its liabilities.[26]

---

[24] For an earlier formulation, see OECD Council, "Draft Decision Concerning the Minimum Pre-Marketing Set of Data in the Assessment of Chemicals," Paris, March 1981.

[25] CMA, Memorandum to the U.S. Department of State, April 2, 1981. See also *Washington Post,* April 23, 1983.

[26] A background paper of the OTA ("The Information Content of Premanufacture

Despite the weakened terms of the MPD agreement, the eight years since the passage of TSCA chronicle considerable progress in establishing comparable national programs of industrial chemical notification in the Atlantic region. Taking advantage of existing institutions for harmonization and previous progress toward economic and political integration, the member nations of the Common Market achieved considerable uniformity in their approaches to this new area of chemical control policy. While less ambitious and ultimately less successful, the OECD negotiators managed to reduce the redundancy of regulatory requirements for new chemicals entering international markets and achieved consensus on much of the technical basis underlying national notification schemes.

The case illustrates how policy innovations in one country diffuse rapidly and spur the development of international norms when vital economic interests are at stake. The passage of TSCA, the culmination of an overwhelmingly domestic political process, provoked a collective response in Europe that in turn provided the basis for broader international negotiation and accommodation. The unilateral initiative of the United States was not taken as an exercise in international leadership, but, indirectly, it had that effect. Once it became apparent that the leading Western nations could not hold off forever in following the American lead, the anticipated economic costs of divergent national schemes provided a powerful incentive for industry representatives and government officials to search for common ground.

But the case also suggests that international policy harmonization can proceed only so far. As illustrated by the confrontation between the British and the Germans during the Sixth Amendment discussions and by the fate of the MPD proposal in the OECD negotiations, "harmonization" is achieved only if the agreement allows sufficient flexibility to accommodate and preserve varying national regulatory styles. As examined at length in previous chapters, these styles reflect longstanding relationships between public authority and the private sector. It is notable that neither the OECD agreements nor even the Sixth Amendment impinged directly on the procedural aspects of national regulatory systems that function to keep these relationships in delicate equilibrium. The interests of international commerce and a common reliance on scientific guidelines provide a substantial foundation for international agreement, but each nation clings to its own arrangements for managing political conflicts and resolving specific regulatory disputes.

Notices," April 1983) documented the advantages to U.S. industry of TSCA as it had been implemented to that time. Nearly one-half of the PMNs surveyed included no toxicity data. Although PMNs for chemicals that would not be exempted under the Sixth Amendment contained a somewhat higher percentage of toxicity test results, about 30 percent of PMNs describing nonpolymer, consumer-use chemicals to be made in amounts greater than ten thousand kilograms annually reported no toxicity results. Only 4.4 percent of all PMNs had been targeted by EPA for follow-up testing or control action.

Other International Programs of Chemical Control: The EC

Instructive as it is, an examination of the effort to align national programs of industrial chemical notification gives only a partial account of the achievements and limits of international harmonization in toxic chemicals policy. In other areas and in less visible forums, steady if hardly spectacular progress has been made to reduce national differences in regulatory approaches and outcomes. Among the many intergovernmental programs in this area, those of the European Community and several specialized agencies of the United Nations have the greatest relevance to the four governments of interest here.[27]

The Community's work outside of the Sixth Amendment has concentrated on the development of uniform regulatory standards to facilitate the free flow of goods among the ten member countries. Possibly its most impressive achievement is a series of directives that set common classification, packaging, and labeling standards for designated substances and mixtures.[28] These requirements now cover more than nine hundred dangerous chemicals as well as paints and related products, solvents, and pesticides. The directives approach "total harmonization," which means, in Community parlance, that compliance with EC requirements is a necessary and sufficient condition for goods to be allowed entry into the market of any EC member country. Nevertheless, in this case governments still remain free to impose the same or additional labeling and packaging requirements on undesignated chemical products, and they can provisionally restrict the use of or prohibit the marketing of a listed product, even if it meets all EC conditions.

Total harmonization is also approached in the case of outright EC bans. One example is the 1978 directive forbidding member countries to market or employ, except for a few specified uses, pesticides that contain designated mercury compounds or several persistent organochlorine compounds.[29] But this directive did not prohibit the manufacture of these products, their export,

---

[27]Prior to negotiations on premarket notification issues, the OECD Council had adopted a decision on the control of PCBs and a recommendation on the reduction of man-made emissions of mercury (see note 18 to this chapter). The Council of Europe, a forum of parliament members from twenty European countries, has also taken some interest in toxic chemicals. Its most notable accomplishment is the publication of guidelines for pesticide registration. In the absence of more formal intergovernmental agreements, these guidelines are credited with achieving a measure of cross-national harmonization in testing and application procedures. Council of Europe, *Pesticides,* 4th ed. (Strasbourg: Council of Europe, 1977); interview, Council of Europe, Strasbourg, October 1979.

[28]The first directive concerning the approximation of laws, regulations, and administrative provisions relating to the classification, packaging, and labeling of dangerous substances, has been amended six times, most recently by the "sixth amendment" cited in note 3 to this chapter. Other directives on solvents, paints and varnishes, and pesticides have been or may be amended, primarily to add new preparations.

[29]Council directive 79/117/EEC prohibiting the placing on the market and use of plant protection products containing certain active substances, *OJEC,* L33, 8 (1979).

or their use for research purposes or for emergency crop infestations in general. Other unequivocal bans on marketing and use have been issued for a few consumer goods containing dangerous chemicals, including the flame-retardant Tris, PCBs, and asbestos.[30]

Most Community standards, however, aspire only to "optional harmonization," in effect allowing much more discretion to national implementing authorities. For example, the Community's first standard for a workplace hazardous substance, the 1978 directive on vinyl chloride, set a relatively high maximum allowable level of exposure, permitting member countries to impose more restrictive controls as they saw fit.[31] The result was that Britain, France, and West Germany all adopted different standards, although each stayed under the EC ceiling. The same approach was taken in the long-awaited EC standard on asbestos exposure in the workplace, issued in 1983.[32]

Opportunities for national variation are even greater in the Community's approach to aligning food-additive policies. Here, harmonization results only insofar as member governments can neither entirely prohibit the use of EC-authorized additives nor use any substance not on the EC lists. (By 1981 these lists covered colors, preservatives, antioxydants, and emulsifiers.)[33] But governments can restrict the use of the authorized additive to certain kinds of foodstuffs and/or to certain maximum dosages. Thus, when the French wanted to ban amaranth (Red Dye No. 2), an EC-authorized coloring agent, they effectively achieved their objective by restricting its use to a single, relatively insignificant foodstuff (caviar).

The Community takes a somewhat different tack in setting pesticide residue standards. The member governments did not accept the Commission's proposal to set maximum permissible tolerances for residues on fruits and vegetables, a procedure that would have required each government to prohibit the marketing of produce exceeding the norms. Instead, the final agreement simply requires governments to allow on their markets produce meeting the minimum EC standards, while giving them the option of allowing or refusing products with higher residue levels.[34] In this way, the British policy

[30] Council directive 76/769/EEC on the approximation of the laws, regulations, and administrative provisions of the member states relating to restrictions on the marketing and use of certain dangerous substances and preparations, *OJEC*, L262, 27 (1976). This directive has since been amended five times to cover additional substances or uses.

[31] Council directive 78/610/EEC on the approximation of the laws, regulations, and administrative provisions of the member states on the protection of the health of workers exposed to vinyl chloride monomer, *OJEC*, L197, 22 (1978).

[32] See *International Environment Reporter*, July 13, 1983.

[33] For a review of Community programs in this area, see R. Haigh, "Harmonization of Legislation on Foodstuffs, Food Additives, and Contaminants in the European Economic Community," *Journal of Food Technology*, 13 (1978), 255–64 and 492–509.

[34] Council directive 76/895/EEC relating to the fixing of maximum levels for pesticide residues in and on fruit and vegetables, *OJEC*, L340, 9 (1976). This directive was first

preference of avoiding official standards for pesticide residues was accommodated and Community trade in agriculture was undisturbed.

In two cases, the European Community has attempted to move beyond standard setting toward more comprehensive regulatory regimes for chemicals. But in neither case has the effort culminated in an agreement as ambitious and sweeping as the Sixth Amendment. In 1978 the Community expanded its involvement in worker health and safety protection, an area long confined to the specific problems of the nuclear, coal, and steel industries that had been addressed in the original EC treaties.[35] Given in 1978 a broad and explicit mandate to further the protection of workers in the EC countries from health and safety hazards, the Commission placed an initial priority on the control of dangerous substances. Its first achievement was the adoption in 1980 of a Framework Directive on "the risks related to exposure to chemical, physical and biological agents at work."[36]

Unlike the Sixth Amendment, the Framework Directive does not require member governments to pass conforming legislation. Instead, it sets forth general principles intended to provide guidance for future national laws and regulations. These principles include obligatory official consultations with workers' and employers' associations prior to promulgation, allowing workers to monitor regulatory compliance in the plant, and providing other jobs to workers temporarily displaced for medical reasons. For ten specified substances or categories, the directive requires medical surveillance before and after exposure and stipulates that workers be informed of the nature of hazards, be notified when exposure limits are exceeded, and have access to medical records. In addition, the directive specifically instructed member governments to set up a system of health surveillance related to lead and asbestos exposure and to require employers to notify workers of the dangers associated with five designated substances. Finally, the directive authorized the EC bodies to develop Community standards for ten substances; by the end of 1983, these had appeared for lead and asbestos.

Efforts to create a Community-wide regime of pesticide registration have so far produced fewer results. Under the Commission's plan,[37] first proposed in 1976, manufacturers would have the choice of applying for national registration, according to each member country's criteria and procedures, or apply-

---

proposed in 1969, but its adoption was delayed by the enlargement of the community in 1973. In 1980 two additional proposals, on pesticide residues in cereals and meats, were before the council.

[35] Council resolution on an action program of the European Communities on safety and health at work, *OJEC*, C165, 11 (1978).

[36] Council directive 80/1107/EEC on the protection of workers from the risks related to exposure to chemical, physical, and biological agents at work, *OJEC*, L327, 3 (1980).

[37] Commission proposal for a council directive concerning the placing of EEC-accepted plant protection products on the market, *OJEC*, C212, 9 (1976).

ing for "European Community acceptance," which would be granted by national authorities according to the provisions of the EC directive. A successful application in the latter case would entitle the manufacturer to market his product anywhere in the Community for a ten-year period. The scheme would establish a looser form of harmonization than that achieved by the Sixth Amendment, primarily because the proposal presents only vague criteria to guide national authorities in deciding whether or not to accept the product. (The Sixth Amendment largely avoids this problem since marketing is assured, barring exceptional restrictive action, forty-five days after notification.) Thus, uniformity in national implementation is far from guaranteed, raising the possibility that manufacturers would gain entry to the EC market through the door of the least stringent regulatory authority. This concern and the fear that the scheme would deprive national authorities of their ability to adapt the use of pesticide products to local conditions have delayed adoption of the plan.

Viewed as a whole, these programs suggest substantial Community participation in the development of the chemical control policies of its member countries. But the significance of the EC as a force of policy harmonization is somewhat less than meets the eye. In many instances, Community programs do little more than reaffirm established national practices or settle for the least offensive or most inconsequential solution to all parties. The frequent recourse to "optional harmonization" agreements attests to the Community's tendency to accommodate, rather than to eliminate, divergent national policies and preferences.

In other cases, however, Community agreements have gone beyond the status quo to effect detectable changes in national policy. The most common format is the generalization of a policy initiative in one country to all member countries. Clear examples are the limited number of bans on consumer products, prompted in each case by unilateral action of a member government. Similarly, the 1978 restrictions on certain pesticides had little effect in Germany and France but did result in a number of withdrawals in Britain. Earlier, the French introduced their first pesticide residue standards in anticipation of imminent Community action. In some cases, the EC has preempted existing national programs with more elaborate and formally conceived EC-wide programs, such as those setting labeling and packaging requirements.

The checkered accomplishments of the Community in the area of chemical control derive from somewhat contradictory impulses. Despite increasing attention to issues of social policy, the Community remains above all a common market, and this fact dominates its efforts in chemical regulation. On the whole, its programs more effectively remove or prevent trade barriers than guarantee the citizens of member countries equal protection from harm. Yet, paradoxically, the net effect of Community involvement is almost always a gain in public protection. Even the lowest of the "lowest common denominator" solutions leads generally to a tangible extension of public regulatory authority somewhere in the Community. For example, the Framework Directive on workplace hazards, although reading like a composite list of each government's good intentions, did commit the British to a more Continental view of the role of medical surveillance in worker protection programs. The French, in turn, agreed to extend coverage to the self-employed, a group that had been neglected in French law. While the advances are often far from spectacular, Community standards that effectively change national policy do so in the direction of tightening, rather than loosening, existing controls. Thus, in promoting the interests of free trade, the Community also manages to promote the interests of public protection.

There are three principal reasons for this anomalous outcome. First, the economic interests that are keen on reaping the rewards of free trade may sometimes be more willing to tolerate high regulatory costs emanating from an international regime than from a purely domestic negotiation. Second, international negotiations are typically in the hands of officials whose primary responsibility is public health and the environment rather than trade. These include not only the Community's own staff but also national regulators, who enjoy a freedom from bureaucratic and political pressures in Brussels that they seldom experience at home. Since domestic pressures tend to push national regulators into a cautious stance in dealing with domestic issues (see chapters 4 and 9), Community negotiations open up opportunities to take more adventurous positions while obscuring accountability.

Finally, the nature of the European Community as a federal lawmaking entity favors the assumption of a certain kind of regulatory role. Without an effective enforcement capability of its own, the Community has evolved a legalistic approach to harmonization in all areas, spelling out in precise rules the criteria for compliance by its member governments and constituents. In toxic substances policy, this approach favors such regulatory techniques as numerical tolerance levels, lists of approved substances, and detailed guidance on such matters as packaging and labeling. A more informal, voluntary approach to toxic substances policy, such as that followed in Britain, is scarcely suitable as a model for international policy harmonization. (Partly for this reason, the British are often at odds with EC programs and intentions, while the Germans see in Brussels an orientation more compatible with their federal tradition.) The Community was given strong legal instruments to build a common market; these are now put to good purpose in aligning national policies of chemical control.

Harmonization in the United Nations

Several specialized agancies of the United Nations engage in activities bearing on chemical risk assessment and control. The focus and purpose of these activities are quite different from those of the EC efforts just reviewed. Only a few UN programs, for example, attempt to establish formal international standards for toxic chemicals.

Most prominent of these is the Codex Alimentarius Commission, a body of delegates from more than one hundred countries. Since 1962, this commission has developed international norms for food additives and pesticide residues.[38] The technical work is performed by expert committees sponsored jointly by the World Health Organization and the Food and Agriculture Organization. These committees regularly publish hazard evaluations that in themselves provide guidance for national regulatory authorities. But the evaluations are also used as technical support for the recommended standards of the Codex Commission. To have official weight, entailing a commitment to allow circulation in domestic markets of goods meeting the norm, a recommendation requires formal endorsement by member governments. Endorsements by the governments of the industrialized nations are infrequent (among the four governments of interest here, by 1977 only the United States had accepted any Codex standards on pesticide residues).[39] But officials do give serious consideration to the Codex standards in developing national regulations. West German authorities appear particularly attentive to Codex recommendations and expert evaluations.

The International Labor Organization has a long and uneven history of standard setting for workplace hazards. Since the adoption of an international convention on white lead exposure for painters in 1921, the organization has fashioned agreements on such matters as worker compensation for occupational diseases (1925, 1934), occupational health services (1959), and radiation protection (1960).[40] In the early 1970s, ILO turned its attention to occupational carcinogens. Its first achievement in the area was an international convention and accompanying recommendation on benzene that, among other provisions, called for an exposure limit of 25 ppm. (The French, alone among the four governments, incorporated the convention into national law.)[41]

---

[38] For background into these programs, see G. Vettorrazzi, *International Regulatory Aspects for Pesticide Chemicals* (Boca Raton, Fl.: CRC Press, 1979); David A. Ray, *The International Regulation of Pesticide Residues in Food,* Report to the National Science Foundation, NSF-RA-X-75-003 (Washington, D.C.: NSF/RANN, 1975); David M. Leive, *International Regulatory Regimes,* vol. 2 (Lexington, Mass.: Lexington Books, 1976), pp. 497–522.

[39] WHO/FAO, Codex Alimentarius Commission, *Acceptations des normes codex mondiales et régionales et des limites maximales codex recommandées pour les résidus de pesticides, tableaux récapitulatifs* (Rome: FAO, 1977).

[40] ILO, International Occupational Safety and Health Information Centre (CIS), "Fifty Years of International Collaboration in Occupational Safety and Health" (Geneva: CIS, 1969); interview, ILO, Geneva, July 1980.

[41] Preliminary reports leading to the ILO standard are ILO, "Protection against Hazards Arising from Benzene," Report 6, no. 1, International Labour Conference, 56th sess., Geneva, 1970, and Report 6, no. 2, 1971.

The ILO benzene standard was followed by a more ambitious initiative directed to the control of occupational carcinogens generally. A 1974 convention and recommendations called on ratifying nations to make every effort to replace carcinogens by less harmful substances, to reduce the number of exposed workers, and to prescribe and regularly review preventive measures. Other provisions covered record keeping, worker information, health surveillance, and inspection.[42] The convention did not list carcinogens, a task left to a later advisory report.[43] Britain adopted the basic terms of the ILO convention in a 1975 parliamentary resolution, followed by a HSE guidance note incorporating recommended precautions.[44]

In addition to these standard-setting efforts, UN agencies concentrate their efforts related to toxic chemicals on the gathering, evaluation, and dissemination of information on chemical risks. The Environmental Health Criteria Program, for example, compiles and analyzes the available information on the health effects of a limited number of selected pollutants. These evaluations are published in a series of reports, some of which conclude with regulatory recommendations. WHO has established a similar program on workplace hazards. The International Agency for Research on Cancer, a unit of WHO created in 1965, undertakes authoritative scientific assessments of known and suspected carcinogens, as well as performing its own research.[45] Two UN programs focus more on dissemination than on evaluation. The International Register of Potentially Toxic Chemicals (IRPTC) is charged with developing an international data bank on toxic chemicals, particularly common agrochemicals.[46] ILO publishes bibliographies and an encyclopaedia of occupational health and safety, both of which contain information on chemical hazards.[47] A more recent entrant on the UN toxic chemicals scene is the International Program on Chemical Safety (IPCS), an effort cosponsored by

[42] See ILO, "Control and Prevention of Occupational Cancer," Report 7, nos. 1 and 2, International Labour Conference, 58th sess., Geneva, 1973; and "Control and Prevention of Occupational Hazards Caused by Carcinogenic Substances and Agents," Report 6, nos. 1 and 2, International Labour Conference, 59th sess., Geneva, 1974.

[43] ILO, "Occupational Cancer: Prevention and Control," Occupational Safety and Health Series no. 39, Geneva, n.d.

[44] "International Labour Conference: Proposed action by Her Majesty's Government . . . ," presented to Parliament by the Secretary of State for Employment, September 1975, Cmdn. 6236 (London: HMSO, 1975).

[45] IARC, *Annual Report, 1980* (Lyon: IARC, 1980); interview, IARC, Lyon, December 1979; IARC, *IARC Monographs on the Evaluation of the Carcinogenic Risk of Chemicals to Humans,* IARC Monographs Supplement 1 (Lyon: IARC, September 1979).

[46] See *IRPTC Bulletin,* 4, no. 1 (January 1981), 2; and IRPTC, *Instructions for the Selection and Presentation of Data for the International Register of Potentially Toxic Chemicals with Sixty Illustrative Chemical Data Profiles* (Geneva: IRPTC, 1979).

[47] ILO, *Encyclopaedia of Occupational Health and Safety,* 2 vols., 3d ed. (Geneva: ILO, 1983).

WHO, ILO, and the United Nations Environment Program (UNEP). The task of IPCS is to enlist national institutions as lead agencies in a coordinated program of new research on specific hazards.[48] EPA, for example, agreed in 1980 to develop chemical scoring systems and study improvements in risk evaluation techniques.

In contrast to the programs of the European Community or even the OECD, these efforts of UN agencies in the area of toxic substances control can appear rather inconsequential, fragmented, and duplicative. They go far to achieve, however, what is undoubtedly their principal purpose and value: to render service to those countries that lack an indigenous capability to gather and evaluate the world literature on chemical hazards. In fulfilling this function, the UN agencies help to extend the benefits of scientific information and increased sophistication in controlling risks to less advantaged regions of the world. But these activities can also serve economic goals. Codex standards, for example, not only reassure less developed countries that imported food meets minimum safety norms, they also reassure food processors and agricultural interests that their export markets will not be disrupted by arbitrary bans or seizures.

Moreover, the UN programs perform a valuable networking function, even for the industrialized countries. They bring together scientists, regulators, and other interested parties into a common forum of information exchange and discussion, whose value in promoting cooperation and consensus goes beyond formal agreements or program outputs. Some prominent participants in UN activities, such as Truhaut from France or Fairwether from Britain, are in a position to transfer the results of international discussions directly into domestic policy making. As for the actual results of UN agency efforts, possibly the most significant for the national programs of interest here is IARC's work on carcinogenic risk analysis (see p. 206). These evaluations, while seldom if ever displacing a government's own assessments for regulatory purposes, are slowly being accepted as authoritative international standards.[49] With such prominence, however, have come greater public notoriety and even controversy over how the agency makes its judgments.[50]

[48] WHO, "WHO's Human Health and Environment Programme: Evaluation of the Effects of Chemicals on Health," Document A 32/12, March 13, 1979; *IRPTC Bulletin,* 4, no. 1 (January 1981), 6–8.

[49] In the United States, for example, the IARC list was one source used to draw up the list of candidate substances for review under OSHA's generic cancer policy (45 FR 157, August 12, 1980). Its listings are also included in the NTP annual reports on carcinogens.

[50] IARC came under public scrutiny in the United States in 1982, when it appeared that the agency altered its risk evaluation of benzene following alleged pressures from NCI officials. See *Science,* 217, September 3, 1982.

Transnational Networks

Recent scholarly work on the dynamics of international cooperation has called attention to the important role of nongovernmental or informal linkages among advanced industrial nations. These transnational networks constitute much of the fabric of social and economic interdependence. They often lay the groundwork for intergovernmental agreements and channel international developments and considerations into the domestic policy process. Since these networks are clearly operative in the area of chemical control, their impact deserves some attention.

Informal ties among governmental regulators themselves form one such network. Mutual participation in the programs of international organizations provides one opportunity for exchange, but some officials have also organized their own regular contacts. For example, food-safety officials in the United States, Britain, and Canada meet about twice a year to discuss regulatory developments and to exchange data. Governments may also convene special international meetings to discuss a particular problem, as the United States did in 1977 to consider a coordinated response to the problem of chlorofluorocarbons.[51] These initiatives are often more than occasions of collegial good will. Evidence of an emerging international consensus can strengthen the hand of regulators who are engaged in difficult domestic proceedings. In the case of chlorofluorocarbons, the initiative translated the desire of the United States government to spread the costs of abating a transnational environmental threat.

Other key national players in chemical control policy—the business, public interest and scientific communities—have developed their own transnational networks to serve particular purposes. Each helps in its own way to shape the international harmonization process and to bring international perspectives into domestic policy debates.

Among these groups, the chemical industry has perhaps the greatest stake in international policy negotiations, but its positions also reflect an underlying ambivalence. The history of negotiations on notification schemes in the EC and the OECD testifies to industry's interest in aligning national regulatory requirements as a means of furthering international trade. National chemical industries can find common ground in working for agreements that remove highly threatening nontariff barriers to trade without imposing unduly high regulatory costs.[52]

---

[51] Thomas B. Stoel, Jr., Alan S. Miller, and Breck Milroy, *Fluorocarbon Regulation: An International Comparison* (Lexington, Mass.: Lexington Books, 1980).

[52] In September 1980, for example, leading chemical manufacturers in Europe banded together in creating the European Chemical Industry Ecology and Toxicology Centre

But this coalition can come under strain when national industries view agreements in the light of varying domestic situations. The industries that are dealing with a relatively unfavorable regulatory environment at home can see international agreements as a means to control dangerous tendencies in domestic policy and politics; to them, detailed and unambiguous international directives are often preferable. Others, such as British industry in the EC negotiations or American industry in the later years of the MPD discussions, are reluctant to give up the advantages of a congenial home environment in exchange for an internationally imposed regime. From their viewpoint, agreements must be weakened or allow sufficient flexibility in their implementation to preserve domestic advantages. Also, relative position in international sales influences how much national industries are willing to give up in generalizing regulatory burdens for gains in equalizing trade opportunities. With foreign sales ranking far behind domestic sales, American firms can afford to treat the international harmonization process somewhat lightly, judging its virtues primarily in terms of the likely impact on the domestic regulatory scene. German industry, in turn, with a substantial export market, has taken a leading role in the harmonization process, even if progress means the imposition of new regulatory burdens at home.

At the level of national policy, chemical industries also keep an attentive eye on international impacts. As noted in chapter 9, governments are sensitive to industry's arguments that new regulatory initiatives will put them at a competitive disadvantage in world commerce. Industry has also lobbied with some success to ensure that domestic requirements also pertain wherever possible to competing imports and to exempt exports from health and environmental controls.[53] All these industry-generated pressures help to keep national regulatory programs in rough alignment.

Compared to the chemical industry, public interest associations and even unions have not become an effective presence in international negotiations on chemical control issues. These groups focus their attention almost exclusively on the domestic policy scene. Apart from undertaking coordinated campaigns on specific ecological threats, environmental and consumer groups

---

(ECETOC), which was intended to coordinate views on technical issues in the regulatory limelight. Clearly responding to OSHA's cancer policy and to the somewhat muted calls for similar initiatives in Europe, ECETOC in 1980 issued a report entitled "A Contribution to the Strategy for Identification and Control of Occupational Carcinogens." The document affirms the prevalent view of European industry that "the assessment of carcinogenic risk is too complex a subject for simple generic rules to be laid down, and expert judgment of the evidence is required in each case" (ECETOC, Monograph no. 2, Brussels, September 1980).

[53] See Philip Alston, "International Regulation of Toxic Chemicals," *Ecology Law Quarterly* (special issue, "Hazardous Substances in the Environment: Law and Policy"), 7, no. 2 (1978), 397–456, for an analysis of the treatment of imports and exports in U.S. law.

appear to develop international ties primarily for reasons of organizational solidarity and to facilitate the exchange of information that can be useful in domestic battles. Through the exchange of publications and other forms of communication, domestic groups learn of favorable regulatory developments abroad and gain other information that can be used to increase pressure on national authorities.

The growing policy role of the European Community did encourage the creation in Brussels of bureaus representing many of the environmental, consumer, and labor associations of the member nations. The European Environmental Bureau (EEB) now represents some fifty national environmental groups. Consumer groups have joined together in the European Bureau of Consumer Unions (BEUC), and organized labor is represented by the European Trade Union Confederation (ETUC). A large part of the efforts of these groups is devoted to monitoring EC activities for their members, so that national governments, in the words of one EEB report, cannot so easily "use the Community as a scapegoat for their policies."[54] While these associations frequently take positions on pending Community business, it is difficult to ascribe to them much direct influence over international policy developments. Besides their informational role, they serve as a useful organizational embodiment of those currents of public opinion that are sympathetic to public health and environmental protection. When national and international officials look for support for such viewpoints, these associations are there to provide it.

The highly developed international networks of the scientific community influence international policy harmonization at several levels. Well-established universal norms for the generation and dissemination of research results have been crucial in developing a common scientific base for harmonized policies. It was this common legacy of a scientific language, standardized methodologies, and accumulated knowledge that the OECD negotiators drew on to reach agreement on international test guidelines and laboratory practices.

A sophisticated system of international communication in science also helps to ensure that research breakthroughs in one country will be rapidly known elsewhere. The research results obtained by the B. F. Goodrich Company linking vinyl chloride exposure to liver cancer, for example, were available to the world scientific community within a matter of days. This rapid diffusion of research results serves to align regulatory agendas and makes

---

[54]European Environmental Bureau, *Annual Report, 1979,* Brussels, 1980. The International Organization of Consumers Unions (IOCU) has set up an international network for the exchange of information on hazardous products. See *Toxic Substances Control Newsletter,* National Audubon Society, New York, Fall/Winter 1981.

available to national authorities a similar array of scientific information on which to base decisions.

But the international efforts of scientists in the area of chemical control go beyond the normal routines of scientific research and testing. Scientists have also probed the frontiers of science in order to reach consensus on key assumptions guiding chemical risk assessment. As early as the 1950s, for example, a group of European toxicologists formed the Permanent European Committee for Research on the Protection of the Population against Chronic Toxicity Hazards (EUROTOX) to seek a common ground on some of the critical issues of toxicological evaluation.[55] International organizations such as WHO and FAO have sponsored a series of conferences and reports designed to foster international scientific consensus on important questions of interpretation.[56] In the late 1970s, the International Commission for Protection against Environmental Mutagens and Carcinogens (ICPEMC) was formed "to identify and promote scientific principles in the fields of environmental mutagenesis, carcinogenesis and genetic toxicology . . . that may serve as a basis for guidelines and regulations in the national or international context."[57] In its classification and evaluation of known and suspected carcinogens, IARC relies on international expert panels that necessarily make judgments going beyond demonstrable scientific fact.

In short, the international scientific community has attempted to bring its superior mechanisms of professional consensus building to bear on science-related questions that also have important social implications. But so far these efforts have had only limited success. The many intractable uncertainties of chemical risk assessment and the high stakes associated with the way these uncertainties are resolved thwart the best intentions of scientists to eliminate scientific controversy from either national or international decision making on chemicals.

Conclusion: International Harmonization and Policy Convergence

Chapter 2 concluded that while the four governments had evolved remarkably dissimilar procedures to formulate national policies and resolve specific dis-

[55] DFG, "Summary of a Meeting of West European Scientists on the Prophylaxis of Cancer," Bad Godesberg, 1954; EUROTOX, "Report of the Third Meeting," *Travaux de Chimie Alimentaire et d'Hygiène*, 48, no. 4 (1957).

[56] See, for example, Joint FAO/WHO Expert Committee on Food Additives, "Evaluation of the Carcinogenic Hazards of Food Additives," 5th report, FAO Nutrition Meetings Report Series, no. 29, Rome, 1961, p. 5.

[57] See *Journal of Environmental Pathology and Toxicology,* 1, no. 6 (July–August 1978), 941–43, for more details on this commission.

putes, they had taken on quite similar missions of chemical control and compiled comparable records in regulating specific substances. The analysis of this chapter helps to explain this finding. Despite the diversity, fragmentation, and sometimes only modest role played by them, all of the international linkages reviewed operate ultimately as a force of cross-national policy convergence. Formal international cooperation is one important component of the convergence process, helping in particular to reduce national disparities in the regulatory hurdles facing new products and in the standards covering already marketed products. But just as important are the independent, less structured efforts of nongovernmental groups: chemical industries, in seeking open foreign markets and international competitive advantage; public interest groups, in the pursuit of domestic political advantage; and the scientific community, forming a common international base for hazard assessment and stretching consensus to the frontiers of science. Separately but cumulatively, these ties sustain international cooperative efforts and prod domestic policies in the direction of cross-national convergence.

The momentum toward international policy convergence is hardly overpowering, however. There is still far more policy making and regulatory initiative taken in response to purely domestic circumstances than there is either formal intergovernmental agreement or spontaneous coordination. Governments show particular resistance to forgoing their policy prerogatives in favor of international regimes when these impinge on deeply embedded regulatory traditions and institutional arrangements. They can more readily defer to international policy frameworks when these do not entail significant departures from existing national practices or policy, as indicated by their ease in reaching agreement on technical matters or on "optional harmonization" proposals.

If international processes are to result in binding agreements or coordinated initiatives that go against the grain of national regulatory styles and policy inclinations, additional incentives are needed. One such incentive is simply the leverage that national authorities can gain over domestic policy making. Agency officials sometimes have more influence over the course of international negotiations than they have over their own regulatory proceedings. This is especially true for European regulators who, although they do not have to face the hostile and contentious environment of their American counterparts, are nonetheless constrained by tightly integrated consultative mechanisms. But American officials also use international developments, although less often and less consistently, for their own purposes. EPA authorities under the Carter administration, for example, were able to make headway on introducing generic testing requirements for new chemicals under TSCA that probably would have been impossible without international backing.

International economics provides another powerful incentive for elevating decision making on chemicals to the international level. Almost invariably, economic interests provide the mortar for building international regimes of chemical control. Where divergent national regulations are most economically threatening, progress in policy harmonization is most rapid and successful. Within both the European Community and the OECD, major agreements on premarket notification issues countered the most serious threat to international trade in chemicals in the postwar period. In turn, there have been few achievements in harmonizing workplace protection policies in any forum, reflecting the lower international economic stakes involved.

In view of the highly integrated market in chemicals that has developed in the North Atlantic region over the past thirty years, the role of economic factors in driving harmonization efforts is hardly surprising. The serious potential of divergent regulatory requirements to disrupt marketing, investment, and trade quickly alerts the private sector, government leaders, and international bureaucrats to the advantages of cooperation.[58] In the European Community, where economic interdependence has progressed the furthest, virtually any policy innovation in a single country has market ramifications that surpass domestic impact and almost invariably triggers EC-level delibertions. Consistent with earlier theoretical work on the processes of EC integration, the imperatives of a common market have drawn chemical regulation policies into the sphere of legitimate and necessary domains of Community intervention and have given the Community strong tools with which to forge alignment.[59] Yet the limited progress achieved to date in this area suggests that the threshold of market disruption justifying Community rather than separate national action remains fairly high.

Finally, one cannot discount the role of international organizations as an independent force of policy harmonization. Once created, the programs of these organizations have a tendency to grow and multiply, seeking new opportunities to expand their functions and relevance. The tendency to expand is supported not only by the international staff but also by a network of sympathetic national officials and other cultivated clientele groups. As a rule, these international bureaucrats and networks define their mission as one of environmental and public health protection; in this respect, they serve as a partial counterweight to economic considerations in international decision making on chemicals. But the impact of these organizations as promoters of international regulation and defenders of health and environmental values is

[58] See Keohane, "The Demand for International Regimes," *International Organization*, 36, no. 2 (Spring 1982), 325–55.

[59] See, for example, Ernst B. Haas, "International Integration: The European and the Universal Process," *International Organization*, 15 (Summer 1961), 366–92; David Mitrany, *A Working Peace System* (Chicago: Quadrangle, 1966); Leon N. Lindberg and Stewart A. Scheingold, *Europe's Would-Be Polity* (Englewood Cliffs: Prentice Hall, 1970); and Joseph S. Nye, *Peace in Parts: Integration and Conflict in Regional Organization* (Boston: Little, Brown, 1971).

limited by their ultimate subservience to the wills of member governments and by their own complex administrative and decision-making processes, which often seem only to magnify the difficulties of taking collective action.

At various points, this analysis has cited the special status of the United States in international processes related to chemical control. Rather than taking the lead, the United States government has consistently shown less inclination than have the European governments to subordinate domestic policy making to an international perspective. The relative size of the domestic market and the correspondingly reduced importance of international trade for the U.S. chemical industry are one important reason. The paramount role of the United States in generating relevant research and in obtaining test results and refining their interpretation also makes access to international information and expertise less crucial. Moreover, the United States has not made the general commitment to economic integration and coordinated policy that the three European governments have made as members of the European Community. The international orientation of U.S. public interest groups and labor is if anything even weaker than it is for European groups. As a result, the politics of U.S. chemical control tends to work itself out more autonomously than the chemical control politics of the European countries, and the role of international factors in explaining domestic policy choice is relatively less pronounced.

Yet, paradoxically, the United States undeniably plays a leadership role in the cross-national alignment and evolution of chemical control policies. Its leadership does not result from formal initiatives of international cooperation or from superior negotiating skills; instead, it derives naturally from a series of features that set American regulatory philosophy and procedures apart from those of the European countries. These features of the American regulary setting (examined at length in previous chapters)—the openness of decision making, the heavy investments in regulatory programs and on health effects research, and a political process that feeds on controversy—serve to uncover and dramatize the hazards of chemical technology. They also produce policy initiatives, such as full-blown notification schemes covering new industrial chemicals and generic cancer policies, which tend to arise more slowly, if at all, in European regulatory settings.

Once launched in the United States, however, these initiatives typically force a European response. In the case of notification schemes, TSCA provoked a collective reaction that later paved the way for broader international negotiation and compromise. More often, the regulatory turbulence from the United States is felt at the national level, as one or more European interest groups focus on American developments to suit their own purposes. Through the multiple channels of interdependence, the unique processes and politics of chemical control in the United States influence the setting of regulatory agendas abroad.

Cross-National Analysis and Regulatory Reform

In chapters 3–11, we analyzed the impact of national and international institutions on chemical control policies in Britain, France, West Germany, and the United States. Domestic political structures, legal and scientific traditions, interest groups, and international organizations were separately examined in an effort to determine how each contributes to convergences and divergences among the four countries. In this concluding chapter, we attempt to synthesize the elements from earlier chapters into larger patterns of explanation. We then present a composite picture of the most significant costs, benefits, successes, and failures of the American and European approaches to chemical regulation. Finally, we suggest ways in which these cross-national comparisons can be brought to bear on discussions about regulatory reform in the United States.

Toward a Coherent Explanation

Across four frameworks for chemical regulation—food additives, pesticides, chemicals in the workplace, and premarket testing of industrial chemicals—striking cross-national divergences in regulatory process coexist with relatively minor differences in the objectives and outcomes of regulation. The U.S. approach, in particular, departs sufficiently from those of the European countries to be identified as a distinctive national model. The openness, complexity, and divisiveness of American decision making have no parallel in

Europe. Yet, regulatory power has been directed at very similar ends in the four countries, particularly in the selection and control of carcinogens.

That chemical regulation occupies an equally firm position on the political agendas of the four countries follows from their parallel economic, social, and technological development and the powerful forces of interdependence in modern industrial society. Flourishing cross-national communication among scientists, the sensitivity of the news media to chemical disasters, and pressure from groups concerned about health and the environment elicited an active regulatory response from the governments of all four countries. In recent years, the discovery of latent risks presented by toxic substances intensified the demand for more comprehensive and effective programs of chemical control.

The success of the Atlantic community in creating and sustaining liberal economic arrangements also helps explain the convergent regulatory response concerning toxic substances. The international integration of modern chemical markets gave national industry leaders a growing interest in the trade-related policies of other states and prompted concerted initiatives by the chemical industry on behalf of harmonization. The importance of chemical trade to Western economies made national governments receptive to the idea of common regulatory policies on chemical hazards. France's willingness to delay implementation of a chemical notification law and Germany's decision to postpone national legislation until after agreement on a European directive can be seen as symptomatic of such concerns.

International organizations like the EC and OECD have provided indispensable institutional frameworks for building a common response. Membership in the EC not only commits the European countries to avoiding trade-distorting regulatory action, it also provides numerous mechanisms for drawing member states into negotiations aimed at developing congruent policies. Representing a larger group of nations and exercising less political power, OECD serves as a complementary forum to the EC. By virtue of its long-standing interest in environmental protection, OECD has been able to take the lead in harmonizing chemical control policies, particularly with respect to technical matters such as standardized test protocols and laboratory practices.

The gap between U.S. and European chemical regulation appears especially narrow when the chemicals actually controlled under the four regulatory frameworks are compared. This convergence can be explained partly in terms of technological and economic determinism. Evidence generated about specific substances in any one country is quickly available to all, and, where the hazards are clear, different procedural arrangements do not lead to different interpretations of the scientific data. The chemical industry's desire to minimize differential treatment for products across national lines provides a powerful economic impetus for the selection of common regulatory targets. By collecting, storing, and disseminating scientific evidence, and by making limited standard-setting efforts, international organizations also contribute to the uniformity of response.

Political and institutional factors also promote convergence toward a relatively conservative position in regulating carcinogens. In the three European countries, the regulatory process contains numerous features that foster caution: a stable, professional civil service that sees no advantage in radical innovation, a concern with minimizing administrative costs, a structuring of scientific input that discourages adventurous views from surfacing and excludes more radical elements from advisory forums. Participation in the EC and other international arenas furthers the European tendency to seek "lowest common denominator" solutions. There are few political incentives for abandoning the reactive, case-by-case approach to dealing with toxic hazards.

The absence in the United States of many of these moderating influences could steer regulators toward more rapid and comprehensive control. Yet, in spite of many innovative and energetic policy initiatives, the United States has regulated few suspected carcinogens that have not also been controlled in Europe. The reason for this anomaly is the subordination of American regulatory policy to a political dynamic that prevents full realization of the potential for state intervention. The complex procedures devised for the administrative agencies by Congress, the courts, and the White House place an effective brake on regulatory action. Both industry and its political adversaries have proved adept at exploiting these procedural checks to promote their positions on major rule-making initiatives. Attempts to regulate in the face of uncertainty have run into special difficulties, since the demands of private interests and reviewing courts have forced regulators to engage in a time-consuming, yet largely inconclusive, exploration of technical issues. Even the generous resources committed to regulation are a debility in the U.S. context, encouraging the compilation of ever more detailed factual records and supplying a plausible excuse for inaction. These delays are compounded by the rapid turnover of high-level personnel and the shifts in policy approach which prevent steady progress in rule making and enforcement.

Differences in regulatory process among the four countries are substantially more difficult to explain. To account for them in detail would require an exploration of legal, political, and social history going well beyond the compass of this book. But even a limited inquiry reveals the significance of the way in which regulatory power is divided in each country, not only within government, but between the state and established societal interests.

The power to make policy is most fragmented in the United States, where Congress, the president, the executive agencies, and the courts all have separate and distinctive roles in decision making. Their overlapping jurisdictions create robust competition that undercuts the authority of each. For example, the ambiguous delegations of power in U.S. chemical control legislation reflect continuing congressional distrust of the executive agencies. Responding to the environmental consciousness of the 1970s, Congress greatly expanded agency authority to intervene in the affairs of the chemical industry. But it circumscribed these broad delegations by systematic checks in the form of complex rule-making procedures, economic analysis requirements, implementation deadlines, and expanded judicial review. The adversarial relationship between Congress and the agencies also accounts for the former's liberal and frequently disruptive use of its oversight and reauthorization powers to control the details of administrative performance.

The fragmentation of political authority leaves U.S. administrators in a peculiarly vulnerable position. They are confronted with demanding statutory mandates, which are often enacted without great attention to bureaucratic or economic reality. These must be implemented under the critical eye of other governmental institutions, and in full view of warring private interests, each advancing interpretations of law, science, and economics consistent with its narrower objectives. Unable to strike bargains in private, American regulatory agencies are forced to seek refuge in "objectivity," adopting formal methodologies for rationalizing their every action. Calls for quantification and specificity, particularly in accounting for economic costs and benefits, emanate not only from Congress, but also from a White House eager to assert centralized control over regulatory policy.

The active supervisory role played by the federal judiciary vis-à-vis the agencies also reflects the competitiveness of U.S. policy making. Though judges in all four countries can respond to persons injured by administrative action, the jurisdiction of the U.S. courts has been systematically enlarged by legislation authorizing citizen groups to seek judicial review. Through these citizen suit provisions, Congress has tried to ensure that regulators will be legally accountable to the public as well as to the industries they seek to regulate. Liberal standing rules, coupled with elaborate legal definitions of agency responsibilities, have generated a multitude of lawsuits that keep American administrators continually on the defensive. Taking their cue from Congress, the courts have adopted an adversarial posture toward the agencies. Their searching review of the decision-making record has forced administrators toward greater formality and rigor in building the evidence to support their decisions.

In contrast to the situation in the United States, the political regimes of Britain, France, and West Germany effectively fuse the state's executive and legislative responsibilities, giving the executive unquestioned leadership in formulating policy. The ties of party membership bind legislature and executive into a cooperative rather than competitive relationship. Because the executive controls the process of drafting legislation, statutory objectives conform closely to the government's actual regulatory agenda. Parliament ratifies the broad outlines of policy in enabling legislation, committing details of implementation to the discretion of the executive. The absence of legislative-executive competition eliminates the pressure for rigorous procedural and judicial controls on the bureaucracy.

Since parliaments have neither the means nor the incentive to exercise effective postlegislative control, European regulators enjoy considerable independence in implementing chemical control laws. They are free to structure and manage access with relatively few statutory constraints. A confidential process of consultation and accommodation permits government officials to mediate among conflicting private interests. As a result, regulators are able to make the necessary trade-offs and compromises without presenting reasoned public justification or drawing open political fire. Peripheral groups that are excluded from the European regulatory process are reluctant to press for more liberal access, either through fear of co-optation or out of a traditional deference toward the bureaucracy. Demands for policy change are expressed primarily through the medium of electoral politics, and because information is kept under careful administrative control, specific regulatory issues seldom achieve a high political profile.

Both institutional history and staffing traditions reinforce the relative independence of the European decision maker. While U.S. agencies are hampered by inexperience and by frequent changes in the upper echelons, European bureaucracies, particularly those with technical expertise, remain better insulated against the winds of electoral politics. Regulatory agencies are staffed by professional civil servants who are not subject to removal with every change in government. At the same time, they are steeped in the history and tradition of bureaucratic decision making, so that their actions arouse less controversy than those of top U.S. administrators, who often approach their tasks with a highly individualistic sense of mission.

Among the three European countries, there are differences in regulatory approach stemming from differences in the configuration of political power. In each country, the legal system and bureaucratic tradition interact to channel or diffuse state power in different ways, reinforcing characteristic national patterns of decision making. In many respects, chemical regulation in France offers the starkest contrasts to the U.S. pattern. Technical committees, staffed largely by public officials and scientists, carry out routine, case-by-case processing of registrations and notifications with little open controversy and with no incentive to explain their actions or to change their regulatory priorities. The absence of public questioning is one manifestation of a system in which regulatory power is extraordinarily concentrated, even by European standards. The constitutional relegation of "regulatory" responsibilities to the executive severely restricts the role of parliament, effectively denying it a voice in determining the institutional and procedural framework of regulation. The power of the executive is reinforced by the Conseil d'Etat, a unique hybrid institution that serves both as the nation's highest administrative court and as its chief adviser on the legality or practicality of proposed administrative decisions. A highly developed tradition of interministerial consultation further centralizes the exercise of executive power. Yet the bureaucracy, dominated by an elite administrative corps, maintains the appearance of impartiality and enjoys steady public confidence in the day-to-day implementation of regulatory policy.

In Germany, more than in France or Britain, state action derives its legitimacy from law. The Basic Law demands specificity both in the formulation of statutory delegations and in the design of regulatory controls. The preference for explicit legal norms brings Germany's chemical control policies surprisingly close to those of the United States in several particulars, such as the adoption of numerical, hence measurable and enforceable, standards for pesticide residues and chemicals in the workplace. German policy on occupational carcinogens most clearly illustrates the regulatory system's demand for precise standards. In contrast to the French and British governments, German federal authorities have promulgated "technically directed" standards for a long list of carcinogens in order to establish uniform duties for employers and to permit effective monitoring and control. Germany's federal structure also works in favor of such policies. With enforcement authority constitutionally assigned to the states, the federal government has to fall back on standard setting as the primary means of establishing national uniformity in the regulation of toxic substances.

Though constrained to act within limits laid down by Parliament, British administrators operate in a far less restrictive legal environment than do their German counterparts. Free from constitutional or statutory demands for explicit standards, British officials can tailor policy to meet the needs of individual industrial concerns. Negotiation takes the place of formal rule making, and the success of the policy machinery depends on the maintenance of mutually trusting relations between government and the private sector. Consultation does not have to be required by law, since both public officials and private interests derive important benefits from the process. Governmental regulators use consultation to promote consensus and to legitimate policy decisions, while private interests participate in the process because it leads to individualized and flexible policy.

British occupational safety and health policies strikingly illustrate the national tendency to avoid legal instruments wherever possible. Controls on workplace hazards are cast in the form of voluntary standards and codes of practice rather than enforceable regulations. The success of such nonbinding rules depends on close supervision of the chemical industry by the relevant health and safety inspectorates. Though these institutions enjoy extensive legal rights to enter and inspect premises, their preference, now as in the past, is to rely more on conciliation than coercion to achieve policy objectives.

Considering the decision-making frameworks of each country as a whole, the inescapable linkages among legal traditions, bureaucratic practice, and the configuration of power within each government become clear. Formality of process in the United States goes hand in hand with the fragmentation of political power. Each branch of government seeks to constrain administrative discretion by means of legally enforceable procedural and analytical requirements. Because power is more effectively concentrated in the executive branch, German decision makers experience far fewer demands for procedural complexity. But the legalism fostered by the Basic Law requires specificity in the formulation of policy goals and instruments and helps create distance between regulators and private interests. In Britain, the insistence on political rather than judicial legitimation of policy is reflected in the informality of the consultation process and the maintenance of close, confidential relations between government and major interest groups. The constitutionally mandated concentration of power in the French executive branch, reinforced by an elite bureaucratic tradition, fosters a more routine and technocratic approach to decision making than is possible in any of the other three countries.

The different configurations of power and the differences in legal and bureaucratic practice within each country are conditioned in turn by the larger context of state-society relationships. A distinctive feature of American policy, for example, is the legislature's willingness to authorize wide-ranging programs for chemical regulation coupled with its steadfast reluctance to grant any single institution enough power to resolve the detailed problems of implementation. This is not an unexpected finding. Both the belief that government should be generously responsive to popular demands and the distrust of centralized authority are deeply rooted in U.S. society. Public problems are best resolved, following the American liberal conception, through clash and compromise among individuals and groups pursuing their own self-interests. The authority of the state is required to put an imprimatur on particular regulatory decisions, but its power to implement a consistent policy direction is undercut by elaborately constructed checks and balances.

Modern programs of social regulation, however, presuppose that the central government must play a dynamic and authoritative part in policy making. For a variety of reasons—the high political saliency of toxic chemicals, their transboundary effects, the dearth of reliable health and safety data, the absence of adequate resources or enforcement authority in the states—the power to regulate chemicals has been centralized in the U.S. federal government. But the complexities and ambiguities built into the enabling laws reflect continuing insecurity about the state as a potent regulator of private activity, and their effect has been to magnify and perpetuate public mistrust of centralized power. Required at every step to expose its innermost workings, the American regulatory process reveals all the weaknesses and imperfections that other political environments take pains to conceal. This tendency feeds the debate about the propriety of entrusting federal agencies with massive rule-making responsibilities and fuels demands for wholesale deregulation.

In Europe, no such skepticism about the state's regulatory role interferes with the task of chemical control. A general acceptance of the state as policy maker keeps the public from questioning the need for expanded control of chemical hazards or from demanding the curtailment of regulatory power through procedural constraints. In turn, the incremental establishment of goals maintains social equilibrium and prevents sudden and dramatic shifts of power into the hands of regulatory officials. The process of regulation has drawn the least critical comment in France, where state control of social policy making is perhaps most firmly established. Regulation in Britain has been absorbed into the consultative mode of policy making and shielded against protest by the public's confidence in the civil service. In contrast, charges of "overbureaucratization" are frequently heard from a more mistrustful German public. Both industry and environmental groups have attempted to change the legal contours of the regulatory process in Germany, the former by trying to delimit the powers of government and the latter by demanding greater access.

Fitting chemical regulation into the broader context of state-society relationships helps explain some of the problems and limitations of international harmonization discussed in chapter 11. While the forces of interdependence account for progress in the area of technical harmonization, the failure to converge on more fundamental policy issues reflects deep-seated differences among the chemical-producing nations about the proper forms and boundaries of state intervention. Some of the conflicts that surfaced during the Sixth Amendment negotiations in the EC illustrate the possible consequences of such cross-national variation. For example, in keeping with a greater regard for specificity and legal norms, Germany advocated a step-sequence plan in which more onerous testing obligations would automatically be triggered at certain production thresholds. Britain, however, argued that such requirements should only be imposed at the discretion of implementing officials. The two sides eventually reached an accommodation. But the disagreement is symptomatic of tensions that are bound to arise as pressures for harmonization collide with different national conceptions of the regulatory state.

Science and Interest Group Politics

We have argued that the participation of scientists and interest groups in the regulatory process takes its shape in each country from the overarching structure of legal and institutional relationships. In the United States, where the relationship between state and society is most antagonistic, the fear of cancer has elicited the most pointed policy responses from elected officials. The Delaney clause and President Nixon's "war on cancer" are but two examples of political action undertaken in response to public anxiety. Both regulatory and research promotion agencies in the United States have proved exceptionally sensitive to such political impulses, responding with ambitious programs for identifying carcinogens that have no analogue in Europe. With this massive investment in cancer research and risk assessment, the United States now provides much of the scientific basis for carcinogen regulation in Europe and elsewhere, in effect generating a free good for regulatory authorities in other industrial nations. However, the impact of these R & D programs on the overall direction of U.S. chemical regulation remains uncertain and is quite limited, at least in the short term. R & D sponsored by American regulatory agencies has proved of little relevance in setting the national agenda for chemical control, and the questionable predictive value of most research on long-term hazards dilutes its usefulness in establishing regulatory standards and priorities.

The expansion of the government's scientific research capacity in response to political pressure is one aspect of a more general phenomenon in the United States. American regulators, being more politically exposed than their European counterparts, have a greater need to support their actions through formal analytical arguments. Their demand for expertise necessitates a continuing build-up of technical capabilities and the development of more sophisticated and detailed analytical methodologies. The structure of the American rule-making process subjects the analytical case for regulation to intense political scrutiny. Any weaknesses are quickly exploited, and the uncertainties and shortcomings of the relevant scientific base are readily exposed. Since there are few forums for directly negotiating political demands, areas of scientific uncertainty and the merits of alternative analytical tools become focal points of controversy.

In this adversarial setting, participating scientists often appear as advocates of particular regulatory outcomes rather than as disinterested experts. When scientists testifying before the agencies espouse positions that can be clearly identified as "pro-" or "anti-" regulation, their contribution tends to merge with that of overtly political interests, such as industry, labor, and environmental groups. Consequently, in the protracted controversy surrounding carcinogen regulation in the United States, science has lost much of its aura of objective authority.

The polarization induced by the U.S. regulatory process has tainted even the federal government's own research institutions, undermining their credibility as a source of unbiased expertise. On a range of scientific issues with important policy implications, scientists from NCI, NIOSH, NIEHS, and the regulatory agencies have advocated positions that are more "proregulation" than those of industry experts, though less extreme than those advanced by environmentalists. Yet, far from reducing conflict, opinions offered by governmental scientists have tended to compound the disagreements surrounding carcinogen identification and risk assessment. In particular, the controversy stirred up by the NCI-NIOSH-NIEHS paper on occupational cancer risks has not yet been stilled. Political fallout from that event continues in the form of demands for stricter peer review of scientific analyses prepared by government agencies.

The structure of decision making in Europe discourages open polarization of expert opinion. A preference for negotiated solutions fosters reliance on pluralistic advisory committees that can resolve both technical and political issues. In societies generally more tolerant of elites, such groups command public respect by virtue of their training and experience. More important, these multipartite expert groups, working out of the public eye, avoid the identification of scientific disputes with different sides in a policy debate. The effect of this institutional approach is to protect the image of science as a neutral and rational decision-making tool, a goal that U.S. agencies have unsuccessfully pursued.

While the forms of expert participation are conditioned largely by factors lying outside science, the patterns of interest group activity reflect conscious attempts by industry and the advocates of regulation to manipulate the political "rules of the game" to their own advantage. In Europe, where regulators occupy reasonably secure positions, interest groups usually seek to influence policy by cultivating good relations with the bureaucracy. In so doing, they reinforce the inclination of governmental officials to operate through informal procedures and flexible control strategies. Groups unable to achieve their objectives through consultation often seek to mobilize political support by taking their case to the public, but their ability to influence regulatory outcomes through such tactics appears neither uniform nor assured.

In the United States, where regulatory power is highly fragmented and access to the regulatory process is easily available at all levels, private interests distribute their resources correspondingly, simultaneously directing their attention to Congress, the agencies, and the courts. Tailoring their actions to the adversarial format of rule making, they maintain a combative and competitive stance against each other as well as against public authorities. Since success in the U.S. process requires meeting and countering the opponents' arguments, it is important for both industry and proregulation groups to acquire independent expertise, particularly on scientific, legal, and economic matters. Their tactics intensify the debate on technical issues and increase the pressure on regulators to respond with equally complex arguments. In short, interest group activity in the United States reaffirms the existing pattern of regulation, exploiting but not altering the distribution of power within government and setting a seal of approval on the formal, adversarial model of decision making.

Evaluating the Two Models

Any attempt to compare the effectiveness of European and American chemical regulation faces formidable difficulties. To begin with, inadequate exposure data do not permit ready comparison of the risks to which people in the four countries are actually exposed. Even where risks are roughly comparable, as for workers in the chemical industry, it is difficult to judge the impact of radically different control instruments, such as medical surveillance, respirators, and engineering controls. It is also unclear whether similar control strategies are equally effective in the four countries, since different monitoring and enforcement practices and cultural attitudes may produce great variations in the level of compliance with health and safety requirements. Without detailed investigation of these issues, it is only possible to guess at the extent of risk reduction achieved by divergent national policies.

It is somewhat easier to compare the impact of chemical control policies on government and private interest groups in the four countries. The costs incurred by the chemical industry in complying with regulatory prescriptions can be analyzed separately from the indirect costs and benefits accruing to government agencies and public interest groups involved in formulating chemical control policy.

In terms of the number of products restricted by state regulation, the chemical industry in Europe and the United States seems to bear a quite comparable burden. Though differences in policy emphasis, such as the greater concern with existing chemicals and carcinogens in the United States, threaten to produce uneven costs for industry, these divergences have not led American administrators to regulate many more substances or to control targeted substances more stringently. Testing burdens for American chemical manufacturers also compare favorably with those of their European competitors, in spite of TSCA's uniquely comprehensive mandate concerning the testing and regulation of existing chemicals. For the present, it appears that U.S. legislative and regulatory policies have created only a potential for higher costs than are likely to be imposed on industry in Europe.

With respect to the administrative costs of complying with regulations, however, there is little question that U.S. industry has to spend considerably greater sums than its European counterparts. American chemical firms enormously expanded their staff and financial commitments to health and environmental issues during the 1970s. Industry attributes much of this development to the growing demands of federal regulators, particularly in the form of required paperwork. Given the obsession of the U.S. regulatory process with formalism and rational justification, these claims carry the ring of truth. It is clear, by contrast, that the less structured process of European regulation keeps formal information exchanges, and the attendant cost of generating and distributing documents, to a minimum.

But industry's total expenditures in the regulatory arena cannot be attributed solely to the administrative costs of compliance. A conscious strategy of combating state intervention wherever possible has also contributed to the costs incurred by American chemical firms. Not all of these costs can be assessed in purely monetary terms. It is probable, for example, that the high priority given to fighting social regulation in the past decade has diverted needed managerial talent from other matters of critical importance, such as the reorientation of R & D investments to take account of changes in product cycles. Persistent opposition to regulatory initiatives has also prolonged the period of market uncertainty surrounding products and processes targeted for control. With outcomes dependent on a court decision or a new directive from Congress, American firms have found themselves less able to predict and plan for regulatory developments than have their counterparts in Europe.

The cost of intervening in U.S. regulatory politics is also high for parties other than industry. The fragmentation of state power forces all interest groups to mount a series of interlocking maneuvers in order to advance their position with all three branches of government. Faced with a simpler configuration of power, European pressure groups can marshall their resources more efficiently, gaining most of their objectives through bargaining with the executive branch. Administrative procedures oriented toward consensus, coupled with high legal and social barriers to litigation, rule out the costly strategy of appealing to the courts. For European groups, therefore, cost is less of a problem than access. Established social forces, such as organized labor, enjoy guaranteed rights of participation, but the same is not always true for newer political coalitions. While their exclusion may promote efficiency and continuity in the short run, failure to integrate them into the bureaucratic decision-making process in the longer term may lead to wider political conflict.

Looking at chemical control from the standpoint of governmental expenditure, it is evident that the U.S. approach is the most costly. Federal agencies incur significant expenses in complying with legally mandated procedures, particularly in preparing rigorous scientific and economic analyses that can withstand sustained critical review. Agencies must not only develop their internal capability for generating and interpreting information, but must also employ outside consultants for supplementary expertise. Voluntary participation by independent experts, a commonplace in Europe, is relatively rare in the United States. Moreover, like private interest groups, American agencies must commit substantial resources to litigation and to meeting challenges from Capitol Hill. Yet the amounts appropriated for federal regulatory programs, although more generous than corresponding European authorizations, seldom take into full account these special complexities. The insufficiency of resources exacerbates the misfit between policy expectations and the pace of implementation, leading to widespread public disenchantment with agency performance.

The costs of the American approach to regulation in terms of time, money, and public dissatisfaction are relatively easy to document. The benefits are less tangible. Seen in cross-national perspective, these have less to do with the quality of technical decisions than with much broader attributes of good government. For adherents of the Jeffersonian ideal, the U.S. regulatory process displays a praiseworthy commitment to the proposition that an informed citizenry is the best safeguard against arbitrary exercises of governmental power. Recourse to a more confidential decision-making process would be viewed, in light of this political paradigm, as a threat to democratic decision making and a symptom of collusion between government and powerful private interests. Similarly, procedural formality, including the right to cross-examine technical witnesses, is seen by many as indispensable protection against the control of policy by politically unaccountable experts. The production of scientific information is regarded as an important public benefit in its own right, justifying substantial governmental expenditure and providing a defense against monopolization of health and safety data by vested commercial interests.

Whether these benefits are considered reasonably proportional to the costs depends largely on the normative criteria brought to the evaluation. Judging the American regulatory process solely by the yardstick of efficiency, for example, a critic might dismiss OSHA's generic policy on occupational carcinogens as thoroughly misguided. It can be persuasively argued that the policy was years in the making, that it diverted resources from the regulation of specific chemicals, and that it completely misconceived the problems of scientific uncertainty. Proponents of OSHA's strategy, however, note that the failure to promulgate workable regulations may be less important than the advancement of certain less tangible social policies. Their appraisal emphasizes the agency's successful shift away from the "body-count" approach and toward the categorization of carcinogens on the basis of positive animal experiments. OSHA's supporters also congratulate the agency on raising public consciousness about the problem of occupational cancer. Both in the United States and abroad, the OSHA cancer policy provided the impetus for a critical reappraisal of governmental policies related to cancer in the workplace.

Regulatory Comparisons and Directions for Reform

To the American regulator attempting to meet the demands of Congress, the courts, and the public, the relatively conflict-free terrain of European regulatory politics beckons as an enticing vision. We have attempted to show, however, that the surface characteristics of other regulatory systems, such as the absence of conflict, cannot be purchased through purely cosmetic changes in legislative or administrative practice. The processes and outcomes of regulation in each country depend on unique configurations of state power, private rights, and public expectations, which constrain the possibilities for regulatory reform and limit the advisability of turning to other countries for new institutional or procedural models. Yet a comparison of U.S. and European chemical control policies suggests that the American approach carries some needlessly high costs. While European solutions cannot be directly applied in the American political setting, they can offer some guidance in designing less wasteful alternatives.

We have argued that much of the malaise of the U.S. regulatory agencies can be laid at the doors of Congress. Legislative goals show little regard for administrative and economic reality, and agencies have to thread their way through a mine field of ambiguous standards, unrealistic timetables, complicated analytical requirements, and crippling rule-making procedures. Aggressive congressional oversight offers legislators obvious political rewards but reinforces the intrinsic shortcomings of the U.S. regulatory process, adding to delay, uncertainty, and conflict. The political structures that permit more careful dovetailing of legislative and administrative interests in Europe can hardly be duplicated in the United States. Open-ended legislation in the European style should in any case be avoided in a political context that offers the agencies relatively little protection against capture. Yet the comparison with European cases suggests that significant improvements could be made in the clarity, consistency, and logic of American chemical control laws without sacrificing the essential elements of the U.S. regulatory approach.

An especially promising direction for reform, in light of the preceding analysis, is the design of procedures not merely to illuminate, but to mitigate, conflict in the administrative process. Much of the delay and uncertainty in U.S. regulation results directly or indirectly from the nature of public participation. Administrative hearings, veering continually toward the adjudicatory model, not only draw out the process leading to a final rule, but darken the prospects for politically acceptable compromise. The European pattern of participation is more restrictive, with the state determining what interests have a "legitimate" voice in policy making and limiting their channels of access. However unappealing this approach may appear to U.S. observers, the European experience with chemical regulation suggests that a more orderly approach to participation may be needed in order to create acceptable points of equilibrium among a wide array of centrifugal political forces. The variety of procedures for participation, for example, could be thinned by adopting more uniform approaches to rule making, and the chances for consensus could be improved by providing more opportunities for negotiation among competing interests.

In Europe the task of legitimating regulatory policy is often delegated to advisory committees that not only evaluate relevant information, but also manage the political conflict latent in technical controversies. The most notable characteristic of these bodies is that they frequently combine technical expertise with political interest representation. U.S. proposals to establish independent scientific review panels in the regulatory agencies would move technical decision making somewhat in the direction of the European model. But the European experience suggests that such groups will be most likely to reach genuine accommodations if they are pluralistic in structure and are granted real decision-making authority, for example, through a legal presumption of validity for their recommendations. In the U.S. regulatory context, such bodies could still be subject to legal and political control through open procedures, judicial review, and the requirement that final decisions be made by the politically accountable agency head. At the same time, such representative committees could help rationalize "mixed" decisions of science and policy, thus relieving administrators and judges of exclusive responsibility for making difficult political decisions. Prospects for such institutional reform are perhaps most attractive in the area of occupational safety and health regulation, since the number of interests needing representation is relatively small. But if European examples are any guide, it appears that pluralistic committees can serve a useful function in other areas as well.

While most U.S. analysts support the open, adversarial model of public participation, their attitude to the role of the courts is more ambivalent. Proposals to reduce the power of federal courts to intervene in the formation of social policy are continually placed before Congress. Yet a countervailing trend can be discerned in suggestions that would increase judicial authority in relation to the regulatory agencies, for example, by legislatively eliminating the presumption of validity traditionally accorded by the courts to agency interpretations of the law. There is strong support as well for the liberal U.S. standing rules, which allow virtually any private individual to question the legality of administrative decisions in court. Recent opinions of the Supreme Court have failed to clarify the proper role of the courts in relation to the administrative agencies, particularly in cases requiring judicial review of technical decisions. In view of these contradictions, and the continuing skepticism about the technical sophistication of the courts, a clearer redefinition of the judicial role seems vitally necessary. Our analysis of toxic substance controversies indicates, however, that proposals governing access to the courts will make little sense unless they are coordinated with reforms in other parts of the regulatory system, such as the use of alternative procedures and institutions to defuse or resolve conflict within the administrative rule-making process.

The U.S. tendency to go it alone in the field of chemical control is evident not only in the distinctive American administrative process, but also in the exceptional attention paid to carcinogens and existing chemicals. Yet in spite of extensive legal support and systematic expenditure of resources, American agencies have not scored spectacular successes in their attempts to regulate these substances. The record we have reviewed suggests that both the United States and the European countries could benefit from a more coordinated strategy on existing chemicals. Laboratory facilities, for example, are limited in all four countries, and separate national plans for identifying and testing substances lead to wasteful use of scarce resources. By establishing internationally agreed-on lists of priority substances and rationally allocating responsibilities for testing and risk assessment, chemical-producing nations might promote more comprehensive regulation of existing chemicals than is possible through unilateral initiatives. The United States would stand to gain in two ways from such cooperation. International sharing of testing obligations would keep the United States from shouldering a disproportionate burden in producing information about existing chemicals. Multilateral efforts in this field could also generate a common fund of knowledge about specific substances and help reduce political resistance to regulation.

The foregoing analysis reflects certain key premises that deserve to be explicitly reiterated in conclusion. The indisputable shortcomings of American chemical control policy grow out of a political system that is remarkable for its reluctance to commit final decision-making authority to any single institution. The fragmentation of political power deeply influences strategies for legitimating regulatory decisions. The techniques consistently favored by American politicians, including unrestricted participation, formal regulatory analysis, and activist judicial review, are all conceived as checks against possible abuses of power. They demand perpetual questioning of administrative authority by the public and by other governmental actors. These adversarial mechanisms exacerbate the weaknesses of policy making at the frontiers of science by exposing uncertainties to critical scrutiny while perpetuating demands for rational explanation of every administrative choice.

European experiences in the field of chemical control are based on a model of legitimation that is radically at odds with prevailing American norms. In the European scheme, administrative decisions achieve political acceptability through institutional continuity, accumulation of technical and political expertise, and the insulation of policy makers from public observation and criticism. We have amply developed the theme that regulatory reform in the United States cannot be accomplished by thoughtlessly borrowing European institutional or procedural models. Nonetheless, cross-national comparison illuminates a possibility that American regulatory reformers have hitherto been reluctant to acknowledge or act on. The credibility of the regulatory agencies may be strengthened in the long run, not by subjecting them to more aggressive external controls, but by eliminating some of the tangled constraints on their exercise of discretionary power. The removal of these checks and balances may well require the imposition of other, less disruptive forms of control, such as clearer legislative guidance or new forms of interest group participation. In short, chemical regulation points to the need for a holistic reappraisal of the American regulatory process in order to avoid contradictory and ultimately ineffectual suggestions for reform. We hope that this book marks one step forward in this endeavor.

APPENDIX

Tables of
Regulated Substances

Table A. Regulatory Histories of Fourteen Selected Substances

The following table presents the most significant regulatory action taken by the four governments and the European Community on each of fourteen potentially carcinogenic substances, as of the end of 1980.

Selection of Substances

Substances selected for this table are not representative of any larger set of chemicals. Each substance has been selected partly because questions have been raised about its carcinogenic properties in at least one of the four countries. Further, for illustrative purposes, we have chosen at least one substance that has been controlled under each of the four regulatory frameworks. Four of the chemicals are found primarily in the workplace; one heavy metal appears as a pesticide ingredient, as a food contaminant, and in the workplace; six of the chemicals are pesticides; and three of the chemicals are food additives.

Regulatory Histories

Entries indicate significant action taken with regard to each substance by each of the four countries and the European Community, the date of the action, and the responsible agency. Action taken under regulatory frameworks other than the four considered in this study are not included. All information except that of the European Community pertains to action taken at the national (federal) level.

Abbreviations

MAK = Maximum Workplace Concentration
Min. Ag. = Ministry of Agriculture
Min. Lab. = Ministry of Labor
R = Recommendation
TRK = Technical Guiding Concentration
TWA = Time Weighted Average

TABLE A1.

Regulatory Histories of Fourteen Selected Substances

Substance	Britain		France		Germany		United States		European Community	
	Date	Action	Date	Action	Date	Action	Date	Action	Date	Action
Acrylonitrile	1978	HSC (R) 20 ppm TWA	1948	Min. Lab. Label required	1974	Min. Lab. Restricted	1971	OSHA 20 ppm TWA	1967	Classified "toxic" and "flammable"
	1979	HSC (R) 5 ppm TWA	1963	Min. Lab. Monitoring of workers	1979	6 ppm (13.23 mg/m³) TRK	1977	Banned in beverage containers	1980	Worker exposure to be kept as low as possible. Medical checks and monitoring
	1979	Classified "toxic"	1978	Min. Lab. 1 ppm TWA (new factory); 3 ppm TWA (old factory). Not to contaminate food at 0.01 detectable level. Min. Ag. 1 mg/kg in materials in contact with food; no new uses.			1978	OSHA 2 ppm TWA (ceiling: 10 ppm/15 min)		
			1979	Min. Lab. Label and packaging requirement						
Aldrin/Dieldrin	1957	MAFF (R) Regulated as seed dressing	1971	Min. Ag. Not to be added to food or administered to animals for human consumption	1971	Min. Ag. Restricted	1974	EPA Banned (except some limited uses)	1967	Classified "toxic"
	1961–71	MAFF (R) Further restrictions	1972	Min. Ag. Banned	1974	Min. Ag. Further restrictions	1976	OSHA 100 mg/m³ TWA	1978	Classified "harmful"
	1973	MAFF (R) Labeling requirement			1979	Min. Ag. 0.25 mg/m³ MAK	1980	OSHA Candidate list	1978	Banned (except very limited uses)
	1978	HSC (R) 0.25 mg/m³ TWA								

TABLE A1.—continued

Substance	Britain Date	Britain Action	France Date	France Action	Germany Date	Germany Action	United States Date	United States Action	European Community Date	European Community Action
	1979	Classified "toxic"								
	1980	MAFF (R) Most remaining uses banned								
Amaranth (Red Dye Number 2)	1973	Permitted (must not contain <0.2% water-insoluble matter)	1964	Min. Ag. On positive list food colorings	1977	Min. Health Appears on positive list (must not contain certain heavy metals)	1903	Subject to certification	1962	Appears on positive list
			1976	Min. Ag. Banned (except in caviar)	1977	Min. Health Label requirements. Restricted to certain foods	1960	FDA Appears on list of permitted colorants		
							1975	FDA (R) Removal from list		
							1976	FDA Banned		
							1980	FDA Ban reaffirmed		
Asbestos	1932	"Dust-datum" standard adopted	1975	INRS (R)	1979	Min. Lab. Respirable dust standards—fibers not to exceed a length >5μm and diameter >3μm (ratio L/D 3:1) New installation: 0.05 respirable fib/cm³ Other: 0.10 respirable fib/cm³	1951	Walsh-Healy 5 mppcf max. concentration	1978	Priority for control
	1969	Min. Lab. Asbestos regulation: most forms, 2.0 fibers/ml in air over 10 min	1977	Min. Lab. Set concentration limits not to be used in residences			1971	OSHA 12 fib/cc 5 m(2 ppcf TWA)	1980	Worker protection
	1978	HSC (R) All forms: 5 fibers/cc >5μm (more stringent for some forms)	1977/8	Min. Lab. Banned use above 1% concentration for spraying buildings			1971	OSHA Temp. standard 5 fib/cc >5μm TWA		
	1979	HSC (R) Sets more stringent stan-	1979	Min. Lab. Monitoring of workers			1972	FDA Bans use in clothes		
							1972	OSHA 5 fib/cc >5μm TWA; 10 fib/cc >5μm ceiling		

Substance					
(Asbestos, cont.)	…dards. Bans new applications of crocidolite			1976 OSHA 2 fib/cc >5μm TWA 1977 CPSC Banned use in patching compounds and fireplaces 1979 EPA Proposed water-quality criteria	
Benzene	1978 HSC (R) 10 ppm TWA 1979 Classified "highly flammable and toxic"	1939 Min. Lab. 25 ppm (80 mg/m³) max. 1948 Min. Lab. Ban use certain solvents 1969 Min. Lab. Banned as dissolving agent 1973 Min. Lab. Adopt ILO convention 25 ppm TWA	1979 Min. Health 8 ppm (26 mg/m³) TRK	1971 OSHA 10 ppm (in air) TWA 1977–78 OSHA Attempts to raise standard to 1ppm TWA—revoked	1967 Classified as inflammable 1976 Classified "toxic" 1980 Worker exposures to be kept as low as possible. Medical checks and monitoring
Cadmium	1956 Bans cadmium plating on food utensils 1978 HSC (R) 0.05 ppm (0.05 mg/m³) in cadmium oxide production		1974 Min. Ag. Banned in pesticides	1951 Walsh-Healy 0.1 mg/m³ max. concentration; EPA 0.01 mg/litre in drinking water 1971 OSHA 0.01 mg/m³ TWA for fumes; 0.02 mg/m³ TWA for dust 1980 OSHA Candidate list	1976 Appears on list of controlled substances 1978 Priority list toxic and dangerous waste 1979 Classified "noxious" 1979 Discharge into ground water to be prevented 1980 Workers' information
Chlordane	1969 MAFF (R) Restricts home use, labeling required	1971 Min. Ag. Not to be added to feed or administered to ani-	1974 Min. Ag. Banned	1974–78 EPA Phases out most uses	1967 Classified "noxious" 1976 Classified "tox-

TABLE A1.—*continued*

Substance	Britain		France		Germany		United States		European Community	
	Date	Action	Date	Action	Date	Action	Date	Action	Date	Action
	1970	MAFF (R) Further restrictions		mals for human consumption						ic"
	1973	MAFF Labeling required	1972	Min. Ag. Banned					1976	Classified "harmful"
	1978	HSC (R) 0.5 mg/m³ TWA							1978	Banned (except very limited uses)
	1979	MAFF (R) Further restrictions								
	1979	Labeling required								
DDT	1969	MAFF (R) Restricts use	1947	Min. Ag. Banned on fruit; use restrictions	1971	Min. Ag. Restricted	1969	Secretary of Agriculture issues cancellation for nearly all uses		
	1973	Labeling required	1969	Min. Ag. Not to be used to disinfect animal pens or food preparation areas	1972	Min. Ag. Banned	1970	U.S. District Court suspends cancellation		
	1978	HSC (R) 1 mg/m³ TWA	1971	Min. Ag. Not to be used on animals or animal feed	1974	Min. Ag. Banned	1971	EPA Banned		
	1979	Classified "toxic"	1972	Min. Ag. Banned (except on corn)	1979	Min. Health 1 mg/m³ MAK	1980	OSHA Candidate List		
			1974	Min. Ag. Banned						
Heptachlor	1961	MAFF (R) Ban as cereal seed dressing	1971	Min. Ag. Not to be added to food or administered to animals for human con-	1971	Min. Ag. Restricted	1974–78	EPA Phases out most uses	1967	Classified "toxic"
	1964	MAFF (R) Bans			1974	Min. Ag. Further restrictions	1980	OSHA Candidate list	1978	Classified "harmful"

	use in food storage bins 1973 Labeling required 1978 HSC (R) 0.5 mg/m³ TWA 1979 Classified "toxic"	sumption 1972 Min. Ag. Banned	1979 Min. Health 0.5 mg/m³ MAK		1978 Banned (except very limited uses)
HCH/Lindane	1979 Classified "toxic"	1969 Min. Ag. Not to be used to disinfect animal pens or food preparation areas 1971 Min. Ag. Not to be added to food or administered to animals for human consumption. Banned	1974 Min. Ag. Restricted 1977 Min. Ag. Banned	1967 Classified "toxic" 1978 Classified "harmful" 1978 Banned	
Nitrites/Nitrates (Potassium and Sodium)	1974 MAFF Max. levels in cured meat: sodium nitrite 200 mg/kg; nitrate 500 mg/kg 1978 MAFF (R) Lower levels 1979 MAFF Cheese (w/exceptions) sodium nitrate 100 mg/kg; sodium nitrite 10 mg/kg	1964 Min. Ag. May be used in meat if less than 10% level in treated food is 150 mg/kg	1977 Nitrates: 30 mg/kg; Nitrites: purity criteria 1977 Only permitted in certain species fish to max. 200 mg/kg	1925 USDA Nitrate 500 ppm; Nitrite 200 ppm 1978 FDA/USDA Proposed nitrate phase-out; USDA regulations to reduce and monitor preformed nitrites in bacon 1980 FDA Revokes proposed phase-out	
Saccharin	1953 MAFF Authorized sweetener 1969 MAFF Only permitted artificial sweetener	1902 Min. Ag. Banned 1914–18 Min. Ag. Authorized 1939–45 Min. Ag.	1977 Label required w/sugar equivalent 1977 Restricted to certain foods/beverages. Must be	1912 Secretary of Agriculture advised that 0.3 mg/day was safe 1955 (R) Max. toler-	1978 Recommendation on use issued

325

TABLE A1.—continued

Substance	Britain		France		Germany		United States		European Community	
	Date	Action	Date	Action	Date	Action	Date	Action	Date	Action
				Authorized		labeled		ance 1 mg/day		
			1950	Min. Ag. Banned (except as a nonprescription drug)			1972	FDA Removed from GRAS list and limits imposed		
							1977	FDA Proposed ban		
							1977	Congress stays FDA ban, label requirements		
							1979	NAS report (R) Not to ban		
							1980	OSHA: Candidate list		
							1980	Congress stay extended		
2,4,5-T	1970	MAFF 0.1 mg/ kg max. level dioxin	1975–77	Min. Ag. Use restrictions. Must contain less than 0.001 mg/kg 2,3,7,8-T and cannot be applied aerially	1971	Min. Ag. Restricted	1969	Presidential advisory commission links dioxin to birth defects	1967	Classified "noxious"
	1973	MAFF Label required			1974	Min. Ag. Banned (w/some exceptions)	1969	EPA Bans use on food crops, domestic use	1978	Classified "harmful"
	1978	HSC (R) 10 mg/ m³ TWA			1979	Min. Health 10 mg/m³ MAK (max. level dioxin 0.01 mg/ kg)	1973	EPA Public hearing		
	1979	Classified "harmful"					1975	EPA Initiates dioxin implementation plan		
	1980	MAFF 0.01 mg/ kg max. level dioxin					1978	EPA Issues RPAR (dioxin: 1 mg/ kg)		

Vinyl Chloride

1972 200 ppm 1975 25 ppm TWA (50 ppm ceiling) 1975 10 ppm TWA (30 ppm ceiling) 1978 HSC (R) 5 ppm TWA 1981 HSC (R) 2 ppm	1975 INRS (R) 5 ppm TWA (15 ppm TWA triggers intervention) 1977 (R) 1 ppm concentration all installations. 5 ppm concentration, evacuation. 15 ppm concentration, intervention. 1978 EC Food directive endorsed 1980 1 ppm (new factory); 3 ppm (old factory)	1979 Min. Health Existing installation: 5 ppm (13 mg/m³) TRK; others: 2 ppm (5 mg/m³) TRK 1980 Min. Health 3 ppm/1 year; labeling requirements	1979 EPA Oregon study. Emergency suspension remaining uses 1980 OSHA Candidate list	1938 FDA Aerosol packaging requirement 1952 Walsh-Healy 500 ppm max. concentration 1958 FDA Bans use in packaging, water pipes 1962 FDA Bans use in drug aerosols 1966 CPSC Bans use in home aerosols, paint 1971 National consensus standard adopted: 500 ppm max. concentration 1974 OSHA: Temp. standard 50 ppm ceiling 1974 FDA: Banned in aerosols 1974 OSHA: 1 ppm TWA (5 ppm/15 min) 1976 EPA/TSCA Controls over PVC sludge waste 1979 EPA Water quality criteria	1967 Classified "flammable" 1976 Classified "toxic" 1976 Banned in aerosols 1978 Monitoring, medical check and unit values: 3 ppm/1 year; 5 ppm/1 month; 6 ppm/1 week; 7 ppm/8 hours; 8 ppm/1 hour 1978 1 mg/kg in materials in contact with food

Table A2. Regulatory Status of Thirty-Six Substances Reviewed by the International Agency for Research on Cancer (IARC)

Selection of Substances

Substances examined in the following table are those reviewed by IARC as of September 1979 and classified by the agency into one of the four following categories:

1. chemicals, groups of chemicals, and industrial processes recognized as carcinogenic for humans;
2a. chemicals and groups of chemicals that are probably carcinogenic for humans, and for which the evidence is "sufficient";
2b. chemicals and groups of chemicals that are probably carcinogenic for humans, and for which the evidence is "suggestive"; and
3. chemicals and groups of chemicals that could not be classified as to their carcinogenicity for humans.

Of the fifty-four entries in the 1979 IARC listing, eighteen have been excluded from this table because the chemical or process comes under a regulatory framework other than those analyzed in this study. Most of these excluded substances are drugs.

Regulatory Status

The regulatory status of each substance as of the end of 1980 is indicated with reference to the following commonly employed methods of intervention.

Bans: Prohibitions on production or use or both. Exceptions pertaining solely to exports and imports have not been taken into account. Bans that apply only to some uses or to certain forms of the substance are indicated as "partial bans" (PB).

Use Restrictions: Measures that allow the substance to be produced and used but that impose conditions (other than tolerance levels and labeling) on its manufacture or utilization. Use restrictions are typically imposed on the permitted uses of substances which are also subject to partial bans. In addition, substances banned under one regulatory framework may be subject to use restrictions under others. Restrictions may take a variety of forms, depending on the category into which the regulated substance falls. Some typical examples are indicated below:

Food additives: purity criteria, permissible concentrations in preparations, solubility standards, etc.

Pesticides: permissible concentration of active ingredient, purity criteria, applicator certification, method of application, quantities applied, etc.

Occupational and industrial chemicals: engineering controls on production
and handling, protective equipment, work practices, warning notices,
information programs, etc.

Tolerance Levels: Numerical standards indicating the levels of permissible
human exposure. For food additives and pesticides, these standards are typically expressed in terms of maximum allowable concentrations in parts per
million by weight in the product; for workplace chemicals, tolerable exposure
levels for workers are calculated as a time-weighted average, using variable
intervals, often in conjunction with a "ceiling value" that must not be exceeded under any circumstances.

Labeling: Requirement to label chemicals (or products containing them) as
hazardous.

Notification: Legally imposed duty of producers or users to provide competent public authorities with information concerning the substance, for example, the fact that the substance is being produced or used, test data,
expected uses and production quantities, health records of exposed workers,
etc.

Monitoring: Requirement that producers or users monitor the conditions
of exposure to the substance, for example, through obligatory medical examinations of exposed workers.

Worker Compensation: National rule requiring that compensation be made
to workers who have developed cancer from exposure to the substance.
Compensation for health effects other than cancer is not noted.

Other Guidelines

Other guidelines used in compiling the table are as follows.

Controls triggered only by "general duty clauses" are not indicated unless
they are invoked through official and explicit reference to a specific
substance.

Separate entries have been made for substances controlled under more
than one of the relevant regulatory frameworks.

Recommendations (rather than legal requirements) are indicated by "R."

Abbreviations

Regulatory frameworks are indicated by the following abbreviations:

FA = Food Additive
P = Pesticide
O = Occupational Chemical and/or existing Industrial Chemical

TABLE A2.

Regulatory Status of Thirty-Six Substances Reviewed by IARC

Country	Banned	Use Restrictons	Tolerance Levels	Labeling	Notifi-cation	Monitoring	Worker Compensation
Group 1: Carcinogens							
4-Aminobiphenyl (O)							
U.S.							
G.B.	X		X	X	X	X	X
Fr.		X					
W.G.		X					
Arsenic and Compounds (O)							
U.S.		X	X	X	X	X	
G.B.			R	X	X	X	
FR.			X	X	X	X	
W.G.			X	X	X	X	X
Arsenic and Compounds (FA)							
U.S.			X				
G.B.			X				
Fr.		X	X				
W.G.		X					
Asbestos (O)							
U.S.		X	X	X		X	
G.B.		X	R	X		X	
Fr.		X	X		X	X	X
W.G.		X	X	X	X	X	
Auramine (O)							
U.S.						X	
G.B.				X	X	X	
Fr.		X	R				
W.G.							X
Benzene (O)							
U.S.		X	X	X	X	X	
G.B.			R	X	X	X	
Fr.		X	X	X	X	X	
W.G.		X	X	X	X	X	X

Substance	Country							
Benzidine (O)	U.S.		X		X	X	X	X
	G.B.					X	X	X
	Fr.					X	X	X
	W.G.					X	X	X
Bis (chloromethyl) ether Chloromethyl-methyl ether (O)	U.S.				X	X	X	
	G.B.				R	X		
	Fr.							
	W.G.			X	X	X	X	X
Chromium and Chromium Componds (O)	U.S.			X	X	R	X	R
	G.B.			X	R	X	X	
	Fr.			X	X	X	X	X
	W.G.			X	X	X	X	X
Diethylstilboestrol (DES) (FA)	U.S.	PB		X	X			
	G.B.	PB		X	X			
	Fr.							
	W.G.							
Haematite (O)	U.S.				R			
	G.B.				R			
	Fr.							
	W.G.							
Isopropyl Oils (O)	U.S.				R			
	G.B.							
	Fr.							
	W.G.				X			
2-Naphthylamine (O)	U.S.		X		X	X	X	X
	G.B.			X		X	X	X
	Fr.			X		X	X	X
	W.G.			X		X	X	X

331

	Country	Banned	Use Restrictons	Tolerance Levels	Labeling	Notification	Monitoring	Worker Compensation
Nickel and Nickel Compounds (O)	U.S.			X	R		R	
	G.B.			R	X (Nickel; tetra-car-bonyl)	X	X	X
	Fr.							X
	W.G.							
Soots, Tars, and Mineral Oils (O)	U.S.			X		X	X	
	G.B.	X Min-eral oil spinning				X	X	X
	Fr.		X					
	W.G.							
Soots, Tars, and Mineral Oils (FA)	U.S.	X (carbon black)				X	X	X
	G.B.				X	X	X	
	Fr.			X (carbon black)				
	W.G.		X					
Vinyl Chloride (O)	U.S.		X	X	X	X	X	
	G.B.			R		X	X	
	Fr.			X		X	X	X
	W.G.			X			X	X

Vinyl Chloride (FA)	U.S.					
	G.B.					
	Fr.		X			
	W.G.	X		X	X	X
Group 2a: Probable Carcinogens ("Sufficient" Evidence)						
Aflatoxins (FA)	U.S.		X			
	G.B.					
	Fr.		X			
	W.G.					
Cadmium and Cadmium Compounds (O)	U.S.		X	X		
	G.B.		R		X	
	Fr.				X	X
	W.G.	X		X		
Group 2b: Probable Carcinogens ("Suggestive" Evidence)						
Acrylonitrile (O)	U.S.	X	X	X	X	X
	G.B.		R	X		
	Fr.		X	X	X	X
	W.G.	X	X	X	X	X
Amitrole (P)	U.S.	X				
	G.B.	X		X		
	Fr.	X		X		
	W.G.					
Beryllium and Beryllium Compounds (O)	U.S.		X			
	G.B.		R	X	X	
	Fr.	X		X	X	X
	W.G.	X		X	X	X
Carbon tetrachloride (O)	U.S.		X			
	G.B.		R	X		X
	Fr.	X		X		X
	W.G.	X	R (pesticide residue)	X		X

TABLE A2.—*continued*

Chemical	Country	Banned	Use Restrictions	Tolerance Levels	Labeling	Notifi-cation	Monitoring	Worker Compensation
Dimethyl-carbamoyl chloride (O)	U.S.							
	G.B.							
	Fr.					X	X	
	W.G.		X					
Dimethyl sulphate (O)	U.S.			X				
	G.B.			X	X			
	Fr.			R	X			
	W.G.		X		X			
Ethylene Oxide (O)	U.S.			X				
	G.B.			R				
	Fr.				X	X		
	W.G.		X	R	X		X	
Polychlorinated biphenyls (PCBs) (O)	U.S.		X	X (as FA)	X			
	G.B.		X	R	X			
	Fr.				X			
	W.G.							
Group 3: Carcinogenicity for Humans Undetermined								
Chlordane/Heptachlor (P)	U.S.							
	G.B.	X	X	R	X			
	Fr.	X						
	W.G.		X	X				
Chloroprene (O)	U.S.			X	X			
	G.B.			R	X			
	Fr.							
	W.G.			X	X			

Substance								
DDT (P)	U.S.	X		X	R		X	
	G.B.	X					X	
	Fr.	X			X (residue)			
	W.G.							
Dieldrin Aldrin (P)	U.S.	PB			R			
	G.B.	PB; R						
	Fr.	X		X	X			
	W.G.	X			X			
Epichlorohydrin (O)	U.S.			X	X	X	X	
	G.B.				X	X	X	
	Fr.				R	X	X	X
	W.G.							
Hexachlorocyclohexane (technical grade HCH/lindane) (P)	U.S.			X	X			
	G.B.							
	Fr.							
	W.G.	X		X				
Lead and Lead Compounds	U.S.			X	X	X	X	
	G.B.			X	X	X	X	
	Fr.			X				
	W.G.			R				
N-Phenyl-2-naphthylamine (O)	U.S.			X	X	X		
	G.B.							
	Fr.							X
	W.G.							
Styrene (O)	U.S.			X	X	X		
	G.B.			X				
	Fr.	R						
	W.G.	R						

TABLE A2.—*continued*

	Country	Banned	Use Restrictions	Tolerance Levels	Labeling	Notification	Monitoring	Worker Compensation
Trichloroethylene (O)	U.S.			X				
	G.B.			R	X			
	Fr.		X		X		X	
	W.G.			R			X	
Tris (aziridinyl)-p-benzoquin- one (triaziquone) (O)	U.S.			X				
	G.B.			R	X			
	Fr.				X		X	
	W.G.			R				

Index

acrylonitrile, 40, 49, 123n, 142, 239n, 321, 333
Agent Orange, 212
aldrin/dieldrin, 120, 121–22, 198n, 203, 255, 321–22, 335
amaranth. *See* Red Dye No. 2
Ames, Bruce, 134–35
arsenic, 142, 330
asbestos, 256
  European Community, 287–88, 322–23
  France, 47, 322–23, 330
  Great Britain, 42, 142–43, 166, 178n, 254, 322–23, 330
  United States, 49, 120, 322–23, 330
  West Germany, 41, 149, 178n, 322–23, 330

Barnes, J. M., 133
benzene, 40, 47, 49, 119n, 122–26, 291, 323, 330
beryllium, 40, 333
Bingham, Eula, 80, 85, 171

cadmium, 143n, 149, 323, 333
caffeine, 265
Canada, 248
cancer, environmental, 131, 134, 144–45, 147, 151, 188–94. *See also* carcinogens; *individual countries*
carcinogens
  animal studies, 60, 134, 140–41, 150, 154, 187, 197–204, 215, 262
  epidemiological studies, 131–32, 140, 147, 188–94, 205, 212–23, 215
  experimental research and testing, 132–34, 140, 142, 144, 148, 150
  generic classification, 41–42, 80–81, 191, 200–201, 205–7, 244–48, 256, 313–14
  government-sponsored research, 138–44, 151–52, 156
  identifying, 195–204, 297
  International Labor Organization and, 292–93
  mutagenicity studies, 130, 134–35, 195–97, 297
  NCI-NIEHS-NIOSH "estimates paper," 190–92, 194
  risk assessment, 152–53, 187, 204–11, 293
  safe threshold of exposure, 39, 47, 122–24, 207–11
  See also carcinogens *and* worker safety *under individual countries*
carrageenan, 140

Carter, Jimmy (administration of), 40, 79, 192, 257, 283, 298
chemical disasters, 21, 31, 154, 212, 263, 302
chemical industry, 19–21, 45, 98, 175, 260
  and carcinogen regulation, 135, 191–92, 193–94, 201, 207, 209–10, 216
  impact of regulation on, 218–49, 311–12
    adverse effect on international trade, 224–25, 233, 295
    decline of R & D, 222–23, 224n, 232
    endangerment of trade secrets, 224
    increased production costs, 20, 221, 239n
  impact on regulation, 247–49
  innovation in, 220, 221–23, 232
  and international harmonization, 224–25, 229, 233, 237, 279, 294–95, 298
  self-regulation of, 32–33, 47–48, 151–52, 221, 231, 239
chlorinated hydrocarbon pesticides, 198–99, 216
chlorofluorocarbons, 36n, 294
chloroform, 142
chlorophenols, 142
cost-benefit analysis, 40, 53, 58–59, 70, 98, 176–77

DBCP (dibromochloropropane), 40, 153–54n
DDT, 67, 106, 198n, 253, 261, 324, 335
Delaney clause. *See* Delaney clause *under* United States
DES, 120, 255
dioxin, 212
Doll, Richard, 131, 191, 194

economic analysis, 40, 58–59, 159, 172–73, 176–77
enforcement, 49–52, 237
Environmental Protection Agency. *See* Environmental Protection Agency *under* United States
Epstein, Samuel, 137–38, 192
ethyleneimine, 121
European Chemical Industry Ecology and Toxicology Centre (ECETOC), 207, 294–95n
European Community (EC),
  influence on members' regulatory policies, 55, 60, 61, 66–67, 72
  policy harmonization in, 23, 26, 276–81, 286–90, 299

Sixth Amendment, 32, 37, 60n, 195–96, 233, 276–81, 281–82, 283, 284, 286n, 288, 289, 308
executive-legislative relations, 55–64, 71–72
expertise in regulatory decision making
  economic, 40, 159, 172–73, 176–77, 181, 243
  and fears of technocracy, 157–58, 178–79, 185–86
  impact of, 168–74
  legal, 159, 161, 171–72, 177, 181
  management and planning, 159, 173, 177–78
  medical, 168, 169–70, 181
  political debate about, 174–80
  role of civil service, 85, 161–62, 182–83, 303
  safety engineering, 170–71
  scientific/technical, 25, 79–86, 131, 159–61, 175–76, 179, 181, 258–59, 283
  shortage of, 131, 136–38
  sources of, 158–68
  see also individual countries

Federal Republic of Germany. *See* West Germany
federalism, 64–67
food additives, 31, 33, 209n, 287, 291. *See also individual countries*
Food and Drug Administration. *See* Food and Drug Administration *under* United States
formaldehyde, 120, 125, 154
France
  Act on Control of Chemical Products, 37, 61–62, 84, 86, 235, 236, 278, 280
  carcinogens
    parliamentary inquiries, 94
    regulation, 38–39, 48–49, 137, 138, 204, 208–9, 210, 211
    regulatory priority not accorded to, 38–39
    research, 132–33, 136, 137, 138, 143–44, 148, 204
    risk assessment, 207, 208–9, 210, 211
  2,4,5-T controversy, 212
  chemical industry, 207, 225, 233–38, 247–48
  Conseil d'Etat, 90, 97, 101–2, 113, 161, 306
  expertise in regulatory decision making, 61, 160n, 161, 163–65, 169–70, 171
  food additives, 46–47, 84, 94, 138, 163,

France *(cont.)*
  food additives *(cont.)*
      171, 265, 287
  French Consumers Union (UFC), 255,
      260, 268
  industrial chemicals, 35, 61–62, 67, 163
  interest groups
      consumer associations, 255, 260, 268
      environmental groups, 252, 254, 262,
          263–64, 270
      standing to sue, 45–46, 90, 109, 111–12,
          117
      trade unions, 252, 255, 268
  international harmonization, 237, 277–78,
      280, 287, 289–91, 302
  judicial review of regulation, 101–2, 104,
      109, 113, 117
  legal tradition, 70, 71, 305
  Ministry of Industry, 235–36, 237
  National Assembly, 56, 57, 61
  National Institute of Research and Safety
      (INRS), 84, 143, 161, 208–9
  pesticides, 34–35, 84, 143, 163, 180, 289
  public participation in decision making,
      43–45, 90–91, 92–93, 117, 305
  regulatory priorities, 38–39, 148, 204
  resources for regulation, 86
  Service of Fraud Repression and Quality
      Control, 50, 84, 161–62, 171
  simplicity of regulatory procedures, 178,
      305–6
  worker safety, 43, 47, 84, 161, 163, 169–
      70, 209, 235, 291

gentian violet, 140
Great Britain
  Administrative Procedure Act, 104
  Advisory Committee on Pesticides
      (ACP), 174, 179, 205, 214, 229
  Association of Scientific, Technical, and
      Managerial Staffs (ASTMS), 138,
      193–94, 204, 209–10, 216, 229, 256,
      262, 263
  British Agrochemical Association (BAA),
      228, 229
  carcinogens, 46–47
      animal studies, 203–4, 215–16
      and the NCI-NIEHS-NIOSH "esti-
          mates paper," 192–94
      parliamentary inquiries, 94–95
      regulation, 38–39, 48–49
      regulatory priority not accorded to, 38–
          39, 170, 209

research, 38–39, 133, 135, 142–43, 148,
    215–16
risk assessment, 209–10, 211
2,4,5-T controversy, 94–95, 203, 205,
    209, 214, 229, 260
Chemical Industries Association (CIA),
    193–94, 204, 209–10, 226, 229
chemical industry, 135, 193–94, 225, 226–
    29, 247–48
Employment Medical Advisory Service
    (EMAS), 160, 170, 174, 179
expertise in regulatory decision making,
    40, 63, 92, 160, 161, 163–66, 170,
    171, 194
food additives, 35, 37–38, 42, 163, 171
Friends of the Earth (FOE), 92, 252, 258–
    59
General and Municipal Workers Union
    (GMWU), 192–93, 229, 253
Health and Safety at Work Etc. Act
    (HSW Act), 35, 37, 44, 62–63, 68,
    69, 82, 91
Health and Safety Commission (HSC),
    40, 42, 81–82, 86, 91
Health and Safety Executive (HSE), 50,
    82, 86, 135, 142–43, 160, 161, 171,
    209, 226–27, 256, 280–81
House of Lords, 57, 105
Imperial Chemical Industries (ICI), 226
industrial chemicals, 22n, 37, 62, 163, 280
inspectorates, 50, 81–82, 83, 161, 170,
    171
interest groups, 111–12, 216
    consumer associations, 180, 254
    environmental groups, 92, 180, 252,
        258–59, 270
    standing to sue, 111–12
    trade unions, 138, 179, 193–94, 204,
        209–10, 214, 253, 255–56, 262,
        268, 272
international harmonization, 276–77, 278,
    279, 280–81, 287–90, 292, 308
judicial review of regulation, 104, 105,
    108–9, 111–12, 114, 117
legal tradition, 68–69, 305
Medical Research Council (MRC), 133,
    148
Ministry of Agriculture, Fisheries, and
    Food (MAFF), 42, 81–82, 143, 203
National Union of Agricultural and Allied
    Workers (NUAAW), 174, 214, 229
Parliament, 56, 57, 62–63, 93–94, 97, 104,
    105, 306

Great Britain *(cont.)*
  pesticides, 42, 47, 51n, 143, 161, 163,
     174, 203, 287–88, 289
    Pesticide Safety Precaution Scheme
       (PSPS), 33, 228
    2,4,5-T controversy, 94–95, 203, 205,
       209, 214, 229, 260
  public participation in decision making,
     44, 90, 92
  resources for regulation, 86
  Robens Committee, 62–63, 166, 277
  and TSCA, 276–77
  worker safety, 22n, 265, 268, 306–7
    carcinogens and, 39n, 137–38, 142–43,
       192–94, 214, 292
    controversy concerning, 174, 229
    experts and, 163, 166, 170
    HSW Act and, 35, 44, 62–63, 68, 82, 86
    medical surveillance and, 47, 290

haloethers, 142
harmonization. *See* international harmoni-
     zation *and individual countries*
HCH/Lindane, 255, 325, 335
Henschler, Dietrich, 137, 202
heptachlor/chlordane, 121–22, 198n, 324–
     25, 334

industrial chemicals, 33, 276–85. *See also*
     European Community; *individual*
     countries
Infante, Peter, 137, 216
interest groups
  consumer associations, 251–52, 256, 260,
     268, 272, 295–96
  environmental groups, 19, 251, 252, 256,
     257, 260, 263–64, 265, 267, 270,
     272, 295–96
  expertise in, 258–59, 262, 269
  ideologies of, 267–69, 270
  impact on regulatory policy, 25–26, 164–
     66, 260–64, 271–73
  and the policy-making context, 219n,
     269–71, 310
  policy objectives of, 253–56, 270
  and public opinion, 264–66, 270
  resources of, 266–67
  standing to sue, 109–10, 257–58
  tactics, 45–46, 256–60, 266, 270–71, 312
  trade unions, 19, 251, 252–53, 255–56,
     260, 262, 266–68, 272, 295, 296
  See also chemical industry; *individual*
     countries

International Agency for Research on Can-
     cer (IARC), 48, 132, 206, 293, 297,
     330–35
international harmonization, 26, 66, 274–
     300, 302–3, 308, 316
  chemical industry, 224–25, 229, 233, 237,
     279, 294–95, 298
  European Community, 276–81, 286–90
  nongovernmental networks, 294–97, 298
  notification requirements, 276–81
  Organization for Economic Cooperation
     and Development (OECD), 281–
     85, 296
  United Nations, 290–93
International Labor Organization (ILO),
     206–7, 291–93

judicial review
  to compel administrative action, 110–12
  to enforce procedural rights, 115–18
  for factual determinations, 112–15
  jurisdictional limits on, 103–6
  scope of, 112–19
  standing for, 106–10

lead, 67, 142, 288, 291, 335
Lederberg, Joshua, 150
legal system and legal tradition, 23, 67–71
Leventhal, Harold, 115
litigation. *See* judicial review
Love Canal, 154, 263

Marshall, Thurgood, 119n, 124n
media, 31, 200, 214, 262–63, 265, 266, 302
mercury compounds, 140, 286
Mirex, 198n, 261

Nader, Ralph, 251–52
neocorporatism, 24–25, 98, 184
Newberne, Paul, 141
nitrites, 49, 81n, 154, 254, 255, 265, 325
Nixon, Richard, 40, 309

occupational hazards. *See* worker safety
Occupational Safety and Health Adminis-
     tration. *See* Occupational Safety and
     Health Administration *under* United
     States
ochratoxin, 140
Organization for Economic Cooperation
     and Development (OECD), 224, 276,
     281–85, 286n, 296, 299

parliaments, 45, 55, 59–60, 63–64, 71–72, 93–95, 305
PCBs, 36n, 121, 140, 253, 255, 261, 263, 286n, 287
pesticides, 31, 33, 37, 47, 48, 78, 166, 286, 287–88, 288–89, 291, 292. *See also individual countries*
Pontanel, Gounelle de, 138
Powell, Lewis, 124
public access to information, 44–45, 114
public opinion, 94, 127, 151, 181, 215, 239n, 249, 262–63, 264–66, 270, 310
public participation in decision making, 26, 43–44, 46, 87–93, 217. *See also* interest groups

Rall, David, 197, 216
Reagan, Ronald (administration of), 40, 77n, 85, 192, 200, 216, 257, 283
Red Dye No. 2, 47, 49, 121, 138, 255, 287, 322
regulatory priorities, 35–39, 152, 265–66
Rehnquist, William, 118
research and development, 25, 41–42, 81, 125–26, 153–55, 296–97, 298, 309–11
risk assessment, 25, 34–35, 42–43, 175, 232, 254
for carcinogens, 124, 152–53, 187, 200, 204–11, 245n
quantitative, 41, 46, 47, 53, 207, 211

saccharin, 41, 47, 81n, 96, 140, 154, 200, 255, 325–26
Selikoff, Irving, 137
Silvex, 261
sulfamethazine, 140

TCDD, 212
Todhunter, John, 85
Toxic Substances Control Act. *See* Toxic Substances Control Act *under* United States
Tris (flame retardant), 42, 196, 287
Truhaut, René, 137, 138, 204, 211, 293
2,4,5-T (trichlorophenoxyacetic acid), 41, 42n, 94–95, 120, 178n, 203, 205, 209, 211–15, 229, 260, 261, 326–27

United Nations, 26, 224, 290–93
United States
Administrative Procedure Act (APA), 58, 88, 90, 98, 105, 110, 114–15, 118

American Conference of Governmental Industrial Hygienists (ACGIH), 168, 175, 207
American Industrial Health Council (AIHC), 175, 191–92, 199, 201, 245–47
carcinogens
animal studies, 38, 121, 134, 140, 141, 150, 197–201, 215
defining safe exposure, 122–24
identifying, 38, 41, 42, 191, 195, 196–201
judicial review of regulation, 119–26
mutagenicity studies, 134–35
National Cancer Act, 145
National Cancer Institute (NCI), 134, 145–47
NCI-NIEHS-NIOSH "estimates paper," 190–94, 310
regulatory priority accorded to, 38, 89–90, 99, 152–53, 266, 309, 311, 316
risk assessment, 152, 205–8, 210–11
2,4,5-T controversy, 212–13, 215
See also Occupational Safety and Health Administration
chemical industry
and carcinogen regulation, 189–90, 191–92, 197, 199, 216
and international harmonization, 225, 283, 284, 295
regulatory burdens, 20, 311–12
tactics, 225, 242–47, 247–49, 284
Chemical Manufacturers Association (CMA), 242, 284
Congress, 34, 45, 55–56, 57–58, 65, 70–73, 111, 127
supervision of administrative agencies by, 93, 95–97, 99, 304, 312, 314
D.C. Circuit Court of Appeals, 103, 110–11, 115, 118, 120–21, 121–22
Delaney clause, 34, 38, 39, 47, 59, 81, 120–21, 155, 254, 309
drugs, 223n, 224n
economic analysis, 40, 58–59, 98, 159, 172–73, 176–77, 243, 246
Environmental Defense Fund (EDF), 196, 252, 253, 258, 261, 269
Environmental Protection Agency (EPA), 58, 76, 77, 78, 89, 261, 293, 298
and carcinogens, 80, 121–22, 142, 153–54n, 158–59, 198–200, 206, 212–13

United States *(cont.)*
  Environmental Protection Agency *(cont.)*
    criticized for overanalysis, 178
    economic analysis by, 40, 59
    founding of, 19, 79–80
    generic procedures and, 37, 99
    outside consultants and, 159–60
    personnel increases at, 86–87
    and pesticides, 34, 37, 78, 95–96
    powers of, 36
    and TSCA, 34, 243–44, 282–84
  expertise in regulatory decision making,
      55–56, 315
    impact of, 169, 170–71, 172–74
    legal, 159, 172, 174, 177
    management and planning, 173, 177–78
    political debate concerning, 175–76,
        176–79, 309–10
    sources of, 158–60, 162–68
  food additives, 34, 37–38, 59, 65, 158,
      163, 175, 239
    cyclamates, 41
    nitrites, 141, 144, 155
    and public interest groups, 251–52
    saccharin, 41, 47, 96, 140, 154, 155, 200
  Food and Drug Administration (FDA),
      19–20, 38, 45, 76, 158, 166, 261
    carcinogens and, 34, 81, 96, 120, 139–
        41, 200
  Food, Drug, and Cosmetic Act, 120
  Food Safety Council, 175
  Freedom of Information Act (FOIA), 44
  General Accounting Office (GAO), 45,
      55, 86–87, 96, 178
  Health Research Group, 261
  industrial chemicals, 65, 76, 163
  Interagency Regulatory Liaison Group
      (IRLG), 197, 199, 200, 208
  interest groups
    consumer associations, 251–52, 268
    environmental groups, 19–20, 78, 120,
        190, 197, 216, 252, 254, 258, 261,
        266, 272, 310
    expertise in, 184, 258, 262, 269–70, 311
    impact on regulatory policy, 184, 262–
        63, 264
    resources of, 266–67, 312
    standing to sue, 45–46, 108, 110–11,
        120, 126, 257–58, 261–62, 269,
        271
    tactics, 256–58, 269–70, 271–72, 310–
        11, 312
  trade unions, 78, 189–90, 252–53, 258,
      261, 267–68
  international harmonization, 241, 282–85,
      300
  judicial review of regulatory policy, 45–
      46, 73, 88–89, 103–8, 110–11, 114–
      15, 117–28, 257–58, 304, 315–16
  legal and procedural complexity, 23, 46,
      52, 54, 178, 301–2, 303, 317
    delays caused by, 59, 89, 98, 112, 173,
        249, 313, 314
    expense of, 89, 91, 248–49, 312, 313
    reasons for, 58, 69–71, 88–89, 103, 118,
        119, 127, 172, 174, 181, 304
  legal tradition, 68, 69–70, 71, 172
  National Academy of Sciences (NAS),
      167, 175
  National Cancer Institute (NCI), 38, 134,
      139, 142, 145–47, 151, 190, 196,
      199, 204, 310
  National Institute of Environmental
      Health Sciences (NIEHS), 135,
      147, 190, 310
  National Institute for Occupational
      Safety and Health (NIOSH), 80,
      139–40, 141–42, 159, 190, 310
  National Institutes of Health (NIH), 145,
      151
  National Research Council (NRC), 167
  National Toxicology Program (NTP), 147
  Natural Resources Defense Council
      (NRDC), 252, 253, 254, 261, 269
  Occupational Safety and Health Act
      (OSH Act), 34, 50, 57–58, 77n, 80,
      89
  Occupational Safety and Health Adminis-
      tration (OSHA)
    benzene standard, 122–26
    and carcinogens, 41, 76–77, 80–81, 89,
        122–26, 139–42, 153–54n, 196–
        201, 211, 261
    economic analysis by, 40
    founding of, 19, 80
    generic policy on carcinogens, 38, 41–
        42, 80–81, 99, 191, 200–201,
        205–6, 244–48, 256, 313–14
    ideology of, 169–71
    NIOSH and, 139–40, 159
  Office of Management and Budget
      (OMB), 40, 77n, 97, 98
  pesticides, 34, 37, 65, 163, 222–23, 244
    carcinogens in, 80, 120, 122, 198–99

United States *(cont.)*
pesticides *(cont.)*
DDT, 106
and EPA, 34, 37, 78, 95–96
registration of, 40, 239
public participation in decision making,
43, 44–45, 46, 88–90, 118, 300,
310, 313, 315
recommendations for regulatory reform,
127–28, 314–17
resources for regulation, 86–87, 313
scientific societies, 167–68
Supreme Court, 34, 97, 107–8, 118, 119n,
122–26, 127
Toxic Substances Control Act (TSCA),
34, 35–36, 50, 77, 254, 282, 284,
311–12
enactment, 58, 86, 242–44
European response, 32, 276–79
provisions for public participation, 43,
44, 107
worker safety, 33, 47–49, 65, 163, 169–71,
175, 267–68, 315
and carcinogens, 41, 42, 76, 122–25,
189–92, 314
See also Occupational Safety and
Health Administration

vinyl chloride, 47, 49, 120, 142, 143n, 152n,
287, 296, 327, 332–33

West Germany
Basic Law, 66, 71, 102, 306, 307
Berufsgenossenschaft (BG), 83, 207
Bundesrat, 56, 66, 95, 97
Bundestag, 56, 60–61, 189
carcinogens
and judicial review of regulation, 125–
26
research, 39, 132, 137, 144, 148–49,
201–3
risk assessment, 206, 208, 210, 211
2,4,5-T controversy, 213–14
and worker safety, 47, 49, 194, 206–7,
306
chemical industry, 194, 225, 230–33, 247–
48, 279, 295, 308
Chemical Industry Association (VCI),
231, 233, 236, 242
Chemicals Act (ChemG), 35, 50, 60–61,
75, 82–84, 232, 280
Committee on Hazardous Substances in

the Workplace (AGA), 163–65,
207, 208
DFG commission on workplace hazards,
83, 163–65, 170, 175, 206, 208, 211
expertise in regulatory decision making,
160–61, 163–66, 167–68, 170, 172
Federal Biological Research Center
(BBA), 41, 82–83, 84, 203
Federal Environmental Agency (UBA),
41, 84, 86, 144
Federal Health Office (BGA), 83, 84, 86,
144, 161
Federal Institute for Occupational Safety
and Accident Research (BAU), 83,
86, 161
federalism, 64, 66
Federal Ministry for Labor and Social
Affairs (BMAS), 83
Federal Ministry for Research and Technology, 149
food additives, 82–83, 163, 166
Frauenhofer Gesellschaft, 149
German Research Society (DFG), 39, 41,
83, 148–49, 161, 167, 170, 194,
208, 217
Green party, 252, 256n, 263
industrial chemicals, 82, 163
interest groups
consumer associations, 255
environmental groups, 252, 262, 263–
64, 270, 308
standing to sue, 109–10, 112, 253
trade unions, 252, 255, 268, 272
international harmonization, 277, 278–79,
280, 287, 289, 302, 308
judicial review of regulation, 102, 104–5,
106–7, 113–14, 116, 125–26, 253
Länder, 49–50, 56, 66, 97, 306
legal tradition, 70–71, 113n, 172, 233,
305, 306
Max-Planck Gesellschaft, 149
pesticides, 35, 78, 82–83, 163, 289
public participation in decision making,
41, 43–44, 90, 92–93
resources for regulation, 86
scientific societies, 167–68
worker safety
carcinogens and, 39, 47, 95, 137, 167,
170, 194, 202, 206–7, 217, 306
Chemicals Act and, 82
exposure limits, 47, 49, 137, 167, 202,
208, 306

West Germany *(cont.)*
  worker safety *(cont.)*
    resources for regulation, 83, 163, 170
worker safety, 31, 33, 47, 49, 299
  European Community guidelines, 287,
      288, 290
  and the International Labor Organiza-
      tion, 291–93
  protective equipment, 170, 221
  and trade unions, 255–56, 267–68
  See also individual countries
World Health Organization (WHO), 48,
    132, 138, 188, 292, 293, 297

Library of Congress Cataloging in Publication Data
Brickman, Ronald.
    Controlling chemicals.

    Includes index.
    1. Chemicals—Law and legislation—United States.
2. Hazardous substances—Law and legislation—United
States.   3. Chemicals—Law and legislation—Europe.
4. Hazardous substances—Law and legislation—Europe.
I. Jasanoff, Sheila.   II. Ilgen, Thomas.   III. Title.
K3672.5.B75   1985   344.73′0424   84-29340
ISBN 0-8014-1677-9   347.304424